GW00507261

Abu Dhabi
EXPLORER

Kicking Boredom's Butt Since 1785!

EXPLORER

EXPLORER

Editorial

Senior Editor	Lena Moosa
	Lena@Explorer-Publishing.com
Editor	Katie Hallett-Jones
	Katie@Explorer-Publishing.com
Proofreader & Photographer	Pamela Grist
	Pamela@Explorer-Publishing.com
Proofreader	Linda Peterson
	Linda@Explorer-Publishing.com

Sales & Advertising

Advertising Manager	Hema Kumar
	Hema@Explorer-Publishing.com
Advertising Executive	Wendy Menzies
	Wendy@Explorer-Publishing.com
Corporate Sales	Nadine Laurent
	Nadine@Explorer-Publishing.com

Production & Design

Production Manager	Cathy McKernan
	Cathy@Explorer-Publishing.com
Designer	Pete Maloney
	Pete@Explorer-Publishing.com
Research	Helga Becker
	Helga@Explorer-Publishing.com
Research	Wendy D'Souza
	Wendy@Explorer-Publishing.com
Research	Geraldine Fernandes
	Geraldin@Explorer-Publishing.com
Research	Melodie Minty
	Melodie@Explorer-Publishing.com
Layout	Jayde Fernandes
	Jayde@Fxplorer-Publishing.com
IT Manager & Layout	Derrick Pereira
	Derrick@Explorer-Publishing.com

Distribution

Distribution Manager	Ivan Rodrigues
	Ivan@Explorer-Publishing.com
Distribution Executive	Abdul Gafoor
	Gafoor@Explorer-Publishing.com
Distribution Executive	Mannie Lugtu
	Mannie@Explorer-Publishing.com

Administration

Publisher	Alistair MacKenzie
	Alistair@Explorer-Publishing.com
Public Relations Manager	Amanda Harkin
	Amanda@Explorer-Publishing.com
Accounts Manager	Yolanda Rodrigues
	Yolanda@Explorer-Publishing.com
Administrator	Nadia D'Souza
	Nadia@Explorer-Publishing.com

Front Cover Photograph	Pamela Grist
Printer	Emirates Printing Press
Website	Internet Solutions

Explorer Publishing & Distribution

Dubai Media City   Phone (+971 4) 391 8060 Fax 391 8062
PO Box 34275, Dubai   Info@Explorer-Publishing.com
United Arab Emirates   www.Explorer-Publishing.com

Third Edition 2003   ISBN 976-8182-38-5
Copyright © 2003 Explorer Group Ltd

Capital Move!

If you've bought this book, you're a genius.

What you have in your hands is the third edition of the *Abu Dhabi Explorer* – completely revised, revamped and updated – and the key to a life of excitement, adventure, convenience and bliss.

If you're anything like us and harbour an obsessive eye for detail, you will be delighted by the new and easy to read format. The restaurant reviews now have ratings for easier assessment and the updated satellite maps chart out all that has changed on the geographical front.

In the past two years (since our previous edition), the capital has gone through quite a transformation: new buildings sprouting, old diners shutting down, location shifts and civic breakthroughs. We are immensely grateful for our dedicated team of researchers, writers and reporters who have been silently taking note, mapping and plotting, crawling and unearthing, collecting and cramming information till our hard drives screamed 'sweet mercy'!

Finally, these bits and bytes have been converted into printed info: pages and pages teeming with more restaurants, hip bars and clubs, extensive business information, numerous activities, endless shopping and leisure tips... the list is endless.

However, if you still don't find the answers to life, the universe and everything, give us a shout. Log on, join our community and unleash any pure or impure thoughts – cuss, praise, suggest and advise your heart out. This book's for you, so whether good or bad, your comments are crucial and can only help us improve.

Dive in, enjoy the ride (follow the maps please) – and grab a life!

Kicking Boredom's Butt Since 1785!

DIGITAL EXPLORER

Web Updates

A tremendous amount of research, effort and passion goes into the making of our books. However, in this dynamic and fast paced environment, decisions are swiftly taken and quickly implemented. We will try to keep you abreast of the flux with current updates on those things that have changed DRAMATICALLY.

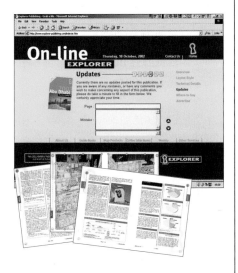

1 To view any changes, visit our Website: **www.Explorer-Publishing.com.**

2 Click on **Guidebooks -> Abu Dhabi Explorer -> Updates** to check on any updates that may interest you.

3 All updates are in Adobe PDF* format. You may print in colour or black & white and update your guidebook immediately.

4 If you are aware of any mistakes, or have any comments concerning any aspect of this publication, please fill in our online reader response form. We certainly appreciate your time and feedback.

*If you do not have Adobe Reader, free versions may be downloaded from **www.adobe.com** or use the link from our Website.*

Who Are You?

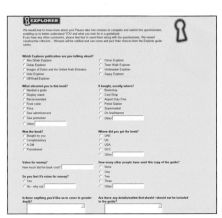

We would love to know more about you. We would equally love to know what we have done right or wrong, or if we have accidentally misled you at some point.

Please take ONE whole minute to fill out the Reader Response Form on our Website. To do so:

1 Visit **www.Explorer-Publishing.com**

2 At the top right, click on Response Form

3 Fill it out and enlighten us

Explorer Community

Whether it's an idea, a correction, an opinion or simply a recommendation, we would like you to tell us about it. Log on and be part of the **Explorer Community** – let your opinions be heard, viewed, compiled and printed.

MEDECINS SANS FRONTIERES
أطبّـــاء بـلا حـدود

Unconditional Medical Aid. where needed. when needed.

WINNER OF THE UAE HEALTH FOUNDATION PRIZE

MSF has been counting on you, and millions have been counting on MSF. Your continuous support has helped relieve pain and suffering of thousands of people around the world.

YOUR DONATIONS are actually supplying medicine, aiding war casualties, administrating vaccinations, providing prenatal care, fighting epidemics, and improving water and sanitation practices and facilities.

YOUR DONATIONS help MSF be an aid against, and a witness to all that endanger humanity, where needed and when needed.

PLEASE DONATE. Help us help them

YOUR DONATION WILL MAKE A DIFFERENCE

The

Art

of

Comfortable

Living

Furniture & Interior Decoration

eldiar
IMPORT & EXPORT

Al-Shaheen Tower, Khaldiya, P.O.Box: 72077, Abu Dhabi, Tel: 02 6814100, Fax: 02 6816556, e-mail: eldiar@emirates.net.ae

Wendy Menzies
Wheeler Dealer

A native of Siberia, Wendy is a bit too cheery for most of us here at Explorer, so we try to limit her drop-ins from Abu Dhabi to days when it rains really really hard. This means we have a hard time keeping tabs on her productivity, but she works for chocolate, so it's not a problem.

Hema Kumar
Primo Peddler

We didn't find Hema so much as she just showed up one day and told us we were going to give her a job. We were hesitant until she incapacitated our security guard (twice her size at six feet) with a wickedly precise judo kick. We reckoned she would be perfect selling advertisements.

Yolanda Rodrigues
Chief Bean Counter

After her retirement from racing alcohol-fuelled funny cars, this beautiful daredevil came to us in desperate need of cash, having spent her entire fortune on Versace wardrobes for her darling kittens. A born linguist, she can say "and shoes to match" in 37 languages.

Lena Moosa
Big Ed

'Dreadlocks' was found sleeping on a bench in the car perk with her backpack for a pillow. We took her in, gave her a saucer of milk and asked her to be our editor. She subsequently replaced her lactose diet with dictionaries for breakfast and developed an unhealthy obsession with full stops and commas – last spotted proofing post-its from the garbage.

Jayde Fernandes
Master Craftsman

We found Jayde working as a dance instructor/party planner for Motown Records. He has threatened to leave us once he finds a rich wife. We're betting that his ponytail will reach the floor first.

Nadine Laurent
Queen Customiser

In the late 90s, Nadine wrote a series of bitterly sarcastic editorials about men who wear black shoes with white socks, which consequently landed her on the government's '10 Most Wanted List'. We granted her an asylum of sorts and in exchange, she has promised to share her 'dress for success' secrets with the rest of the team.

ocolate, have helped us create this guide with their invaluable contributions:

aeme W, Helga & Peter, Hema & Karl, Janet G, John & Vuokko, Joseph & Kara, Karen, Kathy, Lea, Len,

Alistair MacKenzie

Media Mogul

The 'brains' behind the operation, Al arrived here on holiday in 1982, but traded his passport for a shisha pipe and a treasure map, which he subsequently misplaced. In an effort to find it, he has managed to cross paths with every person in Dubai, as well as record the GPS coordinates for every shawarma stand in the Emirates.

Cathy McKernan

Princess Terminator

This little Canadian bag of grins was smuggled in by her circus performer parents. Having travelled the world since birth, Cathy's body clock has never had a chance to set itself, leading to an acute case of jet lag. We're not sure what she does here, but she produces a lot of colourful graphs, so it must be important.

Pete Maloney

Pencil Pusher

Having dated every woman in Manchester, Peet decided to move to Dubai where he is blessed with a new batch of flight attendants every couple of months. He keeps track of his complex diet by dribbling a sample of each meal on whatever 'trendier-than-thou' t-shirt he happens to be wearing.

Derrick Pereira

Techno Guru

A certified IT whiz kid, Derrick quickly grew tired of performing butt shots as Enrique Iglesias' body double and agreed to come and work for us under the proviso that once he finishes his MBA, we will be silent partners in his 'video emporium'.

And a great big thanks to all the following people who, with only a few small bribes of fizzy pop and c
Aidan F, Alan P, Anthony, Cathy, CB, Deborah, Donald, Ed, Emma G, Fred & Valerie, Gillian, G

Explorer's Latest Products

Off-Road Explorer (UAE)

20 adventurous off-road routes.

With clear and easy to follow instructions, this is an invaluable tool for exploring the UAE's 'outback'. Satellite imagery of every stage of the route is superimposed with the correct track to follow. For each route, points of interest are highlighted, along with distances and advice on driving the more difficult parts. Remarkable photography peppers this guide and additional information on topics such as wildlife and archaeology complement the off-road routes.

Images of Dubai & the UAE

A stunning collection of images of Dubai and the United Arab Emirates.

This three time award winner is a visual showcase, sharing the secrets of this remarkable land and introducing newcomers to the wonders of Dubai and the United Arab Emirates. Journey along golden beaches under a pastel sunset, or deep into the mesmerising sands of the desert. View the architectural details of one of the most visually thrilling urban environments in the world, and dive undersea to encounter the reef creatures that live there. This book is for all those who love this country as well as those who think they might like to.

Underwater Explorer (UAE)

Ideal for divers of all abilities with 58 top dive sites.

Detailing top 58 dive sites covering both coastlines and the Musandam, this dedicated guidebook contains suggested dive plans, informative illustrations, shipwreck circumstances and marine life photographs. Written by avid divers who want to share their passion and local knowledge with others, the **Underwater Explorer** includes all that crucial information diving enthusiasts need to know about diving in the UAE.

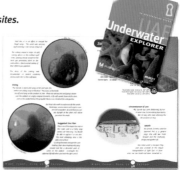

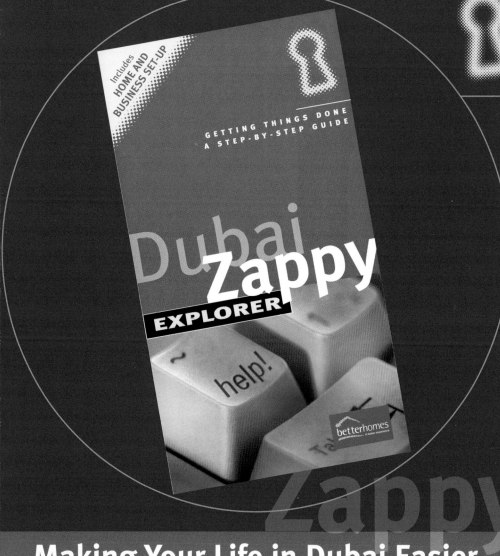

Amanda Harkin

Publicity Junky

When Amanda marched into our office wearing pin stripes and heels, we thought she'd come to audit our books – so we held her hostage! But since no one will pay her ransom, she now spends her time chewing through her shackles and sending out subliminal help messages embedded in Explorer press releases.

Mannie Lugtu

Distribution Demon

When we discovered Mannie, he was smuggling lingerie catalogues into Iran aboard a modified Sea-Doo and using the money to finance his sinister plot to make everyone in the world as friendly and happy as he is.

Helga Becker

Fantasy Foodist

After years of playing with letters in her alphabet soup, Helga decided to continue her career in food by wow-ing Explorer with her unparalleled expertise of fruity teabags. She now spends her time perfecting the art of 'catching the waiter's eye' and researching her first recipe book – '1001 Ways to Boil Water'.

Nadia D'Souza

Nosey Parker

Nadia came to us as part of a two-for-one package. Unfortunately, her parents couldn't bear to see her go, so she commutes every day from India. Although the air miles are great, she's growing bored of 'chicken or beef' and has plans to open an Explorer branch office in her parents' spare bathroom.

Louise D, Mark & Fiona W, Melanie & Stuart G, Pamela, RW, Sarah V, Tony & Vicki G, Wendy. And extra

Abdul Gafoor

Ace Circulator

We couldn't actually afford to buy the Mona Lisa, so we got the next best thing in Gafoor, whose smile has proven as perpetual, even if we can't get him to grow his hair out and wear a dress.

The Explorer 'B' Team

Legends in their own office

We tirelessly searched the far corners of the earth to assemble a crack staff for this edition of the **Abu Dhabi Explorer**. This is the best we could do...

Ivan Rodrigues

Head Honcho

A natural born electrical genius, we decided Ivan would make an excellent Distribution Manager?!? As a test, we once challenged him to deliver a shipment of books to a remote corner of the Emirates with nothing but his eleven beloved Toy Poodles to guide him. Not only did he make it, but he also caught a movie on the way.

Pamela Grist

Happy Snapper

Living among cannibals for the past 15 years has given Pam the ability to eat absolutely anything she wants. An insatiable carnivore, her constitution is so impressive, she is usually referred to as "iron gut". She also has a keen eye for visuals, and is one of the world's finest photographers... or so she keeps telling us.

pecial gold stars go to: AML, Annette, CB, Graeme W, Melodie.

Sharjah's Architectural Splendour

A striking photographic exploration into the architectural splendour of Sharjah.

Take a guided tour of the beauty of Sharjah's architecture and some of the highlights of this remarkable city. From small aesthetic details to grand public compounds, mosques to souks, striking photographs capture and unfurl the civic and historic wonders of this cultural city. Whether you are a long-term resident or a brief visitor, this volume will undoubtedly surprise and delight.

Family Explorer (Dubai & Abu Dhabi)

The ONLY family handbook to Dubai and Abu Dhabi.

Catering specifically to families with children between the ages of 0 - 14 years, the easy to use **Explorer** format details the practicalities of family life in the northern emirates, including information on medical care, education, residence visas and hundreds of invaluable ideas on indoor and outdoor activities for families and kids.

Dubai Explorer

The seventh edition is firmly established as the leading annual lifestyle guidebook to Dubai.

Comprehensive, fun and easy to use, this book covers everything worth knowing about Dubai and where to do it. Meticulously updated by a resident team of writers, photographers and lovers of life, the result is the most in-depth, practical and accurate coverage around. This is the insiders' guide to what's hot and what's not in Dubai and the Emirates and an essential resource for residents as well as business people in this vibrant and surprising city.

For a complete list of Explorer Products, please refer to the back of this guidebook.

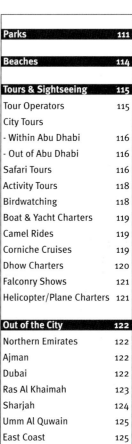

Introduction

Table of Contents

Introduction

Table of Contents

Reach your destination in style.

For a comfortable and memorable journey, rent your vehicle from Eurostar. From luxury cars and sports coupes to economy saloons and 4X4's, we'll fit your choice of car into your wallet.

EuroStar
R·E·N·T·-A·-C·A·R

Best Deals on Wheels®

www.eurostarrental.com

Get into your bank

NBAD now offers you the convenience of managing your personal & business account online. Your First Choice for Online Banking, Anytime, Anywhere.

- Real Time Account Information
- Easy Download of Statement
- Online Fund Transfers
- Online Bill Payments
- Remittance
- Trade Finance*
- Money Market Deposits*
- Foreign Exchange Deals*
- Payroll Management*
- RSA SecurID Protection*
- E-mail

* Service currently available for corporate customers only.

nbad Online

WWW.nbad.com

Total Financial Management is now just a click away!

For more information call us Toll Free 800 2211

بنـك أبـوظـبي الوطنـي
NATIONAL BANK
OF ABU DHABI
The Number One Bank

Branding

Guidebooks

Company Profile

Prestige art books

Brochures

Catalogues

pmdesign

Corporate Identity • Brochures & Reports • Packaging • Advertising • Print • Web

T: 04 391 8924   F: 04 391 8926   E: pmd@emirates.net.ae

General
Information

EXPLORER

General Information

UAE OVERVIEW

Geography

Situated on the northeastern part of the Arabian Peninsula, the United Arab Emirates (UAE) is bordered by the Kingdom of Saudi Arabia to the south and west, and the Sultanate of Oman to the east and north. The UAE shares 457 kilometres of its border with Saudi Arabia and 410 kilometres with Oman. It has a coastline on both the Gulf of Oman and the Arabian Gulf, and is south of the strategically important Strait of Hormuz. The geographic co-ordinates for the UAE are 24 00 N, 54 00 E.

The country is made up of seven different emirates (Abu Dhabi – the capital, Ajman, Dubai, Fujairah, Ras Al Khaimah, Sharjah and Umm Al Quwain), which were formerly all independent sheikhdoms. The total area of the country is about 83,600 square kilometres, much of which lies in the Abu Dhabi emirate.

Golden beaches dot the country's 1,318 kilometres of coastline, of which 100 kilometres are on the Gulf of Oman. The Arabian Gulf coast is littered with coral reefs and over 200 islands, most of which are uninhabited. Sabkha (salt flats), stretches of gravel plain and desert characterise much of the inland region. To the east of the country rise the majestic Hajar Mountains; lying close to the Gulf of Oman, they form a backbone through the country, from the Musandam Peninsula in the north, via the eastern UAE, and into Oman.

Emirs or Sheikhs?

While the term emirate comes from the ruling title of emir, the rulers of the UAE are called sheikhs.

Much of the Abu Dhabi emirate is made up of the infamous Rub Al Khali or Empty Quarter desert which is common to the Kingdom of Saudi Arabia and the Sultanate of Oman. This arid, stark desert is famous for its spectacular sand dunes, broken by an occasional oasis.

Al Ain, the second city of the emirate of Abu Dhabi, lies to the east on the border with Oman. Primarily an oasis town, this 'Garden City' (as it is also known), is a vision of cool tranquillity surrounded by the hostile desert. The other main region of the emirate is the Liwa oasis, which is at the centre of the Al Dhafra area. Liwa is set amidst towering red dunes and is the last main inhabited outpost before the great western desert of the Rub Al Khali.

Visitors to Abu Dhabi will find a land of startling contrasts – from the endless stretches of desert, to the green paradise of irrigated farmland, and vast tracts of sabkha. The city of Abu Dhabi, located on a low lying, 'scorpion shaped' island, is a modern garden city, graced with tree lined streets and futuristic skyscrapers, and surrounded by the sparkling turquoise waters of the Arabian Gulf.

Abu Dhabi City

The city itself is a large, modern metropolis of sophisticated high rise buildings, rich shopping malls, international luxury hotels and cultural centres. The 'Manhattan' skyline reflected in the azure waters of the Arabian Gulf along the Corniche, is a striking contrast to the large gardens and green boulevards. Together with its rich desert heritage and bygone days as a fishing village, Abu Dhabi has become a truly unique and diverse destination – a symbiosis of modernity and traditional Arabian customs.

History

Less than 50 years ago, the emirate of Abu Dhabi was little more than an empty desert inhabited by nomadic Bedouin tribes, with just a sprinkling of villages in the more fertile areas. The capital, Abu Dhabi, was located on the northern side of the island and consisted of two or three hundred palm ('barasti') huts, a few coral buildings and the large, white Ruler's fort. Looking at today's modern city and emirate of Abu Dhabi, it is hard to reconcile with the extent of changes in the intervening years.

In 1761, the leader of the Bani Yas Bedouin tribe moved his people to this 'secure' island, which was not much altered till the discovery of oil in 1950. The abundant wildlife won the island its name – Abu Dhabi translated means 'Father of the Gazelle'. Despite offering good chances for fishing and grazing, it was not until the discovery of a freshwater well in 1793 that the ruling Al Nahyan family, based in the south of the country at Liwa Oasis, moved here. At Liwa, on the edge of the stark Empty Quarter desert, they lived a traditional Bedouin life with animal husbandry and small scale agriculture as their main livelihood. Descendants of the Al Nahyan family, in alliance with other important Bedouin tribes in the region, have ruled the emirate of Abu Dhabi ever since.

By the 1800's, the town had developed considerably and prospered, mainly from pearling, which brought important trade and revenue to the island. From 1855 to 1909, under the reign of Sheikh Zayed bin Mohammed (also known as 'Zayed the Great'), Abu Dhabi rose in prominence to become the most powerful emirate along the western coast of the Arabian Peninsula. His influence was profound, and it was during his rule that Abu Dhabi and the other emirates to the north accepted the protection of Britain in 1892. The British regarded the Gulf region as an important communication link with its empire in India and wished to ensure that other world powers, in particular France and Russia, did not extend their influence in the region. The area then became known as the Trucial States (or Trucial Coast), a name it retained until the departure of the British in 1971.

The death of Zayed the Great lead to a conflict among his descendants for leadership, and the emirate fell into decline. In the 1930s, due to the world recession and the creation of cultured pearls in Japan, pearl trade in the Gulf collapsed. No longer able to rely on this valuable commodity for income, Abu Dhabi slid from a position of relative wealth to the poorest of all the emirates.

The ascension of Sheikh Shakhbut bin Sultan brought a reasonable degree of stability along with the realisation that oil might be the answer to their economic problems. In 1939, he granted concessions to a British company to search for oil, but it was not until 1958 that huge reserves were discovered offshore by an Anglo-French consortium. Four years later, exports began and Abu Dhabi was on its way to becoming an incredibly wealthy state. Sheikh Shakhbut's rule, however, was considered rather idiosyncratic and in 1966, the British, who still had a certain degree of influence in the country helped replace him with his brother Sheikh Zayed bin Sultan Al Nahyan, the governor of the oasis town of Al Ain.

Two years later the British announced their withdrawal from the region and encouraged the separate states to consider uniting under one flag. The ruling sheikhs, in particular Sheikh Zayed and the ruler of Dubai, realised that by joining forces they would have a stronger voice in the wider Middle East region. Negotiations began to try to form a single state consisting of Bahrain, Qatar and the Trucial States, but the process collapsed when Bahrain and Qatar chose to become independent states. Still, the Trucial States remained committed to forming an alliance and in 1971 the federation of the United Arab Emirates was created (excluding the emirate of Ras Al Khaimah which joined in 1972). Under the agreement, each emirate retained a certain degree of autonomy, with Abu Dhabi (and to a lesser extent, Dubai) giving the most input into the federation. The leaders of the new federation elected Sheikh Zayed bin Sultan Al Nahyan as their first president, a position he has held ever since.

HH Sheikh Zayed bin Sultan al Nahyan

The creation of what is basically an artificial state hasn't been without its problems, mainly caused by disputes over boundaries between the different

emirates. At the end of Sheikh Zayed's first term as president in 1976, he threatened to resign if the other rulers didn't settle the demarcation of their borders. The threat was an effective way of ensuring co-operation and although more focus is now given to the importance of the federation as a whole, the degree of independence of the various emirates has, to date not been fully determined. It is however, led by Abu Dhabi, whose wealth and sheer size make it the most powerful of the emirates.

The massive oil reserves that lie below Abu Dhabi allowed Sheikh Zayed to make the most of the revenue from his own emirate. With a population of only 15,000 in 1962, there was a lot of wealth to go around amongst a small number of people. Even today, the population of Abu Dhabi at the last census in 1995 was just under 1 million, of which only 27% are Nationals, and this in an area twice the size of Belgium!

Under Sheikh Zayed's vision and careful guidance, this new found wealth was wisely used to create an economic and social infrastructure which is the basis of today's modern society. The welfare of his people has always been the most important factor and hence, there are excellent hospitals and a health service that is free to the national population, and very low cost to expatriate residents. Education, roads, housing, and women's welfare were all priorities that continue to be developed under Sheikh Zayed's farsighted leadership. As a result, UAE Nationals have a deep admiration and regard for the leader that brought about such a radical transformation to their way of life.

ECONOMY

UAE Overview

Today the UAE has an open economy with one of the world's highest per capita incomes estimated at Dhs.69,000 in 2002 (more than US $22,000), although this is far from being spread evenly amongst the population. Its wealth, once chiefly based on the oil sector, now sees an oil contribution of 27.7% of the country's gross domestic product (GDP). The GDP for 2002 was approximately Dhs.261 billion, compared with Dhs.156 billion in 1995. Abu Dhabi and Dubai contribute most to the country's GDP – the figures for 2002 put these at 57% and 26% respectively.

Over 90% of the UAE's oil reserves lie in Abu Dhabi, and there is enough at the current rate of production (just over 2.5 million barrels per day) to last a further 100 years. However, although there is a heavy dependence on the oil and gas industry, trade, manufacturing, tourism and construction also play an important part in the national economy. Investment in infrastructure and development projects exceeded an estimated Dhs.62 billion in 2002. The UAE's main export partners are Saudi Arabia, Iran, Japan, India, Singapore, South Korea, and Oman. Last year, the UAE's trade outflow was Dhs.143.7 billion. The main import partners are Japan, USA, UK, Italy, Germany and South Korea.

The situation in the Emirates is radically different to that of 30 - 40 years ago, when the area consisted of small, impoverished desert states. Visitors will find a unified and forward looking state with a high standard of living and a relatively well-balanced and stable economy.

Current reports note that the country's economy is roughly 36 times larger than it was in 1971, a mere 32 years ago. With an annual growth rate of 13.2%, the UAE has one of the fastest GDP growth rates in the world and the UAE's credit rating was ranked first in the Middle East for 2001; at the global level, the UAE sits at 26th place.

Abu Dhabi Overview

Abu Dhabi's traditional economy was based around pearl diving, fishing and cultivating the date palm. However, the discovery of oil brought about a radical change. With exports beginning five years later, the die was cast and the new wealth, coupled with enlightened leadership, gave a complete turnaround to Abu Dhabi's fortunes. A modern city was created with an infrastructure built virtually from scratch.

Ongoing exploration in Abu Dhabi, both onshore and offshore, has so far identified 10% of the world's known crude oil resources. Maintaining the present rate of production, there is enough to generate over two million barrels a day for the next 100 years at least. This makes Abu Dhabi the third largest oil producer in the Gulf after Saudi Arabia and Kuwait. It also has 4% of the world's known natural gas reserves. Hence, the infrastructure has been expanded considerably to support the marine crude resources – processing oil and gas is now big business. The Government runs the Abu Dhabi

National Oil Company (ADNOC) which was set up to develop the reserves and to administer the industry.

Etisalat

However, the Government is trying to diversify the economy to give less dependence on oil wealth. In Abu Dhabi, both government and private sector investment in agriculture, industry, fishing, water and electricity supply, transport, construction, warehousing and retailing, has grown at a breakneck pace. Communications are the responsibility of the federally run Emirates Telecommunication Corporation (Etisalat) which, although a monopoly organisation, is continuously building and expanding services. Tourism in Abu Dhabi is also expected to play a major part in the future economy. At present, it still lags behind the emirate of Dubai in this respect.

Really Tax Free?

Taxes? Do they exist in Abu Dhabi? Well, yes and no. You won't pay income or sales tax, unless you purchase alcohol from a licensed liquor store, and then you'll be hit with a steep 30% tax. The main taxes that you'll come across are a municipality tax, in the form of a 5% rent tax and 10% on food, beverages and rooms in hotels. The rest are hidden taxes in the form of 'fees', such as your car registration renewal and visa/permit fees.

Other initiatives to diversify the economy include the relatively new development of Sadiyat Island as a free trade zone. This zone gives investors certain tax and ownership incentives, such as exempting goods being imported or exported into the zone from customs duties. Free zones, such as the Jebel Ali Free Zone in the Dubai emirate, have

General Info

Economy

proved a very successful concept, and undoubtedly, Sadiyat will offer the same attractions to foreign businesses.

Export of non oil related products has grown threefold since 1990 and continues to rise. Private and overseas investment is actively encouraged. While the recent upheavals in world oil prices have affected the emirate's economy, it is to a degree far less than in other countries in the region.

Do not, however, be blinded by the healthy economy into believing that the average expat coming to work in Abu Dhabi will necessarily be on a huge salary. Except for highly skilled professionals, the salary for most employees is dropping and this downward trend is attributed in part to the willingness of workers to accept jobs at very low wages. While per capita income was Dhs.64,400 in 1998, this figure included all sections of the community, and the average labourer can expect to earn as little as Dhs.600 (US$165) per month.

Unemployment levels in the national population are high, partly due to the desire of Nationals to work in the public sector (where salaries and benefits are better), and partly because their qualifications do not match the skills required in the private sector. However, the Government is trying to reverse unemployment with a 'nationalisation' or 'emiratisation' programme (this is common to countries throughout the region). The aim is to rely less on an expat workforce by putting the local population to work. This is being achieved by improving vocational training and by making it compulsory for certain categories of companies, such as banks, to hire a determined percentage of Emiratis. Another step the Government has taken to make employment in the private sector more attractive to Nationals is to implement a pension scheme; private companies are now required to provide a pension for their National employees.

Tourism Developments

Abu Dhabi's economic and social transformation from a breakwater fishing village to international tourist destination and global marketplace can be credited to the President, His Highness Sheikh Zayed Bin Sultan Al Nahyan, who is considered the modern architect and visionary of the emirate and the UAE Federation. Planning department figures show that more than Dhs.100 billion have been pumped into the development of Abu Dhabi,

particularly into infrastructure projects, since Sheikh Zayed took over as Ruler in 1966.

Abu Dhabi has recently upgraded a number of its five star hotels, while several more are being expanded, are under construction, or are at the planning stage. The Abu Dhabi National Hotels Company (ADNHC) owns and administers five star hotels, and a variety of other hotels and resorts in Abu Dhabi and Al Ain. Most hotels have private beaches where guests can indulge in a wide range of water sports with state of the art facilities. ADNHC also supervises the duty free complexes at Abu Dhabi and Al Ain international airports, and provides transport services through Al Ghazal (taxis), a wholly owned subsidiary.

Also active in hotel management is the National Corporation for Tourism and Hotels (NCTH) which is responsible for promoting Abu Dhabi as a tourist and international destination.

Marina Mall

With more than 40 airlines touching down at the Abu Dhabi International Airport, Abu Dhabi has become a widely accessible tourist destination. The planning and execution of a $250 million satellite terminal is now underway. This ambitious project, overseen by Sheikh Hamdan bin Mubarak Al Nahyan, Chairman of the Department of Civil Aviation, is expected to be implemented by 2005. The airport intends to double its passenger and cargo capacity (to over 7 million passengers and over 300,000 cargo tonnes annually) with the construction of a new terminal, a second runway and additional facilities.

Abu Dhabi's developing reputation as a trend setting retail paradise can be traced to the opening of the Abu Dhabi Mall and Marina Mall in

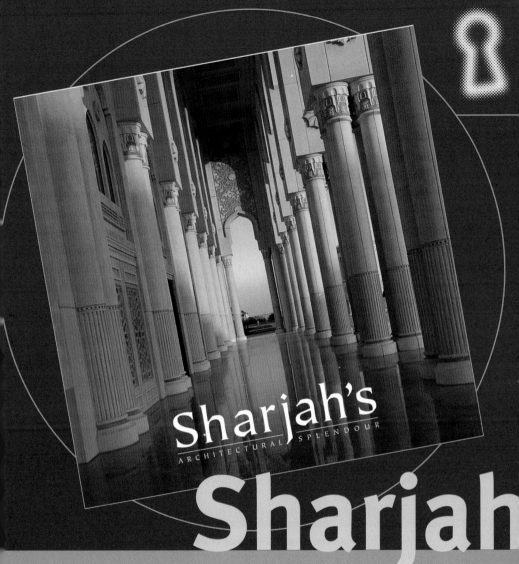

Sharjah's ARCHITECTURAL SPLENDOUR

Sharjah

General Info

Economy

2001. Abu Dhabi Mall is located downtown, within the emirate's residential and Tourist Club area. A main attraction of the mall is the Abu Dhabi Co-op, a 16,000 square metre hypermarket. Over 200 retail outlets, restaurants, an extensive food court, coffee shops and a multi-screen cinema occupy the three upper floors. Located near the rapidly developing breakwater area opposite the Corniche, Marina Mall is the new shopping and recreational landmark of Abu Dhabi, attracting crowds with the famous CineStar Marina nine screen cinema megaplex, IKEA, and a Carrefour hypermarket.

Abu Dhabi has become a prominent centre for leisure and sports tourism, especially for the golfing enthusiast. The capital offers a variety of golf facilities to suit all tastes and budgets, including world class courses designed by top golf course designers.

The Futaisi Island Resort is an imaginative scheme that has transformed the 45 square kilometre Futaisi Island off the Abu Dhabi coast into a popular tourist resort. Housing fifteen luxurious chalets, two villas and a nature reserve, the club boasts a restaurant, an Arabic Fort, horse riding around the island, beaches and a swimming pool. There are also facilities to hold private functions such as concerts and gala dinners. Future plans include a horse riding track and more chalets.

The Khalifa Park in Abu Dhabi, due for completion in September 2003, is currently under construction on the site of the old airport, near the Maqta Bridge. The 430,000 square metres of land will be dedicated to promoting tourism and highlighting the emirate's cultural heritage.

When completed, it will be the first of its kind in the Middle East. It will feature a marine natural history museum, several public gardens and oases, a mosque, a huge open air amphitheatre seating 1,500, games, a water garden and a festival stand. The museum will incorporate a 'time tunnel ride', depicting cultural, historical and exploration aspects of the UAE, taking visitors from the copper mining beginnings of the UAE up to the present day. These leisure and entertainment facilities are part of the Abu Dhabi Municipality's plans to provide more recreational centres in the capital, thus helping to promote tourism in the emirate.

International Relations

In its foreign relations, the UAE's stance is one of non-alignment, but it is committed to the support of Arab unity. The country became a member of the United Nations and the Arab League in 1971 and is a member of the International Monetary Fund (IMF), the Organisation of Petroleum Exporting Countries (OPEC), the World Trade Organisation (WTO), and other international and Arab organisations.

The UAE also shares membership of the Arab Gulf Co-operation Council (AGCC, also known as the GCC) with Bahrain, Kuwait, Oman, Qatar and Saudi Arabia. Led by Sheikh Zayed bin Sultan Al Nahyan, the UAE had a leading role in the formation of the AGCC in 1981 and the country is the third largest member in terms of geographical size, after Saudi Arabia and Oman. All major embassies and consulates are represented either in Abu Dhabi or Dubai, or in both.

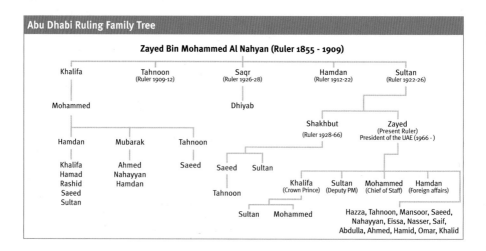

Abu Dhabi Ruling Family Tree

8

Dhs.100 ~ € 26

2003 | **ABU DHABI** EXPLORER

Government & Ruling Family

The Supreme Council of Rulers is the highest authority in the UAE, comprising the hereditary rulers of the seven emirates. Since the country is governed by hereditary rule, there is little distinction between the royal families and the Government. The Supreme Council is responsible for general policy matters involving education, defence, foreign affairs, communications and development, and for ratifying federal laws. The Council meets four times a year and the Abu Dhabi and Dubai rulers have effective power of veto over decisions.

The seven members of the Supreme Council elect the chief of state (the President) from among its members. The President of the UAE is HH Sheikh Zayed bin Sultan Al Nahyan who is also Ruler of Abu Dhabi. He has been President since independence on 2nd December 1971, and ruler of Abu Dhabi since 6 August 1966. The Supreme Council also elects the Vice President, who is HH Sheikh Maktoum bin Rashid Al Maktoum, Ruler of Dubai. The President and Vice President are elected and appointed for five year terms. The President appoints the Prime Minister (currently HH Sheikh Maktoum bin Rashid Al Maktoum) and the Deputy Prime Minister.

The Federal Council of Ministers is responsible to the Supreme Council. It has executive authority to initiate and implement laws, and is a consultative assembly of 40 representatives who are appointed for two years by the individual emirates. The council monitors and debates government policies, but has no power of veto.

The individual emirates still have a degree of autonomy, and laws that affect everyday life vary between the emirates. All emirates have a separate police force, with different uniforms and cars. Additionally it is possible to buy alcohol in Abu Dhabi, but not in Sharjah. Abu Dhabi has consistently been in favour of increasing the strength of the federation and, due to its wealth and size, has always been the most powerful and therefore able to press its point. The current move is towards greater interdependence and the increasing power of the federation, especially in the less oil rich emirates, which increasingly look to Abu Dhabi for subsidies.

FACTS & FIGURES

National Flag

In a nation continually striving for world records, when 30 year anniversary celebrations were marked on National Day 2001, the world's tallest flagpole was erected in Abu Dhabi and the world's largest UAE flag was raised in Dubai. The flag consists of three equal horizontal bands: green at the top, white and black at the bottom. A thicker vertical band of red runs down the hoist side.

The UAE Flag

Population

Emiratis make up only 20% of the population according to the most recently available data, and demographic trends within the country are driven by the Emirates' reliance on foreigners to provide the workforce for their growing economy. During the 1990s, the population grew by an average of 5% a year, reaching 3,247,000 by 2000 — an increase of almost 50% on the 1990 level. The boom in oil prices in 1999 and 2000 led to a sharp increase in demand for foreign labour and, as a result, the population rose to 3,488,000 by the end of 2001, a year on year increase of 12%. Recent UN estimates suggest that the UAE's population will double by 2029.

Abu Dhabi has the largest population within the Emirates at over 1,200,000 compared with just over 1,000,000 in Dubai and 599,000 in Sharjah. Abu Dhabi also has the highest male to female ratio of 2.48 men to every woman.

Population by Emirate

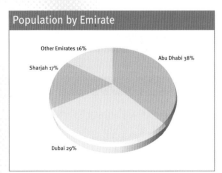

Other Emirates 16%

Sharjah 17%

Abu Dhabi 38%

Dubai 29%

Population Age Breakdown

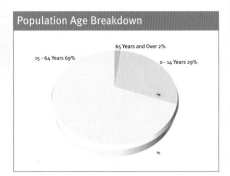

65 Years and Over 2%

15 - 64 Years 69%

0 - 14 Years 29%

Education Levels

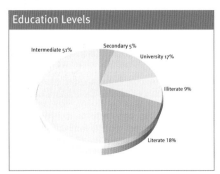

Intermediate 51%

Secondary 5%

University 17%

Illiterate 9%

Literate 18%

Source: Ministry of Planning

According to the United Nations Development Program (UNDP), the UAE has the highest life expectancy in the Arab world at 72.2 years for males and 75.6 years for females.

Local Time

The UAE is four hours ahead of UCT (Universal Co-ordinated Time – formerly known as GMT). There is no summer time saving when clocks are altered. Hence, when it is 12:00 in Abu Dhabi, it is 03:00 in New York, 08:00 in London, 13:30 in Delhi, and 17:00 in Tokyo (not allowing for any summer time saving in those countries).

Social & Business Hours

Social hours are very Mediterranean in style – in general, people get up early, often have an afternoon siesta and eat late in the evening. The attitude to time, especially in business, is often very different from the 'time is money' approach in other parts of the world. So, don't get frustrated if your business meeting happens a day late – the 'Inshallah' (God willing) attitude prevails!

Traditionally there is no concept of the weekend, although Friday has always been the holy day. In modern UAE, the weekend has established itself on different days, generally according to each company. Until recently, government offices had Thursday afternoon and Friday off, however, a 1998 ruling established a five day week for government offices and schools, which are now closed all day Thursday and Friday. Some private companies still take a half day Thursday and Friday, while others take Friday and Saturday as their weekend. Understandably, these differences cause difficulties, since companies may now be out of touch with international business for up to four days, plus families do not necessarily share weekends.

Government offices are open from 07:30 - 13:30, Saturday to Wednesday. In the private sector, office hours vary between split shift days, which are generally 08:00 - 13:00, reopening at either 15:00 or 16:00 and closing at 18:00 or 19:00; or straight shifts, usually 09:00 - 18:00, with an hour for lunch.

Shop opening times are usually based on split shift hours, although outlets in many of the big shopping malls now remain open all day. Closing times are usually 22:00 or 24:00, while some food shops and petrol stations are open 24 hours a day. On Fridays, many places are open all day, apart from prayer time (11:30 - 13:30), while larger shops in the shopping malls only open in the afternoon from either 12:00 or 14:00.

Embassies and consulates open from 08:45 - 13:30. They are closed on Fridays and in most cases on Saturdays, but generally leave an emergency contact number on their answering machines.

During Ramadan, work hours in most public and some private organisations are reduced by two to three hours per day, and business definitely slows during this period. Many offices start work an hour

or so later and shops are open much later at night. The more popular shopping malls are crowded at midnight and parking at that time is tough to find!

Public Holidays

The Islamic calendar starts from the year 622 AD, the year of Prophet Mohammed's (Praise Be Upon Him) migration (Hijra) from Mecca to Al Madinah. Hence the Islamic year is called the Hijri year and dates are followed by AH – After Hijra.

The Hijri calendar is based on lunar months; there are 354 or 355 days in the Hijri year, which is divided into 12 lunar months, and is thus 11 days shorter than the Gregorian year.

As some holidays are based on the sighting of the moon and are not fixed dates on the Hijri calendar, the dates of Islamic holidays are notoriously imprecise, with holidays frequently being confirmed less than 24 hours in advance. Some non religious holidays are fixed according to the Gregorian calendar.

Public Holidays – 2003

New Year's Day (1)	Jan 1[Fixed]
Eid Al Adha (4)	Feb 12[Moon]
Islamic New Year's Day (1)	Mar 5[Moon]
Prophet Mohammed's Birthday (1)	May 13[Moon]
Accession of H.H Sheikh Zayed (1)	Aug 6th[Fixed]
Lailat Al Mi'Raj (1)	Sept 23[Moon]
Ramadan begins	Oct 27[Moon]
Eid Al Fitr (3)	Nov 25[Moon]
UAE National Day (2)	Dec 2[Fixed]

The different emirates also have some different fixed holidays, such as the accession of HH Sheikh Zayed, which is only celebrated in Abu Dhabi on August 6. The number of days a holiday lasts is in brackets in the table above. However, this applies to the public sector only, since not all listed holidays are observed by the private sector and often the public sector gets a day or two more.

Electricity & Water

Other options → Utilities & Services [p.72]

Electricity and water services in Abu Dhabi are excellent and power cuts or water shortages are practically unheard of. Both of these utilities are provided by Abu Dhabi Water and Electricity Authority (known as ADWEA).

The electricity supply is 220/240 volts and 50 cycles. The socket type is the same as the three point British system. Most hotels and homes have adapters for electrical appliances.

The tap water is heavily purified and safe to drink, but most people prefer to drink the locally bottled mineral waters, of which there are several different brands available. Bottled water is usually served in hotels and restaurants.

Photography

Normal tourist photography is acceptable but, like anywhere in the world, it is courteous to ask permission before photographing people, particularly women. In general, photographs of government buildings, military installations, ports and airports should not be taken.

There is a wide choice of film available and processing is usually cheap and fast, although the quality of reproduction can vary. Ultraviolet filters for your camera are advisable. APS, 35mm negative and slide film can all be processed, although the cost of processing and developing APS film is still high, and very few places around town deal with slide film.

ENVIRONMENT

Climate

Abu Dhabi has a sub-tropical, arid climate and sunny blue skies, and high temperatures can be expected most of the year. Rainfall is infrequent and irregular, falling mainly in winter – November to March (12 cm per year). Temperatures range from a low of around 10° C (50° F), to a high of around 48° C (118° F) in the summer. The most pleasant time to visit is in the cooler winter months when temperatures are around 24° C (75° F) during the day and 13° C (56° F) at night.

During the winter there are occasional sandstorms (the wind is known as the 'shamal'), when the sand is whipped up off the desert. More surprisingly, fog occasionally sets in on winter mornings, however, by mid morning, the sun invariably burns the cloud away. The humidity can be a killer in the summer, approaching 100% – prepare to sweat!

Abu Dhabi Temperature & Humidity

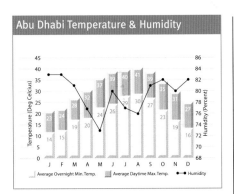

Average Number of Days With Rain

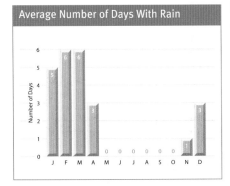

Flora & Fauna

Other Options ➜ Protection [p.14]

As you would expect in a country with such an arid climate, the variety of flora and fauna in the Emirates isn't as extensive as in other parts of the world. However, a variety of plant life and creatures have managed to adapt themselves to life with high temperatures and little rainfall.

In the city of Abu Dhabi, as in all the emirates to a lesser extent, the local municipality has an extensive 'greening' programme underway. Areas along the roads are incredibly colourful for such an arid region, with grass, palm trees and flowers being constantly maintained by an army of workers and watered around the clock. The road from Abu Dhabi to Al Ain covers a distance of 150 km and is green most of the way. The cities also boast a large number of attractive and well kept parks.

Sheikh Zayed was the chief architect behind the greening of the cities, and it is an ongoing process. In the south of the country at the oasis of Liwa on the edge of the Rub Al Khali, the objective is to 'push back' the desert. Each year the tarmac inches forward and each side of the road has extensive agricultural projects bringing employment, fresh produce and wealth to the region, as well as making a more fertile and green environment.

Al Ain, the second city of the emirate, has won various international awards for the quality of its parks, gardens and roadsides, often beating far more fertile regions of the world. Without doubt, it lives up to its label as the 'Garden City'.

The region has about 3,500 endemic plants – quite amazing, considering the high salinity of the soil and the harsh environment. The date palm is the most obvious of the indigenous flora, and this provides wonderful seas of green, especially in the oases. Heading towards the mountains, flat topped Acacia trees and wild grasses give a feel of African 'savannah'. The deserts are often surprisingly green, even during the dry, summer months, but it takes an experienced botanist to get the most out of the area.

Indigenous fauna includes the Arabian leopard and the ibex, but sightings of them are extremely rare. Realistically, the only large animals you will see are camels and goats (often roaming dangerously close to roads). Other desert life includes the sand cat, sand fox and desert hare, plus gerbils, hedgehogs, snakes and geckos. However, a visit to the Arabian Wildlife Centre in Sharjah guarantees a viewing of all the animals mentioned above.

Arabian Leopard (courtesy WWF)

Birdlife in the city is limited – this isn't the place for hearing a 'dawn chorus', unless you are lucky with where you live. However, recent studies have shown that the number of species rises each year, due in part to the increasing lushness of the area. This is most apparent in the parks in spring and autumn as the emirate lies on the route for birds migrating between Central Asia and East Africa.

Off the coast, the seas contain a rich abundance of marine life, including tropical fish, jellyfish, coral, the dugong ('sea cow') and sharks. Eight species of whales and seven species of dolphins have been recorded in UAE waters. Various breeds of turtle are also indigenous to the region, including endangered species of the loggerhead, green and hawksbill turtles. These may be seen by divers off both coasts or, if you are lucky, near the East Coast at Kalba (see Khor Kalba [p.127]). The best known local fish is hammour, which is a type of grouper and can be found on most restaurant menus.

Protection

The UAE's and specifically Sheikh Zayed's commitment to the environment is internationally recognised. At the Environment 2001 Conference and Exhibition in Abu Dhabi, a statement was made that the UAE would invest US $46 billion on projects related to the environment over the next ten years. Sheikh Zayed set up the Zayed International Prize for the Environment, and has already been awarded the World Wild Fund for Nature's Gold Panda Award.

The Hajar Mountains

Various organisations have been formed to protect the environment as well as to educate the population on the importance of environmental issues. The Environmental Research and Wildlife Development Agency (ERWDA) was established in 1996 to assist the Abu Dhabi Government in the conservation and management of the emirate's natural environment, resources, wildlife and biological diversity. There is also a branch of the World Wide Fund for Nature in the UAE. Working closely with the government, NGOs and

businesses, the WWF recently awarded a 'Gift to the Earth' to the first internationally recognised marine protected area in the Arabian Gulf – the island of Qarnein (180 km northwest of Abu Dhabi).

Sir Bani Yas Island in Abu Dhabi has an internationally acclaimed breeding programme for endangered wildlife. The Arabian Wildlife Centre in Sharjah also has a successful breeding programme for endangered wildlife, particularly the Arabian Leopard.

- *Environmental Research and Wildlife Development Agency (02 681 7171)*
- *World Wide Fund for Nature (02 693 4510)*

The UAE is party to international agreements on biodiversity, climate change, desertification, endangered species, hazardous wastes, marine dumping and ozone layer protection. In addition to emirate wide environmental controls, Abu Dhabi has strictly enforced laws governing the use of chemical insecticides.

Despite all the efforts being made, there are still some serious environmental issues facing the UAE. With very little rainfall to speak of for the past few years, the water table is at record low levels and desalination plants work overtime to satisfy a thirsty population, and keep the numerous parks and verges green. Desertification and beach pollution from oil spills are other areas of worry.

See also: *Environmental Groups [p.216]*

CULTURE & LIFESTYLE

Culture

Other options ➜ Business [p.92]

Abu Dhabi's culture is firmly rooted in the Islamic traditions of Arabia. Islam is more than just a religion; it is a way of life that governs even the minutiae of everyday events, from what to wear to what to eat and drink. Thus the culture and heritage of the UAE is tied to its religion. In parts of the world, Islamic fundamentalism has given the 'outside' world an extreme, blanket view of the religion. However, in contrast to this image, the UAE is tolerant and welcoming; foreigners are free to practice their own religion, alcohol is served in hotels and the dress code is liberal. Women face relatively little discrimination and, contrary to the policies of neighbouring countries, are able to drive and walk around unescorted. Among the most highly prized virtues are courtesy and hospitality, and visitors are sure to be charmed by the genuine warmth and friendliness of the people.

Connected!

'Wasta' means connections. If you've got them, all power to you – they'll take you far! However, most people in Abu Dhabi don't have wasta – it is reserved for the select few who have somehow managed to establish the 'right' contacts, either through family or friends. It's pretty much the same as in any other country (very much like an old boys' network), only here it's more pronounced, as rules and regulations aren't always set in stone.

The rapid economic development over the last 30 years has changed life in the Emirates beyond recognition in many ways. Nevertheless, the country's rulers are very aware that their traditional heritage faces the danger of being eroded by the speed of development and increased access to outside cultures and material goods. Hence, they are keen to promote cultural and sporting events that are representative of their past, such as falconry, camel racing and traditional dhow sailing. Ironically though, a large proportion of local entertainment focuses less on traditional pastimes and more on shopping! However, traditional aspects of life are still apparent, most obviously in the clothes (see National Dress [p.17]). Arabic culture in poetry, dancing, songs and traditional art is encouraged, and weddings and celebrations are still colourful occasions of feasting and music.

Language

The official language of the country is Arabic, although English, Urdu and Hindi are spoken and, with some perseverance, understood. Arabic is the official business language, but English is widely used and most road and shop signs, restaurant menus etc, are in both languages. The further out of town you go, the more Arabic you will find, both spoken and written, on street and shop signs. See [p.16] for a quick list of useful Arabic phrases to get you around town.

Arabic isn't the easiest language to pick up – or to pronounce. But if you can throw in a couple of words of Arabic here and there, you're more likely to receive a warmer welcome or at least a smile. Most people will help you out with your pronunciation – they're happy you're putting in the

effort, so it certainly won't hurt to try, and definitely helps when dealing with officials of any sort.

Arabic Family Names

Arabic names have a formal structure that traditionally indicated the family and tribe of the person. Names usually start with that of an important person from the Koran or someone from the tribe. This is followed by the word 'bin' (son of) for a boy or 'bint' (daughter of) for a girl, and then the name of the child's father. The last name indicates the person's tribe or family. For prominent families, this has 'Al' (Arabic word 'the') immediately before it. For instance, the President of the UAE is HH Sheikh Zayed bin Sultan Al Nahyan. When women get married, they do not change their name. Family names are very important here, and extremely helpful when it comes to differentiating between the thousands of Mohammeds, Ibrahims and Fatimas!

Religion

Islam is the official religion of the UAE, but other religions are respected. Abu Dhabi has a variety of Christian churches: St Joseph's Roman Catholic Church, St George's Orthodox Church, St Andrew's Protestant Church, Evangelical Community Church and Arabic Evangelical Church. In Al Ain there is St Mary's Church.

Ramadan

In Islam, Ramadan is the holy month in which Muslims commemorate the revelation of the Holy Koran (the holy book of Islam, also spelt Quran). It is a time of fasting when Muslims abstain from all food, drinks, cigarettes and unclean thoughts between dawn and dusk. In the evening, the fast is broken with the Iftar feast. Iftar timings are found in all the daily newspapers.

All over the city, festive Ramadan tents are filled to the brim each evening with people of all nationalities and religions enjoying shisha and traditional Arabic meze and sweets. In addition to the standard favourite shisha cafés and restaurants around town, the five star hotels erect special Ramadan tents for the month.

The timing of Ramadan is not fixed in terms of the western calendar, but each year it occurs approximately 11 days earlier than the previous year, with the start date depending on the sighting

Basic Arabic

General

Yes	na'am
No	la
Please	min fadlak [m] / min fadliki [f]
Thank you	shukran
Please (in offering)	tafaddal [m] / tafaddali [f]
Praise be to God	al-hamdu l-illah
God willing	in shaa'a l-laah

Greetings

Greeting (peace be upon you)	as-salaamu alaykom
Greeting (in reply)	wa alaykom is salaam
Good morning	sabah il-khayr
Good morning (in reply)	sabah in-nuwr
Good evening	masa il-khayr
Good evening (in reply)	masa in-nuwr
Hello	marhaba
Hello (in reply)	marhabtayn
How are you?	kayf haalak [m] / kayf haalik [f]
Fine, thank you	zayn, shukran [m] / zayna, shukran [f]
Welcome	ahlan wa sahlan
Welcome (in reply)	ahlan fiyk [m] / ahlan fiyki [f]
Goodbye	ma is-salaama

Introduction

My name is	ismiy ...
What is your name?	shuw ismak [m] / shuw ismik [f]
Where are you from?	min wayn inta [m] / min wayn inti [f]
I am from ...	anaa min
America	ameriki
Britain	braitani
Europe	oropi
India	al hindi

Questions

How many / much?	kam?
Where?	wayn?
When?	mata?
Which?	ayy?
How?	kayf?
What?	shuw?
Why?	laysh?
Who?	miyn?
To/ for	ila
In/ at	fee
From	min
And	wa
Also	kamaan
There isn't	maa fee

Taxi / Car Related

Is this the road to ...	hadaa al tariyq ila
Stop	kuf
Right	yamiyn
Left	yassar
Straight ahead	siydaa
U-turn	Urjah
North	shamaal
South	januwb
East	sharq
West	garb
Turning	mafraq
First	awwal
Second	thaaniy
Road	tariyq
Street	shaaria
Roundabout	duwwaar
Signals	ishaara
Close to	qarib min
Petrol station	mahattat betrol
Sea/ beach	il bahar
Mountain/s	jabal / jibaal
Desert	al sahraa
Airport	mataar
Hotel	funduq
Restaurant	mata'am
Slow Down	schway schway

Accidents

Police	al shurtaa
Permit/ licence	rukhsaa
Accident	Haadith
Papers	waraq
Insurance	ta'miyn
Sorry	aasif (m) / aasifa (f)

Numbers

Zero	sifr
One	waahad
Two	ithnayn
Three	thalatha
Four	araba'a
Five	khamsa
Six	sitta
Seven	saba'a
Eight	thamaanya
Nine	tiss'a
Ten	ashara
Hundred	miya
Thousand	alf

of the moon (see Public Holidays [p.12]). In 2003, Ramadan should commence around October 27th.

Non-Muslims are required to refrain from eating, drinking or smoking in public places during daylight hours as a sign of respect. Visitors and new residents should note that in Abu Dhabi there is no sale of alcoholic beverages whatsoever in restaurants or hotels during the holy month of Ramadan or during any religious festival or holiday. Many venues are actually closed for the full month. In addition, entertainment such as live music is stopped and cinemas limit daytime screenings of films.

Islam

The basis of Islam is the belief that there is only one God and that Prophet Mohammed (Peace Be Upon Him) is his messenger. There are five pillars of the faith, which all Muslims must follow: the Profession of Faith, Prayer, Charity, Fasting and Pilgrimage. Every Muslim is expected, at least once in his/her lifetime, to make the pilgrimage or 'Hajj' to the holy city of Mecca (also spelt Makkah) in Saudi Arabia.

Additionally, a Muslim is required to pray five times a day. The times vary according to the position of the sun. Most people go to a mosque to pray, although it's not unusual to see them kneeling by the side of the road if one is not close by. It is not considered polite to stare at people praying, or to walk over prayer mats.

The modern day call to prayer, through loudspeakers on the minarets of each mosque, ensures that everyone knows it's time to pray. Friday is the holy day.

Business hours tend to be shorter during this period, while shops usually open and close later. Expatriate women are advised to be more modest in their dress during this time.

Ramadan ends with a three day celebration and holiday called Eid Al Fitr, or 'Feast of the Breaking of the Fast'. Seventy days later is another Eid holiday and celebration called Eid Al Adha, or 'Feast of the Sacrifice' and this marks the end of the pilgrimage season to Mecca. For Muslims, Eid has similar connotations as Diwali for Hindus and Christmas for Christians.

National Dress

On the whole, the National population still chooses to wear their traditional dress. For men this is the 'dishdash(a)' or 'khandura' – a white full length shirt-dress, which is worn with a white or red checked headdress known as a 'gutra'. This is secured with a black cord, 'agal'. Sheikhs and important businessmen may also wear a thin black or gold robe or 'mishlah', over their dishdasha at important events, equivalent to the dinner jacket in Western culture.

National Weddings

Weddings in the UAE are a serious and very large affair. Homes are lit from top to bottom with strings of white or yellow fairy lights, and the festivities last up to two weeks. Men and women celebrate separately, normally in a hotel ballroom or convention centre, depending on the number of guests. High dowries and extravagant weddings may be a thing of the past though, as the Government has placed a ceiling of Dhs.50,000 on dowries, and lavish weddings can result in a prison sentence or Dhs.500,000 fine!

The Government-sponsored Marriage Fund, based in Abu Dhabi, assists nationals in everything to do with marriage - from counselling and financial assistance (long-term loans up to Dhs.70,000 for UAE national men marrying UAE national women), to organising group weddings to lower costs. While marriage between a national man and a non-national woman is legally permissible (but frowned upon), national women are not allowed to marry non-national men. One of the main aims of the marriage fund is to lessen the number of foreign marriages by UAE nationals.

In public, women wear the black 'abaya' – a long, loose black robe that covers their normal clothes, plus a headscarf, called the 'sheyla'. The abaya is often of very sheer, flowing fabric and may be open at the front. Some women also wear a thin black veil hiding their face and/or gloves, while older

Prayer Time

women sometimes still wear a leather mask, known as a 'burkha', which covers the nose, brow and cheekbones. Underneath the abaya, women traditionally wear a long tunic over loose, flowing trousers ('sirwall'), which are often heavily embroidered and fitted at the wrists and ankles. However, these are used more by the older generation and modern women will often wear trousers or a long skirt beneath the abaya.

Food & Drink

Other options ➜ Eating Out [p.234]

Abu Dhabi offers pretty much every type of international cuisine imaginable. While most restaurants are located in hotels and are thus able to offer alcohol, some of the best places to eat are the small street side stands around town. Refer to the Going Out section for more details on everything available to quench both hunger and thirst.

Arabic Cuisine

Modern Arabic cuisine is a blend of many types of cooking, from Moroccan, Tunisian, Iranian, Egyptian to Afghani, but in Abu Dhabi modern 'Arabic cuisine' invariably means Lebanese food. Sidewalk stands selling 'shawarma' (lamb or chicken sliced from a spit and served in pita bread) and 'falafel' (small savoury balls of deep fried beans), are worth a visit at least once. Generally, this cuisine is excellent for meat eaters and vegetarians alike. A popular starter is a selection of dishes known as 'meze', which is often a meal in its own right. It's a variety of appetisers served with pita bread, a green salad and 'radioactive' pickles. Dishes can include 'humous' (ground chickpeas, oil and garlic), 'tabouleh' (parsley and cracked wheat salad, with tomato etc), 'fatoush' (lettuce, tomatoes etc, with grilled Arabic bread) and 'fattayer' (small, usually hot pastries filled with cottage cheese and spinach).

Charcoal grilling is a popular style of cooking. However, a Ramadan favourite is 'Khouzi' (whole lamb served on a bed of rice, mixed with nuts), an authentic local dish, also served at the 'Mansaf', a traditional, formal Bedouin dinner with dishes placed on the floor in the centre of a ring of seated guests. Other typical dishes include 'kibbeh' (deep fried mince, pine nuts and bulgar or cracked wheat) or a variety of kebabs.

The meal ends with Lebanese sweets, which are delicious, but extremely sweet. The most widely known are 'baklava' (filo pastry layered with honey and pistachio nuts) and 'umm Ali', or 'mother of Ali' in English, a dessert with layers of milk, bread, raisins and nuts.

Pork

Pork is not included on the Arabic menu. Do not underestimate how taboo this meat is to a Muslim. Its restriction is not just in eating the meat, but also in the preparation and service. Thus to serve pork, restaurants need a separate fridge, equipment, preparation and cooking areas etc, while supermarkets need a separate pork area in the shop and separate storage facilities. Images of pigs can also cause offence.

Shisha Pipes

Additionally, in Islam it is forbidden to consume the blood or meat of any animal that has not been slaughtered in the correct manner. The meat of animals killed in accordance with the Islamic code is known as 'halaal'.

Alcohol

Alcohol is only served in licensed outlets that are associated with hotels (ie, restaurants and bars), a few clubs (such as golf) and associations. Restaurants outside of hotels, that are not part of a club or association, are not permitted to serve alcohol.

Permanent residents who are non-Muslims may obtain alcohol for consumption at home without difficulty under a permit system. By law, you are required be have this permit with you whenever transporting liquor or drinking alcohol at licensed premises.

See also: Liquor Licence [p.58]; Alcohol Outlets [p.136].

Shisha

Throughout the Middle East, smoking the traditional 'shisha' (water pipe) is a popular and relaxing pastime, usually savoured in a local café while chatting with friends. They are also known as hookah pipes or hubbly bubbly, but are properly called a 'nargile'.

Shisha pipes can be smoked with a variety of aromatic flavours, such as strawberry, grape, apple etc, and the experience is quite unlike smoking a normal cigarette or cigar. The smoke is softened by the water, creating a much more soothing effect. This is one of those things in life that should at least be tried once, and preferably during Ramadan, under the festive tents set up throughout the city, filled with people of all nationalities and the fragrant smell of shisha tobacco.

ENTERING ABU DHABI

Visas

Other options ➜ Residence Visa [p.54]
Entry Visa [p.52]

Visa requirements for entering the UAE vary greatly between different nationalities, and regulations should always be checked before travelling, since the details can change with little or no warning.

All visitors except Arab Gulf Co-operation Council nationals (Bahrain, Kuwait, Qatar, Oman and Saudi Arabia) require a visa. However, citizens of the countries listed below will be granted a free visit visa on arrival.

"No Visa Required"

Citizens of Andorra, Australia, Austria, Belgium, Brunei, Canada, Cyprus, Denmark, Finland, France, Germany, Greece, Hong Kong (with the right of abode in the United Kingdom), Iceland, Ireland, Italy, Japan, Liechtenstein, Luxembourg, Malaysia, Malta, Monaco, New Zealand, the Netherlands, Norway, Portugal, San Marino, Singapore, South Korea, Spain, Sweden, Switzerland, United Kingdom, United States of America and Vatican City receive an automatic, free visit visa on arrival in Abu Dhabi. The visa is usually stamped for 30 days but entitles the holder to stay in the country for 60 days. This can be extended for a further 30 days upon payment of approximately Dhs.500.

Expat residents of the AGCC who meet certain criteria may obtain a non renewable 30 day visa on arrival. Residents of Oman of certain nationalities may enter the UAE on a free of charge entry permit.

Tourist nationalities (such as those from Eastern and Western Europe, Thailand, China and South Africa may obtain a 30 day, non renewable tourist visa sponsored by a local entity, such as a hotel or tour operator, before entry into the UAE. Other visitors may apply for an entry service permit in advance (for 14 days exclusive of arrival/departure days), valid for use within 14 days of the date of issue, or for a 60 day visit visa (renewable once for a total stay of 90 days) sponsored by a local company. This visit visa costs Dhs.120, plus a visa delivery fee of Dhs.10. Allow 2 weeks for processing.

If you are flying to or from Europe or the USA, to Asia or Africa and passing through UAE airports, a special transit visa (up to 96 hours) may be obtained free of charge through any airline carrier operating in the UAE, though you MUST have a valid ticket for your onward flight.

A multiple entry visa is available for business visitors who have a relationship with a local business. It is valid for visits of a maximum 30 days each time, for six months from the date of issue. It costs Dhs.1, 000 and should be applied for after entering the UAE on a visit visa. However, if you are a German citizen (both tourist and business visitors), you may apply to the UAE Embassy in Germany for a one or two year multiple entry visa. No sponsor is required and the maximum duration of stay should not exceed three months in any one year. The fee for this visa is Dhs.1, 500. Citizens of the USA may apply to the UAE Embassy in the USA for a 1 - 10 year multiple entry visa. A sponsor is required and the visa will be granted free of charge. Maximum duration of stay of each visit should not exceed six months.

Airlines may require confirmation (a photocopy is acceptable) that a UAE visa is held before check in at the airport. If you have sponsorship from a UAE entity, ensure they fax you a copy of the visa before the flight. The original is held at the Abu Dhabi International Airport for collection before passport control. Your passport should have a minimum of three months validity left. Israeli nationals will not be issued visas.

Costs: Some companies may levy a maximum of Dhs.50 extra in processing charges for arranging visas.

Note: Visit visas are valid for 30 or 60 days, not one or two calendar months. If you overstay, there is a Dhs.100 fine for each day overstayed.

Visa Renewals

Visit visas may be renewed for a total stay of up to 90 days. Renewals are usually made by paying for a month's extension (Dhs.500) at the Immigration Department, Saeed bin Tahnoon Street in Abu Dhabi (446 2244), and Aditaba Road, near Dubai Islamic Bank in Al Ain (03 762 5555/751 0000) . After the third month, you must either fly out of the country on a 'visa run' (see below) and collect a new visit visa on return to the airport, or leave the country and arrange a new visit visa from your home country.

Visa Run

The 'visa run' (or 'visa change' flight) basically involves exiting and re-entering the country to gain an exit stamp and new entry stamp in your passport. Unfortunately, driving over the border into Oman is not an option, since you will not receive a UAE exit stamp in your passport. Hence the visa run is a flight to a neighbouring country and back to Abu Dhabi.

The flight is invariably to Doha or Muscat and it returns an hour or so later. Passengers remain in transit and hence do not need a visa for the country they fly to. Gulf Air (633 2600) and British Airways (622 4540) are the only airlines to offer this service from Abu Dhabi and there are flights daily. The cost is about Dhs.400 for a return flight, depending on the season. The low price is only offered for the

visa flight and is not available if you want to spend any time in the country to which you are travelling. There is no visa flight service offered from Al Ain, although a regular flight can be made from Al Ain to Muscat at a cost of Dhs.1,070 return

These flights are the cheapest option for those who need to change their visa status after their residency application has been approved by the Immigration Department.

The visa run is also an opportunity to stock up on good value duty free, and there are sales outlets in both the departure and arrival halls of the airports.

Holders of passports that are allowed a visit visa on arrival at the airport currently have the option of making a visa run indefinitely.

Until 2000, the visa run was an option for all nationalities with sponsors willing to arrange for a new visit visa. Now, unless the situation reverts, a visa run is only possible for nationalities who can gain a visa stamp on arrival at the airport. This was implemented in a crackdown on people working in the country illegally without sponsorship or residency.

Meet & Greet

In keeping with the Arabian tradition of hospitality, meet and greet services are offered at Abu Dhabi airport to assist passengers with airport formalities.

Sunshine Tours (444 9914) helps arrivals through Customs and Immigration, and offers a one way transfer to any hotel in Abu Dhabi for an all inclusive cost of Dhs.100. This can be particularly helpful to passengers who fit the categories of unaccompanied children, the disabled or elderly, although anyone can use the service.

Golden Class Service assists departing and arriving passengers (575 7466 or fax 575 8070). They offer a dedicated check in counter, help with Immigration and use of facilities in the VIP lounge, which includes use of the health club or secretarial services in the Business Centre. Individual annual membership and company membership are also available for the year. For individuals, prices range from Dhs.60 for an arriving or departing passenger. For groups of two or more travelling together, the charge is Dhs.45 each, and children from 2 - 12 years are Dhs.25 each for arrival or departure. Additional offers include a limousine service and fresh flowers for arrivals. This useful service may be booked and paid for at the City Terminal opposite the Beach Hotel.

Customs

No customs duty is levied on personal effects when entering Abu Dhabi. It is, however, strictly forbidden to import drugs and pornographic items.

At Abu Dhabi International Airport, your bags are x-rayed after collection from the arrivals hall. Videos, DVDs, CDs, books and magazines are sometimes checked, and suspect items, usually movies, may be temporarily confiscated for the material to be approved. Unless it is offensive, it can be collected at a later date. The airport duty free has a small sales outlet in the arrivals hall.

There has been talk of restrictions on the import or export of large amounts of any currency since the events of 11 September 2001. We recommend that you check this out before you try it! In addition, a new anti money-laundering law has come into effect, which not only penalises individuals who violate the law, but also financial institutions. The penalty for money laundering will be a prison sentence of up to seven years or a maximum fine of Dhs.300,000. The Central Bank is also due to set a limit for the amount of undeclared cash that can be brought into the country.

Duty Free allowances:

- *Cigarettes - 2,000*
- *Cigars - 400*
- *Tobacco - 2 kg*
- *Alcohol (non-Muslim adults only) - 2 litres of spirits and 2 litres of wine*
- *Perfume - a 'reasonable amount'*

TRAVELLERS' INFO

Health Requirements

No health certificates are required for entry to the Emirates, with the exception of visitors who have been in a yellow fever or cholera infected area in the previous 14 days. However, it is always wise to check health requirements before departure as restrictions may vary depending upon the situation at the time.

There are very few mosquitoes in the towns and cities, and since the risk of contracting malaria is low, tablets are rarely prescribed for travel in the UAE. However, if you are camping near the mountains, or exploring wadis or date groves in the evening, mosquitoes will find you! So cover up and use a suitable insect repellent; it is always safer to avoid being bitten. Tetanus inoculations are usually recommended if you are considering a long trip. Polio has virtually been eradicated in the UAE, and hepatitis is very rare and can be avoided by taking precautions. Check requirements before leaving your home country.

Health Care

The quality of medical care in the Emirates is generally regarded as quite high and visitors should have little trouble obtaining appropriate treatment whether privately or, in case of an emergency, from the government run hospitals. Tourists and non residents are strongly recommended to arrange private medical insurance before travelling since private medical care can become very expensive.

There are no specific health risks facing visitors, though the climate can be harsh, especially during the summer months. It's advisable to drink plenty of water (replace lost salts with energy drinks or salty snacks), and cover up when out in the sun. Use the appropriate factor sunscreen – sunburn, heat stroke and heat exhaustion can be very unpleasant.

If you need a doctor, ask at your hotel, or ring your embassy for recommendations. If you need emergency treatment and are unable to contact a doctor directly, try one of the major hospitals listed below in the table.

Emergency Medical Services	
Abu Dhabi Central Hospital	621 4666
Al Ahliya Hospital	626 2666
Al Mafraq (main govt hospital)	582 3100
Al Manara International Hospital	621 8888
Al Noor Hospital	626 5265
Al Salama Hospital	671 1220
Corniche Hospital	672 4900
Dar al-Shifaa Hospital	641 6999
New Medical Centre	633 2255
Al Ain Hospital (Al Jimi)	03 763 5888
Al Hayat Hospital	03 766 2999
Emirates International Hospital	03 763 7777
Oasis Hospital	03 722 1251
Specialised Medical Hospital	03 766 2291
Tawam Hospital	03 767 7444

Most medicines are readily available at pharmacies and many without prescription – even antibiotics. Each emirate has at least one pharmacy open 24 hours a day. Check the Gulf News for information. Dial 998 or 999 for ambulance service.

Travel Insurance

All visitors to the Emirates should have travel insurance – just in case. Choose a reputable insurer and a plan that suits your needs and the activities you plan to do while in the UAE. Make sure this insurance also covers 'blood money' (see [p.33]) in the event of an accident involving a death and you are found at fault.

Female Visitors

Women should face few, if any, problems while travelling in the UAE. Single female travellers who don't want extra attention should avoid wearing tight fitting clothing and should steer clear of lower end hotels and seedy nightclubs. No matter what, most females receive some unwanted stares at some time or another, particularly on the public beaches. If you can ignore it, you'll save yourself some aggravation! The police are very helpful and respectful – call them if you face any unwanted attention or hassles.

Travelling with Children

Abu Dhabi is a great place for kids of all ages. Parks and amusement centres abound, and if that's not enough for the little ones, there's always the beach. The Activities section will give a better idea of what there is to do with kids, as will the *Family Explorer*.

Shopping Mall Fun for Kids

Hotels and shopping malls are well geared up for children, offering everything from babysitting services to kids' activities. Restaurants, on the other hand, have children's menus but tend not to have many high chairs; it's best to check when making reservations. Discounted rates for children are common – just ask.

Disabled Visitors

Most of Abu Dhabi's five star hotels have wheelchair facilities but, in general, facilities for the disabled are very limited, particularly at tourist attractions. Wheelchair ramps are often really nothing more than delivery ramps, hence the steep angles. When asking if a location has wheelchair access, make sure it really does – an escalator is considered 'wheelchair access' to some! The Abu Dhabi International Airport is equipped for disabled travellers (see also: Golden Class Service [p.20]). As for parking, good luck! Handicapped parking spaces do exist, but are often used by ignorant drivers who don't need the facility.

Hotels with specially adapted rooms for the disabled include: Le Royal Meridien Abu Dhabi, Al Diar Gulf Hotel & Resort, Crowne Plaza, Millenium Hotel, Hotel Intercontinental, Hotel Intercontinental (Al Ain)

Dress Code

For visitors to the country, lightweight summer clothing is suitable for most of the year, but something slightly warmer may be needed for the winter months. Be sure to take some sort of jacket or sweater when visiting hotels or the cinema, as the air conditioning can be pretty fierce.

Although the attitude towards dress is fairly liberal throughout the Emirates, Abu Dhabi is rather more conservative than neighbouring Dubai. There still isn't much that you can't wear, but, as in all countries, a healthy amount of respect for local customs doesn't go amiss, especially when shopping or generally sightseeing. Like anywhere in the world, the rural areas have a more conservative attitude than in the cities. Short or tight clothing may be worn, but it will attract attention – most of it unwelcome. For ladies it is advisable to wear short sleeved rather than sleeveless tops and dresses, especially if travelling by local taxi on your own. During the day, as in any place with loads of sun, good quality sunglasses, hats and buckets of sunscreen are needed to avoid the lobster look!

In the evenings, the restaurants and clubs usually have a mixture of styles – western, Arabic and Asian – anything goes. Again, ladies are advised to take a shawl or jacket, not only for the journey home, but also because of the cold blasts from the air conditioning.

If you plan to visit Sharjah, beware, for a Decency Law has recently been implemented penalising all those who do not abide by a certain dress code and moral behaviour. 'Indecent dress' includes anything that exposes the stomach, back, or legs above the knees. Tight fitting, transparent clothing is also not permitted, nor are acts of vulgarity, indecent noises or harassment. If you are deemed to have offended the law, you will initially be given advice by the police on what decency is, and warned to abide by the law in future. If the police find you breaking the law again, a more severe penalty will be imposed.

Do's and Don'ts

Do make the most of your stay in Abu Dhabi. Have fun, but don't break the law. It's a simple and easy rule, and common sense will keep you out of trouble. In the UAE, drugs are illegal and carry a jail sentence. If you are caught bringing drugs into the country, you will be charged with trafficking, which can result in a life sentence. Pornography of any sort is also illegal and will be confiscated immediately.

The best rule of thumb is to respect the local laws, culture and Muslim sensibilities of the UAE; remember that you are a visitor and treat the local population with the same respect you'd expect back home.

Safety

While the crime rate in Abu Dhabi is very low, a healthy degree of caution should still be exercised. Keep your valuables and travel documents locked in your hotel room or in the hotel safe. When in crowds, be discreet with your money and wallet; don't carry large amounts of cash on you and don't trust strangers offering to double your money with magic potions. Money and gem related scams are on the increase – be warned!

With a multitude of driving styles converging on Abu Dhabi's roads, navigating the streets either on foot or in a vehicle can be a challenge. Here are some quick tips to make your experience on the streets safer: if your taxi driver is driving too aggressively, tell him to slow down. Cross the roads only at designated pedestrian crossings, and before you cross, make sure all cars have actually stopped for you. Learn the rules of the road before getting behind the wheel and drive defensively. Make sure you have insurance!

Lost/Stolen Property

To avoid a great deal of hassle if your personal documents go missing, make sure you keep one photocopy with friends or family back home, and one copy in a secure place such as your hotel room safe.

If your valuables do go missing, first check with your hotel, or if you've lost something in a taxi, call the taxi company lost and found department. There are a lot of honest people in Abu Dhabi who will return found items. If you've had no luck, then call the Abu Dhabi Police to report the loss or theft; you'll be advised on the next steps to follow. If you have lost your passport, your next stop will be your embassy or consulate. For a list of all embassies and consulates in Abu Dhabi, see [p.95].

PLACES TO STAY

Visitors to Abu Dhabi will find an extensive choice of places to stay, from hotels to hotel apartments, youth hostels and even an eco-tourist hotel (the Al Maha resort, located amongst the dunes on the road between Dubai and Al Ain).

The growth in the number of hotels and hotel apartments is constantly on the rise and you can expect excellent service and facilities – at least at the higher end of the market.

One service that hotels offer is to act as sponsor for those needing a visit visa. This service should cost about Dhs.180 (including mark up) for a regular and Dhs.280 for an urgent visa, and the visa is deposited at the airport for collection on arrival. However, the visitor is then expected to stay at the hotel.

Abu Dhabi Airport Hotel
Map ref ➜ 2-B2

Situated at the Abu Dhabi International Airport, this convenient stopover is a great bonus for travellers. Having expanded in 2002, the hotel offers all the facilities you would expect. There are five bars/restaurants, a well equipped children's play area and a Nautilus gym to work out while you wait for your onward flight.

Al Diar Capital Hotel
Map ref ➜ 8-B2

Now a part of the Al Diar Hotel Group, the Capital Hotel opened in late 2002. Well positioned in the centre of Abu Dhabi, it offers 140 standard/deluxe rooms and 60 executive suites (with an equipped kitchenette). The hotel also boasts seven bars and restaurants, including the happening nightspot, Rock Bottom.

Al Maha Rotana
Map ref ➜ 8-B1

Located near the Corniche, these studios and residential suites are modern and good value for money. With all the conveniences of a hotel, they offer an apartment-style stay with your own kitchen/microwave and in-room laundry facilities. For a quick coffee, the City Café is a good choice.

Beach Rotana Hotel & Towers
Map ref ➜ 4-B3

This luxury hotel has recently undergone major expansion. Now boasting a conference centre and additional luxury sea-facing rooms (bringing the total to 558), it also offers a plethora of dining options from Trader Vic's to Italian, Japanese, German and Lebanese. Direct access to the Abu Dhabi Mall is an added bonus.

Crowne Plaza
Map ref ➜ 8-C1

In the heart of the city and only minutes' walking distance from Abu Dhabi's shopping district, this hotel also won the Quality Excellence Award in 2000. Some of their rooms are equipped for disabled travellers. Restaurants include the popular Heroes Diner and there's a well-maintained private beach that is accessible to guests.

Hilton Baynunah Tower
Map ref ➜ 9-A2

Undoubtedly one of the most impressive towers on the Corniche, the Hilton Baynunah Tower has the accolade of being the tallest residential complex in Abu Dhabi. Forty storeys of blue glass house deluxe suites, a restaurant/coffee shop and a health club. However, unlike the impressive exterior, the interior has a somewhat dated feel.

Hilton International Abu Dhabi
Map ref ➜ 10-C2

Conveniently located near Abu Dhabi's financial and business district, the Hilton was refurbished in 2000 and now has 350 guestrooms with first class executive floors. However, it's the Hiltonia Beach Club and famous Hemingway's and Jazz Bar nightspots, along with nine other restaurants and bars that make this hotel a favourite.

Hotel Inter-Continental
Map ref ➜ 10-C1

Adjacent to the marina, this hotel is surrounded by lush parks and gardens. With 5 restaurants, 4 bars and 330 deluxe rooms offering views of the city and the Arabian Gulf, this ageing hotel draws many conference and business visitors. Located out of the city centre, some of the outlets here are definitely worth the trek.

Le Meridien Abu Dhabi
Map ref ➜ 7-D1

Renovated in 1998, this hotel has a vast choice from standard five star rooms to studios, plus residence, diplomatic, deluxe suites and even a presidential suite. However, the hotel is best known amongst residents for its modern health club & spa, private beach, and Culinary Village with excellent food & beverage outlets.

Le Royal Meridien Abu Dhabi
Map ref ➜ 8-B2

Recently taken over by Le Meridien Hotels, this landmark, known to most as the Abu Dhabi Grand, has 187 rooms/suites, most of which are Corniche and sea-facing. Originally opened in 1993, current refurbishments are due to finish in 2004. Offering spectacular views, it also has the only revolving restaurant in the capital.

Abu Dhabi 5 Star Hotels

Millennium Hotel
Map ref ➔ 8-C2

This modern Millenium Hotel, located near the famous Corniche, has great views of the city. It has 325 elegantly decorated rooms and 3 restaurants serving Moroccan, Italian and international cuisine. However, the hotel is more widely known for opening Abu Dhabi's first ever champagne & cigar bar - Cristal.

Sands Hotel
Map ref ➔ 8-C1

Previously known as the Holiday Inn, this hotel reopened as the Sands Hotel in 1996. Located in the city centre with 253 rooms/suites, it has convenient access to the business district as well as both the Abu Dhabi & Marina Malls. The Sands has six restaurants and bars, including Chequers, La Piazza and Imperial Chinese.

Sheraton Abu Dhabi
Map ref ➔ 8-A3

Situated on the Corniche, the Sheraton has recently undergone renovations and is a favourite in Abu Dhabi with both residents as well as business travellers. Apart from the 259 rooms, most with a sea view, their Italian restaurant, La Mamma, draws many regulars. It also has a private beach and health club.

Conference Palace Hotel
Map ref ➔ 10-D4

Will be completed in 2004.

Al Ain 5 Star Hotels

Al Ain Rotana Hotel
Map ref ➔ 14-E4

Set in the heart of the garden city, this hotel allows easy access to Al Ain's tourist attractions. The 100 spacious rooms, suites and chalets are comfortable and the fitness centre is state-of-the-art. On the cuisine front, their restaurants cover everything from Lebanese to the ever-popular Polynesian Trader Vic's.

Hilton Al Ain
Map ref ➔ 15-C4

Located near the heart of Al Ain, this ageing hotel, built in 1971, is a base from which to explore the zoo, museum, Jebel Hafeet and the Hili Tombs. The 202 guestrooms, suites and villas look over landscaped gardens, and five bars and restaurants, floodlit tennis/squash courts, a health club and a nine-hole golf course offer plenty to do.

Hotel Inter-Continental Al Ain
Map ref ➔ 15-E4

A recent multi-million dollar refurbishment has transformed this hotel into one of the most impressive inland resorts in the UAE. Landscaped gardens, swimming pools, guestrooms, deluxe villas and a Royal Villa with a private jacuzzi, along with restaurants and bars only make this an even greater leisure retreat - highly recommended.

Mercure Grand Jebel Hafeet
Map ref ➔ 17-B4

Having taken seven years to build, thanks to its precarious location on Jebel Hafeet, the Mercure Grand finally opened its doors in 2002. Simply decorated rooms, offer the best views over Al Ain. Diners at Le Belvedere can admire stunning vistas of the city at night, as can those out for a stroll through the hotel gardens below.

General Info

Places to Stay

Al Ain Palace Hotel
Map ref ➜ 8-B3

The Al Ain Palace is one of Abu Dhabi's more established hotels (fondly known as the 'Ally Pally'). It offers international restaurants and theme bars, 110 deluxe rooms and suites, plus self-contained studios and chalet-style rooms. Situated on the waterfront with a private beach, it's a good base from which to discover Abu Dhabi.

Al Diar Dana Hotel
Map ref ➜ 4-B4

Located in the tourist club district a short way from the new Abu Dhabi Mall, this hotel has 112 spacious rooms, each with their own kitchenette for self sufficiency coupled with the perks of a hotel. On the dining front, it offers a choice of European pub, pizzeria, karaoke bar, and 49ers – the only Wild West rooftop restaurant and bar.

Al Diar Gulf Hotel & Resort
Map ref ➜ 1-D3

This resort offers a range of amenities to distinguish it from others. Opened in 1977, it has 273 rooms and 4 restaurants, and boasts the largest beach on the island. The hotel's Palm Beach Club offers every activity imaginable, from numerous water sports to tennis, squash and even mini golf – great for family vacations.

Al Diar Palm Hotel
Map ref ➜ 5-A2

Situated on Al Murror Street near the shopping districts, this hotel comprises 72 apartment-style suites offering more than just hotel facilities. All rooms are spacious and have a kitchen equipped with a washer/dryer, fridge and cooker – great for extended stays. There's also a coffee shop on the ground floor.

Grand Continental Flamingo Hotel Map ref ➜ 8-B2

Open for five years, this 'boutique' hotel looks and feels pretty much the same as many other four star hotels in the city. The many rooms and the Flamingo Club showcase views of the city, but it may be the popular Peppino's restaurant that attracts the crowds. A pub and international restaurant caters mostly to guests and lunch diners.

Howard Johnson Diplomat Hotel Map ref ➜ 8-B2

This hotel is decent value for money. Repackaged as the Howard Johnson in 2000, it has 125 apartment-style rooms and 20 suites, all above average in size and each with a kitchenette for self-sufficiency - good for longer staying guests. The hotel has over 11 food/entertainment outlets including the European pub, Cellar.

International Rotana Inn
Map ref ➜ 8-A1

Opened in 1978 and especially known for their breakfast, lunch and dinner buffets at Windows Café, this spacious hotel offers visitors 130 guestrooms and a location handy to the Exhibition Centre. The Red Lion Pub with its traditional pub fare is a firm favourite with the western community in Abu Dhabi.

Khalidia Palace Hotel
Map ref ➜ 10-E2

This hotel is a kid's holiday come true. Apart from the 120 rooms and suites, they have beach chalets each with a kitchen, private garden and direct beach access. The children can enjoy the mini zoo, bouncy castles and go-karts as well as the usual water sports. For the adults, there are four restaurants and a health club.

Mafraq Hotel
Map ref ➜ UAE-A4

Built in 1996 and conveniently located 10 minutes from Abu Dhabi International Airport, and 20 minutes from the city centre, this quiet hotel featuring 120 rooms and four suites offers relaxed, landscaped surroundings and a decent range of good value restaurants.

Novotel Centre Hotel
Map ref ➜ 8-D2

One of the better known city centre hotels, the Novotel is located in the heart of Abu Dhabi on Sheikh Hamdan Street, near the Liwa shopping mall. It has 201 rooms and 7 suites, but the restaurants are the main draw, covering some of Europe's finest cuisine. Le Beaujolais and L'Opera are perennial favourites with residents.

Al Diar Hotels
COMMITTED TO MEETING SUCCESS

Take your next meeting to Al Diar, where the business travellers' convenience is our concern. With a choice of 8 deluxe hotels, your business soujourn in the UAE couldn't be more comfortable. Al Diar Hotels have redefined standards for business travel, with state-of-the-art communications, professional service, fine dining, an array of recreational options and perfect conference solutions.

Al Diar Hotels & Resorts

A DIVISION OF ABU DHABI NATIONAL HOTELS
www.aldiarhotels.com

P.O.Box: 46806, Abu Dhabi, U.A.E. Tel.: 00971 2 4447327, Fax: 00971 2 4444048

- **AL DIAR CAPITAL HOTEL** (Newly Opened)
- **AL DIAR SANDS HOTEL**
- **AL DIAR GULF HOTEL & RESORTS**
- **AL DIAR SIJI HOTEL** (Fujairah)
- **AL DIAR PALM HOTEL**
- **AL DIAR REGENCY HOTEL**
- **AL DIAR MINA HOTEL**
- **AL DIAR DANA HOTEL**

General Info

Places to Stay

Hotels – Abu Dhabi

Five-Star	Beach Access	Phone	Map	Double	Email
Abu Dhabi Airport Hotel		575 7377	2-B2	587	airphotl@emirates.net.ae
Al Diar Capital Hotel		678 7700	7-E2	371	adcaphtl@emirates.net.ae
Al Diar Mina Hotel		678 1000	8-A2	350	minahotl@emirates.net.ae
Al Maha Rotana		610 6666	8-B1	230	almaha.suites@rotana.com
Beach Rotana Hotel & Towers	✔	644 3000	4-B3	1,100	sales.abudhabi@rotana.com
Crowne Plaza		621 0000	8-C1	522	cpauh@emirates.net.ae
Hilton International Abu Dhabi	✔	681 1900	10-C2	673	auhhitw@emirates.net.ae
Hilton Baynunah Tower		632 7777	9-A2	766	baynunah@emirates.net.ae
Hotel Inter-Continental	✔	666 6888	10-C1	1,102	abudhabi@interconti.com
Le Meridien Abu Dhabi	✔	644 6666	7-D1	928	sales@meridien-abudhabi.co.ae
Le Royal Meridien Hotel		674 2020	8-B2	580	info@leroyalmeridien-abudhabi.com
Millenium Hotel		626 2700	8-B2	1,032	sales.abudhabi@mill-cop.com
Sands Hotel		633 5335	8-C1	1,102	sandshot@emirates.net.ae
Sheraton Abu Dhabi	✔	677 3333	8-A3	696-812	sheraton@emirates.net.ae
Four-Star					
Al Ain Palace Hotel		679 4777	8-B3	500	aphsales@emirates.net.ae
Al Diar Dana Hotel		645 6000	4-B4	450	danahotel@emirates.net.ae
Al Diar Gulf Hotel & Resort	✔	441 4777	1-D3	522	adglfhtl@emirates.net.ae
Al Diar Palm Hotel		642 0900	5-A2	450	diarpalm@emirates.net.ae
Al Diar Regency Hotel		676 5000	8-A2	450	regencyh@emirates.net.ae
Grand Continental Flamingo Htl		626 2200	8-B2	754	grndconh@emirates.net.ae
Howard Johnson Diplomat Htl		671 0000	8-B2	300	diplomathojo@hotmail.com
International Rotana Inn		677 9900	8-A2	300	rotanainn@emirates.net.ae
Khalidia Palace Hotel	✔	666 2470	10-E2	325	kphauh@emirates.net.ae
Mafraq Hotel		582 2666	UAE-A4	638	mafraq@emirates.net.ae
Novotel Centre Hotel		633 3555	8-D2	580	novoad@emirates.net.ae
Three-Star					
Emirates Plaza Hotel		672 2000	7-E2	450	eph@emirates.net.ae
Zakher Hotel		627 5300	8-B2	265	zakhotel@emirates.net.ae

Hotels – Al Ain

Five-Star	Beach Access	Phone	Map	Double	Email
Al Ain Rotana Hotel		754 5111	15-A3	812	alain.hotel@rotana.com
Hilton Al Ain		768 6666	15-D4	754	aanhitwrm@hilton.
Hotel Inter-Continental Al Ain		768 6686	15-E4	696	alain@intercont.com
Mercure Grand Jebel Hafeet		783 8888	17-B4	690	rdv@mercure_al ain.com
Three-Star					
Ain Al Fayda		783 8333	na	165	na
Jazira					
Al Diar Jazira Beach Resort	✔	562 9100	na	300-350	jazbeach@emirates.net.ae
Ruwais					
Dhafra Beach Hotel		877 1600	na	638	dbhotel@emirates.net.ae

Hotel Apartments – Abu Dhabi

Deluxe	Phone	One B/room Apts (Weekly)	(Monthly)	Two B/room Apts (Weekly)	(Monthly)
Al Hamra Residence	678 8000	1,750	5,000	3,500	9,000
Al Maha Rotana Suites	610 6666	3,724	9,500	na	16,000
Al Rawda Rotana Suites	445 7111	2,100	6,000	na	na
Beach Rotana Suites	644 3000	na	8,000	na	13,000
Baynunah Residence	632 7777	3,654	9,000	7,308	14,000
Corniche Residence	627 6000	2,436	8,000	6,049	9,000
Corniche Towers Residence	681 0088	3,000	6,500	4,000	8,500
Golden Tulip Dalma Suites	633 2100	1,925	5,000	na	na
Khalidia Hotel Apartments	666 2470	2,800	6,000	5,250	15,000
Oasis Residence	641 7000	1,225	4,500	na	na
Park Residence	674 2000	1,050	3,300	na	na
Platinum Residence	634 4463	2,800	8,000	4,900	10,000
Royal Residence	627 2300	2,450	4,500	4,200	6,500
Sahara Residence	631 9000	1,575	5,000	2,100	7,000
Sheraton Residence	666 6220	2,450	8,400	4,200	13,500

Note The above prices are the hotel apartment's peak season published rack rates and are inclusive of tax and service charge. Many hotels offer a discount off the rack rate if asked. Peak or high season is from October - April (except during Ramadan, refer to Ramadan & Public Holidays, General Information, for further details).

The Conference Centre Hotel

Hotels

Although the choice of good quality, cheap hotels is limited, visitors can be assured of an excellent selection of hotels at the higher end of the market.

Hotels in Abu Dhabi can be split into 'city hotels' and 'beach hotels', and the majority are located around the northern end of the island near the Corniche. The journey from the airport to the centre takes about 40 minutes and the taxi ride to most hotels will cost Dhs.70 in specially registered airport taxis. Larger hotels offer an airport shuttle service. Road transport in Abu Dhabi is usually pretty fast and the majority of journeys on the island will only be of 10 - 15 minutes duration, costing about Dhs.5 - 10.

In Al Ain there are four main hotels, the Hilton, the Inter-Continental, the Al Ain Rotana and The Mercure Grand Hotel. Trips from the airport take 15 - 20 minutes to the Hilton, costing Dhs.15 in normal taxis or Dhs.40 by special airport taxi. The Al Ain Rotana is about five minutes nearer the airport, the Inter-Continental about five minutes further from the Hilton and The Mercure Grand is situated near the top of Jebel Hafit and will take about 30 minutes to get to from the airport.

Remember that, as is the case the world over, a discount on the 'rack rate' or published price is often given.

The rates listed in the table [p.28] are peak season discounted rates (discount off the rack rate). Where applicable, the 16% municipality tax has been included in the listed price.

Hotel Apartments

A cheaper alternative to staying in a hotel is to rent furnished accommodation. This can be done on a daily/weekly/monthly or yearly basis and there are a number of agencies offering this service. One advantage is that the place can feel far more like home than a hotel room. Usually the apartments will come fully furnished, from bed linen to cutlery, plus maid service. Additionally, there may be sports facilities, such as a gym and swimming pool in the building.

See also: *Hotel Apartments – Accommodation (New Residents)*

Youth Hostels

The UAE is not a budget destination. Nevertheless, inexpensive accommodation in hostels is available in most of the Emirates. The hostels are networked and they do co-operate as far as advance bookings and other issues are concerned. A Hostelling International membership card is requested of guests, however if you do not have one, you can purchase a yearly membership at the hostels in the UAE for approximately Dhs.100, or alternatively, pay a higher non member rate per night. To apply for membership, you will need to complete an application form and provide a passport copy along with two passport photos. See www.hostels.com/ae.html.

UAE Hostels	
Dubai (Al Qusais Road, Nr Al Ahli Club)	04 298 8161
Fujairah (Nr Supreme Council of Youth Sports Office)	09 222 2347
Khor Fakkan (Nr Oceanic Hotel)	09 237 0886
Sharjah (Nr Sharjah Sports Club)	06 522 5070

Accommodation is available for men, women and families. Single women especially should check availability, since the management reserves the right to refuse bookings from single women when the hostel is busy with men. There are hostels in Dubai, Sharjah, Fujairah and Ras Al Khaimah.

Camping

Other options ➜ Sports [p.167]

There are no official campsites in the UAE, but there are plenty of places to camp outside the cities. Near Abu Dhabi, options include the desert dunes at Liwa or on the way to Al Ain. An hour's drive away in Dubai is the Jebel Ali beach, a popular place in the cooler months. If you get there early enough, you can have your own shelter and shower right on the beach.

Desert Camping

While there are many campers around, the majority are UAE residents. It's rare for someone to show up at the airport, camping gear in hand, ready to set off on a camping holiday in the Emirates.

Pick up a copy of the *Off-Road Explorer (UAE)* for further information. This guide covers everything from where to go and how to get there, to what to bring and how to prepare, and where to buy what you'll need for your camping trip.

GETTING AROUND

Other options ➜ Maps [p.301]
Exploring [p.100]

The car is the most popular method of getting around Abu Dhabi, Al Ain and the Emirates, either by private vehicle or taxi. There is a reasonable public bus service, but walking and cycling are limited and there are no trains or trams (see Bus [p.35], Car [p.32] and Taxi [p.34] entries).

The UAE's road network is excellent, and most of the roads comprise two, three and sometimes four lanes. In addition, roads are generally well signposted, with blue or green signs indicating the main areas or locations out of the city, and brown or purple signs showing heritage sites, places of interest, hospitals etc. For the benefit of both locals and expats, the majority of signs are in Arabic and English.

Lane Discipline?

Lane discipline is yet another challenge to the overall UAE driving experience. As so many different nationalities converge on the roads, there are bound to be some major differences in driving styles, and lane discipline is a particular annoyance of ours! On a highway, the majority of drivers seem to believe that the two far right lanes are reserved for trucks and the two left lanes for cars. This means that with a posted speed limit of 120 km per hour, and drivers flying down the fast lane at sometimes over 200 km per hour, you will find a small car plodding along in the next lane over at far below the speed limit! Now, if you have someone coming up behind you very, very fast, flashing their headlights and swerving dangerously, where do you go?!

In Abu Dhabi, a surprising amount of care has been taken in beautifying the roads and roundabouts; you will find many tree lined avenues and roundabouts decorated with flowers and shrubs,

and sometimes even a dhow or a coffeepot – these often become useful landmarks for getting around.

Roundabout – Abu Dhabi

Visitors should find the UAE's cities relatively easy to negotiate. Be aware though, people usually rely on landmarks to give directions or to get their bearings and most often these are shops, hotels, petrol stations or notable buildings. Roads are named with white road signs, but these are not, with a few exceptions, referred to regularly. Similarly, while there is a street name/numbering system, few people actually use it. In Abu Dhabi in particular, confusion arises since some streets can be called by their street number, their old name or their nickname! For example Sheikh Zayed the Second Street, is also known as Seventh Street, but is also popularly called Electra Street.

Hence, a little bit of insider knowledge and broad facts will help you get from A to B. The island's roads are built on a grid system and linked to the mainland by two bridges – Al Maqta Bridge and Mussafah (or Al Ain) Bridge. As you come onto the island, the first areas you'll pass are chiefly residential. Most of the offices, shops, hotels and restaurants are located within four or five blocks of the main Corniche road, which runs along the northern side of the island.

The island is split using New Airport Road as the dividing line. This road runs from Al Maqta Bridge in the east (near the mainland), to the Corniche on the northern side of the island. All roads to the east are in Zone 1 (east) and those to the west in Zone 2 (west). Roads that run parallel with New Airport Road are given even numbers, with the numbers increasing as they move away from New Airport Road to either coast. Roads parallel to the Corniche (ie, at right angles to New Airport Road), are given odd numbers, in ascending order. In addition, the city is divided into districts. And remember, ultimately, Abu Dhabi is built on an island, so if you get lost you'll never be far from the coast roads.

Al Ain is unusual in that it straddles the border with the Sultanate of Oman. There are no border posts within the city and UAE visitors can travel into the Omani part (known as Buraimi) without any problem.

In comparison to Abu Dhabi, Al Ain has developed in a less organised manner but is nevertheless based on a rough grid system. The city is fairly spread out, consisting of about ten main roads, and here too, roundabouts are important landmarks for giving directions (such as Clock Tower in the centre of town). Oases dominate the city; visitors will find walled oases all around and most of these are still farmed. Such popular spots, plus any main heritage and hotel sites are highlighted with large brown or purple signs. However, these are often missing just when you need them the most!

For further details of the road network in Abu Dhabi and Al Ain, refer to the main map section at the end of the book.

Bridge – Al Ain

Car

Other options ➜ Transportation [p.86]

Over the past two decades Abu Dhabi has built, and is still building, an impressive network of roads. So be prepared to come across lots of roadworks! There are two bridges linking the island with the mainland, with a third bridge well under way. The roads to all major towns and villages are of an excellent standard. Al Ain is about 150 km from Abu Dhabi and takes about 1½ hours to reach. A four lane highway heads north from the city to Dubai, which also takes about 1½ hours to reach.

Driving Habits & Regulations

While the infrastructure is superb, the general standard of driving is not. Apparently the UAE has one of the world's highest death rates per capita due to traffic accidents. Drivers often seem completely unaware of other cars on the road and the usual follies of driving too fast, too close, swerving, pulling out suddenly, lane hopping or drifting, happen far too regularly.

Driving & Alcohol

The Abu Dhabi Police exercise a strict zero tolerance policy on drinking and driving. This means that if you have had ANYTHING to drink, you are much better off taking a taxi home or having a friend who has consumed nothing drive you home. If you are pulled over and are found to have consumed alcohol, you are likely to find yourself enjoying the overnight hospitality of a police station - at the very least!

Also note that if you are involved in an accident, whether it is your fault or not, and you are found to have been drinking and driving, your insurance is automatically void. Penalties are severe, so the simple message is to be safe: if you are going to drink, don't even think of driving.

One move to help the situation was a ban on using handheld mobile phone while driving. Predictably, the sales of hands free systems rocketed, but it was only a matter of time before people went back to their old bad habits.

Driving is on the right and it is mandatory to wear seatbelts in the front seats. Children under ten years of age are no longer allowed to sit in the front of a car, and this ban is now countrywide, though you'll still see people driving with their children on their lap.

Fines for any of the above violations are Dhs.100, plus one 'black' point on your licence. Speeding fines are Dhs.400 and parking fines start at Dhs.100. Most fines are paid when you renew your annual car registration. However, parking tickets appear on your windscreen and you have a week or two to pay – the amount increases if you don't pay within the time allotted on the back of the ticket.

Try to keep a reasonable stopping distance between you and the car in front. Ultimately, it also helps to have eyes in the back of your head and to practice skilful defensive driving at all times.

Abu Dhabi Police HQ: 02 446 1461

Speed Limits

Speed limits are usually 60 - 80 km around town, while roads to other parts of the Emirates are 100 - 120 km. The speed is clearly indicated on road signs and there is no leeway for breaking the limit. Both fixed and movable radar traps, and the Abu Dhabi Traffic Police, are there to catch the unwary violator, and slap them with a hefty Dhs.400 fine!

Driving Licence

Visitors to Abu Dhabi have two options for driving. You can drive a rental vehicle with an international driving licence or with a licence from your country of origin, provided you are from one of the countries included in the transfer list (see [p.55]).

If you wish to drive a private vehicle, you must first go to the Traffic Police to obtain a temporary licence. Unless you have an Abu Dhabi driving licence, either permanent or temporary, you are not insured to drive a private vehicle.

Accidents

If you are involved in a traffic accident, however minor, you must remain with your car at the accident scene and report the incident to the Traffic Police, then wait for them to arrive. Unfortunately, when you have an accident in this part of the world, you become the star attraction as the passing traffic slows to a crawl and everyone has a good gawk.

Blood Money

If you are driving and cause someone's death, even in an accident that is not your fault, you are liable to pay a sum of money, known as 'blood money', to the deceased's family. The limit for this has been set at Dhs.100,000 per victim and your car insurance will cover this cost (hence the higher premiums). Moreover, insurance companies will only pay if they cannot find a way of claiming that the insurance is invalid (ie, if the driver was driving without a licence or, for example, under the influence of alcohol). The deceased's family can, however, waive the right to blood money if they feel merciful.

Stray animals (mostly camels) are something else to avoid on the roads in the UAE. If the animal hits your vehicle and causes damage or injury, the animal's owner should pay compensation. However, if you are found to have been speeding or driving recklessly, you must compensate the owner of the animal – this can be expensive.

See also: *Traffic Accidents [p.91].*

Non Drivers

In addition to dealing with the nutters in cars, you will find that pedestrians and cyclists also seem to have a death wish! The few cyclists who do brave the roads will often be cycling towards you on the wrong side of the road, invariably without lights if it is night time. Pedestrians often step out dangerously close to oncoming traffic, and a lack of convenient, safe crossings makes life for those on foot especially difficult. However, the numbers of pedestrian footbridges and pedestrian operated traffic lights are gradually increasing.

Parking

In most cities of the Emirates, parking is readily available and people rarely have to walk too far in the heat. However, in Abu Dhabi, parking can be a problem, particularly in the city centre and the more popular shopping areas. Recently, quite a few underground parking areas have cropped up, and several more are under construction. It's worth paying the Dhs.5 fee just to come back to a cool car.

Street Parking – Abu Dhabi

Petrol/Gas Stations

Petrol stations in the Emirates are numerous and run by Emarat, Emirates, EPPCO and ENOC. Most offer extra services, such as a car wash or a shop selling all those necessities of life that you forgot to buy at the supermarket. Likewise, there are plenty of petrol stations on the main roads around the Abu Dhabi emirate, but the ones on the island itself are mostly tucked away and difficult to find. The Abu Dhabi National Oil Company (ADNOC) runs most of the petrol stations in the emirate.

Most visitors will find petrol far cheaper than in their home countries; the price is about Dhs.4.2 for Premium (unleaded). In an effort to better protect the environment, leaded fuel was replaced by unleaded at the end of 2002. The UAE must be one of the few countries in the world where diesel is actually more expensive than other fuels.

ADNOC Petrol Station

Car Hire

In Abu Dhabi, you will find all major car rental companies, plus a few extra, and it is best to shop around a bit as rates vary considerably. Still, it's worth remembering that the larger, more reputable firms generally have more reliable vehicles and a greater capacity to help in an emergency (an important factor when handling the trying times following an accident). Depending on the agent, cars can be hired with or without a driver, and the minimum hire period is usually 24 hours. Prices range from Dhs.140 a day for smaller cars, up to Dhs.1,000 for limousines. Comprehensive insurance is essential (and make sure it includes personal accident coverage).

Car Rental Agencies	
Abu Dhabi Rent a Car	641 8209
Al Ghazal Transport Co.	644 7787
Avis Rent a Car	632 3760
24 hour airport branch	575 7180
Budget Rent a Car	633 4200
Cars Rent a Car	633 4334
Diamondlease	678 8400
Europcar	631 9922
Inter Abu Dhabi Rent a Car	674 4446
Inter Emirates Rent a Car	645 5855
Mondial Rent a Car	676 8377
Thrifty Car Rental	675 7400
24 hour airport branch	575 7400
Tourist Rent a Car	641 8700
Al Ghazal Transport Co.	03 721 5222
Avis Rent a Car	03 768 7262

The rental company will also arrange a temporary local driving licence for visitors. To rent a car, you are usually required to produce your passport, two photographs and either a valid international driving licence or national licence from one of the following countries: Austria, Belgium, Canada, Denmark, Finland, France, Germany, Greece, Holland, Ireland, Italy, Japan, Norway, Spain, Sweden, Switzerland, Turkey, UK and USA.

Taxi

If you don't have a car, taxis are the most common way of getting around. They are reasonably priced and plentiful, and recognised by the green taxi sign on the roof of the white and gold cars. Some driving school cars have similar markings, which can create quite a bit of confusion (and judging by the standard of some taxi drivers, you'll have a hard job distinguishing which are the real learners anyway). They may be flagged down at the roadside, ideally at the special lay bys, which have been built for picking up and dropping off passengers.

Taxis are metered, with fares starting at Dhs.2, and most trips around the city will cost between Dhs.5 - 10. After midnight, the drivers usually want to negotiate the fare rather than have the meter running, so it's often not much cheaper than taking the more upmarket Al Ghazal taxis, which always have the meter running. For trips outside the city, it is best to agree on a price before travelling; alternatively, shared minibuses can be flagged down from the side of the road and are reasonably cheap. A journey from the airport to the town centre can cost from around Dhs.40 to Dhs.70 (in specially registered airport taxis).

As well as car hire, Al Ghazal runs a taxi service – its luxury cars are white Mercedes with a pale green stripe. The meter starts at Dhs.5, and the service is very professional, with courteous, uniformed drivers. Stretch limos are also available for hire – ideal for special events.

Since Abu Dhabi has a somewhat unused street address system, most people use landmarks as an aid to get around. Unless your destination is well known, taxi drivers will not necessarily be familiar with where you want to go, so you may have to help with directions. Remember that most Abu Dhabi taxi drivers speak very little English. Start with the area you wish to go to and then choose a major landmark, such as a hotel, roundabout or shopping centre. Then narrow it down as you get closer. If you are going to a new place, try to phone for instructions first – you will often be given a distinctive landmark as a starting point. It's also helpful to take the phone number of your destination with you, in case things get too desperate.

Taxi Companies	
Al Ghazal Taxis	444 7787
Al Ghazal Taxis	03 751 6565

Airport Bus

There is a regular bus between the airport and the city centre. The municipal bus service runs 24 hours a day, every 30 minutes from 06:00 to 24:00, and every 45 minutes from 00:00 to 06:00. Buses are air conditioned, green and white in colour, and depart from outside the arrival hall. The fare is Dhs.5 and is paid when boarding the bus. Airport bus route maps are available at the Abu Dhabi International Airport.

For the return journey, Gulf Air passengers can check in at the City Terminal opposite the Beach Rotana Hotel & Towers, up to 12 hours before departure. This means that passengers can check in their luggage early before travelling to the main airport; especially helpful for those with loads of suitcases. There is a 24 hour courtesy shuttle service every 30 minutes from the City Terminal to the airport.

Bus

The Abu Dhabi Municipality operates bus routes all over the emirate, as well as the city. Attempts are being made to make the service more cost effective and organised, with more readily available route information and timetables. The service operates more or less around the clock and fares are inexpensive – recently reduced to Dhs.1 within the Capital.

The main bus station is on Hazza bin Zayed Road, and the main station in Al Ain is behind the Co-Operative Society. Buses between the two cities leave daily on a regular basis and cost Dhs.18 for a one day round trip. Fares are paid to the driver when you board, so try to keep some change ready.

Contact: Abu Dhabi Transport (02 443 1500).

Air

Other options → Meet & Greet [p.20]

The UAE's location at the crossroads of Africa, Asia and Europe makes it easily accessible. London is seven hours away, Frankfurt six, Hong Kong eight, and Nairobi four. Most European capitals and other major cities have direct flights to Abu Dhabi or Dubai, many with a choice of operator.

Abu Dhabi International Airport is located 35 km from the city. Its futuristic satellite passenger hub has been upgraded to handle 11 aircraft simultaneously, with passengers all boarding and disembarking via telescopic walkways – a great bonus against the unrelenting summer heat. Annually it handles over 3,500,000 passengers. Plans are underway for a new terminal, of similar design to the existing one.

A variety of facilities are available at the airport, including a hotel and golf course, which can be used by transit passengers. The large Duty Free is well known for its raffles – the latest raffle sells tickets for Dhs.1,000 to win Dhs.1,000,000! Abu Dhabi is part owner in Gulf Air, along with Bahrain, Oman and Qatar, and is the second biggest hub for Gulf Air outside Bahrain, boasting non stop flights as far as New York and Australia. Emirates, the national airline, only operates out of Dubai.

Al Ain has its own international airport, which opened in March 1994 and is about 20 km west of the centre. While the number of airlines operating out of here is not huge, the introduction of this airport has eased the pressure on Abu Dhabi by redirecting some of the air traffic.

Boat

Other options → Boat & Yacht Charters [p.119]

Opportunities for getting around by boat in the Emirates are limited unless you wish to travel by dhow, in which case your opportunities are limitless. Various companies offer trips by dhow or boat to explore the islands off the coast; alternatively you can try hiring a fishing boat to do this privately. Currently, there are no scheduled passenger services from Abu Dhabi to other countries, or even to Dubai.

General Info

Getting Around

Walking & Biking

Other options ➜ Cycling [p.172]
Hiking [p.184]
Mountain Biking [p.191]

Cities in the Emirates are generally very car orientated and not designed to encourage either walking or cycling. In addition, the heat in summer months, with daytime temperatures around 45° C, makes either activity a rather sweaty experience! However, in Abu Dhabi the relative compactness of the main commercial area makes it a pleasant and more popular way of getting around. The evenings are much cooler and strolling along the Corniche and Breakwater is a popular pastime, even more so in the winter months when temperatures are perfect for the outdoors. Heading back from the Corniche, the first few blocks comprise a range of shopping malls, souks, cafés and cinemas. The central oasis area in Al Ain is also quite similar. Both areas are best explored on foot.

Cycling can be an enjoyable way to explore the cities – you can cover more ground than on foot and still see more than from a car. This is even more appropriate for the quieter areas where the roads are often wide and tree lined and cars infrequent. With the exception of the Corniche in Abu Dhabi, there are no dedicated bike lanes to encourage cycling and the busier parts of the cities or the dual carriageways are probably best avoided. However, many of the footpaths are wide enough to cycle along. A lot of care is needed when cycling in traffic, since drivers often seem very unaware of this method of transport. Also beware the heat in summer, which can easily exhaust the cyclist – not much fun during the day, but it can be quite pleasant at night.

MONEY

Cash is still the preferred method of payment in the Emirates, although credit cards are now widely accepted. Foreign currencies and travellers cheques can be exchanged in licensed exchange offices, banks and hotels – as usual, a passport is required for exchanging travellers cheques.

There is more confidence in cheques these days; strict enforcement of laws concerning passing bad cheques has helped. It is a criminal offence to write a cheque with insufficient funds in the bank account, and a jail term will result.

Exchange Rates

Foreign Currency (FC)	1 Unit FC = x Dhs	Dhs.1 = x FC
Australia	2.05	0.48
Bahrain	9.73	0.10
Bangladesh	0.06	16.67
Canada	2.33	0.43
Cyprus	6.48	0.15
Denmark	0.49	2.04
Euro	4	0.25
Hong Kong	0.47	2.13
India	0.07	14.29
Japan	0.03	33.33
Jordan	5.17	0.19
Kuwait	12.15	0.08
Malaysia	0.97	1.03
New Zealand	1.79	0.56
Oman	9.53	0.10
Pakistan	0.06	16.67
Philippines	0.07	14.29
Qatar	1.01	0.99
Saudi Arabia	0.98	1.02
Singapore	2.08	0.48
South Africa	0.37	2.70
Sri Lanka	0.04	25.00
Sweden	0.41	2.44
Switzerland	2.53	0.40
UK	5.82	0.17
USA	3.67	0.27

Rates updated – November 2002

Local Currency

The monetary unit is the 'dirham' (Dhs.), which is divided into 100 'fils'. The currency is also referred to as AED (Arab Emirate Dirham). Notes come in denominations of Dhs.5, Dhs.10, Dhs.20, Dhs.50, Dhs.100, Dhs.200, Dhs.500 and Dhs.1,000. Coin denominations are Dhs.1, 50 fils and 25 fils, but be

UAE Dirhams

warned, there are two versions of each coin and they can look very similar. Because 5 and 10 fil coins are rarely available, you will often not receive the exact correct change.

The dirham has been pegged to the US dollar since the end of 1980, at a mid rate of US $1 ~ Dhs.3.6725. Exchange rates of all major currencies are published daily in the local newspapers.

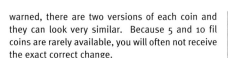
Banks

The well-structured and ever growing network of local and international banks, strictly controlled by the UAE Central Bank, offers the full range of commercial and personal banking services. Transfers can be made without difficulty as there is no exchange control and the dirham is freely convertible.

Union National Bank

Banking hours: Saturday - Wednesday 08:00 - 13:00 (some are also open 16:30 - 18:30); Thursday 08:00 - 12:00

Main Banks

ABN AMRO Bank	633 5400
Abu Dhabi Commercial Bank	696 2222
Abu Dhabi National Bank	611 1111
Bank of Sharjah	679 5555
Barclays Bank Plc	627 5313
Citibank	698 2206
Emirates Bank International	645 5151
HSBC Bank Middle East	615 2330
Mashreq Bank	627 4300
Middle East Bank	446 4000
National Bank of Dubai	639 4555
Standard Chartered	677 7400
Union National Bank	674 1600

ATMs

Most banks operate ATMs (Automatic Teller Machines, also known as cashpoints or service tills) which accept a wide range of cards. For non UAE based cards, the exchange rates used in the transaction are normally extremely competitive and the process is faster with far less hassle than traditional travellers cheques.

Common systems accepted around Abu Dhabi include: American Express, Cirrus, Global Access, MasterCard, Plus System and VISA. ATMs can be found in all shopping malls, at the airport, at petrol stations and at various street side locations.

Money Exchanges

Money exchanges are available all over Abu Dhabi, offering good service and reasonable exchange rates, which are often better than the banks. Additionally, hotels will usually exchange money and travellers cheques at the standard hotel rate (ie, poor).

Money Exchange Hours: Sat - Thurs 08:30 - 13:00 & 16:30 - 20:30; Friday 16:30 - 20:30

Exchange Centres

Al Ansari Money Exchange	622 7888
Al Fardan Exchange	622 3222
Lari Money Exchange	622 3225
Liwa Exchange	622 7366
Thomas Cook Al Rostamani Exchange	672 7717
UAE Exchange Centre	632 2166
Al Ansari Money Exchange	03 766 1363
Al Fardan Exchange	03 765 6325
Lari Money Exchange	03 766 6424
Thomas Cook Al Rostamani Exchange	03 766 5558
UAE Exchange Centre	03 765 4258

Credit Cards

Most shops, hotels and restaurants accept all major credit cards (American Express, Diners Club, MasterCard and VISA). Smaller retailers are sometimes less keen to accept credit cards and you may have to pay an extra five percent for processing (and it's no use telling them that it's a contravention of the card company rules – you have to take it or leave it!). You can, however, call your local credit card company to lodge a complaint if you are charged this five percent 'fee'. Conversely, if you are paying in cash, you may sometimes be allowed a discount – it's certainly worth enquiring.

Tipping

Tipping practices are similar to most parts of the world. An increasing number of restaurants include service, although it is unlikely to end up with your waiter. Otherwise ten per cent is the usual.

MEDIA & COMMUNICATIONS

Newspapers/Magazines

Abu Dhabi has three of its own Arabic language newspapers – Al Ittihad, Al Wahda and Al Fajr. The only English language paper produced in Abu Dhabi, Emirates News, has closed down and it is not known whether it will reopen. Also available in Abu Dhabi are other newspapers printed in Dubai and Sharjah; these include the Arabic papers Al Bayan and Al Khaleej, and in English: Gulf News, Khaleej Times and The Gulf Today (all Dhs.2, and Dhs.3 on Fridays).

Foreign newspapers, most prominently French, German, British and Asian, are readily available in hotel bookshops and supermarkets, although they are more expensive than at home (about Dhs.8 - 12) and slightly out of date. There is also a good supply of hobby magazines such as computing, photography, sports and women's magazines (expect to find censored portions, or even occasionally whole pages or sections missing). They are expensive, usually costing two or three times more than at home (between Dhs.30 - 50).

Newspapers and magazines are available from bookshops, supermarkets and hotel shops. Additionally, newspapers are available at 'corner' shops and are sold at major road junctions.

Further Reading

Visitors will find a variety of books and magazines available on the Emirates, from numerous coffee table books to magazines with details of aerobics classes. Monthly publications range from the free Dubai-based Out & About to Connector and Aquarius (on health and beauty), to the event focused Time Out and What's On magazines. Many magazines here seem to almost merge into one; they have no clear cut identity and the audience always seems the same, no matter which magazine you pick up. Currently the only dedicated Abu Dhabi magazine is Time Out; all others tend to throw in only a few token pages covering Abu Dhabi.

Guides to the region include Explorer Publishing's *Dubai Explorer* as well as the Lonely Planet series. Sharjah The Guide, the Spectrum Guide to the United Arab Emirates and Trident Press' informative United Arab Emirates Yearbook also offer more information on the region.

Recommended Reading

For the finer points on life in the Emirates, books to refer to include: the *Family Explorer (Dubai & Abu Dhabi)*, a family guidebook to life in the UAE; the *Off-Road Explorer (UAE)*, the UAE's ultimate outdoor guide; and the *Underwater Explorer (UAE)*, a detailed guide to scuba diving in the area. These can be found in all good bookstores around town.

Post & Courier Services

Other Options ➜ Postal Services [p.75]

Empost, formerly known as the General Postal Authority (GPA), is the sole provider of postal services in the UAE. In addition, plenty of courier companies operate both locally and internationally, such as Aramex, DHL, Federal Express etc. Empost also operates an express mail service known as Mumtaz Express.

Post within the UAE takes 2 - 3 days to be delivered. Mail takes 7 - 10 days to reach the USA and Europe, 8 - 10 days to reach Australia, and 5 - 10 days to reach India. Airmail letters cost Dhs.3 -

6 to send, depending on weight, and postcards cost Dhs.1 - 2. Letters are a dirham cheaper if they are posted unsealed. Aerogrammes can be bought for Dhs.2 each from post offices, which also saves the bother of buying a stamp before posting your letters

Main Courier Companies

Aramex	627 2888
DHL	800 4004
Empost	621 3526
Federal Express	800 4050
TNT	677 1159
UPS	446 1961

Stamps can be bought from post offices and certain shops – card shops often sell a limited range of stamps. For outbound mail, red postal boxes are located at post offices and near shopping centres. Hotels too will handle your mail if you are staying there.

There's no house address based postal service; all incoming mail is delivered to a PO Box at a central location and has to be collected from there.

Radio

The UAE has a number of commercial radio stations broadcasting in a range of languages, from Arabic and English to French, Hindi, Malayalam or Urdu. Daily schedules can be found in the local newspapers.

Operating 24 hours a day, everyday, the English language stations, Dubai FM (92 FM), Free FM (96.7FM) and Ajman's Channel 4 FM (104.8 FM), play modern music. Operating throughout the UAE, Emirates 1FM (99.3, 100.5 FM) plays music for a 'younger' audience, while Emirates 2FM (90.5, 98.5 FM) broadcasts a mixture of news, talk shows and modern music. Sadly, while there are a few current affairs programs in English, most are sorely lacking in depth.

Ras Al Khaimah's Radio Asia (1152 khz) has programmes in Hindi, Urdu and Malayalam, while Umm Al Quwain's Hum FM (106.2 FM) broadcasts mainly in Hindi with a bit of English.

If you want to hear Arabic music, tune in to 93.9 FM. At times the BBC World Service can also be picked up with the right equipment.

Television/Satellite TV

Other Options → Television [p.76]
Satellite TV [p.76]

Abu Dhabi has thirteen television channels broadcasting mainly in Arabic. It is however, possible to pick up signals from the northern emirates and countries outside the UAE. The local English language channel is broadcast on Channel 48, and you can also tune in to Channel 33, the English language channel in Dubai.

There are a variety of services offered via satellite. Most leading hotels and hotel apartments have satellite television available for residents, and many apartment blocks have dishes preinstalled – residents have to simply acquire a decoder. Satellite programmes that can be received range from international entertainment or films to sports, cartoons and current events.

Telephones

Other options → Telephone [p.73]

Telecommunications are very good, both within the UAE and internationally. All communication is provided by the monopoly Emirates Telecommunications Corporation, commonly known as Etisalat. Calls from a landline to another landline within Abu Dhabi are free of charge, and direct dialling is possible to over 170 countries. GPRS and WAP services are also available in the UAE.

Telephone Codes

UAE Country Code	+971	Directory Enquiries	181
Abu Dhabi	02	Operator	100
Ajman	06	Etisalat Information	144
Al Ain	03	Fault Reports	170
Dubai	04	Billing Information	142
Fujairah	09	Etisalat Contact Centre	121
Hatta	04	Speaking Clock	140
Jebel Ali	04		
Ras al Khaimah	07		
Sharjah	06	To dial a typical Abu Dhabi	
Umm Al Quwain	06	number from overseas it is	
Mobile Telephones	050	00 **971 2** 391 8060	

Public payphones are all over the city; a few accept coins, but most require phone cards, which are available from many shops and supermarkets. They come in a variety of values, although for international calls beware: the units vanish at a truly amazing rate! Etisalat has a new generation of prepaid phone cards called 'Smart Cards', which are available for Dhs.30.

Mobile phones are very popular and widely used – there are more than 1.7 million subscribers in the Emirates. Etisalat has a reciprocal agreement with over 60 countries for international GSM roaming service, allowing visitors whose countries are part of the agreement to use their mobile in the UAE. However, if your country is not on the list or you don't have a GSM phone, Etisalat offers a useful service called 'Wasel'. It is possible to bring the phone with you (or buy it here) and to purchase a SIM card from Etisalat, which enables you to make and receive calls while in the UAE. A local number is supplied and calls are charged at the local UAE rate.

Internet

Other options → Internet Cafés [p.282]
The Internet (Residents) [p.74]

With around one third of the population using the Internet, the UAE is among the top twenty countries in the world in terms of Internet use. Internet or cyber cafés around town provide easy and relatively cheap access.

Etisalat is the sole provider of Internet services within the UAE and in order to maintain the country's moral and cultural values, all sites are provided via Etisalat's proxy server. This occasionally results in frustrated users being unable to access perfectly reasonable sites that, for some reason have been blocked. If you come across such a site, you can report it to Etisalat. Please see [p.43] for helpful sites and numbers.

Most organisations that are connected have an eight character email address. Typical email syntax is: user@emirates.net.ae

You can also surf the Internet without being a subscriber. All that's needed is a computer with a modem and a regular phone line. To avail this facility, simply call 500 5555. For information on charges, see Dial 'n' Surf on [p.75].

Websites

There are numerous Websites about Abu Dhabi and the Emirates in general, and new ones are being uploaded all the time. Some are more interesting, successful and relevant than others, and the table

lists those that the Explorer team has found to be the most useful – let us have your suggestions about others to include in the next edition of the book.

UAE ANNUAL EVENTS

Throughout the year Abu Dhabi, Al Ain and Dubai host a number of well-established annual events. The events described below are the more popular and regular fixtures on the social calendar. But be warned – this is only a general guide since, for the most part, events are not always promoted until closer to the date and some organisers prefer using the 'grapevine' rather than local press and publications.

Al Ain Flower Festival

The Al Ain Flower Festival is a feast of colour taking place each spring. View the stunning landscaping of the park near Jahili Fort, and the amazing flowers and shrubs planted and in bloom for the event. There's also a parade worth attending, participated in by most of Al Ain, particularly the children, dressed in colourful flower costumes. Dates are not available for 2004 as yet but will be available nearer the time from Al Ain Municipality on 03 763 5111.

Abu Dhabi Shopping Festival

The Abu Dhabi Shopping Festival held every year in early March is filled with fantastic bargains, sale and prizes from all the shopping malls. Lesser known than the Dubai Shopping Festival in terms of worldwide exposure, it is still a worthy event for those living in the area. The month is filled with competitions and giveaways, and provides the perfect excuse to make those special purchases you've been waiting for all year.

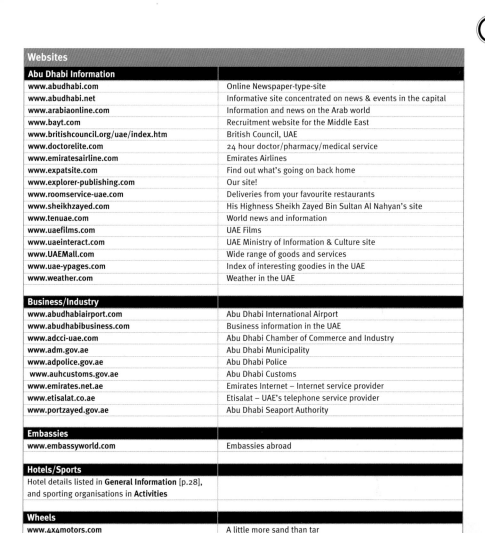

Websites

Abu Dhabi Information

www.abudhabi.com	Online Newspaper-type-site
www.abudhabi.net	Informative site concentrated on news & events in the capital
www.arabiaonline.com	Information and news on the Arab world
www.bayt.com	Recruitment website for the Middle East
www.britishcouncil.org/uae/index.htm	British Council, UAE
www.doctorelite.com	24 hour doctor/pharmacy/medical service
www.emiratesairline.com	Emirates Airlines
www.expatsite.com	Find out what's going on back home
www.explorer-publishing.com	Our site!
www.roomservice-uae.com	Deliveries from your favourite restaurants
www.sheikhzayed.com	His Highness Sheikh Zayed Bin Sultan Al Nahyan's site
www.tenuae.com	World news and information
www.uaefilms.com	UAE Films
www.uaeinteract.com	UAE Ministry of Information & Culture site
www.UAEMall.com	Wide range of goods and services
www.uae-ypages.com	Index of interesting goodies in the UAE
www.weather.com	Weather in the UAE

Business/Industry

www.abudhabiairport.com	Abu Dhabi International Airport
www.abudhabibusiness.com	Business information in the UAE
www.adcci-uae.com	Abu Dhabi Chamber of Commerce and Industry
www.adm.gov.ae	Abu Dhabi Municipality
www.adpolice.gov.ae	Abu Dhabi Police
www.auhcustoms.gov.ae	Abu Dhabi Customs
www.emirates.net.ae	Emirates Internet – Internet service provider
www.etisalat.co.ae	Etisalat – UAE's telephone service provider
www.portzayed.gov.ae	Abu Dhabi Seaport Authority

Embassies

www.embassyworld.com	Embassies abroad

Hotels/Sports

Hotel details listed in **General Information** [p.28], and sporting organisations in **Activities**	

Wheels

www.4x4motors.com	A little more sand than tar
www.diamondlease.com	Car leasing/rental
www.motorhighway.com	Buy a vehicle online
www.valuewheels.com	Buy a vehicle online

General Info

UAE Annual Events

Camel Racing

Camel racing is a spectacular sport and a trip to a race can be one of the most memorable highlights of any visit to the Emirates. A traditional sport, the sight of these ungainly animals, ridden by young boys, is an extraordinary sight. Racing camels can change hands for as much as ten million dirhams! Races normally take place on Thursdays and Fridays during the winter months, with additional races on National Day and other public holidays.

The main race is a two day event held in April each year, which attracts enthusiasts from all over the Emirates. Try to be at the racetracks early on a Friday morning to catch the atmosphere. Watch the local press for details of race dates and times.

Al Wathba Racetrack is about 40 km east of Abu Dhabi, near Mafraq. The Al Ain Racetrack is on the road to Abu Dhabi, about 25 km from the centre of Al Ain. There are also camel races at Sowaihan (130 km from Abu Dhabi on the road to Al Ain).

Call the Emirates Heritage Club on 02 446 6116 for further information on camel racing.

Desert Rallies

The UAE deserts provide the ideal location for desert rallying and many events are organised throughout the year by the Emirates Motor Sports Federation (EMSF) in Dubai. The highest profile event is the Desert Challenge, which is the climax of the World Cup in Cross Country Rallying. It attracts top rally drivers from all over the world and is held the first week of November.

Other events throughout the year include the Spring Desert Rally (4 WD); Peace Rally (saloons); Jeep Jamboree (safari); Drakkar Noir 1000 Dunes Rally (4 WD); Shell Festival Parade; Audi Driving Skills (driving challenge); Federation Rally (4 WD).

For 2003 event details, call EMSF (04 282 7111). For information on the UAE Desert Challenge call (04 282 3441).

See also: *Emirates Motor Sports Federation – Rally Driving [p.193]. UAE Desert Challenge [p.46]*

Dhow Racing

The traditional wooden dhows look very atmospheric when racing. The vessels are usually 40 - 60 ft in length and are either powered by men (up to 100 oarsmen per dhow) or by the wind. As well as fixed races throughout the year, there are often events on special occasions, such as National Day.

Most of the races in Abu Dhabi are short coastal races and the boats, many of which are old pearling vessels, have a shallow draught ideal for sailing closer to the Corniche.

In Dubai there are longer sea-going races, notably in April, the race to Sir Bu Naair Island, which sees as many as 80 boats taking part.

As well as the fixed races, there are often events on special occasions, such as National Day, sponsored by the government in its wish to keep traditional heritage alive. Keep an eye on the local press for further information.

Dubai Desert Classic (Golf)

Incorporated into the European PGA Tour in 1989, this popular golfing tournament attracts growing numbers of world class players. The prestige associate with this event is evident with the past appearance of such players as Tiger Woods, Ernie Els and Thomas Björn.

Traditional Dhow Racing

Dubai Rugby Sevens

This two day event is a very popular sporting and spectator fixture. With alcohol freely available at the stadium, the party atmosphere carries on until the small hours. Top international teams play and the competition also provides a rare opportunity for local teams from all over the Gulf to try their luck in their own games, which run alongside some of the big names in sevens rugby.

Dubai Shopping Festival

A combination of festival and shopping extravaganza, DSF, as it is popularly known, is hard to miss as buildings and roads are decorated with coloured lights and there are bargains galore in participating outlets. Highlights include a spectacular firework show over the Creek each evening, the international wonders of Global Village and numerous raffles. Other attractions include music, dance and theatrical entertainment from around the world, plus animal shows and a huge funfair. Hotels are at 100% occupancy during this month (Jan 15 - Feb 15) and it's cynically dubbed 'Dubai Traffic Festival' due to its success and the resulting traffic congestion in the evenings.

Dubai Summer Surprises

Similar to DSF, but smaller, Dubai Summer Surprises is held to attract visitors during the hot and humid summer months. Aimed at the family,

DSS offers fun packed activities, which are generally held in climate-controlled facilities, such as shopping malls, specially constructed areas and hotels. Events are often based on food, heritage, technology, family values, schools etc.

Dubai Tennis Open

Held in the middle of February, the US $1,000,000 Dubai Duty Free Tennis Open is a well-supported event. It is established on the international tennis circuit and offers the chance for fans to see top seeds, both male and female, in an intimate setting, battling it out for game, set and match.

Dubai World Cup

The Dubai World Cup is billed as the richest horseracing programme in the world – last year's total prize money was over US $15,000,000. The prize for the Group 1 Dubai World Cup race alone was a staggering US $6,000,000. It is held on a Saturday to ensure maximum media coverage in the West, and with a buzzing, vibrant atmosphere, is a great opportunity to dress up and bring out your best hat.

Eid Al Adha

Meaning 'Feast of the Sacrifice', this four day Islamic holiday marks the end of the annual period of pilgrimage to Mecca. Many animals are killed to celebrate this holiday 70 days after the first Eid.

Eid Al Fitr

This Islamic holiday lasts for three days and celebrates the 'Feast of the Breaking of the Fast'. It is held at the end of Ramadan.

Horse Racing

The Abu Dhabi Equestrian Centre provides information on endurance horse racing, horse racing and show jumping. The season lasts from October to April and horse racing takes place every Sunday night during these months. Contact the centre on 02 445 5500.

IDEX

The International Defence Exhibition and Conference is one of the most prestigious of its kind in the world. Suppliers exhibit state of the art weaponry and navies show off their submarines, frigates, minesweepers and so on in the specially developed berthing area. The guest list is a worldwide 'who's who' of defence ministers and high ranking chiefs of staff representing most international governments. According to the website in 2001, contracts negotiated ran into the multi millions, with those involving the UAE alone running to US $255 million! This exhibition is biannual, with the next due to be staged March 6 - 10, 2005

Islamic New Year's Day

Islamic New Year's Day marks the start of the Islamic Hijri calendar. It is based on the lunar calendar and should fall on March 21st in 2004.
   See also: *Public Holidays [p.12].*

Lailat Al Mi'raj

This day celebrates the Prophet's ascension into heaven and is expected to occur on September 23 in 2003.

Horse Racing

General Info

UAE Annual Events

Powerboat Racing

The UAE is well established on the world championship powerboat racing circuit, in Abu Dhabi with Formula I (onshore) and in Dubai and Fujairah with Class I (offshore). These events make a great spectacle – take a picnic and settle in with family and friends to be an armchair sports fan for the day.

Abu Dhabi plays host to the final round of the Formula One series at the end of the season. ADIMSC organises Formula Four races for UAE participants, jet ski races and the Al Shwaheef race, which is designed to encourage the younger generation of Emiratis to remain close to their marine heritage. Each season there are also two open regattas for modern sailing boats (including catamarans, lasers and windsurfers), which are open to all ages and nationalities.

Abu Dhabi International Marine Sports Club has a water racing calendar, which runs from Oct - May. Contact the Race Co-ordinator on 02 681 5566.

Terry Fox Run

Every year, thousands of people around the world run, jog, walk, cycle, and even roller blade their way around a course for this worthwhile charity. All funds raised go to cancer research programmes at approved institutions around the world. Abu Dhabi's next run is expected to be in February 2004 with

exact dates confirmed nearer the time. Al Ain has not had runs for the last couple of years although one of the main receivers of charity money is Tawam Hospital. However, Al Ain is expected to hold a run in 2004. Check the local media for contact details nearer the time or contact the Ambassador's Office, Canadian Embassy on 02 407 1300 for exact dates.

UAE Desert Challenge

This is the highest profile motor sport in the country and is often the culmination of the cross country rallying world cup. Following prestigious events such as the Paris - Dakar race, this event attracts some of the world's top rally drivers and bike riders who compete in the car, truck and moto-cross categories. The race is held on consecutive days over four stages, usually starting in Abu Dhabi and travelling across the harsh and challenging terrain of the deserts and sabkha to finish in Dubai. For more details, check out www.mid-east-offroad.com.

Highrises lining the Corniche

Main Annual Events – 2003/2004

May

1	UAE International Offshore Powerboat Championship Class II & III 6Ltr.
8	St. Andrew's Society chieftan's Ball
	Contact 050 443 5175
10 - 19	Model Exhibition
	Contact 763 0111
15	Abu Dhabi Rugby Football Club May Ball Crowne Plaza Hotel.
	Contact 6275777
13	Prophet's Birthday (Moon)

June

2 - 14	Child World Exhibition
	Contact 626 2639

August

6	Accession of the Ruler of Abu Dhabi

September

23	Lailat Al Miraj (Accession of the Prophet) (Moon)

October

tbc	Camel Races at Sowaihan
	Contact 446 66116
5 - 8	Safety and Security Exhibition
	Contact 444 6900
13 - 16	Emirates Employment and Recruitment Exhibition
	Contact 634 8511
16	BP Pro Am
13 - 15	Power Generation Exhibition
	Contact 444 6900
21 - 25	International Jewellery Exhibition
	Contact 679 5444
27	Ramadan (Moon)

November

7 - 27	Ramadan and Eid Festival
	Contact 444 6900
24 - 26	Eid Al Fitr (Moon)
tbc	St. Davids Ball

December

2	UAE National Day (Fixed)

11	St. Andrew's Night Dinner.
	Contact 050 443 5175
24	Abu Dhabi Rugby Football Club Christmas Ball
	Contact 6275777

January

1	New Year's Day
8 & 9	Sheraton Mixed Amateur Open
	Contact 558 8990
18 - 21	Industrial Exhibition
	Contact 444 6900
22	St. Andrew's Society Burns Night Supper
	Contact 050 443 5175
22 & 23	Sheraton Ladies Amateur Open
	Contact 558 8990

February

tbc	Terry Fox Run AUH & Al Ain
	Contact 407 1300 for dates
tbc	Oilmen's Tournament
	Contact 558 8990
tbc	Eid Al Adha (Feast of Sacrifice) (Moon)
15 - 19	IFEX -Furniture and Interior Design
	Contact 444 6900
21	Islamic New Year's Day (Moon)
26 & 27	Sheraton Junior's Open
	Contact 558 8990

March

tbc	UAE Pro Am
	Contact 558 8990
tbc	Al Hijra (Islamic New Year) (Moon)
tbc	The Irish Society St Patricks Ball
14 - 17	ROADEX
	Contact 444 6900

April

tbc	St. Georges Ball
15 & 16	Sheraton Mens Amateur Open
	Contact 558 8990
tbc	Abu Dhabi Net Ball Club Dinner & Dance
	Contact 050 536 3821

tbc - to be confirmed

General Info

L3_First | L3_Last

Better Homes...

helping you make better choices

apartments

consultancy

interior decoration

retail

international

showrooms

maintenance

villas

offices

warehouses

property management

New
Residents

New Residents

OVERVIEW

Abu Dhabi, the capital city of the UAE, is one of the Gulf's top destinations to which expatriates come for work. Life here can definitely be fun – getting things done can be a headache. Emiratis love paperwork and red tape, and to become an official resident of Abu Dhabi you will need plenty of paper, plenty of patience and a sense of humour!

However, attempts are continually being made to streamline processes, and government departments are being encouraged toward enhanced efficiency and creativity with special focus on the use of the Internet for the issue of documents, such as trade licences or health cards. In fact, 'e-government' is the buzzword everywhere these days, but that said, don't expect to find everything online, and don't expect the general public's paperwork load and woes to be at all reduced! This government directive is taking its time (read: years) to filter through to the individual departments, so you can still expect to be sent from counter to counter with your documents. This can be confusing, but remember, wherever you are, people are invariably ready to help and will point you in the right direction if you are well and truly lost.

The following information is meant only as a guide to what you will have to go through in order to become a car owning, phone owning, Internet connected, working resident. Remember, requirements and laws change regularly and often in quite major ways. Changes are generally announced in the newspapers and can be implemented literally overnight – so be prepared for the unexpected, if that is at all possible.

The following applies only to the Abu Dhabi emirate. While geographically, Abu Dhabi may be close to Dubai, and share many rules and regulations, there are several differences between the emirates.

The Beginning...

To be resident in Abu Dhabi, you need a sponsor – someone to legally vouch for you – this is usually your employer. Once you have residency, you may then be in a position to sponsor your spouse, parents or children.

The first step to acquiring residency is to enter the country on a valid entry visa (refer to: Documents – Entry Visa [p.52], Residence Visa [p.54]). Your new employer will usually provide your visa. If you do not already have a job secured, you may obtain a visit visa to enter the UAE for a short time (see also: Visas – Entering Abu Dhabi [p.19]). If you are already in Abu Dhabi and are applying for a visa for a family member or friend, the application form may be collected from the Immigration Department.

The original entry visa documentation must be presented to airport Immigration on arrival and your passport will be duly stamped.

Once you have entered the country on the correct visa, the next step is to apply for a health card, which requires a medical test, after which you can apply for residency. This should be done within 60 days of entering the country. To work legally, you also require a labour card. Your employer will usually take care of processing all required documentation for you, and sometimes for your family as well.

Labour cards and residence visas are valid for three years and can be renewed. This does not apply to elderly parents or maids (see: Residence Visa [p.54] and Domestic Help [p.71]). Labour cards for employees on their father or spouse's visa must be renewed on an annual basis. Health cards too, are valid only for one year.

If you are a qualified professional with a degree, or have an established employment history, there should be few difficulties in obtaining the necessary paperwork.

Useful Advice

When applying for a residence visa, labour card, driving permit etc, you will always need a handful of Essential Documents (see below) and countless application forms – invariably typed in Arabic. Don't panic. At most government offices such as the Immigration Department, Labour Office, Traffic Police, Ministry of Health, government hospitals etc, there are small cabins full of typists offering their services in English and Arabic, for just Dhs.10 - 15. Most also offer photocopying services and some even take instant passport sized photographs.

Essential Documents

To save repetition in the following section, Explorer has devised a list of Essential Documents. These are standard items that you will invariably need to produce when processing documentation. Additional documents will be referred to in the appropriate paragraph.

- *Original passport (for inspection only)*
- *Passport photocopy (personal details)*
- *Passport photocopy (visa/visit visa details)*
- *Passport sized photographs*

You will need countless photographs over the next few months – up to four per application. Usually two passport photocopies and two passport photos will be required each time. To save time and money, ask for the original negative when you order your first set of photos. Duplicate photos can then be made easily. There are many small photo shops that offer this service; look in your local area.

In addition, you will often have to produce what is commonly known as an NOC, a 'no objection certificate' (or letter) from your employer or sponsor. This confirms who you are and says that they have no objection to you renting a house, getting a driving licence etc. It should be on the company letterhead paper, signed and then stamped, and stamped again (and again!) with the company stamp, to make it 'official'. Remember to take a photocopy of this document.

e-Dirhams

Introduced in late 2001, the credit card sized e-Dirham card, a pre-paid 'smart card', is an electronic payment tool replacing the use of cash payment for procedures done within various federal ministries. Ministries requiring e-Dirham usage that you are likely to visit are the Ministry of Labour & Social Affairs and the Ministry of Health. Private users may purchase fixed value cards from e-Dirham member banks. Currently, the available denominations are Dhs.100, 200, 300, 500, 1000, 3000, and 5000. While they say cash is no longer accepted at these ministries, call ahead before you purchase your e-Dirham card to find out whether they are still accepting cash or only e-Dirhams.

DOCUMENTS

Entry Visa

You must enter the country on the correct entry visa in order to initiate your residence visa application process. This is either a residence or an employment visa. The other two kinds of visa, visit and transit, only allow you to remain here temporarily, as the names imply.

If you enter the country on a visit visa, you can remain in the UAE for up to 60 days after which you can extend your stay once for a further 30 days by applying through the Immigration Department. The cost for renewal is Dhs.500. Nationalities that can obtain a visit visa on arrival at the Abu Dhabi International Airport can stay initially for 60 days and renew once through the Immigration Department or alternatively take a 'visa run' indefinitely (see also: Entering Abu Dhabi [p.19]).

If you manage to secure work whilst on a visit visa, you will need to transfer to an employment visa in order to apply for your residence visa and labour card. You can transfer your visa status through the Immigration Department. You will need the relevant application form typed in Arabic, Essential Documents, a copy of your original labour contract from your new employer and a copy of your sponsor's original passport, plus Dhs.100.

Alternatively, you can fly out of the country on a visa run and re-enter the country on the correct visa – usually cheaper!

Health Card

Once you have the correct visa status (see above), the next step to becoming a resident is to apply for a health card, which is valid for one year. This entitles residents to cheap medical treatment at public hospitals and clinics, (charges are Dhs.20 per visit; Dhs.50 for a visit with a specialist; emergency cases are free). Some employers provide additional private medical insurance and, as in most countries, this is regarded as preferable to state care, although the usual hospital horror stories apply to both sectors.

To apply for your health card, collect an application form from the Ministry of Health, the Central Hospital or any government clinic. Submit the application form (typed in Arabic) along with Essential Documents, a letter of employment and Dhs.300. If you are a dependant and are not employed, you will need your tenancy contract, electricity and phone bills (original and photocopy of all documents), instead of your employment letter. In return, they will issue you with a temporary health card and a receipt for Dhs.300.

You can then go for your medical test. For this, you will need the temporary health card, a copy of the receipt for Dhs.300 and two passport photos. The cost is Dhs.207, which includes Dhs.7 for typing the application form in Arabic (this is done by the hospital). The medical test includes a medical examination, a chest X-ray and a blood test for AIDS, Hepatitis etc. If you are processing a health card for a maid, you will need to pay an additional Dhs.100 to have him or her vaccinated against Hepatitis, and an additional Dhs.10 for typing out the form (refer to Domestic Help [p.71]).

Your temporary health card will be returned to you, and 2 - 3 days later you can collect your medical certificate. The temporary health card will have a date on it stating when to collect your permanent health card. This can take anywhere from a week to a few months; in the meantime, the temporary health card can be used at hospitals should you require treatment.

If you prefer to have your medical test in a private hospital where the conditions tend to be slightly better, you can go to the Al Noor Hospital. At Dhs.650, it's slightly more expensive than going the government hospital route. You will need to present your passport copy and four passport photos along with the fee.

Office Locations:

Abu Dhabi:

• *Public Health Department, Central Hospital (02 633 1300), entrance on Karama St between Al Manhal St (9th) and Sudan St (11th) (Map ref. 5-C2)*

• *Al Noor Hospital (02 626 5265), Khalifa St (Map ref. 9-A3)*

Al Ain:

• *Al Jimi Hospital (03 763 5888), Shakhbut Bin Sultan Rd*

Moving: From A to B

Relocating: From A to Z

Relocating is about more than moving boxes and changing time zones. It's about starting over. New home. New school. New neighbours. Perhaps even a new country. Only a company with offices worldwide can make this transition easier by offering staff to help you on both ends of your move. Crown Relocations. A single source of all your relocation needs, here and abroad. When it comes to beginning life's new chapter, Crown wrote the book.

Helping you begin life's next chapter.

CROWN
RELOCATIONS

Crown Worldwide Movers
Ras Al Khor Complex
Showroom 9, Ras Al Khor, Al Aweer
P.O.Box 51773, Dubai
United Arab Emirates
Tel: (971) 4 289 5152 Fax: (97.1) 4 289 6263
Email: dubai@crownrelo.com
www.crownrelo.com

Crown Worldwide Movers
Seventh Floor, Flat-702
Al Salmein Tower, Electra Street
P.O.Box 44669, Abu Dhabi
United Arab Emirates
Tel: (971) 2 674 5515 Fax: (971) 2 674 2293
Email: abudhabi@crownrelo.com
www.crownrelo.com

Residence Visa

There are basically two types of residence visas: when you are sponsored for employment, and when a family member sponsors you for residency only. As stated, the first step to gaining a residence visa is to apply for a health card.

Once a resident, you must not leave the UAE for more than six months without revisiting, otherwise your residency will lapse. This is not relevant to children studying abroad who are on their parents' sponsorship here, as long as proof of enrolment with the educational institution overseas is furnished.

Office Locations:

Abu Dhabi:

Immigration Department, Saeed Bin Tahnoon St (02 446 2244) (Map ref. 3-C2)

Al Ain:

Immigration Department, Aditaba Road, nr Dubai Islamic Bank (03 762 5555)

See also: *Visas – Entering Abu Dhabi [p.19]*

1. Sponsorship by Employer

Your employer should handle all the paperwork, saving you a lot of hassle. After arranging for your residency, they should then apply directly for your labour card (see: Labour Card [p.55]).

You will need to supply Essential Documents and education or degree certificates. You must have your certificates attested by a solicitor or public notary in your home country and then by your foreign office to verify the solicitor as bona fide. The UAE embassy in your home country must also sign the documents. Of course, it makes life much simpler if you can do all of this before you come to Abu Dhabi, rather than trying to deal with the bureaucracy of your home country from afar.

If you are working for a UAE government body, the certificate must also be verified and certified by the Ministry of Higher Education in the UAE.

2. Family Sponsorship

If you are sponsored and are arranging sponsorship for your family since your employer will not do so, you will have a lengthy and tedious process ahead. Good luck!

Note: it is very difficult for a woman to sponsor her family. Exceptions to this rule are women employed as doctors, lawyers, teachers etc, and earning a minimum stipulated salary. In most cases though, the husband/father will be the sponsor.

To sponsor your spouse or children, you need a minimum monthly salary of Dhs.3,000 plus accommodation, or a minimum all inclusive salary of Dhs.4,000. Only what is printed on your labour contract will be accepted as proof of your earnings.

For parents to sponsor children, difficulties arise when sons (not daughters) become 18 years old. Unless they are enrolled in full time education in the UAE, they must transfer their visa to an independent sponsor or the parents may pay a Dhs.5,000 security deposit (once only) and apply for an annual, renewable visa. If they are still in education, they may remain under parental sponsorship but, again, only on an annual basis.

When sponsoring parents, there are certain constraints depending on your visa status; you should be in a certain category of employment, such as a manager, and earning over Dhs.6,000 per month. In addition, a special committee meets to review each case individually – usually to consider the age of parents to be sponsored, health requirements etc. Even when a visa is granted, it's only valid for one year and is reviewed for renewal on an annual basis.

If you are resident under family sponsorship and then decide to work, you will need to apply for a labour card, and you will also need a second medical test – this should be paid for by your employer.

The Process

To become a resident, collect a residency application form from the Immigration Department and have it typed in Arabic. Then submit the application, along with Essential Documents, your medical certificate and Dhs.100. You may also need a letter from your employer stating your position and salary, your original Arabic contract plus photocopy, attested marriage/birth certificates, dependants' passport photocopies, and your original passport for inspection.

It is essential that you fill out the names of your parents (including your mother's maiden name) in the specified section. Once the application is approved (this may take up to a month), you will be issued with a permit of entry for Abu Dhabi and you must exit and re-enter the country, submitting the entry permit on re-entry to Immigration (ie, passport control), who will then stamp your passport. You should then submit your original passport to the Immigration Department along with your medical certificate, four passport photos and Dhs.300 (e-Dirham) in order to get your permanent residency stamp. This can take anywhere from ten days to 1 - 2 months, or longer. Then you can relax.

For dependants, once the application is approved and the permit of entry has been issued, there are then two options:

a) The dependant can exit and re-enter the country, submitting the entry permit to Immigration on re-entry.

b) Or take the dependant's passport along with the permit of entry and ask for an exemption from departure; Immigration will arrange the stamp internally. Note this facility is applicable to dependants only.

Labour Card

To work in the UAE you are legally required to have a labour card. This can only be applied for once you have residency.

If your employer is arranging your residency, the labour card should be processed directly after residency has been approved. You should not need to supply any further documentation. Before your labour card is issued, you will need to sign your labour contract, which is printed in both Arabic and English. It's a standard form issued by the labour authorities and completed with your details. Unless you read Arabic, it may be advisable to have a translation made of your details, since the Arabic is taken as the legal default if there is any dispute (refer to Employment Contracts [p.62]).

If you are on family residency and decide to work, your employer, not your sponsor, will need to apply for a labour card. Your sponsor must supply a letter of no objection (also known as an NOC or no objection certificate). Ensure your employer does supply you with a labour card – the penalties for dependants working without a labour card are severe.

Documents to supply include Essential Documents, NOC, education certificate/s (if appropriate) and usually a photocopy of your sponsor's passport – they may also require the sponsor's original passport.

Office Locations:

Abu Dhabi: Labour & Social Affairs (02 667 1700).

Al Ain: Labour and Social Affairs (03 762 9999).

CERTIFICATES AND LICENCES

Driving Licence

Taking to the roads of the Emirates is taking your life in your hands! The standard of driving leaves much to be desired.

Until you acquire full residency, you can drive a rental car provided you have a valid driving licence from your country of origin (and not from any other country in which you have resided in the past), or an international licence (this only applies to those countries on the transfer list below). Make sure your driving licence details are registered with the rental company.

To drive private vehicles, you must first apply to the Traffic Police for a temporary Abu Dhabi licence. You will need to fill out the application form and take Essential Documents and Dhs.10 to obtain a temporary licence that is valid for one month (longer periods are also available).

No UAE Licence?

You cannot drive a privately registered vehicle on an international driving licence, as the vehicle is only insured for drivers holding a UAE driving licence.

Once you have your residence visa, you must apply for a permanent UAE licence. Nationals of certain countries can automatically transfer their driving licence, providing the original licence is valid. These countries are:

Licence Transfers

Australia, Austria, Belgium, Canada, Cyprus, Czech Republic, Denmark, Finland, France, Germany, Greece, Holland, Iceland, Ireland, Italy, Japan, Luxembourg, New Zealand, Norway, Poland, Portugal, Slovakia, South Africa, South Korea, Spain, Sweden, Switzerland, Turkey, United Kingdom, United States of America.

Some of the above licences will need an Arabic translation from your embassy or consulate – check with the Traffic Police. You may also be required to sit a short written test on road rules before the transfer takes place.

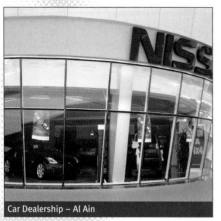

Car Dealership – Al Ain

If you aren't from one of the countries listed in the box, you will need to sit a UAE driving test. To apply for a permanent driving licence, submit the following documents (see below) to the Traffic Police Department, plus your valid Abu Dhabi residence visa and Dhs.200.

If your licence from your country of origin has expired, you will also have to sit the driving test. The alternative is to return home, renew your licence and save yourself the hassle!

Always carry your Abu Dhabi driving licence when driving. If you fail to produce it during a police spot check, you will be fined. The licence is valid for ten years, and if you manage to drive on the UAE roads for that long without going crazy, you deserve a medal!

Driving Licence Documents

- Relevant application form from the Traffic Police typed in Arabic
- Essential Documents
- A copy of your sponsor's passport or a copy of the company's trade licence
- NOC from your sponsor/company in Arabic
- Your original driving licence (as well as a photocopy and translation, if requested by the Traffic Police. This can be done at a legal translator's office – there are several on the road opposite the Novotel Centre Hotel on Hamdan Street).

Sometimes your sponsor's original passport is asked for, along with a copy. However, this seems to depend on whim more than anything concrete.

Office Locations:

Abu Dhabi: Traffic Police Licence Department, Muroor District btw Airport Rd and East Rd (02 446 1461)

Al Ain: Traffic Police Licence Department (03 707 3500)

Driving Test

If your nationality isn't on the automatic transfer list, you will need to sit a UAE driving test in order to be legally eligible to drive in Abu Dhabi, regardless of whether you hold a valid driving licence from your country of origin. If you haven't driven in your country of origin and need to obtain a driving licence, the following information will apply to you as well.

The first step is to obtain a learning permit – apply at the Traffic Police for the application form. You will also need Essential Documents, Driving Licence Documents, Dhs.100 and you will be given an eye test at the Traffic Police. Then find a reputable driving school – check the Yellow Pages or try:

- Abu Dhabi Motor Training School (02 448 4878)
- Al Harbi (02 671 6177)

Some driving institutions insist that you pay for a set of pre-booked lessons. In some cases, the package extends to 52 lessons and can cost up to Dhs.3,000! The lessons must be taken on consecutive days and usually last 30 - 45 minutes. Other companies offer lessons on an hourly basis, as and when you like, for Dhs.35 per hour for an automatic and Dhs.75 for a manual car. If a woman wants to take lessons with a male instructor, she must first obtain NOC's from her husband/sponsor and the Traffic Police. That said, if she has previous driving experience, she will have to sit a test with an instructor (who could be male) before signing up for lessons (no NOC's required for this one).

When your instructor feels that you are ready to take your test, you will be issued with a letter to that effect and can then apply for a test date. You will need to fill out the necessary application form at the Traffic Police and hand in your Essential Documents, Driving Licence Documents, Dhs.100 and, again, you must take an eye test elsewhere and bring the certificate the optician supplies you. The time between submitting your application and the test date can be as long as two months.

You will be given three different tests on different dates. One is a highway code test, the other is an 'internal' test that includes garage parking etc, and the third is a road test. Once you pass all three tests, you will be issued with a certificate (after about five days), which you should take to the Traffic Police to apply for your permanent driving licence.

The Emirates only family handbook

Abu Dhabi Dubai

Family **EXPLORER**

Family

The ONLY Family Handbook to Dubai & Abu Dhabi

Catering specifically to families with children between the ages of 0 - 14 years, the easy to use **Explorer** format details the practicalities of family life in the northern emirates, including information on medical care, education, residence visas and hundreds of invaluable ideas on indoor and outdoor activities for families and kids.

- Listings of the best leisure and entertainment activities
- Practicalities of life in the UAE, from education to medical care
- Indoor & outdoor activities
- Unique birthday parties section
- Shopping information and tips
- General information about family life in the UAE
- Listings and independent reviews of child friendly restaurants

Available from leading bookstores, hotels, supermarkets or directly from Explorer Publishing

Explorer Publishing & Distribution • Dubai Media City • Building 2 • Office 502 • PO Box 34275 • Dubai • UAE
Phone (+971 4) 391 8060 **Fax** (+971 4) 391 8062 **Email** info@Explorer-Publishing.com **Web** www.Explorer-Publishing.com

Insiders' City Guides • Photography Books • **Activity Guidebooks** • Commissioned Publications • Distribution

EXPLORER
www.Explorer-Publishing.com

Liquor Licence

Although Abu Dhabi has a moderately liberal attitude towards the consumption of alcohol by non-Muslims, this should be seen as a privilege, not a right. Residents must have a liquor licence to drink in hotels and social clubs, which should be carried at all times. As it is possible to add your spouse's name to your licence, this is strongly recommended to avoid possible problems. Visitors and non residents who do not have a liquor licence should be very careful about where they drink alcohol (and how much!) as this is a rather grey area. Anyone arrested for being drunk in a public place faces imprisonment and a fine and, believe us, this does happen from time to time!

If you wish to buy alcohol to drink at home, you will need a special liquor licence, which entitles you to buy from a liquor shop (not the local supermarket). Only non-Muslims with a residence visa earning more than Dhs.2,500 per month may obtain a licence. In public, only four and five star hotels and some social clubs are licensed to serve alcohol.

The liquor licence allows you to spend a limited amount on alcohol per month – this amount is calculated based on your monthly salary. To apply, collect an application form from your local liquor store or the Police headquarters, situated between Airport Road and Al Saada Street in Abu Dhabi , or Zayed Al Awwal Street in Al Ain. Your employer must sign and stamp the Arabic form, then submit it to the Police headquarters along with Essential Documents, a religion certificate (available from your embassy/St Joseph's Church if you are Filipino) and your labour contract (stating your salary). Application forms must be typed in Arabic, which can be done in the translation and typing booths opposite the Police Station.

The licence fee is 20% of your permit value. Permits are usually issued on Saturday and Sunday, and can be obtained on the same day. When renewing a liquor licence, the expired licence should be used. If the residence visa has been issued by a different emirate, a letter will be required confirming that no liquor licence has already been issued elsewhere.

Buying alcohol from liquor shops can be expensive, as you have to pay an additional tax of 30% on all items. However, the range of alcohol for sale is excellent. Cheaper, unlicensed alternatives for buying alcohol include Ajman's 'Hole in the Wall' (near the Ajman Kempinski) and Umm al Quwain's Barracuda Resort, next to Dreamland Aqua Park. It is illegal to transport alcohol around the Emirates without a liquor licence; this is particularly enforced in Sharjah.

See also: *Alcohol [p.19]; Liquor Stores [p.136].*

Zero Tolerance

Under no circumstances should you drive if you have had ANYTHING to drink. The authorities in Abu Dhabi have a very strict zero tolerance policy. A jail sentence will be the least of your worries! Also, if you are involved in a traffic accident and are found to have any alcohol whatsoever in your blood, your vehicle insurance will be void, even if you did not cause the accident.

A leaflet describing the law and penalties can be found at the liquor shops. Entitled "For Your Safety, Be Aware of the Alcoholic Beverages Law", it sets out the law and penalties in very clear terms.

Birth Certificates & Registration

Every expat child born in the UAE must be registered with a residence visa within 40 days of birth. Without the correct documentation, you may not be able to take your baby out of the country.

Baby Explorer

The hospital where the baby is delivered will prepare the official 'notification of birth' certificate in English or Arabic upon receipt of hospital records, photocopies of both parents' passports and marriage certificate, and a fee of Dhs.50. Take the notification certificate for translation into English to the Preventative Medicine Department (Central Hospital in Abu Dhabi, Al Ain Hospital/Al Jimi in Al Ain), where you will be issued with an application form, which must then be typed in English. You should also take the certificate to be

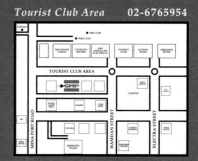

attested at the Ministry of Health (Dhs.10 fee) and the Ministry of Foreign Affairs (Dhs.50 fee).

Once this is done, ensure you register your child's birth at your embassy or consulate. To do this you will require the local notification of birth certificate, both parents' birth certificates, passports and marriage certificate. In addition, you may want to arrange a passport for your baby. Then you must apply for a residence visa through the normal UAE channels.

Before the birth, it is worth checking the regulations of your country of origin for citizens born overseas. (See [p.95] for a list of embassies and consulates in Abu Dhabi.)

Marriage Certificates & Registration

Most people prefer to return to their country of origin in order to get married, but if you are planning to marry in Abu Dhabi you have a number of options.

1. Atheists

Atheists should contact their embassy for information on arranging a local civil marriage.

2. Christians

Christians can either choose to have a formal ceremony at the church with a congregation, or a small ceremony at the church and a blessing afterwards at a different location such as a hotel.

At the official church ceremony, you will need two witnesses to sign the marriage register – the church then issues a marriage certificate (you will also need to take copies of your passport and residence visa). You can then take the certificate and your Essential Documents to your embassy in order to attest the document.

If you are Anglican, you will be required to fill out a number of forms stating your intent to marry, that you are not Muslim, and confirming that you are legally free to marry. Documents required are your original passport and photocopies, passport sized photos and a letter from both sets of parents stating that you are legally free to marry. If you have previously been married, you will need to produce either your divorce certificate or the death certificate of your previous partner.

This marriage is recognised by the government of the UAE and the Chaplain's signature may be authenticated by taking an Arabic translation of the marriage certificate to the Abu Dhabi Court after the ceremony. Filipino citizens are required to contact their embassy before the court will authenticate the marriage certificate. Contact the multi-denominational church of St Andrew's (02 446 1631) for more information.

Catholics must also undertake a Marriage Encounter course, which usually takes place on weekday evenings. You will need to fill out a standard form, and at the end of the course you are presented with a certificate. You should then arrange with the priest to undertake a pre-nuptial ceremony and again you are asked to fill out a form. You will need to take your birth certificate, baptism certificate, passport and passport copies, and an NOC from your parish priest in your home country. If you are a non-Catholic marrying a Catholic, you will need an NOC from your embassy/consulate stating that you are legally free to marry. A declaration of your intent to marry is posted on the public noticeboard at the church for three weeks, after which time, if there are no objections, you can set a date for the ceremony. Contact St Joseph's Church (02 446 1929).

3. Hindus

Hindus can be married through the Indian Embassy – for further details, contact the marriage section (02 666 4800). They publish a booklet with guidelines on how to get married, and you'll have to fill out an application form on the premises. Formalities take a minimum of 45 days.

4. Muslims

As a Muslim marrying another Muslim, you should apply at the marriage section of the Sharia Court, Sheikh Zayed Court (02 665 2000). You will need two male witnesses, and the bride should ensure that either her father or brother attends as a witness. You will require your passports and copies and proof that the groom is Muslim – a fee of Dhs.50 will be charged. You can marry there and then.

Opening hours: 07:30 - 14:00 & 17:30 - 20:30.

For a Muslim woman marrying a non-Muslim man, the situation is more complicated as the man must first convert to Islam. For further information, the Sharia Court can advise. This can be an incredibly long and complicated process (up to six months before the paper work is completed) and many couples end up returning to their country of origin to marry there.

Death Certificates & Registration

In the unhappy event of a death of a friend or relative, the first thing to do is to notify the police of your district. On arrival, the police will make a report and the body will be taken to a hospital, where a doctor will determine the cause of death. A post-mortem examination/inquest is not normally performed, unless foul play is suspected or the death is a violent one. Contact the deceased's embassy or consulate for guidance.

The authorities will need to see the deceased's passport and visa details. The hospital will issue a death certificate declaration on receipt of the doctor's report, for a fee of Dhs.50. Make sure that the actual cause of death is stated. Then take the declaration of death and original passport to the Al Asima Police station, next to Khalidiya Spinneys at the entrance nearest to the Corniche. The police will give permission to release the body in a letter which, along with the death declaration, original passport and copies, should be taken to the Department of Preventative Medicine. In Abu Dhabi, this is at the Central Hospital. In Al Ain, go to the Al Ain Hospital/Al Jimi. Here the actual death certificate will be issued for a small fee. If you are sending the deceased home, you should also request a death certificate in English (an additional Dhs.100), or apply to the legal profession for translation into other languages.

Then take the certificate to the Ministry of Health and the Ministry of Foreign Affairs for registration. Notify the relevant embassy/consulate for the death to be registered in the deceased's country of origin. They will also issue their own death certificate. Bring the original passport and death certificate for the passport to be cancelled.

The deceased's visa must also be cancelled by the Immigration Department. Take the local death certificate, original cancelled passport and embassy/consulate death certificate.

To return the deceased to their country of origin, contact the cargo section of Omeir Travel (02 631 9997). Apparently, they have had the most experience in arranging this and will give you all the necessary information along with the procedure to follow.

The body will also need to be embalmed – and you must obtain a letter to this intent from the police. Embalming can be arranged through the Central Hospital for Dhs.1,000, which includes the embalming certificate (there should be no charge if a copy of the deceased's medical card is supplied). The body must be identified before and after embalming.

The following documents should accompany the deceased overseas: local death certificate, translation of death certificate, embalming certificate, NOC from the police and embassy/consulate death certificate and NOC, and cancelled passport.

A local burial can be arranged at the Muslim or Christian cemeteries in Abu Dhabi. As there are no undertakers in the city, you will need to arrange for a coffin to be made, as well as transportation to the burial site. Advice and guidance for burial in the Christian and non-Muslim cemetery can be obtained from the Parish Clerk at St Andrew's Church (02 446 1631). Only Hindus may be cremated, with the permission of the next of kin.

See also: *Support Groups [p.83]*

WORK

Working in Abu Dhabi

Working in Abu Dhabi is very different from working in America, Asia or Europe. One of the greatest advantages is the general proximity of everything – there are no stuffy trains to catch, no real distances to commute and it's always sunny!

Expatriate workers basically fall into two categories. Those who have been seconded by companies based in their home country, and those who have come to Abu Dhabi in search of the expat lifestyle.

Office Towers, Abu Dhabi

Working Hours

Working hours vary quite dramatically within the emirate, based on straight-shift and split-shift timings. Split shift allows for an afternoon siesta and timings are generally 08:00 - 13:00 and 16:00 - 19:00. Straight-shift timings vary from government organisations' 07:00 - 14:00, to private companies' 09:00 - 18:00.

The work week for many companies is based on a traditional 5½ day week, with Thursday afternoon and Friday off, although more are adopting a two day, Thursday/Friday weekend. Some private companies have a two day, Friday/Saturday weekend, although this is more common in Dubai. Government offices and schools have a two day, Thursday and Friday weekend.

Social Life

Circle of Friends

Try to be open minded and make an effort to get to know people from all backgrounds. Diversity is the spice of life.

The Rumour Mill

Abu Dhabi has a very healthy grapevine and quite often you'll know of people even before you meet them. In the end everyone knows what's going on! If possible, use it to your advantage but remember... walls have ears.

Live it up!

Get ready to live the high life with five star hotels galore in Abu Dhabi and Dubai. You can do more for less in the Emirates, so you've no excuse to stay at home.

Public holidays are set by the Government and religious holidays governed by the moon. During Ramadan most organisations reduce their working hours for their Muslim employees, with the public sector working a six hour day. For more details on public holidays, refer to [p.12].

Finding Work

If you do not have employment on arrival, the best way to find a job is to register with the recruitment agencies and to check the small ads and the employment pages in the main newspapers. An employment supplement is published in the Gulf News on Sunday, Tuesday and Thursday, and in the Khaleej Times on Sunday, Monday and Wednesday.

A note of caution concerning the use of the words 'UK/US educated' in the papers. As far as we can make out, this is an 'accepted' form of discrimination. Basically, it should read 'white, Western educated'.

Recruitment Agencies

There are a number of employment agencies in Abu Dhabi and Dubai that offer recruitment consultancy for Abu Dhabi and Al Ain.

To register, check with the agency to find out if they take walk ins. Most only accept CVs via email these days, and will then contact you for an interview. You'll need an updated copy of your CV or résumé, and passport photographs for the interview, if you get one. You will invariably have to fill out an agency form summarising your CV. The agency takes its commission from the registered company once the position has been filled. It is illegal for a recruitment company to levy fees on candidates for this service.

Don't rely too heavily on the agency finding a job for you; more often than not, they depend on you spotting a vacancy that they have advertised in the paper and telephoning them to submit your interest. Should you be suitable for the job, the agency will mediate between you and the employer and arrange all interviews. Good luck!

Main Recruitment Agencies	
ABC Recruitment Agency	676 8558
Jobscan	627 5592
Nadia	677 4031
Resources	644 2868
SOS Recruitment Consultants	626 7700
Clarendon Parker	04 391 0460
Kershaw Leonard	04 343 4606

Employment Contracts

Once you have accepted a job offer, you may be asked to sign a copy of your contract in Arabic as well as English. Be sure to check the Arabic translation before you sign, as this is taken as the legal default if there is a dispute. There have been instances where the Arabic differed from the English version. You should also refer to a copy of the UAE Labour Law for details of other benefits and entitlements. A copy should be available with your employer or can be obtained from the Ministry of Labour (02 666 6930).

If you are sponsored by your spouse and wish to work, you will need to obtain an NOC from him before signing a contract with your new employer. Your employer will then apply for your labour card.

Labour Law

The UAE Labour Law is a work in progress; the most recent version available is 1980's, though updates and amendments occur from time to time. The Labour Law outlines everything from employee entitlements (end of service gratuity, workers' compensation, holidays etc), to employment contracts and disciplinary rules. The law tends to favour employer rights, but it still clearly outlines any employee rights that do exist in the UAE.

Labour unions are illegal, as are strikes. Recent moves have been made by the Ministry of Labour to assist workers (particularly labourers) in labour disputes against their employers. The Ministry now punishes companies who do not comply with the Labour Law – licences are withdrawn if warnings are not heeded. Non payment of salaries is a common problem, hopefully to be sorted one day soon!

A copy of this useful publication should be available from your employer or can be obtained through the Ministry of Labour & Social Affairs (02 666 6930). The UAE Labour Guide, published by the Ministry in 2002, also outlines workers' rights.

'Banning'

However, before you leap in and sign that job contract, make sure it's the job that you really want. In the UAE there is a cunning little law that aims to stop certain people from job hopping; if you resign from a job, you can potentially receive a minimum six month, maximum two year ban from working in the UAE. You can also potentially be banned from entering the country for six months.

People resigning from a job fall into three groups:

- Those who resign to return to their own country. Their residence visa will be cancelled (if they wish to live/work here in the future, they must find a new sponsor and apply for residency etc, from the beginning).

- Those who resign to go to another company. If they are lucky, their old company will supply an NOC and their residency can be transferred. This too is possible if they have been employed by the company for over one year and they fall into certain categories of employment.

- Those who resign to work for another company and are unable to get the approval of the former company (maybe the new company is a direct competitor or there is ill will between employer/employee), or in rare cases, the labour authorities. Unless they fall into certain, more essential categories of work, they will be liable to a minimum six month ban from working here and their residency will be cancelled. For details of the categories of employee that cannot be banned, refer to the most recent version of the UAE Labour Law.

FINANCIAL & LEGAL AFFAIRS

Other options ➜ **Money [p.36]**

Banks

Abu Dhabi is not short of internationally recognised banks that offer standard facilities such as current, deposit and savings accounts, ATMs (otherwise known as automatic teller machines, service tills or cashpoints), chequebooks, credit cards, loans etc. There are plenty of ATM machines around Abu Dhabi (location details can be obtained from the bank), and most cards are compatible with other Abu Dhabi-based banks; a few also offer global access links.

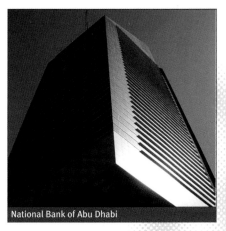
National Bank of Abu Dhabi

To open a bank account in Abu Dhabi, you need to have a residence visa or have your residency application underway. You will need to present the banking advisor with your original passport, copies of your passport (personal details and visa)

Financial & Legal Affairs

and an NOC from your sponsor. Some banks set a minimum account limit – this can be around Dhs.2,000 for a deposit account and as much as Dhs.5,000 for a current account.

Opening hours: *Saturday - Wednesday 08:00 - 13:00; Thursday 08:00 - 12:00. Some banks such as Mashreq and Standard Chartered also open in the evenings from 16:30 - 18:30.*

Financial Planning

Planning for the financial future – unless you take the head in the sand approach – is an important aspect of modern day life, and especially necessary for expats.

Before you do anything, you should contact the tax authorities in your home country to ensure that you are complying with the financial laws there. Most countries will consider you not liable for income tax once you prove your UAE residence or your non residence in your home country (a contract of employment is normally a good starting point for proving non residence). As a non resident, however, you may still have to fulfil certain criteria (such as only visiting your home country for a limited number of days each year).

Generally, the main reason for accepting an expat posting is to improve your financial situation. It is recommended not to undertake any non cash investments until you know your monthly savings capacity, even though this may take up to six months to ascertain. In fact, the first steps you should take with your new earnings are to begin paying back as much debt as possible (starting with your credit card/s!).

If you have a short term contract, stay away from long term investment contracts. Once you have decided that expat life is for you and that you are ready to plan for the future, you might want to establish the following: emergency cash buffer (3 - 6 months salary), retirement home, retirement income, personal and family protection (life insurance, health coverage) etc.

When selecting a financial planner, use either a reputable name, or at least an institution regulated by the UAE Central Bank. If another authority is 'regulating' your advisor, you cannot expect the principal UAE authority to be of assistance to you, and your chances of recourse in the event of a problem may be severely hampered. For financial planners, we recommend word of mouth or any of the major international companies.

Taxation

The UAE levies no personal income taxes or withholding taxes of any sort. The only noticeable taxes you are obliged to pay as an expat are a 30% tax on alcohol bought at liquor stores and a 15 - 16% service tax in hotel food and beverage outlets.

Doing Business

For information on conducting or setting up a business in Abu Dhabi, refer to your local business group or the commercial attaché at your embassy/consulate. For further details, refer to Business Groups and Contacts [p.94].

Legal Issues

For most people, any sort of brush with the 'wrong' side of the law can be a worrying experience, but in a foreign country and with an alien language, this can be particularly unnerving. If you are in really serious difficulties, you should contact your embassy or consulate as soon as possible and follow their advice, plus find yourself a good lawyer.

The UAE is governed by sharia law – this is Islamic canonical law that is based on the traditions of the Prophet Mohammed (PBUH) and the teachings of the Koran – and only a graduate of a sharia college can practice in court here. All court proceedings are conducted in Arabic, so you will find it important to hire legal representation that you can trust.

Legal Consultants	
Al Sayegh Richards Butler	631 3010
Bryan Cave – Al Mehairi Legal Consultants	634 0322
Denton Wilde Sapte	626 6180
Shearman & Stirling	627 4477
Simmons & Simmons	627 5568
Trowers & Hamlins	626 7274

HOUSING

Housing in Abu Dhabi

On the Abu Dhabi and Al Ain property markets, 'rental' is the name of the game. Unless you are born a UAE National or are a national of another GCC country, owning property or land in Abu Dhabi

In the UAE, extremes of temperature and low annual rainfall combine to make a very challenging environment for wildlife. Yet many species show remarkable adaptations to life in such a harsh environment. WWF is working with local government, NGO's and businesses to help in the establishment of protected areas and raise awareness about the UAE's fragile ecosystems.

Let's leave our children a living planet.
www.panda.org   wwfuae@erwda.gov.ae

is not an option (proposals may restrict land ownership further to UAE Nationals only). New residents arriving in Abu Dhabi on a full expatriate package may very well have accommodation included – but don't be fooled by the charm of the 'expat lifestyle' – life here can be expensive.

It is generally best to rent from a real estate agent, as they will handle all the paperwork for you. It's worth noting that single women occasionally have difficulty renting apartments and may need to put their employer's name on the lease.

Search Tips

A Des. Res.?

Check proximity of potential homes to church bells, mosques, rubbish bins and schools.

New Buildings

Look out for buildings under construction – it's often a good way to find a place you like and be one of the first on the waiting list. The guys on site should be able to give you the name of the real estate agent or landlord.

Noise Control

In the areas with lesser construction, beware of the empty plots for they could be ripe for development – few people really appreciate a noisy building site just a few metres from their bedroom window! Construction work starts at about 07:00 and finishes by 20:00 or 21:00, with the odd 01:00 concrete pour, often seven days a week.

Real Estate Glossary

Abbreviations

BR	Bedroom
Ensuite	Bedroom has private bathroom
Fully fitted kitchen	Includes appliances (oven, refrigerator, washing machine)
L/D	Living/dining room area
W/robes	Built-in wardrobes (closets)
Hall flat	Apartment has an entrance hall (ie, entrance doesn't open directly onto living room)
D/S	Double storey villa
S/S	Single storey villa
C.A/C	Central air conditioning (usually included in the rent)
W.A/C	Window air conditioning (often indicates an older building)

Abbreviations

S/Q	Servant quarters
ext S/Q	Servant quarters located outside the villa
Pvt garden	Private garden
Shared pool	Pool is shared with other villas in compound

Renting a Home

Rents over the past few years have consistently risen, and in general are very high in Abu Dhabi. However, it is expected (and hoped) that accommodation at the middle/higher end of the market (Dhs.60,000+ for apartments and Dhs.100,000+ for villas, per annum) will drop eventually due to supply exceeding demand. Prices at the lower/middle end are expected, at the least, to remain firm due to heavy demand. Rents are always quoted for the year, unless otherwise stated.

The Lease

To take out a lease personally, you need to be a resident. The real estate agent will need a copy of your passport and visa, a no objection letter (NOC) from your company, a copy of your salary certificate and an initial signed rent cheque (plus up to three post-dated cheques covering the remaining period of the lease). Unlike elsewhere in the world, rent cheques have to be paid to the landlord up front and not on a monthly basis. This can cause problems, as many new residents do not have the cash available to pay this sort of lump sum in advance. Needless to say, banks are quick to offer loans! To rent through your company, you require a copy of the company trade licence, a passport copy of whoever is signing the rent cheque and, of course, the rent cheque/s itself.

Renter's Nightmare

The majority of leases in Abu Dhabi are fixed for one year, and unless you find a really nice landlord who offers you an opt out clause, you are locked in till the end of the year. The penalty for breaking your contract? You might not get your deposit back, and you certainly won't get the remainder of your rent back.

Be careful when you sign your lease. Make sure the apartment or villa you've just found is really the one you'd like to make your home for the next year.

Main Accommodation Options

1. Apartment/Villa Sharing

For those on a budget, the solution may be to share an apartment or villa with colleagues or friends. Check the noticeboards in supermarkets such as Abela and Spinneys, or sports clubs for people advertising shared accommodation. The Classifieds section in the local newspapers also advertises accommodation.

2. Standard Apartment

There are generally two types of apartments available for rent – those with central air conditioning (A/C) and those with noisier window A/C where the unit is in the apartment wall. Central A/C accommodation is always more expensive, although in some buildings the charge for A/C is absorbed into the rent. Top of the range, central A/C apartments often come semi-furnished (cooker, fridge, washing machine), boast 24 hour security, satellite TV, covered parking, gym, pool etc. Normally, the more facilities that come with the apartment, the more expensive the rent.

Apartments – Annual Rent	
B/R	Annual Rent
1	30,000 - 38,000
2	40,000 - 55,000
3	70,000 - 80,000
4	90,000 - 130,000

Older villas near the Corniche

3. Villa

The same procedure applies to leasing villas as for apartments. Value for money villas are very hard to find and where you used to be able to find older, cheaper villas in some parts of Karama and Bateen, many are being demolished for redevelopment. As with apartments, villas differ greatly in quality and facilities such as pool, security, compound etc.

Villas – Annual Rent	
B/R	Annual Rent
3	90,000 - 130,000
4	110,000 - 200,000

4. Hotel Apartment

An alternative option is to rent a hotel apartment – ideal if you require temporary, furnished accommodation, although they are expensive. Apartments can be rented on a daily/weekly/monthly or yearly basis. They come fully furnished (from sofas to knives and forks) and serviced (maid service), with satellite TV and are often complemented by sports facilities (pool and gym etc). Water and electricity are also included in the rent.

Hotel Apartments – Rates			
B/R	Daily	Weekly	Monthly
Studio	200 - 370	1,350 - 2,600	3,500 - 8,000
1	150 - 522	1,050 - 3,650	3,300 - 9,500
2	300 - 1,040	2,100 - 7,300	6,500 - 14,000

Abu Dhabi Hotel Apartments	
Al Hamra Plaza Residence	678 8000
Al Maha Rotana Suites	610 6666
Beach Rotana Suites	644 3000
Corniche Residence	627 6000
Corniche Towers Residence	681 0088
Golden Tulip Dalma Suites	633 2100
Hilton Baynunah Tower	632 7777
Oasis Residence	641 7000
Park Residence	674 2000
Platinum Residence	634 4463
Royal Residence	627 2300
Sahara Residence	631 9000
Sheraton Residence	666 6220

Desirable Areas

As in all cities, there are obvious areas of desirable residence. The more upmarket area for villas is Khalidiya, with cheaper options in Rhoda, Karama and Bateen, and the mainly Arabic areas of Muroor and Al Dhafra. The most popular areas for apartments tend to be along the Corniche and Khalidiya, with cheaper alternatives found more centrally on Sheikh Hamdan Street, Najda Street

New Residents

Housing

(Bani Yas Street) and Sheikh Zayed 2nd Street, and further out of the town centre on Airport Road and New Airport Road.

A glance through the property pages in the newspapers will give you an idea of what's available where, and for how much. However, the best deals are still found by word of mouth. Many people even approach the security guard of buildings they are interested in to check availability.

Check out the following areas plus the maps at the back of the book to get a feel for the layout of the city.

Airport Road   Map ref → 1-D4, 2-C2, 3-C1

- Mix of old and new high rise apartments
- Lower rents in this area
- Wide mix of nationalities
- Early morning traffic congestion

New Airport Road   Map ref → 2-B3/C3, 3-B1/B3

- Mainly less expensive tower blocks, alongside a few newer, pricier ones
- Good mix of nationalities
- Possible parking problem if not included in rent
- Early morning traffic congestion

Bateen   Map ref → 6-A2,/C3, 9-C1

- Very popular, prestigious, and quiet area
- Larger villas and more expensive low rise apartment blocks
- Mainly expat Arabs and UAE Nationals
- Roadside parking usually available

Help for Renters

The Khalifa Committee

When seeking accommodation, this is one of the best sources in town. Commonly known as the Khalifa Committee, the proper name is The Department of Social Services and Commercial Buildings. This government organisation acts as a commission free clearinghouse for flats, villas, and other real estate rentals. Reasonably English friendly and computerised, they list hundreds of properties and can provide pricing details, the owners name and contact number, and a detailed map. Mind the government hours and be prepared for some quirky frustrations. But given the scandalous rental agencies that abound in Abu Dhabi, this office is a godsend.

Location: *In the Union National Bank Building (5th floor), on the Corniche*

Corniche   Map ref → 8-A3/B3

- Beautiful but highly priced sea views
- Parking difficult to find unless your building has underground parking
- Major road works and construction scheduled over the next few years

Views of the Corniche

Electra (Nr Town Center)   Map ref → 8-A1/D1

- Plenty of hustle and bustle within this mix of commercial and residential towers
- Mainly older towers, but some newer executive apartment blocks
- Possible parking problem if not included in rent
- Traffic congestion most of the day
- Mainly Asian men and expat Arabs

Hamdan St (Nr Town Center)   Map ref → 8-B2/D2

- A lively mix of commercial and residential towers
- Mainly older towers, but some newer, more expensive apartments
- Possible parking problem if not included in rent
- Traffic congestion during rush hour
- Good mix of nationalities

Karama & Old Mushrif   Map ref → 3-C4, 5-C1, 3-D3

- Much sought after, long established expat areas
- Mainly low rise flats and older villas
- Near British and International Schools

- Leafy trees and shrubs give pleasant feel to neighbourhood
- Mainly Western expats and Nationals

Green Spaces Abound

Khalidiya   Map ref ➜ 9-D1

- Very expensive, large villas and high rise luxury apartments
- Mainly Western expats, Nationals and expat Arabs
- Near or on the famous Abu Dhabi Corniche
- Quiet, peaceful area
- Near the American Community School

Manaseer   Map ref ➜ 6-A2

- Much sought after older apartments
- Low rise apartments; not cheap but never vacant for long
- Quiet, open area with ample greenery
- Palaces and embassies for neighbours!

Muroor   Map ref ➜ 3-B2

- Well out of town, hence lower rents
- Low rise buildings and large villas along the main roads
- Near the American International School
- Mix of Asians, expat Arabs and Nationals

Rhoda   Map ref ➜ 5-D2, 6-A2

- Villas in this area much sought after by Western expats
- Located near Embassy Road
- Quiet, lush, green open area

Other Rental Costs

Extra costs to be considered are:

- Water and electricity connection fee (Dhs.1,000)
- Real estate commission: 5% of annual rent (one off payment)
- Fully refundable security deposit (Dhs.2,000)
- Some landlords also require a deposit against damage (usually a fully refundable, one off payment)

Real Estate Agents

Asteco	626 2660
Hyatt Real Estate	633 2959
Homestyle Property	645 6242
Pivot	633 1907
Silver Lake Property Management	676 2461

If you are renting a villa, don't forget that you may have to maintain a garden and pay for extra water etc. To avoid massive water bills at the end of every month, many people prefer to have a well dug in their backyard for all that necessary plant and grass watering. Expect to pay around Dhs.1,500 - 3,000 to have a well dug and a pump installed.

Some of the older villas may also need additional maintenance, which the landlord may not cover. Often the more popular accommodation has waiting lists that are years long. To secure immediate tenancy many people offer the landlord 'key money', a down payment of several thousand dirhams to secure the accommodation.

Real Estate Websites

Asteco	www.astecoproperty.com
Colliers International	www.colliersuae.com
Hayatt Real Estate	www.hayattrealestate.co.ae
Homestyle Property	www.homestyle-property.co.ae
Silver Lake Property Management	www.silverlakeuae.com

Moving Services

Two main options exist when moving your furniture and personal effects either to or from Abu Dhabi: air freight and sea freight. Air freight is a better option when moving smaller amounts, but if you have a larger consignment, sea freight is the way to go. Either way, make sure your goods are packed by professionals.

New Residents

Housing

Unless you send your personal belongings with the airline you are flying with, you will need to use the services of a removal company. A company with a wide international network is usually the best and safest option but, more importantly, you must trust the people you are dealing with. Ensure they are competent in the country of origin and have reliable agents in the country to which you are shipping your personal belongings. Most removal companies offer free consultations, plus advice and samples of packing materials – call around.

Moving Tips:

- Book moving dates well in advance
- Don't forget to insure your goods, and purchase additional insurance for irreplaceable items
- Make an inventory of the items you want moved (keep your own copy!)
- Ensure everything is packed extremely well and in a way that can be checked by Customs and repacked with the least possible damage; check and sign the packing list
- Keep a camera and film handy to take pictures at each stage of the move (valuable in case of a dispute)
- Do not pack restricted goods of any kind
- If moving to Abu Dhabi, ensure videos, DVD's and books are not offensive to Muslim sensibilities

When your belongings arrive in Abu Dhabi, you will be called to Customs to be present while the authorities open your boxes to ensure nothing illegal or inappropriate is being brought into the country. Assisting in this process can be exhausting; the search may take place outdoors over a few hours, with your belongings thrown on the ground. After this, depending on the agreement you have with the removal company, either their representative in Abu Dhabi will help you transport the boxes to your new home, or you can make the arrangements locally.

Relocation Experts

Relocation experts offer a range of services to help you settle into your new life in Abu Dhabi as quickly as possible. Practical help ranges from finding accommodation or schools for your children to connecting a telephone or information on medical care. In addition, they will often offer advice on the way of life in the city, putting people in touch with the social networks to help them establish a new life.

Moving Services

Relocation Companies	
Chestertons Property Management	676 7181
Colliers International	626 4543
Crown Relocations	674 5155
Gulf Agency Company (GAC)	673 0500
In Touch Relocations	04 332 8807
Removal Companies	
Allied Pickfords	677 9765
Al Moherbie Clearance and Transport	672 2004
Colliers International	626 4543
Crown Worldwide Movers	674 5155
Gulf Agency Company(GAC)	673 0500

Furnishings

Other options → **Furniture & Household Items [p.146]**

Good quality furniture and household items can be found at reasonable prices here. The most popular furniture outlets in Abu Dhabi are ID Design, IKEA, Marlin, THE One, Home Centre and Pan Emirates. Other favourites for Indian teak and wrought iron are Marina Gulf Trading or Heritage Touch in Khalidiya.

Household/furniture shopping

For cheap second hand furniture, you can often buy from the previous tenant through 'garage' sales or small ads in the newspapers, or from supermarket noticeboards. The souks have plenty of shops selling inexpensive, basic furniture, pots, pans and ironing boards etc.

Household Appliances

Carrefour, Jashanmal, Jumbo Electronics and Plug Ins have decent selections of heavy household appliances. Make sure that your purchases come with a warranty. All the main brands are found in the UAE, but the fittings are made for the European market, and thus North American makes can be harder to find.

Prices are quite reasonable for new appliances, but if you would prefer to buy second hand, have a look at the noticeboards at the various supermarkets around town. Of course, there is no guarantee with second hand goods, so beware.

Household Insurance

No matter where you live in the world and how 'safe' a place may seem, it is always wise to insure the contents of your home. There are many internationally recognised insurance companies operating in Abu Dhabi – check the Yellow Pages or Hawk Business Pages for details.

When forming your policy, insurance companies need certain general information, such as your home address in Abu Dhabi, a household contents list and valuation, and invoices for items over Dhs.2,500. Cover usually extends to theft, storm damage, fire etc. For an additional fee you can insure personal items outside the home, such as jewellery, cameras etc.

Laundry Services

Whilst there are no self service launderettes in Abu Dhabi there are many small outlets, plus larger supermarkets, some hotels and The Club (673 1111), offering laundry and drycleaning services at reasonable rates and next day delivery. You can also choose to simply get your clothes ironed at approximately Dhs.1 per item. It's always a good idea to speak to the laundry man himself if you have a preference on how you want an item ironed (or if you would like to avoid the 'shiny' look!).

Domestic Help

Although you may never have considered hiring a domestic helper before, many people in Abu Dhabi do, as the service is comparatively cheap and easy to arrange. For the busy or the lazy, it means the house is spotless and shirts are always pressed.

To employ the services of a full-time live in domestic helper, you must have a minimum monthly salary of Dhs.6,000. The helper cannot be related to you, or of the same nationality as you. In fact, the list of acceptable nationalities can also change from time to time. At the time of print, the rules are as follows – only Filipino, Ethiopian and Indonesian maids can be brought from overseas; all other nationalities already in the country can remain. Check with the Immigration authorities before starting the process – just in case.

Domestic Help Agencies	
Delight Cleaners	678 9216
Solutions	443 0445

As the employer, you must sponsor the person and deal with all residency papers, including the medical test etc. Singles and families in which the wife isn't working may face difficulties sponsoring a helper. It is normally best to find someone through an agency dedicated to hiring domestic helpers. You will be asked to sign a contract stating that you will pay your employee a minimum salary of about Dhs.750 each month with an airfare to his/her country of origin once a year. There may also be a small fee if you are hiring via an agency.

The residence visa for a maid will cost around Dhs.5,000 (Dhs.4,800 for the government fee, Dhs.100 for the residence visa and Dhs.100 for the labour card). Residency is only valid for one year. You can obtain a residence visa card through the normal channels, after which some embassies (eg, the Philippines) require to see the labour contract of your newly appointed maid. This is to ensure that all paperwork is in order and that the maid is receiving fair treatment. It is illegal to share a maid with another household.

An alternative and cheaper option is to have part-time home help and there are a number of agencies that offer domestic help on an hourly basis. The standard rate is about Dhs.20 - 25 per hour, with a minimum of two hours per visit. The number of hours required would obviously depend on the size of your accommodation and the level of mess. The service includes general cleaning, washing, ironing and sometimes babysitting.

Pets

Bringing Your Pet Here

There are only restrictions on bringing pets with you to Abu Dhabi if you are entering the country from certain parts of Asia (including India and Pakistan). This includes a 21 day quarantine, and your pets are required to be micro chipped. When travelling from Asia or other parts of the world you will first require an import permit from the Ministry of Agriculture and Fisheries. The permit normally takes about a week to process.

You will need the following documents:

- A copy of your pet's vaccination certificate showing valid rabies vaccination (if this is the first injection, you will have to wait 30 days before the pet can travel)
- A copy of your passport

The British Veterinary Centre (02 665 0085) can help you obtain an import permit, customs clearance and collection from the airport, delivery and/or boarding of your pet, if required. If you choose not to use their services, the airline you are travelling with should be able to advise you of the necessary requirements. There is no quarantine for properly documented pets brought into the UAE (though see exception above).

Taking Your Pet Home

The regulations for 'exporting' your pet depend on the laws of the country of destination. Basic requirements are:

- A valid vaccination card, not older than 1 year, but not less than 30 days
- A health certificate from your local vet 10 days or less before departure
- A government export permit, obtained from Abu Dhabi Airport Departures
- A travel box, normally wooden or fibreglass, that meets airline regulations

Your local vet, kennels or the airline that you are travelling with can inform you of the specific regulations pertaining to your destination, such as quarantine rules etc. Again, the British Veterinary Centre can assist you with this process. Check out their Website for all pet travel information.

Veterinary Clinics	
American Veterinary Clinic	673 3337
British Veterinary Centre	665 0085

Cats & Dogs

The Municipality controls Abu Dhabi's huge stray population by trapping and eliminating animals. All pets should be sterilised and kept safely on your premises. Once sterilised, they will wander less and

will therefore be less exposed to the dangers of traffic and disease. If you feed the stray population around your home, you will simply create a problem for yourselves and your neighbours with a growing stray population. To do some proactive help, or if you see an injured cat and need assistance, contact Feline Friends (02 673 2696 – voicemail). For any help with stray or injured dogs, call K9 Friends (04 347 4611)

Pet Shops

Though regulations governing the sale of animals in pet shops exist, they are rarely actively enforced. Animals are often underage (although their papers state differently), sick or even pregnant, and the conditions in which they are kept leave a lot to be desired. Rather than encouraging this trade, you would do better to give a home to one of the many stray animals in Abu Dhabi. Contact Feline Friends or K9 Friends to see who needs a home or check out the special Feline and K9 Friends page in the Saturday edition of the Gulf News.

Animal Souks

There is an animal souk in the Meena area, on the way to The Club. This souk, as with others in the UAE, is not for the faint hearted. The CITES protected list is disregarded in these souks, and animals are often diseased and kept in very cramped, overcrowded cages. Give this one a miss!

UTILITIES & SERVICES

Electricity & Water

These services are provided by the government run Abu Dhabi Water and Electricity Department (commonly known as ADWEA). The authority provides excellent service, with extremely rare electricity or water shortages/stoppages.

Water and electricity deposits, as well as monthly bills, can be paid at any office or through various banks. Those offering this service are listed on the reverse of the bill. Bills are 'assessed' one month and the meter read the next month.

Location:
Abu Dhabi: Madinat Zayed, beh Central Post Office (02 642 3000).
Al Ain: Beh Municipality (03 763 6000).

Opening hours: *Sat - Wed 07:00 - 19:00 (bill payments); 07:00 - 14:00 (inquiries); Thursday 07:00 - 17:00 (bill payments) and 07:00 - 19:00 (inquiries).*

Electricity

There's plenty of it! The electricity supply in Abu Dhabi is 220/240 volts and 50 cycles. The socket type is identical to the three point British system. Adapters can be purchased at any grocery or hardware store.

Water

More expensive than oil! The tap water is safe to drink, but not always pleasant, and visitors generally prefer the locally bottled mineral water, which is widely available. Bottled water is usually served in hotels and restaurants.

Buying 20 litre water bottles, rather than small 1½ litre bottles, is more environmentally friendly and can make a considerable cost saving for drinking water. The bottle deposit is usually Dhs.25 - 35, and refills Dhs.5 - 7. These large bottles can be used with a variety of methods for decanting the water. Choices include a hand pump available from supermarkets and costing about Dhs.3. A fixed pump can be bought for about Dhs.60 and a variety of refrigeration units are also available. Prices vary depending on the model, but on average are about Dhs.400. Water suppliers will deliver to your door, saving you some serious backache.

One of the slightly crazy aspects of life in the Emirates is that during the summer months, if your water tank is on the roof, you won't need to heat water – it's already hot when it comes out of the cold tap! Indeed the only way to have a cold(ish) shower is to keep the immersion heater off and use the hot tap.

Water Suppliers

Water Suppliers	
Abu Dhabi: Oasis Water	558 2030
Al Ain: Oasis Water	03 782 5181

Gas

While a mains gas supply does not exist in Abu Dhabi, there is the option of buying individual gas canisters for cooking if required. These can be connected to a gas oven and generally cost about Dhs.220 per new canister and Dhs.25 for a refill. Some newer buildings supply central gas from rooftop storage tanks. If you live away from the centre of town, you can hear the gas delivery van's bell ringing in the morning and afternoon as they go on their rounds.

Gas Suppliers

Gas Suppliers	
Al Ruwais Industrial Gases	555 3809
Milky Way Trading	446 2130
Zubair Gas Distribution	679 2205
Majed Gas	03 762 2199

Telephone

Emirates Telecommunications Corporation (known as Etisalat) is the sole telecommunications provider in the Emirates – its headquarters are located in the buildings next to the Fatouh Al Khair Centre (Marks and Spencer building) situated in the centre of the city and in between Hamdan and Electra Streets. The tallest block has the huge white trademark golf ball on its roof. They are responsible for telephones (both landlines and mobiles) and Internet (through its sister company, Emirates Internet & Multimedia).

Etisalat, Abu Dhabi

Etisalat is generally an efficient and innovative company, constantly introducing new services and even cutting bills to the consumer from time to time. You should have few problems in processing paperwork, receiving services or rectifying problems. Recent public mutterings about Etisalat's monopoly over the telecom market has not yet received any sort of official response.

Opening hours: *Saturday - Wednesday 07:00 - 15:00*

Bill payments only: Saturday - Wednesday 15:00 - 19:00; Thursday 08:00 - 13:00

New Residents

Utilities & Services

Landline Phones

To install a regular landline phone connection in your home, you need to apply directly to Etisalat with the following: Etisalat application form in English (hand written is acceptable), copy of passport and residence visa, NOC from your employer, Dhs.250, and a copy of your tenancy agreement. Once you have submitted the application, it takes between 2 - 3 days until a phone connection is installed. Even if you have your own phone handset, Etisalat will provide one, and it's usually bright pink, green or blue. If you require additional phone sockets, order them at the same time, and pay a further Dhs.50 for the first socket and then Dhs.15 per socket thereafter. The procedure is usually extremely efficient and streamlined.

Etisalat offers many additional services, such as call waiting, call forwarding, a 'follow me' service – for more information contact you nearest Etisalat branch or check the Etisalat home page (www.etisalat.co.ae).

Quarterly Rental: Standard landline (for all sockets) is Dhs.45. All calls made locally within Abu Dhabi on and to a landline are free. For international and mobile rates, check the phone book.

Discount Long Distance Rates: Standard landline: all day Friday and government declared national public holidays.

Weekdays: outside GCC, 21:00 - 07:00; GCC only 19:00 - 07:00.

Mobile Phones

Most people in Abu Dhabi seem to own a mobile phone, if not two. Etisalat puts the number of GSM subscribers in the UAE at well over 1.7 million. Mobiles can be purchased from Etisalat, specialised telecommunications shops, most electronics shops and large supermarkets, such as Carrefour.

Etisalat GSM assistance telephone service: dial 101 for enquiries.

Missing Mobile

If you lose your mobile or have it stolen, call 101 to deactivate your SIM card temporarily. You might need to know your passport number for security. To disconnect your number permanently, you will have to go to Etisalat to fill in a line disconnection application form.

Non resident

(ie, visa not fully processed/visit visa)

If your visa is not fully processed, or if you are visiting the country and want to use your mobile, your only option is Wasel GSM service.

This is a popular variation of GSM service, available to both non residents and residents, allowing you to decide on the amount of outgoing calls that can be made on your phone, but allowing unlimited incoming calls. This service also provides international roaming for incoming calls (you will be charged the international rate).

The subscription is for one year and payment for outgoing calls needs to be made in advance. The cost is Dhs.185 for one year's subscription and you can apply at any branch office. The annual renewal charge is Dhs.100. Fill out the application form and provide Essential Documents, although, as mentioned, you do not need to be a resident to avail this service. The service includes connection, one year's rental, SIM card charges and Dhs.10 free credit. You may 'recharge' your card for outgoing calls in Dhs.30 units or Dhs.50 in cash. The minimum amount that you can recharge your card at an Etisalat machine is Dhs.50.

Resident

If you are a resident applying for a mobile phone connection, collect an application form from any Etisalat office. Submit the application to any Etisalat branch office, along with your passport and residence visa copy and Dhs.215. This amount includes rental for the first quarter. You should receive your SIM card there and then, and once installed, you're ready to dial. An alternative to the standard mobile phone agreement is to apply for the Wasel GSM service (see above).

Rental charges: Quarterly rental charge for the standard mobile phone service: Dhs.90.

Local rates: Peak rate: 30 fils per minute (06:00 - 14:00 & 16:00 - 24:00); off peak rate: 21 fils per minute.

International discount rates: All day Friday and government declared national public holidays; Weekdays: 21:00 - 07:00 (outside GCC); 19:00 - 07:00 (GCC only).

Internet

For connection to cyberspace, Etisalat's sister company, Emirates Internet & Multimedia (EIM) is the sole provider of Internet services through its UAE proxy server. With the proxy server in place, some sites are restricted (if you find a blocked site that you believe is perfectly reasonable, you can report it to Etisalat on help@emirates.net.ae).

You can access Emirates Internet from any standard telephone line using an appropriate modem at speeds in excess of 56 Kbps. If you require higher speed access, you can apply for an ISDN line (64 Kbps) or an ADSL line (128 Kbps); for more information contact Etisalat (800 6100).

Numerous Internet sites about the Emirates exist; check out the Website listing on [p.43].

To get yourself connected, you will require a landline in your name or your company's name, a copy of your passport and residence visa, and the Internet application form from Etisalat.

Registration charge: Dhs.100 for dialup or ISDN; Dhs.200 for ADSL (plus Dhs.100 for optional software installation by the Etisalat technician).

Rental: Standard Internet connection: Dhs.20 per month; ISDN line: Dhs.100 quarterly; ADSL line: Dhs.250 per month

Additional user charge for the standard and ISDN connection: peak rate, Dhs.1.8 per hour (06:00 - 01:00); off peak, Dhs.1 per hour.

With an ADSL line, you are logged on 24 hours a day and pay no further charges.

Dial 'n' Surf

This facility allows you to surf without subscribing to Internet service. All that's needed is a computer with a modem and a regular phone (or ISDN) line – no account number or password is required. In theory you then simply dial 500 5555 to gain access. However, in practice it may not be quite so straightforward, since there are different set ups depending on your software. If you have difficulties, contact the helpdesk (800 5244).

Internet Help

abuse@emirates.net.ae for reporting on hacking, illegal use of Internet, spamming etc.

watch@emirates.net.ae for reporting inappropriate sites

custserv@emirates.net.ae for comments, billing disputes and general Internet inquiries

help@emirates.net.ae for technical support

www.emirates.net.ae to visit the Etisalat homepage & for Emirates Internet & Multimedia products and services, billing inquiries, online change of passwords, change of ISDN access speed

Tel 800 6100 for Internet Help Desk

Charges: a charge of 15 fils per minute is made for the connection and billed to the telephone line from which the call is made.

Bill Payment

Bills are mailed monthly and are itemised for international and mobile calls, SMS (short message service) and service charges. All bill payments can be made at Etisalat branch offices, on the Internet, and certain banks such as Emirates Bank International and HSBC (details can be obtained through Etisalat). Etisalat also has cash payment machines at several sites, saving you the hassle of queuing at Etisalat or the bank; again, details can be obtained from Etisalat. You can also recharge your Wasel service using these machines.

If you don't pay your landline telephone bill within the first ten days of the month, or your GSM bill within 45 days, you outgoing calls will be blocked, although you will still receive incoming calls for up to 15 days afterwards. Before the final disconnection, Etisalat very kindly automatically calls landlines and sends an SMS to mobiles to remind people to pay up.

Bill Enquiry Service

Etisalat provides a useful bill enquiry service, enabling customers to obtain the current amount payable on their phone/s up till the end of the last month. The aim is to help customers budget their calls and to facilitate prompt settlement of bills, leading to fewer disconnections.

The information is only available for the phone that the call is made from (in theory) and the cost of the call inquiry is charged at the normal rate. To use the service, dial 142 (English) or 143 (Arabic). You may also use Etisalat cash payment machines for this service, and Etisalat's 'online billing service' to pay Internet bills.

Postal Services

Other options ➜ **Post & Courier Services [p.38]**

There is no house address based mailing system in the UAE – all mail is delivered to the Central Post Office and then distributed to centrally located post office boxes. While many residents direct mail to a company mailbox, it is also possible to rent a personal PO Box. To apply for one, you require an application form from the Central Post Office and

Dhs.160. You can then select a PO Box at a convenient location near your home (if available).

Emirates Postal Service (Empost) will send you notification by email when you receive registered mail or parcels in your PO Box. There is no charge for this service, but you do have to register your email address and details with Empost. They will tell you the origin, arrival date, type of mail and location, and for Dhs.9, you can have your parcel or registered mail delivered to your door – all you have to do is reply to the mail with your address attached.

Location:

Abu Dhabi: Central Post Office (02 621 5415), East Road, Madinat Zayed Area

Al Ain: Central Post Office (03 764 2200), Main Street, nr Clock Tower

Opening Hours: *Saturday - Thursday 08:00 - 20:00; Friday 17:00 - 21:00*

Television

UAE television is divided amongst the emirates with Dubai, Abu Dhabi, Sharjah and Ajman all broadcasting terrestrially and via satellite. Dubai has four channels; Dubai 2, 10 and 41 show Arabic programmes, whilst Dubai 33 broadcasts mainly in English. It offers a mixture of serials, documentaries and films (chiefly American, British and Australian), as well as films from 'Bollywood'. Programme details are published daily in the local press.

Emirates Dubai Television broadcasts by satellite throughout the world in Arabic and English. Abu Dhabi has an English language channel, while Sharjah and Ajman TV transmit mainly Arabic programmes, with some in English.

There are numerous video/DVD rental stores around and the latest releases from Hollywood and Bollywood are widely available, usually in English or Hindi with Arabic subtitles. Anything that offends the country's moral code is censored – be prepared for some interesting continuity!

The Emirates Cable TV & Multimedia (E-Vision) is UAE's cable TV network and a subsidiary of Etisalat. There are approximately 70 Arabic, Asian and Western channels to choose from, though this will rise to 100 channels in the future. The basic subscription fee is Dhs.50 and for an extra charge, you can add pay satellite channels. For further information, contact 800 5500, or log on to www.emiratescatv.co.ae.

Television, video and DVD in the Emirates follows the European PAL system, though most new televisions, video recorders and DVD players now have dual systems, allowing you to play both PAL and NTSC formats.

Satellite TV

The digital in home entertainment revolution is sweeping through the Middle East, and Abu Dhabi is its epicentre judging by the number of satellite dishes in the city. Satellite TV offers viewers an enormous number of programmes and channels to watch and there is a confusing choice of options available. Most leading hotels offer satellite in their rooms, showing news, sports, movies, documentaries, cartoons etc. Considering the diversity of people watching, it's not surprising that programmes of all hues, flavours and tastes are available. Couch potatoes will have to first decide the types of programmes they want to watch and then whether they are willing to pay for them. The various channels available can be split into two types:

1. Pay TV Satellite Channels

These are channels that require payment for installation and equipment, such as the decoder, dish etc, followed by a viewing subscription for the channels you choose to watch. Generally, subscriptions can be paid monthly, quarterly or annually. Take your time making the right choice because the Middle East has a competitive pay TV market, with four pay TV networks all offering a range of channels.

2. Free to Air Satellite Channels

These are channels that require payment for the installation and reception equipment, but there is no viewing subscription. There are more than 200 of these types of channels.

Equipment

Equipment can be bought from various locations; directly from the main dealers, electrical shops, second hand shops or classified ads. The majority of dealers offer installation. For apartment blocks or buildings with a large number of viewing points, a central system is recommended, making it economical as well as offering more choice. Persuade your landlord to install the system if the block does not already come with satellite receiving equipment.

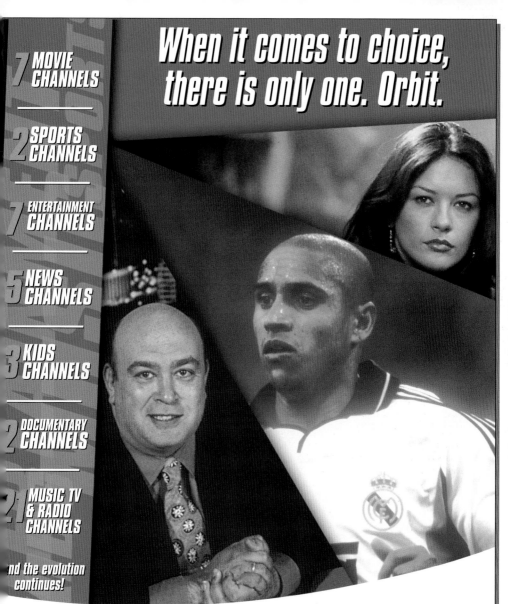

Satellite Main Dealers

Eurostar	634 7357
Hayat Electronics	676 6094
Star Distributions – Orbit – Bond Communications	633 3377
1st Net Bouquet – Satellite World	03 751 5212
Star Distributions – Orbit (Digital) – Bait Al Ezz	03 751 2831

HEALTH

General Medical Care

The quality of medical care in the Emirates is generally regarded as quite high and visitors should have little trouble in obtaining the appropriate treatment whether privately or, in case of an emergency, from the government run hospitals. Tourists and non residents are strongly recommended to arrange private medical insurance before travelling since private medical care can become very expensive.

Al Noor Hospital, Abu Dhabi

There are no specific health risks facing visitors, although the climate can be harsh, especially during the summer months. It is advisable to drink plenty of water (and to replace lost salts with energy drinks or salty snacks), to cover up when out in the sun and use the appropriate factor sunscreen – sunburn, heat stroke and heat exhaustion can be very unpleasant.

UAE Nationals and expatriate residents are allowed healthcare for a minimal cost at the government hospitals and clinics.

In Abu Dhabi, the Department of Health and Medical Services runs the Abu Dhabi Central Hospital, the Corniche Maternity Hospital and the Al Jazeera, although the latter is mainly for use by Nationals only. Al Ain has the Al Jimi and Tawam hospitals.

There are also various private medical hospitals and clinics. All are required to display a price list in Arabic and English for patients.

Each emirate has at least one pharmacy open 24 hours a day. The location and telephone numbers are printed in the daily newspapers. The pharmacies attached to the Al Noor and New Medical Centre and the Al Rizi Pharmacy at the Hamdan Centre are open 24 hours. Opening times: Saturday - Thursday 08:30 - 13:30 and 16:30 - 22:30; Fridays 16:30 - 22:30 Some pharmacies may be open on Friday mornings, 09:00 - 13:00.

Hospitals/Clinics

Hospitals

Al Noor Hospital Emergency	626 5265
The Corniche Hospital (maternity only) Emergency	672 4900
Golden Sands Medical Hospital	642 7171
Mafraq Hospital Emergency	582 3100
National Hospital Emergency	671 1000
New Medical Centre Hospital Emergency	633 2255
Sheikh Khalifa Medical Centre Emergency	633 1000
Al Ain Hospital (Al Jimi) Emergency	03 763 5888
Emirates International Hospital	03 763 7777
Oasis Hospital Emergency	03 722 1251
Specialised Medical Care Centre Emergency	03 766 2291
Tawam Hospital Emergency	03 767 7444

Private Centres/Clinics

Centre Medical Franco – Emirien Emergency	626 5722
Gulf Diagnostic Centre	665 8090
Al Aheed Medical Centre	03 764 2791
Al Dhahery Clinic	03 765 6882
Emirates Medical Clinic Centre	03 764 4744
Family Medical Clinic	03 766 9902
Hafeet Medical Centre	03 764 1565
Hamdan Medical Centre	03 765 4797
Mahboob Clinic	03 765 4631
New Al Ain Medical Clinic	03 764 1448
Sulaiman Clinic	03 764 1009

Emergency **Denotes 24 hour Emergency Service**

YOUR SMILE IS OUR CONCERN

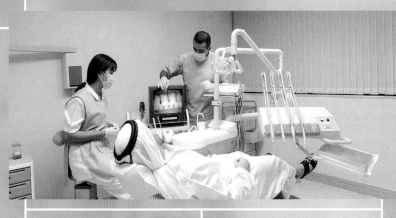

BESIDES GENERAL DENTISTRY SUCH AS COSMETIC FILLINGS, CROWNS
AND BRIDGES, VENEERS AND PEDIATRIC DENTISTRY, WE OFFER THE
FOLLOWING SPECIAL SERVICES:

✔ 40 minute Bleaching (Apollo 95).
✔ Root canal treatment in one visit only
(Root ZX).

✔ Painless sedation using Nitrous Oxide.
✔ Air Disinfecting System (Stery Box).

Hamdan Street,
Liwa Center
Tower B. Floor O
Abu Dhabi

FIRAS DENTAL CLINIC

Tel: 02 6335990 - 02 6335988

www.firasdental.com

Maternity

Every expatriate child born in the UAE must be registered at the Ministry of Health within two weeks, and have a residence visa within four months of birth. Without the correct documentation, you won't be able to take your baby out of the country. The hospital you deliver at will prepare the birth certificate in Arabic upon receipt of hospital records, photocopies of both parents' passports, the marriage certificate and a fee of Dhs.50. Take the birth certificate for translation into English to the Ministry of Health Department of Preventive Medicine (there's one in every emirate). They will endorse and attest it for a fee of Dhs.10. Once this is done, ensure you register your child at your embassy or consulate (you may also want to arrange for a passport for your baby at this time), and then apply for a residence visa through the normal UAE channels. Before the time of birth, it is worth checking out the regulations of your country of origin regarding citizens born overseas.

Abu Dhabi Hospital

Gynaecology & Obstetrics

Al Noor Hospital	626 5265
Corniche Hospital	672 4900
Gulf Diagnostic Centre	665 8090
New Medical Centre	633 2255
Al Ain Hospital (Al Jimi)	03 763 5888
Emirates International Hospital	03 763 7777
Oasis Hospital	03 722 1251
Specialised Medical Care Centre	03 766 2291
Tawam Hospital	03 767 7444

Ante Natal/Post Natal Care

Al Noor Hospital	626 5265
Corniche Hospital	672 4900
Dr McCulloch Clinic	633 3900
Gulf Diagnostic Centre	665 8090
New Medical Centre	633 2255
Emirates International Hospital	03 763 7777
Oasis Hospital	03 722 1251
Specialised Medical Care Centre	03 766 2291
Tawam Hospital (ante Natal only)	03 767 7444

Mental Health

Psychology/Psychiatry

Al Noor Hospital	626 5265
Gulf Diagnostic Centre	665 8090
New Medical Centre (Psychiatry only)	633 2255
Al Ain Hospital (Al Jimi)	03 763 5888
Specialised Medical Care Centre	03 766 2291
Tawam Hospital	03 767 7444

Dentists / Orthodontists

The standard of dentistry in Abu Dhabi is generally very high. Practitioners and specialists of all nationalities offer services on par with or better than those found 'back home'. Prices, however, match the level of service and most health insurance packages do not cover dentistry, unless it is emergency treatment as the result of an accident. Word of mouth works particularly well for finding a suitable dentist. Alternatively, phone around to find out what methods and equipment are used.

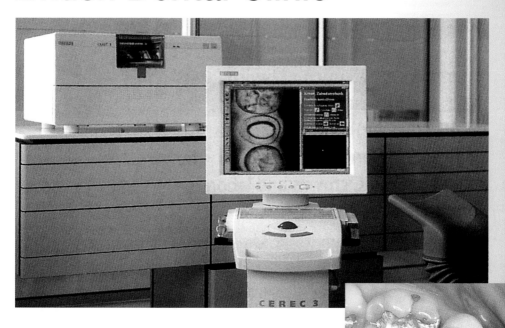
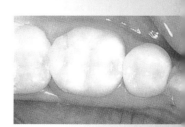

Private Dentists/Orthodontists

Advanced Dental Clinic	681 2921
American Dental Clinic	677 1310
Austrian Dental Clinic	621 1489
Barbara Dental Clinic	626 9898
British Dental Clinic	677 3308
Dr Elisabeth Dental Clinic	626 7822
Dr Firas Dental Clinic	633 5988
Gulf Diagnostic Centre	665 8090
Faxius Dental Clinic	672 3445
International Dental Clinic	633 3444
Maher Dental Clinic	666 3588
Swedish Dental Clinic	666 5444

Al Bahri Dental Clinic	03 764 3273
Al Hijjar Dental Clinic	03 765 8155
Canadian Dental Clinic	03 766 6696
City Dental & Medical Centre	03 764 2252
Gulf Dental Clinic	03 765 4373
Modern Dental Clinic	03 766 4764
New Al Ain Dental Clinic	03 766 2059
Swedish Dental Clinic	03 766 6227
Tabrizi Dental Clinic	03 766 2133
Thabit Medical Centre	03 765 4454

Alternative Therapies

The UAE has finally permitted the practice of alternative medicine, including homeopathy, Ayurveda, osteopathy, herbal medicine and traditional Chinese medicine. An office of Complementary & Alternative Medicine has been set up at the Ministry of Health, which examines and grants licences to practitioners of alternative medicine before they are able to legally practice here.

With the granting of licences for alternative therapists, Abu Dhabi residents now have a range of healing methods to choose from in addition to the more conventional approach to medicine. As always, word of mouth recommendation is the best way of establishing who might offer the most appropriate treatment and approach. The following are some of the treatments offered and the main practitioners in Abu Dhabi.

Acupressure/Acupuncture

These are two of the oldest healing methods in the world. Acupressure is a system where manual pressure is applied by the practitioner at specific points along the body's energy lines, whereas acupuncture employs needles to stimulate various points along the body's energy lines. Despite the fact that needles are used, this ancient method of healing can be a pleasant experience and can assist with many ailments.

Abu Dhabi Health and Fitness Club	443 6333
Gulf Chinese Medical Centre	634 3538
Gulf Diagnostic Centre	665 8090

Back Treatment

Without your back, you're nothing! Luckily, treatment is widely available in the UAE, with many top notch specialists from around the world practising here.

Chiropractic/Osteopathy/Craniosacral Therapy/Pilates

The first two treatments concentrate on manipulating the skeleton in a non intrusive manner to improve the functioning of the nervous system or blood supply to the body. Chiropractic is based on the manipulative treatment of misalignments in the joints, especially those of the spinal column, while osteopathy involves the manipulation and massage of the skeleton and musculature.

Abu Dhabi Health and Fitness Club	443 6333
Chiropractic Speciality Clinic	634 5162
Gulf Diagnostic Centre	665 8090

Craniosacral therapy aims to relieve pain and tension by gentle manipulations of the skull to balance the craniosacral rhythm.

Pilates is said to be the safest form of neuromuscular reconditioning and back strengthening available.

Homeopathy

Homeopathy uses natural remedies to help with both physical and emotional problems. It strengthens the body's defence system, helping eliminate many health issues. Currently, there is only one licensed homeopath in the UAE, Dr. Ludmila Vassileva, who is located in Dubai.

• Holistic Healing Medical Centre (04 228 3234)

Massage Therapy/Reflexology

Reflexology is a science based on the premise that zones and reflex areas in the feet and hands correspond to all parts and systems of the body. Pressure applied to these reflex areas results in stress reduction and improved health. While many salons and spas in Abu Dhabi offer massage and some of them offer reflexology, the following focus more on holistic healing. For a listing of spas offering massage, see Activities [p.166].

| Abu Dhabi Health and Fitness Club | 443 6333 |
| Gulf Diagnostic Centre | 665 8090 |

Help on the Web

www.doctorelite.com is a Website run by doctors and health professionals in the UAE, containing information on where to find a doctor who speaks your language, health tips, which pharmacies are open late at night etc. Basically, the main function of the Website is to provide a search engine that allows you to look for practitioners in the UAE and internationally. It details their qualifications, specialities, medical degrees etc – very helpful!

Support Groups

Even the most resilient of personalities can be affected by culture shock or simply a change in circumstances, whether this is the stress of settling into a new environment and adjusting to new places and faces, or coming to terms with a more personal problem. Abu Dhabi can be a challenging place to live and, with many residents originating from overseas, there is often a lack of the family support that people are used to. Taking the first step to reach out for help can be tough, however, there are groups out there offering a hand through the difficult patches.

Check out the back of any of the monthly health focused magazines that are usually available in surgeries, nutrition stores etc, for updates of support groups. If possible, get personal recommendations first as standards can vary enormously, especially if a group or workshop is linked to a business. Be wise and use your discretion.

Support Groups in Abu Dhabi:

- *Al Anon Family Groups* (050 668 4640) Meet Saturdays at 18:15.
- *Alcoholics Anonymous (AA)* (02 443 6325 – hotline) Meet every Saturday, Monday and Wednesday at 20:00 and Fridays at 10:00.
- *Overeaters Anonymous* (050 668 4640) Meet Sundays at 20:00.
- *Twins, Triplets or More!* (050 654 0079 – Paula) (050 641 2776 – Francesca) (http://uk.groups.yahoo.com/group/TTOM/)

Community of support, advice and information for families of multiples.

- *Abu Dhabi Mums* (02 448 2562 – Revi Bernard) (revibern@emirates.net.ae). A voluntary organisation providing support and activities for parents and children.
- *Mums and Toddler Group* (050 667 5220 – Janet) Meet every Monday, Wednesday and Saturday from 10:00 - 12:00 at St. Andrews Church Community Hall.
- *Eating Disorder Support Group* (02 665 8090 or 050 641 2776 – Francesca Bonta at Gulf Diagnostic Centre)
- *Parentcraft* (02 665 8090 – Head Nurse Dee Holme-Werner at Gulf Diagnostic Centre) A support group and a series of lectures for mums and dads to be on Tuesdays from 19:30 - 21:00.
- *Abu Dhabi Ladies* (02 667 3024 or 050 621 6213 – Angie Cummings) A support group open to ladies of all ages, helping them find new friends and offering many activities on a very informal basis. Meet every Wednesday at Sands Hotel, plus once a month at different venues.
- Upcoming support groups at the Gulf Diagnostic Centre include a Breast Cancer Support Group and Diabetes Support Group. For further information about these groups contact Head Nurse Dee Holme-Werner on 02 665 8090.

EDUCATION

In Abu Dhabi, due to the diverse expat culture, the education system is extremely varied and there are many schools from which to choose, all of which require fees from expats. For further information on the education system, schools, fees etc, refer to the *Family Explorer (Dubai and Abu Dhabi)*, published by Explorer Publishing.

It is always best to seek advice from friends or colleagues about a school's reputation. Many schools operate a waiting list and families are not necessarily able to enrol their child at their preferred school.

School terms: autumn (mid September - mid December); spring (early January - early April); summer (mid April - early July).

Generally, to enrol your child at a school the following information is needed:

New Residents

Education

- School application form
- Copies of student's and parents' passports – both information page/s and residence visa stamp
- Passport size photos (usually eight)
- Copies of student's birth certificate
- School records for the past two years
- Current immunisation records and medical history
- An official transfer certificate from the student's previous school detailing his/her education
- Some schools also require a student questionnaire to be completed

Original transfer certificates must contain the following details:

- Date of enrolment
- Year placement
- Date the child left the school
- School stamp
- Official signature

The Ministry of Education also requires the following documentation for any student enrolling at any school in any emirate:

- Original transfer certificate (to be completed by the student's current school)
- A recently issued original report card

If the student was attending a school in any country other than the UAE, Australia, Canada, European nation or the USA, the transfer certificate and the most recently issued original report card must be attested by the Ministry of Education, Ministry of Foreign Affairs and the UAE embassy in that country.

Nursery & Pre-School

(Age: babies - 4½ years)

Nursery schools usually like to interview a child before accepting him/her. Most nurseries adopt English as their common teaching language and annual fees can vary dramatically, depending on the level of establishment you approach.

Fees: *approximately Dhs.3,000 - 12,000 per annum.*
Hours: *most nurseries run for 4 - 5 hours in the morning.*

Primary & Secondary School

(Age: 4½ - 11 years) (Age: 11 - 18 years)

Most schools require proof of your child's previous school academic records. You will also need an official letter from the school in your home country detailing your child's education to date. Some schools even ask for a character reference! The child may also be required to take a short entrance exam and there may even be a physical examination as well as a family interview.

Depending on your nationality and educational requirements, most national curriculum syllabuses can be found in Abu Dhabi schools, covering GCSE's, A levels, French and International Baccalaureate and CNEC, as well as the American and Indian equivalent.

Standards of teaching are usually high and schools have excellent facilities, with extracurricular activities on offer. The Ministry of Education regularly inspects schools to ensure rules and regulations are being upheld, and most schools insist on a school uniform. Some school fees include books and transport to school by bus, but mostly, fees only cover the basic education.

Hours: *most are Saturday - Wednesday from 08:00 - 13:00 or 15:00.*

Fees: *Primary: approximately Dhs.10,000 - 20,000 per annum. Secondary: approximately Dhs.15,000 - 43,000 per annum. Other costs may include a deposit or registration.*

The British School Al Khubairat	446 2280
First Steps Kindergarten	445 4920
Giggles	641 6255
Humpty Dumpty	666 3277
Sesame Street Private Nursery	641 2300
Stepping Stones	681 5583
Al Adhwa'a Private School	03 766 7667
Al Ain Juniors	03 766 7433

Al Nahda National School	445 4200
Al Rabeeh	448 2856
American Community School	681 5115
American International School	444 4333
Cambridge High School	552 1621
International School of Choueifat	446 1444
The British School Al Khubairat	446 2280
Al Ain English Speaking School	03 767 8636
Al Dhafra Private School	03 767 1123
International School of Choueifat	03 767 8444

University & Higher Education

Most teenagers at university or higher education level return to their 'home' country to enrol in further education there. However, for those who wish to stay in the Emirates, a few choices exist.

British School, Abu Dhabi

A number of universities and colleges around the UAE with American, Australian and European affiliates offer degree and diploma courses in Arts, Sciences, Business & Management, and Engineering & Technology. Many commercial organisations also offer higher education courses for school leavers, mature students and adults. Details of these establishments can be found in the Hawk Business Pages or Yellow Pages. Both the American University of Dubai and the University of Wollongong in Dubai are accredited, and offer undergraduate and graduate degrees.

Special Needs Education

If you have a child or children with special needs, then before embarking on your adventure in the Emirates, we recommend that you first contact one or more of the following schools/centres, as student spaces are limited. All centres are charities, rather than government run, and thus rely on donations, sponsorship, grants and a certain amount of voluntary work from outside helpers. Entry into most is generally between the ages of 3½ to 5, unless the child was in a special needs school previously. Most of the teaching is generally in English, but Arabic language instruction is also available and, in most cases, each child receives an individual programme. All charge tuition fees.

- Al Noor Speech, Hearing and Development Centre (02 449 3844) is partially a charity organisation

as it takes in students who cannot afford to go to other centres in Abu Dhabi. Students are accepted with all types of disabilities and are of all ages. The centre provides formal and informal education and also vocational training which may further help the students to be self dependent. Staff are mainly Arab, with a few staff members of other nationalities.

- Future Centre (02 445 3324) is a 'not for profit' charitable institution for all nationalities between the ages of 3 and 20. Classes exist for students with DD/behavioural disorders, Downs Syndrome, Cerebral Palsy and Traumatic Brain Injury. There is a small Autism unit. The combination of education, therapies and care enables specialised and holistic services to be offered to children and young people with complex needs, degenerative conditions and additional sensory impairments whilst also supporting the rest of the family.

- Indian Ladies Association Special Care Centre for Handicapped Children (02 627 6070) aims to provide comprehensive educational, therapeutic, self help skills, social skills and a vocational training programme for handicapped children. The centre now has 70 children.

- Additionally, there is a therapeutic horse riding programme in Dubai for children with special needs – Riding for the Disabled (04 336 6321).

Note that in general, the UAE is not set up for those with special needs, and you won't find many wheelchair ramps around. Those ramps that we have seen appear to be there to assist with construction rather than with wheelchairs, as they all seem to be at a 60 degree angle. When considering employment in the Emirates, check with your future employer to see if the medical insurance programme they offer covers special needs children, as many do not.

See also: *Disabled Visitors [p.22]*

Learning Arabic

Can you speak the lingo? While it is relatively easy to pick up a few local words of greeting, if you are keen to learn more, there are a number of private institutions that offer very good Arabic language courses. Refer to Language Schools [p.218].

If you want just a few words to help you get by, have a look at the Arabic expressions table on [p.16].

TRANSPORTATION

Other options → Car [p.32]
Car Hire [p.34]

Cars are the most popular mode of transport in Abu Dhabi, and those who have a license and can afford it, generally have one. The main options if you wish to drive here for any length of time, are to buy a vehicle (for which you will need residency), or to lease. Visitors (short or long term) have the option of renting a vehicle from one of numerous rental companies.

The following section covers leasing, buying (new or used vehicles), registration, fines, insurance and traffic accidents.

The Traffic Department recorded information line (900 921 111) (English/Arabic) tells you all you ever wanted to know about fines, speeding tickets, registering vehicles, applying for driving licences, emergency numbers, suggestions etc.

Office locations:

• *Abu Dhabi: Traffic Police HQ/Traffic Department, Eastern Ring Road (02 448 6100)*

• *Al Ain: Traffic Police, Zayed Al Awwal Street (03 707 3500)*

Vehicle Leasing

Leasing a vehicle has many advantages over buying. Not only is it a financially viable option for shorter periods, there are also fewer hassles when it comes to breakdowns, re-registration etc, since the leasing company deals with everything. All services are provided inclusive of registration, maintenance, replacement, 24 hour assistance and insurance (comprehensive with personal accident is advisable). You may find that your employer has connections with a car hire company and can negotiate better rates for long term hire than you can on an individual basis.

Leasing is generally weekly, monthly or yearly. Cars typically range from Mitsubishi Lancers or Toyota Corollas to Mitsubishi Pajero 4 wheel drive vehicles. Monthly lease prices range from Dhs.1,600 for a small vehicle, and Dhs.1,800 to Dhs.3,000 for larger cars to Dhs.5,500 to Dhs. 7,500 for a 4 wheel drive. As the lease period increases, so the price decreases.

For short term rental there are many companies offering daily services – check the Hawk Business Pages for the most competitive. To hire any vehicle you will need to provide a passport copy, credit card and a valid driving licence from your home country or a valid international driving licence.

Vehicle Leasing Agents

Al Ghazal Rent a Car	634 2200
Avis	621 8400
Budget	633 4200
Diamond Lease	622 2028
Europcar	631 9922
Eurostar	645 5855
Fast Rent a Car	632 4000
Thrifty	634 5663
Avis	03 768 7262
Europcar	03 721 0180
Fast Rent a Car	03 768 8640

Buying a Vehicle

In Abu Dhabi, the car rules as the most popular method of getting around, and buying one gives you far greater flexibility than relying on other means of transport. Choosing a car here can be a tough decision as the market is huge – should it be second-hand, a 4 wheel drive, which one has a good A/C, what colour's best...?

Only those with a residence visa can own a vehicle in the UAE. Most people will find that cars are far cheaper here than in their home countries and with the low cost of petrol and maintenance, they can afford something a little more extravagant than they would otherwise think of buying.

New Vehicles

If you are going to invest in a brand new vehicle, you will find most models available on the market through the main dealers.

New Car Dealers

Audi	Ali & Sons	681 7770
BMW	Abu Dhabi Motors	558 2400
Chrysler	Trading Enterprises	623 3400
Dodge	Trading Enterprises	622 3400
Ford	Galadari Automobiles	677 3030
Honda	Trading Enterprises	621 3400
Jeep	Al Jallaf Trading	631 2345
Land Rover	Al Otaiba Group	444 3333
Lexus	Al Futtaim Motors	644 7888
Mercedes-Benz	Emirates Motor Company	444 4000

New Car Dealers

Mitsubishi	Elite Motors	642 3686
Nissan	Al Masaood Automobiles	677 2000
Porsche	Ali & Sons	681 7770
Toyota	Al Futtaim Motors	644 7888
Volkswagen	Ali & Sons	681 7770
Volvo	Trading Enterprises	624 3400
Audi	Ali & Sons	03 721 0066
Chrysler	Trading Enterprises	03 724 1838
Dodge	Trading Enterprises	03 725 1838
Ford	Galadari Automobiles	03 721 4775
Honda	Trading Enterprises	03 721 1838
Jeep	Trading Enterprises	03 722 1838
Land Rover	Al Otaiba Group	03 721 8888
Lexus	Al Futtaim Motors	03 721 0888
Mercedes-Benz	Eastern Motors	03 721 7777
Mitsubishi	Elite Motors	03 721 6252
Porsche	Ali & Sons	03 721 0066
Toyota	Al Futtaim Motors	03 722 0888
Volkswagen	Ali & Sons	03 721 0066
Volvo	Trading Enterprises	03 723 1838

Used Vehicles

Where can you go to buy a second hand vehicle? Due to the relative cheapness of cars and the high(ish) turnover of expats in the Emirates, there is a thriving second hand market. Airport Road (both sides of the road between 15th and 19th Streets) is noted for its vast number of second hand car dealers. Expect to pay a premium of about Dhs.5,000 for buying through a dealer, since they also offer a limited warranty, insurance, finance and registration, unlike a less 'official' sale. Sometimes the main dealers will offer good deals on demonstration cars, which are basically new but have been used by the showroom for test drives.

Alternatively, go online and visit www.valuewheels.com.

For other second hand deals, check the classifieds in the newspapers and supermarket noticeboards (mainly Abela or Spinneys).

Used Car Dealers

Obaid Mohd Trading	445 3961
Reem Auto Showroom	446 3343
Al Nuaimi Car Exhibition	03 765 6345
Al Yazreb Cars	03 721 1833

Before buying a second hand car it is advisable to have it checked by a reputable garage – just to 'make sure', especially for 4 wheel drives, which may have been driven off-road rather adventurously! Expect to pay around Dhs.300 for this service, and it is best to book in advance.

All transactions for vehicles must be directed through the Traffic Police. A Dhs.3,000 fine is imposed on both buyer and seller for cars sold unofficially.

Ownership Transfer

To register a second hand car in your name you must transfer vehicle ownership. You will need to submit an application form, an NOC from the finance company, the original licence plates, the valid registration card, the insurance certificate and Dhs.10. The previous owner must also be present to sign the form.

Vehicle Import

A recent requirement for cars imported by individuals or private car showrooms that were manufactured after 1997/8, is an NOC from the official agent in the UAE or from the Ministry of Finance and Industry (if no official agent exists). This is to ensure that the car complies with GCC specifications (or rather that the local dealers are not outdone by any neighbouring competition!).

Additionally, if you are buying a vehicle from another emirate, you will first need to import it. This means lots of paperwork and lots of hassle. You will need to take Essential Documents, the sale agreement, current registration and Dhs.60. You will then be issued a set of temporary licence plates, which are valid for a few days, until you have submitted a new registration application in the emirate where you hold your visa.

Vehicle Insurance

Before you can register your car, you must have adequate insurance, and many companies offer this service. In Abu Dhabi, some of the insurance providers are located at the Traffic Department. The insurers will need to know the year of manufacture and may need to inspect the vehicle. Take along a copy of your Abu Dhabi driving licence, a copy of your passport and a copy of the vehicle's existing registration card.

Annual insurance policies are for a 13 month period (this is to cover the one month grace period that you are allowed when your registration expires). Rates depend on the age and model of your car and your previous insurance history. The rates are generally 4 - 7% of the vehicle value or 5% for cars over five years old. Again, fully comprehensive

One call
and you're covered!

8004845

- Immediate quotation by phone

Norwich Union Insurance (Gulf) B.S.C. (c)

- Instant cover available

Dubai	Tel:	+9714	324	3434
	Fax:	+9714	324	8687
Abu Dhabi	Tel:	+9712	677	4444
	Fax:	+9712	676	6282
Sharjah	Tel:	+9716	561	3186
	Fax:	+9716	562	0953
Jebel Ali	Tel:	+9714	881	9696
	Fax:	+9714	881	9699

- Discounts for careful drivers
- Call Centre open 8am - 8pm Sat - Wed, 8pm - 4pm Thurs
- Home and holiday cover also available

NORWICH UNION

I'm Covered!

xperience makes all the difference

E-mail: nuigdub@emirates.net.ae

www.nu-me.com

with personal accident insurance is highly advisable. For details of insurance companies look in the Yellow Pages or Hawk Business Pages.

It is wise to check whether your insurance covers you for the Sultanate of Oman, as within the Emirates, you may find yourself often tempted to drive through small Omani enclaves (especially if you are off-road, for example near Hatta, through Wadi Bih and on the East Coast in Dibba). Insurance for a visit to Oman can be arranged on a short term basis, usually for no extra cost.

Registering a Vehicle

All cars must be registered annually with the Traffic Police. If you have the energy to do it yourself, expect to be pushed from counter to counter, filling in form after form. If you do not wish to battle through the red tape, some companies offer a full registration service.

There is a one month grace period after your registration has expired during in which to have your car re-registered.

If the car is more than two years old it must be 'passed' by the Traffic Police. This involves a technical inspection, checking lights, bodywork, fire extinguisher, emissions etc. Remember to take Essential Documents. Once the car has been 'passed' you will receive a certification document. If you have purchased your vehicle brand new from a dealer, they may agree to carry out the registration for you (for a fee).

Once your vehicle is insured, you must submit the insurance documents and vehicle 'passing' certificate to the Traffic Police, along with Essential Documents and Dhs.360. Before starting the registration procedures, ensure that all traffic offences and fines against your registration have been settled – a potentially expensive business.

Traffic Fines & Offences

If you are caught driving or parking illegally, you will be fined (unless the offence is more serious). You can also be fined Dhs.50 on the spot for being caught driving without your licence. If you are involved in an accident and don't have your licence with you, you will be given a 24 hour grace period in which to present your licence to the police station. If you don't, you risk having your car impounded and going to court.

There are a number of police controlled speed traps, fixed and mobile radar cameras around Abu Dhabi (speed cameras only operate in one direction and are set off by speeds of 10 - 20 km/h over the speed limit). There is no leeway for breaking the speed limit – not that it seems to bother many people. The fine for speeding is Dhs.200 (Dhs.400 in Dubai). Parking tickets are Dhs.100 and up. In addition, a black point penalty system operates for certain offences. You do not receive any notification when you are caught, so it can be quite a shock when you re-register your car and collect all the fines in one go.

There is also an additional fine of Dhs.10 a month for non payment. Keep a check on the number of fines against your vehicle by telephoning the Traffic Information Dialling System (900 921 111). You will need to know the licence plate number and colour of your car. If you can leave a fax number, you will be faxed a list of when the offences were committed and the fine. For payment, go to the traffic fines section of the Traffic Police.

Black Points

In addition to a system of fines for certain offences, a black points penalty system operates. If you have a permanent licence and receive 12 black points four times in one year, your licence is taken away and your car impounded. The first time you hit 12 points, you receive a fine and your licence is revoked for anything between two weeks and a month. For the next set of 12 points, the penalty is more severe, and so on.

If you are on a probationary licence and aged between 18 - 21, and receive 12 points within 12 months, your licence is revoked and you have to start the whole process of obtaining a licence from the beginning.

However, it seems that there are no hard and fast rules or amounts when it comes to black points ... if you do something serious, your licence can be taken away immediately. If you run a red light, you receive nine black points instantly.

Breakdowns

In the event of a breakdown you will usually find that passing police cars stop to help, or at least to check your documents. We recommend that you keep water in your car at all times – the last thing you want is to be stuck on the road in the middle of summer with no air conditioning, nothing to drink, and lots of time to kill waiting for help.

The International Automobile Association (AAA) (02 641 5198) offers a 24 hour roadside breakdown service for an annual charge. This includes help in minor mechanical repairs, battery boosting, or help if you run out of petrol, have a flat tyre or lock yourself out. The more advanced service includes off-road recovery, vehicle registration and a rent a car service. It's a similar concept to the RAC or AA in Britain, or AAA in the States.

Recovery Services/Towing	
Ghazal Al Wadi	554 0000
IATC Recovery	632 4400
Ghazal Al Wadi	03 721 5444

Traffic Accidents

Bad Luck! If you have an accident dial 999 (Al Ain 03 707 9999) and wait for the police to arrive. They will assess the accident and apportion blame on site (and if you disagree with their judgement, well, tough!). In this part of the world, if you have an accident, you are the star attraction of a million rubberneckers. Sadly, according to the norm, most let their car block as much traffic as possible till the police tell them to move it.

If there is minor damage, move the vehicles to the side of the road. However, if there is any doubt as to who is at fault or if there is an injury (however slight) do not move the cars, even if you are blocking the traffic. Apparently, if you help or move anyone involved in an accident, the police may hold you liable should anything then happen to that person.

Having assessed the accident and apportioned blame, the police document the necessary details and give you a copy of the accident report. Submit the paper to your insurance company to get the vehicle repaired. A pink accident report means you are at fault, and green means you are not to blame. The police may retain your driving licence until you obtain the necessary documentation from the insurance company saying the claim is being processed. Your insurers will then give you a paper that entitles you to retrieve your licence from the police.

Repairs

According to the law, no vehicle can be accepted for repair without an accident report from the Traffic Police. Usually your insurance company has an agreement with a particular garage to which they will refer you. The garage will carry out the repair work and the insurance company will settle the claim.

New Cars for Sale, Abu Dhabi

BUSINESS

General Business Information

Strategically located between Europe and the Far East, Abu Dhabi is one of a few cities of choice for both multinational and private companies wishing to tap the lucrative Middle Eastern, Indian, and African markets (a combined population of 1.4 billion people).

Customs

Imports to Abu Dhabi (and the UAE) are subject to 5% customs duty, which is applied at the time of delivery at the port or airport; there are no duties on the import of personal effects. No customs duties are payable on goods that do not leave a free zone.

At the beginning of 2003, the Gulf Co-operation Council's GCC Customs Union went into effect. Under the terms of this agreement, all six GCC countries now apply the same rate of 5% to imports.

Taxation

Although UAE law provides for taxation, no personal income taxes or corporate taxes are actually levied and collected, either in the city or the free zones; the free zones offer additional guarantees to companies concerning their future tax free status. The UAE has double taxation treaties with various countries, although the effectiveness of these treaties is limited given that the effective tax rates in the UAE are nil.

The only corporations subject to income taxes in the UAE are courier companies, oil companies, and branches of foreign banks.

Exchange Controls

The UAE Dirham (Dhs.) is pegged to the US Dollar at the rate of about 3.67 dirhams per dollar, and never fluctuates significantly from this level. Due to the strength of the local economy, the large foreign currency reserves, the lack of advanced financial currency products and restrictions on foreign share ownership, the dirham has not been attacked by foreign speculators and is generally perceived to be a safe currency.

There are no foreign exchange controls and there are generally no restrictions on repatriating capital and/or earnings. In an attempt to control problems of money laundering, banks are supposed to report all transactions in excess of Dhs.40,000 to the Government, although pre-approval is not required.

White Collar Crime

Like everywhere in the world, there are instances here of white collar crime, so companies must establish proper audit controls. However, companies exert a greater level of control over their employees because most are expatriates with some employers even holding their passports.

In the UAE, it is considered a crime to issue a cheque for which insufficient funds exist in the bank account – penalties for this offence range from a fine to, in most cases, imprisonment. The authorities tend to favour the more extreme punishment for this crime – be warned!

Infrastructure

The fuel for development is investment in infrastructure. Abu Dhabi has invested some of its oil revenues in basic and advanced infrastructure required to make the city attractive to both local and foreign investors. Equally important, the Government maintains low tariffs (no departure taxes, road tolls etc), which further stimulates demand. This is the catalyst that converts a nation's natural resources into human, intellectual and technological capital – the real capital. For any modern state, the point of arrival is a formidable core of this real capital. The replacement of resources from crude oil to infrastructure to technological dominance is a prolonged process

Abu Dhabi Planning Department

requiring full commitment. From basic initiatives such as water, food and housing to genetics, robotics etc, all are links in the same chain.

International banks such as HSBC, Citibank, Standard Chartered Bank and Lloyds TSB offer advanced financial products for trade and commerce, while the Government controlled Etisalat offers a full range of advanced voice and data telecommunication services. Most government departments have a Website offering some services online.

Housing

Among various other housing development programs, the Abu Dhabi Department of Social Services and Commercial Building oversees the most significant housing initiative. Up to the end of 2000, the Department had spent a total of Dhs.33 billion to build around 6000 buildings with over 93,000 apartments. These have been allocated to citizens and, in most cases, the Department also undertakes management of these buildings.

Land Ownership

Currently, foreign companies and non Nationals are not permitted to own commercial land in the UAE other than in free zones, where leasehold ownership is offered. Commercial property must be either rented or leased, and rates tend to be very high. In Dubai, the year 2002 witnessed significant changes in land ownership rules for residential properties, where leasehold and freehold ownership opportunities have emerged for non Nationals – it remains to be seen if this trend will spill over into the commercial market and into Abu Dhabi.

Public Transportation

Air conditioned buses and taxis with smart card fare technology are as good as it gets in public transportation. The current set up in conjunction with private transportation satisfactorily meets the current transportation needs of Abu Dhabi, and can be easily expanded if warranted.

Electricity & Water

The UAE has the second largest per capita water consumption in the world after the United States. It comes as no surprise then that provision of electricity and water remain top priorities. The Abu Dhabi Water & Electricity Authority (ADWEA) has continued to successfully meet the challenges of an ever increasing demand and as in other developed countries, the buzzword is privatisation. ADWEA has been proactively soliciting domestic and international private sector investment and the reward is an uninterrupted supply of electricity and water at affordable rates.

Seaports and Shipping

The UAE is a maritime nation with 800 kilometres of coastline and, in Abu Dhabi, the main general cargo port is Mina Zayed. Oil industry related marine terminals of Jebel Dhanna, Ruwais, Umm al-Nar, Das Island, Zirku and Mubarraz make up the other major terminals. Dry docks and shipbuilding are other successful initiatives of the Abu Dhabi government.

Airports

ISO certified Abu Dhabi International Airport (ADIA) is rated as one of the most modern airports in the Middle East. ADIA is equipped to receive all types of aircraft and provide a full range of services and management.

Free Zones

Jebel Ali Free Zone Authority (JAFZA), established in 1985 at an estimated cost of over US$2 billion, has become a runaway success, and today is home to almost 2,500 companies from about 100 different countries. The signboards dotting the free zone are a who's who of both Fortune 500 companies and local business houses. The original area between the port and Sheikh Zayed Road is almost full and massive efforts are underway to develop the desert on the other side of the road. JAFZA offers investors 100% control of their business, duty free import of products (for manufacturing/transit/export), leasehold land ownership, and guaranteed freedom from corporate taxation.

Free Zones	
Ajman Free Zone Authority	06 742 5444
Dubai Airport Free Zone Authority	04 299 5555
Dubai Media City	04 391 4615
Dubai Internet City	04 391 1111
Fujairah Free Zone	09 222 8000
Hamriya Free Zone Authority – Sharjah	06 526 3333
Jebel Ali Free Zone Authority	04 881 5000
RAK Free Zone	07 228 0889
Sharjah Airport Free Zone	06 557 0000
Umm al Quwain Ahmed Bin Rashid Free Zone Authority	06 765 5882

New Residents

Business

The success of JAFZA has spawned competing facilities in Sharjah, Ajman, Fujairah, and Ras al Khaimah. Each of these free zones also offers investors 100% control of their business. Abu Dhabi's free zone on Saadiyat Island is currently under development by the Abu Dhabi Free Zone Authority.

Free Zone in Dubai

Business Climate

The pace of economic growth over the past 20 years has been incredible and the emirate stands poised for future strong growth with a multitude of new business and financial ventures. With the vision of the rulers of the UAE, both the legislation and government institutions have been designed to minimise bureaucracy and create a business friendly environment. Government officials take an active role in promoting investment in the emirate, and decisions are taken (and implemented) swiftly. Government departments have also in recent years placed increasing importance on improving customer service levels.

The commitment of the rulers to economic development is pioneering in the Middle East, and is seen by many as a model for other governments in the region. While Abu Dhabi is among the more expensive business locations in the Middle East, many companies pay this premium to reap the rewards offered. These include no tax collection and low business fees, a high degree of political stability, steady, strong economic growth rates, excellent infrastructure, and a high quality of life for expatriate residents.

Doing Business

Aside from Agency Law (see p.96), which is in many cases avoidable by establishing oneself in one of the various free zones, Abu Dhabi can be an enjoyable and rewarding place to live and do business. There are many exciting business opportunities for companies and entrepreneurs to serve an increasingly sophisticated and growing market.

Business Groups & Contacts

In addition to various departments specifically responsible for providing commercial assistance to enterprises in Abu Dhabi, there are various chambers of commerce and other business groups that help facilitate investments and provide opportunities for networking with others in the community. Refer to the Abu Dhabi Yellow Pages for a full listing.

Trade Centres and Comissions

Australlian Trade Comission	634 6100
British Embassy – Commercial Section	632 6600
Canadian Trade Comission	407 1300
Egyptian Trade Centre	444 5566
French Trade Comission	645 7138
German Office of Foreign Trade	621 1221
Philippine Embassy	634 5664
Romanian Trade Representation	666 6346
Sultanate of Oman Office	446 3333
Thailand Trade Centre	642 1772
Trade Representative of the Netherlands	632 1920
USA Consulate General	443 6691
Cyprus Trade Centre	04 228 2411
Danish Trade Centre	04 222 7699

Business Councils

American Business Council	671 1141
British Business Group	445 7234
British Council	665 9300
Canadian Business Council	407 1300
South African Business Group	633 7565
Australian Business in the Gulf (ABIG)	04 395 4423

Embassies/Consulates

Country	Phone	Map ref
Australia	634 6100	8-E1
Bahrain	665 7500	4-E4
Canada	407 1300	3-D4
China	443 4276	5-D1
Egypt	444 5566	2-C2
France	443 5100	3-D4
Germany	443 5630	3-D4
India	449 2700	9-B2
Iran	444 7618	2-C2
Italy	443 5622	3-D4
Japan	443 5696	3-E4
Jordan	444 7100	2-C3
Kuwait	444 6888	2-C3
Lebanon	449 2100	3-D4
Malaysia	448 2775	6-B1
Netherlands	632 1920	8-C2
Norway	621 1221	10-A2
Oman	446 3333	3-C2
Pakistan	444 7800	2-C3
Qatar	449 3300	2-C3
Saudi Arabia	444 5700	2-C2
South Africa	633 7565	4-C4
Sri Lanka	642 6666	6-A4
Switzerland	627 4636	8-B2
Thailand	642 1772	3-D4
UK	632 6600	9-A2
USA	443 6691	5-E1
Denmark	04 222 7699	UAE-C2

BUSINESS CULTURE

Customs

Despite its cosmopolitan outward appearance, Abu Dhabi is an Arab city in a Muslim country, and people doing business in Abu Dhabi must remember this fact. Even if your counterpart in another company is an expatriate, the head decision maker may be a UAE National who might take a different approach to business matters.

Etiquette

Tea and coffee are a very important part of Arabic life, and it may be considered rude to refuse this offer of hospitality; tilting the small Arabic coffee cup back and forth several times with your fingers will signal that you do not want another refill.

Although proper dress is important for all business dealings, the local climate has dictated that a shirt and tie (for men) is sufficient for all but the most important of business encounters; women usually choose a suit or a skirt/blouse that are not excessively revealing.

In Arab society, a verbal commitment, once clearly made, is ethically if not legally binding and reasonable bargaining is an important part of reaching any such agreement. Finally, it is important to remember that Abu Dhabi is still a relatively small business community, and so confidentiality and discretion are of the utmost importance in all business dealings.

Meetings

A strong handshake should not only start off each meeting, but also end the encounter – a longer handshake at the end is an indication that the meeting has gone well. It is always preferable to start a meeting with a non business discussion, but avoid enquiring after somebody's wife, even if you know the wife. General enquiries about the family are more appropriate.

Don't be surprised if other people walk in and out during the meeting to discuss unrelated matters, and be prepared for the meeting to run longer than expected. While meeting agendas might be important to ensure that all relevant matters are discussed, they are better used as a checklist (at the end) instead of a schedule for discussions during the meeting.

Time

While punctuality for meetings is very important, the visitor must always remember to be patient if the host is delayed due to an unforeseen (and possibly more important) other visitor. Remember traffic accidents are a very predictable event (they happen every day), so plan ahead and don't be forced to use them as an excuse for being late.

Business Hours

Abu Dhabi has no business hours that are set in stone, or even fixed working days for that matter. Government departments generally work between 07:00 - 14:00 from Saturday to Wednesday, although departments providing services to the public sometimes offer extended hours. Many multinational companies prefer the Sunday to Thursday workweek allowing them a greater overlap with other international offices, while other companies work a straight six day week (Saturday to Thursday). Private sector offices normally work a 08:00 - 17:00 or a 09:00 - 18:00 work day, though some take advantage of the Labour Law guidelines and make the most of their employees' time with an 08:00 - 18:00 work day.

Banks remain open until about 13:30 on weekdays but close early on Thursdays, while large supermarkets generally maintain hours between 10:00 and 22:00 throughout the week. Shopping malls are open for about 12 hours starting from 10:00 (later in the day on Fridays), while other shops in the city generally close between 13:00 and 16:30.

During the holy month of Ramadan, working hours for government and some private sector companies are reduced by 2 hours, while shops and malls open later in the day and stay open till much later in the evening – call ahead to avoid frustration.

BUSINESS LAWS

Laws & Regulations

As with many countries in the Middle East, UAE law requires that companies have a local (UAE National) participant holding at least 51% of the shares. While there has been discussion of easing or even removing these ownership restrictions, no change in the regulations is imminent.

Legal Consultants	
Afridi & Angell	627 5134
Al Tamimi & Co	674 4535
Denton Wilde Sapte	626 6180
Emirates Advocates	639 4446
Simmons & Simmons	627 5568
Trowers & Hamlin	626 7274

100% foreign ownership is permitted for the following:

• A company located in a UAE free zone (see below)

• A company with activities open to 100% GCC ownership (Gulf Co-operation Council: Saudi Arabia, Oman, Kuwait, Qatar)

• A company in which wholly owned GCC companies enter into partnership with UAE Nationals

• A branch or representative office of a foreign company registered in Abu Dhabi

• A professional or artisan company practising business activities that allow 100% foreign ownership

Agency Law

By law, foreign nationals intending to set up a company such as a sole proprietorship, a branch of a foreign company, or a professional company must find a National agent and sign a local (National) service agency agreement with him. The local agent is usually referred to as a 'sponsor'.

The sponsor does not have any responsibility for the business, but he is obliged to assist with all government related procedures such as obtaining government permits, trade licenses, visas, and labour cards. His signature will be required for most application forms.

A sponsor may be a UAE National or a company fully owned by UAE Nationals. The choice of a sponsor can be of significant importance, particularly for a larger company. Appointing a sponsor who is considered prominent and influential can open many doors that might otherwise be extremely difficult to access. Local sponsors may be paid a lump sum and/or a percentage of the profits or turnover.

City Centre, Abu Dhabi

A foreign national looking to establish a business in Abu Dhabi must place a lot of trust in this system. Before choosing an agent, it is highly advisable to first investigate his reputation in the market and agree on each party's rights and responsibilities. Once established, it is very difficult to break an agency agreement, except in case of cessation of activity.

The UAE Labour Law

The UAE Labour Law is very employer friendly. Labour issues are administered by the Federal Ministry of Labour and Social Affairs. The law is loosely based on the International Labour Organisation's model and deals with employer/employee relations such as working hours, termination rights, benefits, and repatriation. Little recourse for employees exists and exploitation does occur, particularly amongst blue collar workers and labourers. Trade unions do not exist and strikes are forbidden.

Government workers and employees of quasi-government institutions are not necessarily subject to the UAE Labour Law. Some free zones have their own labour rules and disputes are settled by the free zone authority without recourse to the Federal Ministry.

See also: *Labour Law [p.63]*

SETTING UP

Trade Licence

In order to obtain a trade licence, membership with the Abu Dhabi Chamber of Commerce & Industry must first be obtained. An application for a trade name is submitted as the first step in the membership procedure. Once approved by the Chamber of Commerce & Industry, a copy is then submitted to the Abu Dhabi Municipality along with an application form and all related documents. On the Municipality's approval, a membership letter will be sent by the Municipality to the Chamber of Commerce & Industry. The Abu Dhabi Chamber of Commerce & Industry will assist with this procedure.

Staffing

For companies operating outside free zones, the Ministry of Labour will set a maximum number of expatriate staff that may be hired, according to the size of the business and the business activity. In some cases, such as banks, the Ministry will state that a minimum percentage of the organisation's employees must be UAE Nationals.

Recruitment of staff is an entirely separate challenge. Various agencies can assist with the recruitment of labourers from the Indian subcontinent, while other local recruiters specialise in searches for professional and managerial positions. In reality, however, many positions in Abu Dhabi are filled through word of mouth between friends and business colleagues, and also through 'wasta' (connections).

Work Permits

The employer is responsible for all work permits and related immigration procedures; this can be quite a tedious endeavour, so be warned and start the process early. If setting up in a free zone, the free zone authority will handle all immigration related procedures, which simplifies the process dramatically, but costs slightly more. The company must cover all costs (visa, medical test etc) involved in hiring an employee. Costs for family members are the employee's responsibility, unless otherwise stated in the employment contract.

Labour Contracts

When applying for a work permit, the Ministry of Labour provides a model labour contract in Arabic. It is advisable to draft an additional contract with further employment and benefit details, particularly for senior staff. The employment contract is enforceable in a court of law (except in the case of some free zones) as long as it does not contravene the Labour Law. The Arabic version of the contract will prevail in a court of law.

National Bank of Abu Dhabi

New Residents

Setting Up

What kind of adventure will you have today?

Discover Dubai and the UAE with our exciting range of tours, safaris and activities. Cruise Dubai Creek, dine among the dunes, or get an aerial perspective. Take a city tour, go deep sea fishing, desert driving or explore the *wadis*. We'll even tailor-make a package just for you – from scuba diving to sand-skiing.

Call us on Dubai 303 4888 or Abu Dhabi 633 8111.

www.arabian-adventures.com

Arabian Adventures

Dubai: Tel: +971 4 343 9966, Abu Dhabi: Tel: +971 2 633 811, Fujairah: Tel: +971 9 204 4057, E-mail: arabian.adventures@emirate

Exploring

Exploring

ABU DHABI AREAS

Exploring

Abu Dhabi is a striking modern city of high rise buildings, areas of lush greenery and wide boulevards with bustling centres of commerce. Considering that just forty years ago, before the discovery of oil, Abu Dhabi was little more than a village consisting of the ruler's stone fort and a scattering of barasti (palm) huts, the changes that have occurred are remarkable.

The modern capital is fairly compact due to its unique position on an island. In places, the high rise buildings, wide tree lined roads and greenery almost give it an American feel, with grid ordered streets and 'sidewalks' under shady trees. There are many different areas; the main 'downtown' streets near the Corniche are packed with skyscrapers and look like a little Manhattan with coloured glass and sleek, imaginative designs. However, further inland, the streets are quieter and house magnificent government buildings and homes or palaces tucked behind high walls to deter unwanted scrutiny.

In addition, many of the roundabouts are decorated with giant coffee cups, clock towers, forts and falcons and make excellent photo opportunities. Cannon Square situated near the Clock Tower has a huge cascading water fountain and enormous concrete replicas of traditional Arabic artefacts.

Souks were, and still are, an integral part of life in the Middle East, and a visit to Arabia is not complete without experiencing the hustle and bustle of this traditional and busy market place. Originally, they were not only for trade or shopping, but also a place to meet friends, catch up on gossip, and for the men to sit in adjoining cafés and smoke shisha. Abu Dhabi has a number of thriving souks, selling everything from plastic buckets and fresh fish to carpets from Afghanistan. The Old Central Souk is a sprawling affair with about 500 shops, selling a wide range of items, and the Iranian Souk, surprisingly enough, does sell goods from Iran! The Madinat Zayed Gold Centre sells gold and a variety of exquisite items such as precious stones at excellent prices. Exercise as much self control as you can here, for the bargains are hard to resist (refer to Souks [p.161]).

The following section deals with what there is to see and do in Abu Dhabi and Al Ain – interesting places to visit such as museums and heritage sites, parks and beaches. The list is by no means exhaustive and should be read in conjunction with the rest of the book, but in particular with the Organised Tours section at the end of Out of Abu Dhabi. This section gives information on tour operators, prices and descriptions of various tours that are on offer. Unless otherwise marked for Al Ain, the activities in the book are for Abu Dhabi.

The city of Abu Dhabi grew and developed along the waterfront on the northern side of the island and to date, the waterfront is still the main centre of activity. Most of the hotels, restaurants and places of interest are within four or five blocks of the sea (although this is still quite a wide area). However, since the sea and fishing played an important part in the early lives of the local people, we suggest you start your exploration of Abu Dhabi at the Corniche and Breakwater, then work your way along the coast or inland.

Airport Road

This 'spine' of Abu Dhabi runs through the centre of the island from Al Maqtaa Bridge in the south, to the centre of town in the north. The section that passes through town is extremely busy with high rise apartments on either side, but as you travel away from the city centre, the apartments gradually disappear and are replaced with more suburban green areas and villas. Plenty of shops, independent cafes and restaurants line this road, and car dealerships fill most of 15th to 18th streets.

Al Bateen

On the west side of the island is the area of Al Bateen that houses the Inter-Continental Hotel with its trendy restaurants, along with some large parks that are popular barbecue spots on weekends for Arab families. The Bateen shipyard here is well worth a visit with its smells of freshly cut African and Indian teak emanating from the high piles of wooden planks. Craftsmen use ancient skills to fashion these into traditional dhows and racing hulls that can be seen on special occasions during competitions off the Corniche. Little has changed in this age old craft – some of the building methods look positively medieval! The yard offers unique insight into a city that once thrived on maritime resources such as pearl diving and fishing.

If not too busy, the craftsmen will happily explain their work. The surroundings are ideal for photography with all the wood and construction amidst sawdust – do ask for permission though, before clicking the craftsman.

The yard is open throughout the week except Fridays, however, the best time to visit is around 17:00.

Al Karamah

This green, mainly residential area has numerous villas lining its streets. The Sheikh Khalifa Medical Centre, Central Hospital, Al Jazeirah Hospital and the Kuwaiti and Korean embassies are also located here.

Central Hospital

Al Khalidiyah

The coast road heading north from the south of the island leads to Al Khalidiyah; an upmarket, much sought after area with a mixture of tightly packed high rise apartment buildings and large villas. An Abela and Spinneys supermarket service the needs of the population here, while the Khalidiya Garden and the Khalidiya Children's Garden provide additional green spaces.

Al Maqtaa

On the southern part of the island in the direction away from town, before reaching Umm Al Nar you will see the Grand Mosque. The Officers Club and the Al Diar Gulf Hotel & Resort are nearby and conveniently located for those who happen to live on the outskirts and fancy a pint without the journey all the way into town. Further south is the Al Maqtaa Bridge, taking drivers off the island and on the motorways to Al Ain, Dubai and the Abu Dhabi International Airport.

Exploring

Abu Dhabi Areas

Maqta Bridge

Al Markaziyah

This centrally located business and shopping area has shops – both local and international – lining the streets, along with numerous restaurants and entertainment venues, such as the Al Mariah and Al Massa Cinemas, and a bowling alley. City hotels and apartments share the streets with embassies, the Al Noor Hospital, Etisalat's headquarters and the Fatouh Al Khair Centre.

Al Meena

Located on the northern tip of the island, east of the Corniche, this warehouse and port district also houses the vegetable market, the animal souk and the Iranian souk. The result of recent developments can already be seen with the new Meena Centre that has an Abu Dhabi Co-operative Society, 2XL furniture store, Jarir Bookstore and Cost Less Electronics. Toys R Us and Ace Hardware are also located nearby.

Of interest to many expats is The Club – one of Abu Dhabi's most popular health and sports clubs. With a beach, pool, gym, full sporting facilities, activities, a restaurant, sailing, diving etc, you're bound to find some activity that you fancy.

The international Port Zayed in the area is the main port authority in Abu Dhabi and has an active harbour nearby with a small market along the quay. Business here is thriving with interesting odds and ends. Once the day's catch of hammour or fresh lobster has been secured and new traps laid, the

local fishermen head to their berths in the fisherman's co-operative area. The sight of 200 traditional wooden dhows and weathered launches at sunset conjures up images of crusty seafarers battling the high seas to bring in their booty of exotic herbs and spices. The boats make great photo opportunities and the best time to view the scene is at dusk when they are gently lit. Take permission however, before you click a crewmember.

Meena Market

Also situated in the Dhow harbour is the Al Dhafra Restaurant, a seafood restaurant popular with tourists and locals alike. You can even catch dinner cruises on the Shuja Yacht (see [p.120] for further details) which sails from the harbour along the Corniche every evening. Alternatively, similar companies offer dinner cruises on more traditional old wooden dhow boats.

Al Mushrif

Located near Airport Road and Karamah Street, Al Mushrif is in the centre of the island but still away from the high rises and heavily constructed areas. Popular landmarks and areas include the Abu Dhabi Golf & Equestrian Centre, the Mushrif Gardens (great for walking the dog), some international schools, most of Abu Dhabi's churches and the Immigration Department.

Al Safarat

Located towards the southern side of the island, near Airport Road, this area houses the General Exhibition Centre (GEC) – a purpose built centre hosting international exhibitions. The Grand Stand on the main coast road holds military marches for Sheikh Zayed on a regular basis. All embassies (other than the embassies of Saudia Arabia, Yemen and Qatar), the Sheikh Zayed Sports Centre, the Sharia Courts and the headquarters for Abu Dhabi International Hotels are all based in Al Safarat.

Breakwater

The Breakwater is an area of reclaimed land leading off Abu Dhabi island. The Marina Mall (with CineStar Cinemas), the Abu Dhabi International Marina Sports Club and the Heritage Village are situated here as well as various Arabic style restaurants and cafes along the waterfront. Still developing, the Breakwater will soon house a new marina and luxury housing development, which is presently under construction.

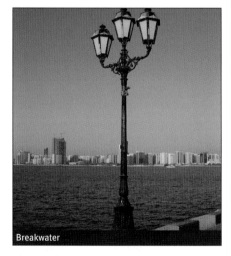
Breakwater

Also coming up next to the entrance of the Breakwater is the enormous Conference Palace Hotel, due for completion in 2004. It should be complete in time for the next GCC Conference.

Corniche

This stretch of the city edges the waterfront and is quite popular with both Abu Dhabi residents and visitors. On any given night, you can expect to bump into one of over 100 different nationalities taking time out to walk, run, roller blade or cycle along. The Corniche has already undergone the first phase of a Dhs.200 million facelift, designed

to enhance its position and add to the beauty of the seafront. The second phase, further land reclamation, has made a bit of a messy construction zone of much of the Corniche, but should be complete mid 2004. *Map reference 8-A3 to 10-D3*

Corniche

On the opposite side of the road from the cycle lane, you will find several well-equipped play areas for younger children under the shade of palm trees. Elegant fountains (the most notable being the Volcano Fountain) are dotted along, with features like the Clock Tower and small folly like rest rooms. In peak tourist winter months, the carefully manicured lawns bordering the Corniche are ideal for picnics and barbecues.

Towards one end of the Corniche, a road by the Hilton Hotel leads to the Breakwater and the reclaimed area beyond. Marina Mall is located here and future plans include the building of a hotel and luxurious villas. The Breakwater itself is a leisure stretch festooned with brightly lit restaurants and miniature fun fairs where children are happily occupied with the small selection of rides. This leaves you free to pick up a pleasure dhow for a cruise along the Corniche, visit the Heritage Village, admire the tallest flag pole in the world, dine at one of the traditional restaurants or sit in your own majlis and smoke shisha pipes. Most of the outlets here are open at night and the Breakwater also provides spectacular views of the entire length of downtown Abu Dhabi – a photo opportunity that shouldn't be missed.

The newly renovated part of the Corniche is generally referred to as the new Corniche.

Exploring

Abu Dhabi Areas

However, for those new to Abu Dhabi, don't confuse this with The New Corniche, (AKA Eastern Lagoon) which runs along the eastern side of the island.

See also: *The New Corniche – Parks and Beaches (Exploring).*

The Islands

One of the unique aspects of the emirate of Abu Dhabi is its islands. There are over 200 of them in varying sizes, and the majority are flat, sandy and uninhabited. A popular activity is to go island hopping, or to spend the day on your own private island, exploring, having a barbecue, or simply enjoying the sun and the peace. If you have a private boat, make sure you keep to the dredged channels to avoid running aground. Any boat over 16 ft must have a licence and a radio.

Directly opposite the Corniche is Lulu Island, a large manmade island protected from the sea by a breakwater. Undergoing an exciting transformation, this once barren island has had a massive facelift with thousands of palm trees planted and sand dunes relocated. A variety of buildings, cafes and restaurants have also been constructed. However at the time of going to print, there was very little information on when it would open to the public.

Sadiyat Island is another island turned beach resort. Popular for weekend breaks as well as day trips, it offers a variety of facilities including an entertainment hall, restaurant, chalets for overnight stays, boat mooring facilities and plenty of water sports. The island can be reached from the Abu Dhabi Tourist Club.

Five kilometres south of Abu Dhabi city is the island of Futaisi, a private island owned by HH Sheikh Hamad Bin Hamdan Al Nahyan. The islanders of this long inhabited island used to supply sweet water and stone for building forts and rulers' houses on Abu Dhabi island. There are still signs of their previous existence such as an ancient mosque, a graveyard and several old wells. There used to be a golf and country club which has now closed down and a leisure destination is being developed in its place with furnished chalets for hire. For just Dhs.50, you can get a motor boat ride to the island. Phone 02 666 1185 to book a boat.

To the west of Abu Dhabi lies Sir Bani Yas island, owned by HH Sheikh Zayed Bin Sultan Al Nahyan. The President has turned it into a nature reserve with a breeding and conservation programme for indigenous and African animals. However, this island can only be visited through organised groups by prior arrangement.

Other popular islands are Bahraini and Cut Islands, which are a 40 and 25 minute boat ride away from the Corniche, respectively. You will need to take all supplies with you since there is nothing there. Horseshoe Island is flat and sandy, and home to a number of foxes. Off its shore is Surf Reef – a great spot for windsurfing. Several of these islands have been earmarked for development so access may soon be limited.

Madinat Zayed

On the east side of the island between Airport Road and Electra Street lies the Madinat Zayed that holds an enormous shopping centre and gold souk of the same name. Located nearby is the central post office along with various government departments such as the Municipality & Town Planning Department, Ministry of Finance & Industry and ADWEA. Both high and low rise apartment buildings dwarf the odd villa, housing numerous businesses (big and small), independent restaurants, dry cleaners etc.

Manasir

Manasir is very popular with Abu Dhabi's expat residents. This green locale has many embassies, including the American Embassy, and various palaces. For the active reader, take note that this is a great area for cycling and jogging.

Blue Dolphin Company LLC	
Location → Htl Inter-Continental · Bainuna St	666 9392
Hours → 08:00 - 13:00 16:00 - 19:00 Closed Fri	
Web/email → sindbadbd@hotmail.com	Map Ref → 10-C1

Blue Dolphin offers two island trips by traditional dhow, one during the day and one in the evening, on the *Saif, Aldhana or Sindbad.*

Cut Island: arrive at a fully equipped island camp, settle in and experience an evening of live music, bellydancing and a traditional barbecue.

Bahraini Island: the sea around this island is too shallow to approach in the dark. However, a visit to this island by day allows you a barbecue lunch and soft drinks.

For the more adventurous, Blue Dolphin can drop you at an island and collect you the next morning.

Dhs.100 ~ € 26   2003 | ABU DHABI EXPLORER

Exploring

Abu Dhabi Areas

However, this isn't an organised trip and is carried out by special arrangement. Take your own tent, equipment and supplies.

Futaisi Island Resort

Location ➜ Futaisi Island Resort · Abu Dhabi	**666 1185**
Hours ➜ Timings on request	
Web/email ➜ halamigr@emirates.net.ae	Map Ref ➜ na

Discover the wonders of Futaisi Island with this tour. While sightseeing, you will have the opportunity to marvel at the natural flora and fauna, as well as the wildlife – gazelles, ospreys, flamingos, wild rabbits and an interesting variety of birds have made the island their habitat. Various points of interest include an authentic Arabian fort, an ancient mosque, a graveyard and a mangrove lagoon. The duration of each trip is about an hour. Tickets can be bought at the resort at Dhs.50 per adult and Dhs.15 per child.

Sunshine Tours

Location ➜ ADNHC · Airport Rd	**444 9914**
Hours ➜ Timings on request	
Web/email ➜ adnh.com	Map Ref ➜ 2-B2

Tours to explore the islands around Abu Dhabi by speedboat are offered for half, full day or overnight trips. For overnight trips, tents and sleeping bags can be provided. In addition, entertainment such as a live band or bellydancer can be arranged.

Crab hunting and fishing trips are also available and the tour operators will provide all the necessary equipment and meals. On request, they can organise island trips around Abu Dhabi for bigger groups too.

Tourist Club Area

Situated on the northeast end of the island at the end of Hamdan and Electra Streets, this very busy area is packed with residential buildings, shops, hotels, and restaurants. It is also home to the Beach Rotana Hotel & Towers, Al Diar Dana Hotel, Emirates Plaza Hotel, Le Meridien Abu Dhabi, International Rotana Inn, Abu Dhabi Mall (with Century Cinemas), Abu Dhabi Marina Yacht Club and the old Abu Dhabi Co-operative Society to name a few. The area is named after the Al Diar Tourist Club – a members club with mostly Arab and family members – offering a beach, pool, gym,

park, sporting facilities and food outlets. Of importance to visitors is the City Terminal bus station located across the street from the Beach Rotana Hotel & Towers. Buses depart from this location on a regular basis to the Abu Dhabi International Airport.

Umm Al Nar

Situated on the outskirts of the city on the road to Dubai and Al Ain, this area houses the Abu Dhabi Golf Club and large villas, and is predominantly inhabited by locals. However, enthusiastic golfers won't mind the 30 - 40 minute drive.

AL AIN AREAS

Al Ain Attractions

Al Ain is the second most important town in the Abu Dhabi emirate and lies 148 km east of the capital, on the border with Oman. The town is often best known as the birthplace of the ruler of Abu Dhabi and President of the UAE, HH Sheikh Zayed Bin Sultan Al Nahyan. The whole area is known as the Buraimi Oasis and the town actually straddles the border with the Sultanate of Oman. The UAE side is known as Al Ain and the Omani side as Buraimi, named after the oasis. There are 18 fortresses in Al Ain, a testament to the town's importance and its position on the ancient trading routes from Oman to the Arabian Gulf.

For many years the oasis was at the centre of territorial disputes between the UAE, Oman and Saudi Arabia; all had a claim to the area as the border had never been properly defined. In the 20th century, the disputes were fuelled by the belief that there might be oil in the region, and in 1952 Saudi Arabia actually occupied part of Buraimi. The dispute was finally settled and in 1966, the border was defined between Oman and Abu Dhabi. However, it was not until 1974 that Saudi Arabia finally dropped its claim to the area.

The oasis is a pleasant stretch of greenery, amidst hostile surroundings and hence Al Ain is often described as the 'Garden City'. Whilst it is not oil rich, it is the most fertile region in the country. In the days before the oil boom, the town was a five day camel ride from Abu Dhabi. Today, it takes about 1½ hours on a modern two lane highway.

Exploring

Al Ain Areas

However, once you're there, watch out for the numerous road humps.

The town has a variety of sights to interest visitors and, like Abu Dhabi, this section of Local Attractions should be read in conjunction with what the tour operators have to offer.

Al Ain Oasis

Location → Nr Al Ain Museum · Al Mutawaa	na
Hours → na	
Web/email → na	Map Ref → 15-B3

Scattered throughout Al Ain are various pockets of palm plantations, many of which are still working farms. Visitors are welcome to wander around the main part near the Al Ain Museum but stick to the paved areas, which weave between the walled in trees.

Al Ain Oasis

The shady palm trees provide a welcome respite from the heat and noise of the town and, at the main entrances into the plantation, picnic tables have been placed for public use. The farms have plenty of examples of falaj – the ancient irrigation system, used for centuries to tap into underground wells and to control scarce water resources.

Al Ain Souk

Location → Zayed Bin Sultan St · Al Ain	na
Hours → 09:00 - 22:00	
Web/email → na	Map Ref → 15-C3

Also known as the Central or Old Souk, the Al Ain Souk is a great place to explore, savour the local

atmosphere, and practise your bargaining skills. A mixture of household goods is on sale, including pots and pans, plastic buckets of every size and colour, and fruit and vegetables, and the prices are excellent. The souk itself is a rather ramshackle affair, but it is certainly different from many of the modern, rather sterile, air conditioned markets that are appearing everywhere.

Al Ain Zoo & Aquarium

Location → Nr Traffic Police · Zoo R/A	03 782 8188
Hours → See timings below Closed Sat	
Web/email → na	Map Ref → 17-C2

Al Ain Zoo & Aquarium is one of the best and largest in the Gulf region, where the animals are well cared for with reasonable amounts of space to roam around. The zoo opened in 1969 and spreads over 400 hectares. The layout may seem confusing, but a decent map near the entrance should ease your way around the place. It's home to a wide variety of both rare and common animals, some indigenous to the Middle East and many from Africa and India. Local species include the Arabian oryx and gazelle, and there are also kangaroos, hippos, monkeys, big cats, reptiles etc. There is a special breeding programme for rare or endangered animals. The zoo also has a large aquarium, with sea lions, penguins and fish.

Entrance fee: *adults Dhs.2; children under four years free.*

Timings: *07:00 - 17:30 winter; 08:00 - 17:30 summer. Saturday closed.*

Buraimi

Location →Al Ain	na
Hours → na	
Web/email → na	Map Ref → 13-D3

Visitors to the UAE do not need a visa to enter the Omani side of the Buraimi Oasis, as there is no UAE customs post. The Omani customs post is about 50 km from the border and visitors will only require an Omani visa if they wish to travel past this. If you are driving and decide to enter this part of the oasis, make sure your car insurance covers Oman.

There's less to see and do in the Buraimi part of the oasis and it's noticeably less affluent than Al Ain, which is fortunate enough to have had money lavished on it by Sheikh Zayed. However, do check out the Buraimi Souk, which is worth a visit for the local atmosphere and colour. On sale is a mixture of food and household goods along with a small selection of souvenir shops selling pottery, woven crafts and silver jewellery. Behind the souk is Al Hilla Fort, which is an interesting starting point to explore the oasis. The other main fort is Al Khandaq Fort, located in Hamasa town in Welayat Buraimi, which is believed to be about 400 years old. Like many of Oman's forts, it has been extensively restored and although there are no displays, it is enjoyable to wander around and admire the view from the battlements.

Camel Market

Location ➔ Al Ain	na
Hours ➔ 10:00 - 22:00	
Web/email ➔ na	Map Ref ➔ 15-C3

Al Ain's camel market is well known throughout the country and is the last of its kind in the Emirates. The market provides an excellent opportunity to view the 'ships of the desert' up close, and to see and hear the traders discussing the price and merits of their animals. The market is open only in the mornings, but is always busy and a great place to enjoy some local colour. It's an excellent photo opportunity, but be careful where you point your lens and always seek permission first.

Hili Archaeological Garden

Location ➔ Mohammed Bin Khalifa St · Hili	na
Hours ➔ 09:00 - 22:00	
Web/email ➔ na	Map Ref ➔ 13-B1

Off the Al Ain - Dubai road, about 10 km outside of Al Ain, is Hili Dig, which is both a public garden and an archaeological site. It is the source of some of the richest finds in the area, many of which are believed to be over 4,000 years old. Most of the land is a garden, with plants and fountains and a small play area for children with swings and slides.

The archaeological site has remnants of a Bronze Age (2500 - 2000 BC) settlement, which was excavated and restored in 1995. It shows the remains of a round building with several rooms and a well. There are other archaeological structures around the park, but the area is chiefly a garden. If you are keen on archaeology, you will find a visit to Al Ain Museum of more interest, since many of the finds are displayed there. Near the site is Fossil Valley, which is rich in fossils

from the days when it was covered by sea thousands of years ago.

Entrance: *Dhs.1.*

See also: *Hili Fun City & Ice Rink (Activities).*

Jahili Fort & Park

Location ➔ Nr Public Garden · Al Jahili	na
Hours ➔ 09:00 - 22:00	
Web/email ➔ na	Map Ref ➔ 15-A3

Jahili Fort is located near the Public Garden and is famous for being the birthplace of Sheikh Zayed, the ruler of Abu Dhabi and President of the UAE. This large restored structure is set in its own walled park and although visitors can walk around the landscaped gardens, entrance to the building itself is not permitted. The fort is notable for its main corner turret, which is round with four levels.

Entrance: *Dhs.1.*

Timings: *09:00 - 22:00*

Jebel Hafeet

Location ➔ South of Al Ain · Al Ain	na
Hours ➔ na	
Web/email ➔ na	Map Ref ➔ 17-B4

One of the highlights of Al Ain is a visit to Jebel Hafeet. It is similar to Ayers Rock in Australia in that it rises abruptly from the surrounding flat countryside, but the comparison ends there. However, the view from the top embraces the surrounding wadis, desert plains and oases, and is absolutely stunning. In the distance, you can see the city of Al Ain, which is situated about 300 metres above sea level, so the height of the mountain at 1,180 metres is quite dramatic.

The road to the top is well lit most of the way and there are viewing points with plenty of car parking. However, the energetic should try cycling – only an hour or two going up, and 20 minutes down! The recently opened Jebel Hafeet Hotel is set in a commanding position with splendid views of the surrounding area, especially from the dining room windows. A visit to the hot springs near the base of the mountain can be coupled with a stay at Ain Al Fayda Resthouse (03 783 8333).

Exploring

Al Ain Areas

Livestock Souk

Location → Nr Al Ain Museum · Zayed Bin Sultan St | na
Hours → 08:00 - 21:00
Web/email → na   Map Ref → 15-C3

Definitely the place to go if you need to pick up a goat or a sheep at a bargain price. Watch the locals arrive in pickups laden with animals and settle in to do some hard bargaining. Arrive early (preferably before 09:00, although there are people milling around all day) to soak up the true essence and atmosphere of this large, bustling market which attracts traders from all over the Emirates. Be prepared, however, to be the object of a certain amount of curiosity, and do not be too upset with the rough treatment of the livestock.

Livestock Souk

Old Prison

Location → Nr Al Ain Museum · Zayed Bin Sultan St | na
Hours → na
Web/email → na   Map Ref → 15-D3

Near the Coffee Pot roundabout, the Old Prison is worth a visit simply for the stunning view of the surrounding town and oasis. The structure is a lone square turret in the centre of a gravel courtyard, surrounded by high walls. Unfortunately, there is no organised system of admittance and the door at the bottom is sometimes padlocked. Hence, admittance is a hit and miss.

Visitor's Checklist

The following is our list of 'must dos' to help you plan your schedule for a visit to Abu Dhabi. While the city isn't exactly over endowed in the cultural and heritage stakes, there are plenty of options to keep most people busy.

Arabic Food

For authentic dining, try the Shamyat restaurant. You could also go for a dune dinner or buy a shawarma from any roadside restaurant. To top off a true 'local experience', eat dates and smoke a shisha pipe.

Exploring/Shopping

Take a day trip to the islands and relax in the sun or dive in and observe life under water. Shop till you drop at the magnificent Abu Dhabi Mall and Marina Mall. Alternatively visit the gold souk, Madinat Zayed, and stock up on the shiny stuff.

The Corniche

Walk, run, roller blade or cycle away in this popular area along the waterfront. Enjoy the stretch of restaurants and miniature fun fairs at the Breakwater. Pick up a pleasure dhow for a cruise, visit the Heritage Village and admire the tallest flagpole in the world.

Sightseeing Tour

While in Abu Dhabi, a trip into the desert is a must. Experience the beauty and fun of this sandy escape as you ride a camel, climb a dune, watch the stars, eat your fill and learn how to bellydance!

Out of Abu Dhabi

Head for the East Coast or the Hajar Mountains near Hatta — both drives take you through great desert and mountain scenery with small towns, forts and mosques. The East Coast has excellent beaches and water sports, while Hatta has spectacular scenery and freshwater pools. Have a look at the Friday Market near Masafi — you may find the deal of a lifetime.

MUSEUMS & HERITAGE

Other options → Art [p.139]
Children's City [p.226]

Al Maqtaa Fort

Location →Al Maqtaa | na
Hours → na
Web/email → na   Map Ref → 1-C3

Heavily renovated, Al Maqtaa Fort is one of the very few remaining examples of its kind in the emirate of Abu Dhabi. You can catch the first glimpse of this monument while crossing the Al Maqtaa Bridge approaching Abu Dhabi island. The 200 year old fort, standing on the edge of the island, was built to fend off bandits and is a wonderful contrast to the modern bridge.

Cultural Foundation

Location → Opp New Etisalat · Shk Zayed 2nd St | 619 5280
Hours → See timings below
Web/email → www.cultural.org.ae   Map Ref → 9-A1

Sprawling over 14 hectares, the Cultural Foundation is the arts centre of the capital and a remarkable monument displaying Abu Dhabi's desire to enrich knowledge, preserve heritage and enhance cultural activities. This simple yet efficient building has grown according to its needs, with a myriad of passages, arches, courtyards and flowering garden pathways providing a relaxing atmosphere – an excellent example of Islamic architecture.

The place consists of three buildings, one of which houses the National Archives. It is also home to the National Library and the Institution of Culture & Art. The publishing side of the foundation produces books relating to the UAE, the Middle East and the Islamic world, and takes part in book fairs all over the world, also hosting Abu Dhabi's biggest annual book exhibition.

For most of the year, except the summer months, the foundation throws open its lecture and exhibition halls to local and international speakers and artists. Programme highlights include visits from international classical musicians, art exhibitions and plays, while embassies regularly hold cultural events and film festivals in the auditorium.

The annual chess festival brings together local, regional and international players, and a cinema in the building screens mainly English language films all year round, weaving film festivals into its calendar of events – a good chance to view classic cinema. Be a part of the centre's activities by subscribing for the free monthly guide (ask for your name to be added to the mailing list). After that, entrance to exhibitions and lectures becomes free.

Timings: 08:00 - 14:00 & 17:00 - 21:00; 09:00 - 12:00 & 1700 - 20:00 Thurs; Closed Fri morning.

See also: Qasr Al Husn (Exploring); Art Classes; Libraries; Family Explorer (Pleasure & Leisure); Cinemas (On the Town).

Heritage Village

Location → Breakwater · Breakwater | na
Hours → na
Web/email → na   Map Ref → 10-B4

Situated on a 1600 square metre site overlooking the Corniche near the Breakwater, the recently opened Heritage Village is organised by the Emirates Heritage Club and offers the visitor a glimpse into the country's past. Many traditional features of Bedouin life such as the camp fire with coffee pots, goat's hair tent, a well and an irrigation system are all attractively displayed in the open museum giving a true feel of what life must have been like in those days. You can even experience the ancient form of air conditioning in traditional houses built of barasti (dried palm leaves) by standing under the wind tower and feeling a breeze even on the calmest day. There will be plenty of great photo opportunities up close and personal with a camel or even the 'Drinkers of the Wind' – the beautiful Arabian horses in their full ornamental regalia. There are interesting workshops where various craftsmen demonstrate their carpentry, pottery and metal work skills, and women can be seen weaving and spinning.

An air conditioned museum houses a collection of artefacts including jewellery, weapons, coffee pots, diving tools, Holy Qurans and folklore garments. There is also a shop for local crafts.

The Heritage Village is open from 09:00 to 14:00 and from 17:00 to 21:00. The entrance fee for adults is Dhs.3 and for children Dhs.1. After visiting the village you can then sample typical Arabic cuisine at the beachside restaurant.

Exploring

Museums & Heritage

Heritage/Bedouin Village

Location ➔ See text · Al Safarat | na
Hours ➔ 08:30 - 17:00
Web/email ➔ na   **Map Ref** ➔ 2-C2

This is a must for all visiting VIPs, including Mikhail and Raisa Gorbachev and Lebanese President Hrawi. According to a guide, they all sat beneath the stars on rush mats at the reconstructed Bedouin camp, slugging the strong 'qawah' (Arabic coffee) which is served to all visitors.

Spread across an area the size of two football pitches, the village faithfully replicates the simple nomadic life in Abu Dhabi before the oil boom. Goats' wool summer tents contain original artefacts like swinging cradles and leather drinking pouches. Enthusiastic guides will soon have you making rope from date palm husks. Aside from the Bedouin encampment, there are also superb examples of more permanent structures like the sheikh's mud brick house and traditional mosque. A good chance to marvel at early air conditioning systems, which trap air using square towers made of jute and wood.

On certain occasions, it's possible to watch traditional agricultural and craft techniques being demonstrated and on Fridays there are demonstrations from falcon handlers. For those who want a memento of their stay, the village boasts its own traditional souk where you can buy a range of handicrafts and exotic Arabic perfumes. For those with intrepid tastes, a camel ride around the village costs an additional Dhs.2. Photography is actively encouraged and when you're not posing by a camel, you can go for some refreshments available on the site. There is sand everywhere, so sensible clothing and shoes are advised. Open from 08:30 to 17:00; entry is free.

> **Location:** *take Mussafah Road, off the Airport Road and follow signs for the Abu Dhabi International Exhibition Centre. The village is behind the centre.*

Petroleum Exhibition

Location ➔ Nr Commercial Bank · Corniche Rd East | 626 0817
Hours ➔ 07:00 - 14:00   Closed Thu & Fri
Web/email ➔ na   **Map Ref** ➔ 8-D3

The Petroleum Exhibition is a must for anyone interested in Abu Dhabi's phenomenal development from a desert oasis to a thriving cosmopolitan city. Spread across three rooms, there are scale models, photographs and maps which chart the earliest oil exploration in the desert and the Gulf, to the first oil export from Das Island in 1962. Interactive displays like giant drill bits and documentary films (dubbed in English, French and German) give some fascinating insight into one of the world's largest oil and gas producers. Entrance is free.

Qasr Al Husn

Location ➔ Cultural Foundation · Shk Zayed 2nd St | 619 5349
Hours ➔ 08:00 - 13:30   17:00 - 20:30   Closed Fri
Web/email ➔ www.cultural.org.ae   **Map Ref** ➔ 9-A1

The White Fort, or Fort Palace as it is also known, dates back to 1793. It was built as the official residence for the rulers of the Abu Dhabi emirate when they moved from the oasis of Liwa to Abu Dhabi island. Since then, the fort has undergone reconstruction and renovation with major work last done in 1983.

Extensions were also made to the existing building, which until recently housed the capital's Documentation and Research Centre. The Centre will eventually be based in a new building along with all the artefacts previously on display in the fort. These include displays of the natural history and old weaponry of the emirate, photographs of Abu Dhabi pre 1960 and a model of the location of the various tribes.

Women's Handicraft Centre

Location ➔ Karama St · Al Mushrif | 447 6645
Hours ➔ 08:30 - 13:00   Closed Thu & Fri
Web/email ➔ na   **Map Ref** ➔ 3-C3

Located on the outskirts of the city, this government sponsored operation is run by the Abu Dhabi Women's Association as a showcase for local craftswomen.

Every item available has been manufactured locally, and if a true scent of Arabia is what you seek, the centre is the ideal place to visit. It's an opportunity for local women to display weaving, handmade souvenirs and traditional artefacts, as well as distinctive Arabian oils, crochet mats, incense and local dress. Most of the items are for sale and while you shop, you can also use this opportunity to watch the women at work. There is also a small museum showing traditional clothing and artefacts.

> **Entrance:** *Dhs.5.*

Museums & Heritage - Al Ain

Other options → **Tours & Sightseeing [p.115]**

Al Ain Museum

Location → Sultan Bin Zayed St · Al Muraba R/A | **03 764 1595**
Hours → 08:00 - 14:00 15:30 - 17:30   Closed Sat
Web/email → na   Map Ref → 15-C3

Opened in 1971, the museum is housed in a low modern structure standing on the edge of the main Al Ain Oasis. There is a variety of displays on life in the Emirates and it is well laid out, with labelling in both Arabic and English. Of particular interest is the selection of photographs taken in the 1960's of Al Ain, Abu Dhabi and Liwa. These strikingly reveal just how much the country has changed and developed in such a short space of time.

Museum, Al Ain

Other exhibits include Bedouin jewellery, weapons and musical instruments, as well as a reconstruction of a traditional majlis, which, it appears, is just waiting for guests to arrive before coffee and dates are served. For those interested in archaeology, there are extensive displays, many from the nearby Hili Gardens, and a visit here before going to the gardens proves quite informative. There are also displays from Garn Bint Saud, a site 12 km north of Hili, comprising of more than 40 tombs dating back to the first millennium BC.

Visitors will also find a reconstruction of how everyday life was before the arrival of oil revenues. It's interesting to note that the figures are dressed with Omani turbans instead of the traditional headdress of the Gulf Arabs. The area around Buraimi was a source of contention between Abu Dhabi, Oman and Saudi Arabia for many years.

The museum shares the same compound as Sultan bin Zayed Fort, or Eastern Fort as it is also known. Built in 1907, it is now open to visitors, although there is little to see beyond the cannon in the courtyard.

There is talk that a new museum will be built on the existing site to allow more room to display artefacts.

The opening times listed below are for the winter period only; during summer months the museum opens and closes an hour later in the afternoon.

Entrance: *50 fils.*

Timings: *08:00 - 13:00 & 16:30 - 18:00 Sunday - Wednesday; 08:00 - 12:00 & 15:30 - 17:30 Thursday; 09:00 - 11:30 & 15:30 - 17:30 Friday; closed Saturday.*

Al Ain University Natural History Museum

Location → Al Khubaisi | **03 767 7280**
Hours → 07:30 - 16:30   Closed Thu & Fri
Web/email → www.uaeu.ac.ae   Map Ref → 14-C1

Aimed at those with a serious interest in the flora and fauna of the Emirates, this is a small but informative centre run by the university. Photography is allowed with permission from the Department of Geology.

Entrance: *free.*

PARKS

Other options → **Beaches [p.114]**

Abu Dhabi is home to nearly 20 parks decorated with fountains, most of which offer lush green surroundings and playground equipment for children. In addition, you will find many grassy areas around the city that are not organised parks and require no entrance fee, but are often just as popular. During the cooler winter months, all areas (even central reservations) come alive with people having barbecues and picnics or knocking a ball around.

They provide welcome areas of peace and greenery and have been provided for all to enjoy, so treat them with respect and leave them as you would wish to find them. Opening and closing times vary considerably amongst the different parks, but there is a standard admission fee of Dhs.1 for adults and free entry for children. During Ramadan, park timings change, generally opening and closing later in the day.

See also: *Corniche – Local Attractions (Exploring)*

Abu Dhabi Park

Al Mushrief Children's Garden

Location → Nr Choueifat School · Airport Rd | na
Hours → See timings below
Web/email → na   Map Ref → 3-C3

Away from the heart of the city but not too far out, this garden is a pleasant refuge in the capital. Attracting the more local population, amusement park rides (with varying fees), simple swings, fountains and ample car parking are all found here. The garden also boasts a cafeteria that is open daily (except Monday) from 17:00 - 21:30. Beware, no video filming is allowed in the park!

Timings: *15:00 - 22:00 Saturday – Thursday; 15:00 - 21:30 Friday. Monday closed for maintenance work. Public holidays 09:00 - 12:00 & 15:00 - 22:00.*

Location: *Mushrief area near the Choueifat School. Driving along Airport Road from the city centre, the turning to the park is marked opposite the National Theatre.*

Al Nahyan Garden

Location → Beh Sheraton Residence · Khalidiya | na
Hours → 16:30 - 23:00 08:00 - 22:00 Fri
Web/email → na   Map Ref → 9-C2

Small but perfectly formed, this no frills park provides yet another retreat from the bustling city. Because of its size, there's no chance your child will

run too far. Entertainment is limited to simple rides such as swings.

Entrance: *adults Dhs.1; kids free.*

Capital Gardens

Location → Opp City Centre Bldg · Khalifa Bin Zayed St | na
Hours → 14:30 - 22:30 09:00 - 22:00
Web/email → na   Map Ref → 8-C2

These immaculately manicured gardens in the middle of the city centre are the ideal bolthole for the whole family. Each little cove of the garden has a small selection of rides including swings, slides and a merry-go-round. A large pond in the middle of the lawn occasionally erupts into stunning fountain bursts (10 metres high) at certain times of the day. Vending machines provide refreshments, while an enclosed cafeteria stocks a range of snacks and drinks. Walls of bougainvillaea make this the perfect city hide away.

Entrance: *adults Dhs.1; kids free.*

Capital Gardens

Khalidiya Children's Garden

Location → Al Khalidiya St · Khalidiya | na
Hours → 09:00 - 12:00 15:00 - 21:30 15:00 - 22:00 Fri
Web/email → na   Map Ref → 9-E1

This is one of the more popular parks for children. Situated near the Abu Dhabi Women's Higher College of Technology, the garden is somewhat typical of other children's parks in the capital but with a greater number of rides and more variety.

Exploring

Parks

Entrance is restricted to women and children only and the entrance fee is standard, but the costs of the rides vary.

Khalidiya Garden

Location ➜ Al Khaleej Al Arabi St · Khalidiya	**666 1281**
Hours ➜ na	
Web/email ➜ na	Map Ref ➜ 9-D1

This carefully manicured large garden does not have a cafeteria on its premises, but vending machines within the grounds provide light refreshments. A particular favourite with the locals, it takes up a whole block on the junction of 30th Street and the main Khalidiya Road. Entrance is restricted to women and children only.

Ladies Park

Location ➜ Zayed Al Awwal St · Al Ain	03 681 3910
Hours ➜ 15:30 - 22:30 10:00 - 22:30 Fri	
Web/email ➜ na	Map Ref ➜ 14-D3

Also known as Basra Park, this quiet and attractive garden is for women and children only (boys up to the age of 10 years are also allowed in). Plenty of benches under shady trees allow you to sit and enjoy the peace. A small dry wadi with wooden bridges runs through the middle of the park where you can find a small snack bar. Abundant greenery attracts a large number of birds in winter.

There are a couple of small play areas with swings, slides and climbing frames and toilet facilities are also available. The standard entrance fee of Dhs.1 applies for adults while children under the age of 10 enter for free.

Mosque Gardens

Location ➜Shk Hamdan St	na
Hours ➜ 15:00 - 23:00 09:00 - late Fri	
Web/email ➜ na	Map Ref ➜ 7-E1

Another serene retreat in the middle of the city, this garden is pleasantly landscaped with hedgerows, and the children can play on swings and slides. It's rarely busy and hence is ideal for families. The standard entrance fee applies.

New Corniche, The

Location ➜ See below · Corniche	na
Hours ➜ na	
Web/email ➜ na	Map Ref ➜ 3-A2

This pristine stretch of immaculate lawns, dotted with ornate shelters and large wooden tables, comes alive as families gather for evening picnics. Well lit and clean, it is especially busy on winter nights and during cooler weather.

This is a great location for birdwatching and an ideal fishing spot (the water and mangroves border one side of the park). A word of warning though. If you are new to Abu Dhabi, it is easy to confuse The New Corniche, which is on the eastern side of the island, with the main Corniche in the north. To further complicate matters, the newly renovated part of the main Corniche, near the Hilton Hotel, has also become known as the New Corniche!

Old Airport Garden

Location ➜ Nr Sheikh Zayed Sport Centre · Airport Rd	**444 4068**
Hours ➜ 06:00 - 22:00	
Web/email ➜ na	Map Ref ➜ 2-B1

Quiet, but an ideal place if you want to relax after taking your kids ice skating at the adjacent rink. One half of the grounds has a number of swings and small but tidy gardens, while the other side is more ornamental with plenty of trees offering shade during the warmer months. If you or the kids are hungry, a KFC outlet is situated right on the edge of the gardens. The side with the swings however, is busy with maintenance workers in the mornings, so it is advisable to stay on the other side until it gets a little quieter.

Public Garden

Location ➜ Zayed Bin Sultan St · Al Mutawaa	03 765 8122
Hours ➜ 16:00 - 23:00 10:00 - 23:00 Fri	
Web/email ➜ na	Map Ref ➜ 15-A3

The main park in the city, the Public Garden is a tranquil and relaxing spot amid the hustle and bustle of town. Walkways meander under shady trees with patches of grass and masses of carefully tended flowerbeds. Fountains are attractively lit up at night for visitors to enjoy, and play areas for younger children offer see saws, swings and

Exploring

Parks

slides. For the older kids, there's a small amusement arcade tucked away by the back entrance. This park is popular with all sections of the community and is especially crowded in the cooler winter evenings.

Around the city, purple road signs in English direct the way to the garden but, once you are there, all signs are in Arabic. Entrance fee is Dhs.1, but children under 12 years are free.

Silmi Garden	
Location → Mohammed Bin Khalifa St · Buraimi	na
Hours → 16:00 - 23:00 10:00 - 23:00 Fri	
Web/email → na	Map Ref → 15-A2

Silmi Garden is a popular spot with local families who come for a stroll in the cool of the evenings. Like all parks in Al Ain, it is well cared for with plenty of trees, shrubs and flowers along with fountains and a limited play area with swings and slides.

Unfortunately, you have to park on the street and all signs are in Arabic. However, even if you're unfamiliar with this language, the park is quite easy to locate, especially at night when the walls are lit with multi-coloured lights. Entrance fee is Dhs.1, and there's no charge for children under 11 years of age.

BEACHES

Other options → **Swimming [p.198]**
Parks [p.111]
Beach Clubs [p.203]

Since Abu Dhabi City is on an island, it is hardly surprising to find a number of beaches dotted along the coast, offering stretches of golden sand and turquoise waters. Some places, such as the two mentioned below, are organised beach parks that offer extra facilities like changing rooms or a café. You will also find various other public beaches that do not require an entrance fee. These include areas around the peninsula near the Khalidiya Palace Hotel and the Breakwater, as well as the beaches along the coast towards the mainland.

Like parks, the beaches too attract more of a crowd during the cooler months (especially at weekends), with people having barbecues or playing cricket or volleyball. Unlike other places in the Emirates, vehicles cannot enter the beaches here, so you won't find people churning up sand as they practise their 4 wheel driving.

Beach, Abu Dhabi

Al Dana Ladies Beach	
Location → Nr Khalidiya Palace Htl · Khalidiya	665 0129
Hours → See timings below	
Web/email → na	Map Ref → 10-E4

Besides the privacy the beach prides itself on, the facilities on site also make it a valuable leisure spot for women in the capital. It has a cafeteria and a recently renovated swimming pool. On Wednesdays, Thursdays and Fridays, the beach is open from 10:00 to dusk (generally around 18:00), and from noon to dusk on other days. Entrance fee: Dhs.10, plus another Dhs.5 if you wish to take your car inside.

Al Raha Beach	
Location → Channel Rd, Abu Dhabi - Dubai Rd · Abu Dhabi	na
Hours → 10:00 - 19:00	
Web/email → na	Map Ref → 1-A1

Al Raha Beach has some of the best amenities of any public beach in the capital. Situated on the Abu Dhabi - Dubai Road past the Umm Al Nar roundabout, the beach is divided into two sections. One section is cordoned off for women only, and the other is open to both men and women. Facilities include a cafeteria and there is no entry fee.

Exploring

Beaches

TOURS & SIGHTSEEING

Other options → Out of the City [p.122]
Weekend Breaks [p.129]

An organised tour can be a great way to discover the UAE, especially if you're only here for a short time, or do not have ready access to a vehicle.

While Abu Dhabi isn't as developed for tourism as other cities in the UAE, there are a growing number of tour companies operating here. Besides the local companies, firms from other emirates either have bases in Abu Dhabi, or will pick up for tours out of Abu Dhabi.

Tours range from a half day city tour, to an overnight safari visiting the desert or mountains and camping in tents. On a full day, evening or overnight tour, meals are generally provided, while on a half day city tour you will usually return in time for lunch. Check what's included when you book, as sometimes there may be an extra charge for meals. Generally all tours include soft drinks and water as part of the package.

Most trips require a minimum of four people for the tour to run. Larger companies may take couples or individuals if there's a group already booked that they can join. If you want a tour or car to yourself, you will probably have to pay for four people, even if there are fewer of you.

It's advisable to book three or four days in advance, although in some cases a shorter notice is not a problem. A deposit of up to 50% is normal, with the balance payable when you are collected. Cancellation usually means losing your deposit, unless appropriate notice is given. This, however, differs from company to company.

On the day of the tour you can be collected from either your hotel, residence or from a common meeting point if you are part of a large group. Tours usually leave on time – no shows do not get a refund, so don't be late! Wear cool, comfortable clothing, plus hats and sunglasses. Also wear strong, flat soled shoes when going on desert or mountain tours, in case you're required to go for longer walks. In the desert after sunset, temperatures can drop surprisingly, especially in winter, so it's a good idea to take some warm clothing. Other necessities include sun protection creams and a camera with spare films and batteries.

Exploring

Tours & Sightseeing

Tour Operators & Travel Agents

Company	Phone	Fax	Email
Abdul Jail Travel Agency	622 5225	622 7395	ajta001@emirates.net.ae
Abu Dhabi Travel Bureau	633 8700	634 6020	atb@emirates.net.ae
Advance Travel and Tourism	627 5750	627 5760	asi@asiuae.com
Advanced Travel and Tourism	634 7900	632 5334	advanced@emirates.net.ae
Al Gaith Travel and Tourism	672 3700	672 7790	-
Al Masood Travel & Services	621 2100	621 9332	masoodt@emirates.net.ae
Al Toofan Travel & Tours	631 3515	631 5055	cyclone_t@hotmail.com
Arabian Adventures	633 8111	631 4116	arabian .adventures.emirate.com
Emirates Holidays	800 5252	634 5511	emirates.holidays@emirates.com
Falcon Tours	677 6775	677 8080	-
Net Tours	679 4656	671 1232	netmerry@emirates.net.ae
OffRoad Emirates	633 3232	633 6642	offroad@emirates.net.ae
Omeir Holidays	626 2526	627 5653	holidays@omeir.co.ae
Salem Travel Agency	627 4424	-	-
Sunshine Tours	444 9914	444 6856	abusun@emirates.net.ae
Thomas Cook Al Rostamani	672 7500	672 8521	tcartauh@emirates.net.ae
VIP Holidays	677 2211	-	-
Al Ain Golden Sands Camel Safaris	03 768 8006	03 768 8005	alhilton@emirates.net.ae
Al Darmakh Travel & Tourism	03 764 2447	-	
Al Mahboob Travel	03 751 5944	03 751 5584	almahbob@emirates.net.ae
Al Rumaithy Travel & Tourism	03 765 6493	03 765 6493	-
Bin Harmal Travel & Tourism	03 764 1111	03 766 0004	-
Emirates Travel Express	03 765 0777	03 751 5747	ete1980@emirates.net.ae
Gulf Air	03 764 3483	-	
Gulf Travel Express	03 764 3697	03 765 7295	-
Middle East Travel	03 764 1661	03 764 2478	-

Desert safaris are a must for anyone who hasn't experienced dune driving before, especially good for friends and relatives visiting the Emirates. Most companies have excellent safety records, but there is always an element of risk involved when driving off-road. Remember you are the client and if the driver is going too fast for your group, tell him to slow down – there shouldn't be any wheels leaving the ground!

Most companies will take an easier route if there are young children, the elderly or anybody who doesn't want to experience the most extreme dunes. Accidents have happened in the past, but with a good driver you should have total confidence in his driving abilities and you'll be in for a thrilling ride.

The following descriptions of the main tours are intended only to give an idea of what is most commonly included. Obviously, each tour operator will have their own style, so the content and general quality may differ from one company to another.

City Tours – Within Abu Dhabi

Abu Dhabi Tour

Go sightseeing around the capital with this tour. Visit the Women's Handicraft Centre, Heritage Village, Petroleum Exhibition and Abu Dhabi's famous landmark – the Corniche. (full day)

Al Ain Tour

Known as the 'Garden City', Al Ain was once a vital oasis on the caravan route from the Emirates to Oman. Many historical sites can be visited from one of the first forts to be built by the Al Nahyan family over 175 years ago, to prehistoric tombs at Hili known to be over 5,000 years old. Other attractions include Al Ain Museum, the camel market, the falaj irrigation system, which is still in use, and the quaint souk. (full day)

City Tours – Out of Abu Dhabi

Dubai City Tour

This tour is an overview of the old and new in the city of Dubai. The souks, the fish market, mosques, abras, Bastakia windtower houses and thriving commercial areas with striking modern buildings are some of the usual inclusions. (half day)

Ajman & Sharjah Tour

Ajman is the place to visit if you want to see traditional wooden dhows being built just as they were hundreds of years ago. Explore and relish the museum before driving to the neighbouring emirate of Sharjah where you can visit the numerous souks. Finish with a stroll around the restored Bait Al Naboodah house for a glimpse into native life before the discovery of oil. (half day)

Ras Al Khaimah Tour

Drive upcountry along what is commonly known as the Pirate Coast, through Ajman and Umm Al Quwain. Explore ancient sites and discover the old town of Ras Al Khaimah and its museum. The return journey passes natural hot springs and date groves at Khatt, via the starkly beautiful Hajar Mountains. (full day)

Shopping Tour

Known as the 'shopping capital of the Middle East', the neighbouring emirate of Dubai is a shopper's paradise. From 'almost designer' clothes at incredibly low prices to electronics, watches or dazzling bolts of cloth in the Textile Souk, everything is available at prices to suit every budget — don't forget to bargain your way through the day. Next, explore the malls; ultra modern and air conditioned, and selling everything you'd expect, plus a lot more! (half day)

See also: Bargaining [p.135], Shopping Malls [p.154].

Safari Tours

Dune Dinners

Late afternoons are ideal for enjoying the thrill of driving over golden sand dunes in a 4 wheel drive vehicle. Departing at around 16:00, the route passes camel farms and fascinating scenery, which provide great photo opportunities. At an Arabic campsite enjoy a sumptuous dinner and the calm of a starlit desert night, then return around 22:00. (half day)

East Coast

Journey northeast to Al Dhaid, a small oasis town known for its fruit and vegetable plantations. Catch glimpses of dramatic mountain gorges before arriving at Dibba and Khorfakkan on the East Coast. Have a refreshing swim, then visit the oldest mosque in the UAE nestling below the ruins of a

watchtower. This tour usually visits the Friday Market for a browse through carpets, clay pots and fresh local produce. (full day)

Full Day Safari

This day long tour usually passes traditional Bedouin villages and camel farms in the desert, with a drive through sand dunes of varying colours and heights. Most tours also visit Fossil Rock and the striking Hajar Mountains, the highest mountains in the UAE. A cold buffet lunch may be provided in the mountains before the drive home. (full day)

Hatta Pools Safari

Modern highways, soft undulating sand dunes and a kaleidoscope of colours lead the way to Hatta in the foothills of the Hajar Mountains. Swim in the Hatta Pools and see the hidden waterfall inside a gorge.

The trip generally includes a stop at the Hatta Fort Hotel, where you can relax and enjoy the swimming pool, landscaped gardens, archery, clay pigeon shooting and 9 hole golf course. Not every tour has lunch at the hotel; some have it in the mountains, especially in the cooler winter months. (full day)

Mountain Safari

Travelling north past Dubai along the coast and heading inland at Ras Al Khaimah, the oldest seaport in the region, you enter the spectacular Hajar Mountains at Wadi Bih. Rumble through rugged canyons onto steep winding tracks, past terraced mountainsides and old stone houses at over 1,200 metres above sea level. It leads to Dibba where a highway quickly takes you to Dubai, stopping at Masafi Market on the way. Some tours operate in reverse, going to Dibba before Ras Al Khaimah. (full day)

Overnight Safari

This 24 hour tour starts at about 15:00 with a drive through the dunes to a Bedouin style campsite. Dine under the stars, sleep in the fresh air and wake to the smell of freshly brewed coffee, then head for the mountains. The drive takes you through spectacular rugged scenery, along wadis (dry riverbeds), before stopping for a buffet lunch and then back to Abu Dhabi. (overnight).

Activity Tours

Arabian Adventures

Location → BHS Bldg, 2nd floor · Shk Hamdan St   **633 8111**
Hours → 09:00 - 17:30
Web/email → www.arabian-adventures.com   Map Ref → 8-C1

Arabian Adventures offers you a chance to venture into the desert or explore the rugged peaks and wadis with experienced guides. Their tours cover the whole of the UAE and are a perfect opportunity to discover the richness of Arabian culture and heritage. The Dune Dinner and Starlight Express are popular full day and overnight safaris.

The company arranges sporting activities such as golf, fishing or scuba diving, as well as special interest activities, such as horse racing. Alternatively, you have the option of requesting an itinerary created just for you.

Arabian Adventures also organises overland explorer programmes to Bahrain, Iran, Oman, Qatar and Yemen. For more information, call 02 631 5888.

Birdwatching

Other options → Falconry Shows[p.121]
Khor Kalba [p.127]
Environmental Groups [p.216]

As a destination for birdwatchers, Abu Dhabi's reputation has grown considerably over the years. The increasing lushness of the area attracts more and more birds, many of which are not easily found anywhere in Europe or the Middle East. Over 80 species breed locally, while during the spring and autumn months over 400 species have been recorded on their migration between Africa and Central Asia.

In the city, the best bird watching sites include the many parks and golf clubs, where parakeets, Indian rollers, little green bee-eaters and hoopoe can easily be spotted. Other species found in the Emirates include the Socotra Cormorant, Striated Scops Owl, Chestnut-bellied Sandgrouse, Crab Plover, Saunders' Little Tern and Hume's Wheatear.

Abu Dhabi is renowned for its excellent birdwatching, both on and off the island. Good areas include the eastern lagoon on the New Corniche, Al Meena Zayed port area, Mushrif Palace

Exploring

Tours & Sightseeing

Gardens and the area around the Abu Dhabi Equestrian Club.

The few resident ornithologists are extremely active and assist visitors in viewing some of the local specialities during individually tailored tours. These are for novices and rampant 'twitchers' alike, and can be for half a day, a day, or a longer duration.

Other excellent places for birding around the Emirates include the mangrove swamps in Umm al Quwain and Khor Kalba on the East Coast. Khor Kalba is the only place in the world where you can spot the rare white-collared kingfisher. Birdwatching tours to the mangroves in a canoe can be arranged through Desert Rangers (see Canoeing [p.169]).

In addition, falconry, the sport of sheikhs, has a deep rooted tradition here. The best opportunity for enjoying these beautiful and powerful birds is on an organised tour when you can see the birds in flight.

Boat & Yacht Charters

Other options → Corniche Cruises [p.119]
Dhow Charters [p.120]

Blue Dolphin Speed Boat Charters

Location → Htl Inter-Continental · Bainuna St | **666 9392**
Hours → Timings on request
Web/email → sindbadbd@hotmail.com   Map Ref → 10-C1

Blue Dolphin has 31 foot Barracuda speedboats that are available for charter. Equipped with two 140 hp engines, they are available anytime, except when being used for fishing or diving. Trips cost Dhs.800 for 4 hours or the boats can be hired on an hourly basis for Dhs.250 (minimum 2 hours).

Shuja Yacht

Location → Nr Al Dhafra Jetty · Al Meena Zayed Port | **695 0539**
Hours → 17:30 - 23:00 20:30 - 23:00   Closed Sat
Web/email → na   Map Ref → 7-D4

The yacht Shuja is a double decker motor cruiser, available for charter for private individuals or parties, and a great way to celebrate in style. It has a maximum capacity of 140 passengers and is chartered out with experienced crewmembers, including the captain.

Charter rates are negotiable, depending on the size of the booking. Call 02 695 0539 for individual reservation and 02 695 0510 for a group (meeting, seminar or private).

Camel Rides

Other options → **Camel Racing**

A visit to Arabia is hardly complete without a close up experience with the 'ship of the desert' – the camel. Several tour operators incorporate a short camel ride on their desert safaris. Alternatively, for a unique adventure, try a camel ride into the spectacular sand dunes. Your guide will lead you to a Bedouin camp, where you can enjoy a rest and some refreshments. Along the way there are stops for photos, so that you can remember this unique experience long after the aches subside! Prices are from Dhs.200 per person.

Al Ain Golden Sands Camel Safaris

Location → Hilton Al Ain · Al Ain | **03 768 8006**
Hours → 10:00 - 13:00 17:30 - 20:00   Closed Fri
Web/email → www.hilton.com   Map Ref → 15-D4

For something a bit more adventurous, Al Ain Golden Sands Camel Safaris offers a selection of tours which include camel rides over the dunes of Bida Bint Saud. The rides usually last for 1 - 2½ hours, and all the tours include transfers from Al Ain, as well as Arabic coffee and dates.

Corniche Cruises

Blue Dolphin Company LLC

Location → Htl Inter-Continental · Bainuna St | **666 9392**
Hours → 08:00 - 13:00 16:00 - 19:00   Closed Fri
Web/email → sindbadbd@hotmail.com   Map Ref → 10-C1

During this hour long cruise, view the spectacular fountain, park areas and multi-coloured skyline of the impressive 8 km long Corniche. Sindbad is a traditional Arabian dhow that departs from near the Al Sofon Restaurant on the Breakwater at 17:30 every evening and then every hour, on the hour, for the rest of the evening. However, it is advisable to check sailing times with Blue Dolphin as occasionally the dhow is chartered for private parties. The fare is inclusive of tea, coffee and soft drinks – don't forget your camera!

Prices: *Dhs.10 adults; Dhs.5 children.*

Shuja Yacht

Location → Opp Al Dhafra Jetty · Al Meena Zayed Port | **695 0539**
Hours → 17:30 - 23:00   20:30 - 23:00   Closed Sat
Web/email → Map Ref → 7-D4

Check out the sunset cruise on the yacht *Shuja*. The route of the cruise is from the jetty along the Corniche, following the Abu Dhabi skyline. At the Breakwater, guests can view the sun setting over the sea (refer to Shuja Yacht – Boat & Yacht Charters [p.119] for details).

Shuja Yacht

Sunshine Tours

Location → ADNHC · Airport Rd | **444 9914**
Hours → Timings on request
Web/email → adnh.com   Map Ref → 2-B2

The sunset dhow cruise offers an hour long scenic journey along the Corniche, with Arabic coffee and dates served on board. The average price is Dhs.80 per person, including coach transfer if required. However, cruises can be suited to fit anyone's tastes and budget, and they can accommodate big and small groups alike.

Dhow Charters

Other options → **Boat & Yacht Charters [p.119]**
Corniche Cruises [p.119]

Large independent groups can try chartering a dhow from the fishermen at Dibba to travel up the coast of the Mussandam. Be prepared to haggle hard – knowing a bit of Arabic will smooth things along. Expect to pay about Dhs.2,500 per day for a dhow large enough to take 20 - 25 people.

Since in theory, you're not entering Oman, visas are not required. It is still possible to arrange a stop along the coast for the night, in which case, it is recommended that you bring your own camping equipment. Alternatively, you can also choose to sleep on board. You will however, need to take your own food, water etc, as you will only be provided with ice lockers, suitable for storing supplies. Conditions on board are pretty basic and you have limited freedom to plan your own route (camping is only allowed in certain areas). It is nevertheless, a good chance to view the beautiful scenery of the Mussandam from a traditional wooden dhow. The waters are crystal clear and, although the weather can seriously reduce visibility, turtles and dolphins can be seen from the boat. It is also ideal for diving, but hire everything before reaching Dibba. Try the Sandy Beach Motel for equipment hire. Alternatively, spend the days swimming, snorkelling and lazing, or hire a speedboat (maximum 6 persons a boat) and explore the coast for an extra Dhs.800 per day.

Al Dhafra

Location → Al Dhafra · Al Meena | **673 2266**
Hours → 12:30 - 16:00   19:00 - 24:00
Web/email → www.aldhafra.net   Map Ref → 7-C4

Al Dhafra operates seven traditional dhows, including a luxurious VIP one, and all are available for charter. They can accommodate a range of parties, from a minimum of ten (Al Tawash) to a maximum of 50 people (the air conditioned Al Falah and Al Sameen). Trips can be made along the Abu Dhabi Corniche or to nearby islands, and timings are adjusted as per the request. The dhows are also available for fishing. If required, a meal or buffet and soft drinks can be served by the crew, although this will come at an added cost. What better place to have a party though?

There are daily dinner cruises along the Corniche with a meat and fish BBQ from 20:30 - 22:30 for Dhs.100 per person. Call to book.

Prices: *range from Dhs.150 per hour for Al Tawash, to Dhs.700 per hour for Al Falah.*

Blue Dolphin Dhow Charters

Location → Htl Inter-Continental · Bainuna St | **666 9392**
Hours → Timings on request
Web/email → sindbadbd@hotmail.com | **Map Ref →** 10-C1

Blue Dolphin's three traditional Arabian fishing dhows are all available for charter. Trips can be customised to suit the client. Alternatively, you can take your pick from the Island Tours and other recommendations, such as a five hour trip around Abu Dhabi island to enjoy the sights.

The Saif is the smallest dhow with a single deck and a total capacity for 30 persons. A four hour trip costs Dhs.2,000 and it can also be chartered on an hourly basis (2 hours minimum) for Dhs.600 per hour. The Aldhana has a double deck and takes up to 60 passengers (Dhs.3,000 per charter or Dhs.800 per hour). Sindbad is the largest, taking up to 120 people costing Dhs.4,000 for a four hour trip or Dhs.6,000 for a weekend. Hourly charters are also available. All dhows are equipped with a buffet, radio, shady deck areas and toilets; 'extras' such as a special menu can be arranged.

Sunshine Tours

Location → ADNHC · Airport Rd | **444 9914**
Hours → Timings on request
Web/email → adnh.com | **Map Ref →** 2-B2

Dhow charters are one of the services offered by Sunshine Tours Dhow Ships. Depending on the number of people, the duration of the trip required and the type of menu, all kinds of occasions can be catered for on their dhows. A great way to celebrate birthdays, staff parties, anniversaries etc.

Falconry Shows

Other options → **Birdwatching [p.118]**

Falconry, the sport of Sheikhs, has a deep rooted tradition in the UAE and is still practised today. At one time, the falcons were used to catch wild prey, such as hares, so that the family would not have to kill any of their valuable livestock for meat. Nowadays, Sheikh Zayed has declared Abu Dhabi a conservation zone to protect the depleted wildlife.

However, the keeping of falcons is still popular and it's not unusual to see these beautiful and valuable birds being transported around the Emirates – even at the airport (where of course they fly first class!). In general, it's not possible to watch them being flown, unless personally invited. However, at the Wedding Grounds near the Abu Dhabi Equestrian Club there are sometimes trainers flying their birds during the cooler months. Make sure you ask before taking photographs. In addition, the Heritage/Bedouin Village has falconers demonstrating their art, and on some tours it's possible to see these impressive birds.

Feathers of Arabia

Location → Throughout the UAE | **050 643 0990**
Hours → Timings on request
Web/email → dandaman@emirates.net.ae | **Map Ref →** na

Dan Daman gives falconry displays throughout the UAE, showing not only falcons, but also birds indigenous to the country such as buzzards, kites, owls and eagles. Usually he flies the birds and gives a short talk about the art, after which, visitors can have a chance at flying the birds themselves under close supervision. Demonstrations are often given as part of an Arabian Desert evening.

Dan operates chiefly between 1st October and 31st May, as the summer months are too hot to fly the birds. He may still, however, display them and give lectures. This multilingual and talented individual can converse in Flemish, German, French and English – so you won't miss a thing. He can be faxed on his Sharjah number (06 766 3193). Private bookings cost approximately Dhs.1,000 for the evening and require two week's notice.

Feathers of Arabia also installs falconariums for hotels and individuals, and is available for advice on falcon breeding.

Helicopter/Plane Charters

Currently there are no companies specifically offering flights for visitors wanting a different perspective of the emirate. However, in the past it has been possible to arrange a charter through some of the tour operators, who use either helicopters or fixed wing aircraft from Abu Dhabi Aviation. Trips are generally into the desert and offer incredible views of the huge, endless golden-red sand dunes of the Empty Quarter. Cameras aren't allowed for security reasons.

OUT OF THE CITY

Other options → **Tours & Sightseeing [p.115]**
Weekend Breaks [p.129]
Camping [p.168]

If you have access to a car, it's worth spending some time exploring places outside the city. To the south of Abu Dhabi lies the Liwa Oasis situated on the edge of the infamous Rub Al Khali desert, also known as the Empty Quarter. This region stretches from Oman, through the southern UAE into Saudi Arabia, and was regarded as the edge of civilisation by the ancients.

North of Abu Dhabi are the six other emirates that form the UAE – Dubai, Sharjah, Ajman, Umm Al Quwain, Fujairah and Ras Al Khaimah. To put the size of Abu Dhabi in perspective, these six emirates cover only 13% of the country's landmass among them!

Also covered in this section is the east coast of the peninsula – a mix of rugged mountains and golden beaches, it's one of the most interesting areas in the country to explore.

For further information on exploring the UAE 'outback', refer to the *Off-Road Explorer (UAE)*, published by Explorer Publishing

Liwa

About a four and a half hour drive from Abu Dhabi is the Liwa Oasis, one of the largest oases on the Arabian Peninsula and home to the ancestors of the current ruling family of Abu Dhabi. Even though a number of small villages are spread over an area span of about 150 km, its resident communities are scattered, so do not expect to find vast tracts of date palms otherwise found in most other settlements in the region. The main attraction of Liwa is the desert with its dramatic red and golden dunes rising to heights of over 300 metres. This area has become increasingly popular for short weekend breaks among visitors to the UAE and Oman as well as Nationals.

> **See also:** *Wadi & Dune Bashing; Desert Driving – Deserts & Mountains (Exploring)*.

Northern Emirates

Other options → **Weekend Breaks [p.129]**

Further north of Abu Dhabi, are the emirates which make up the rest of the country. As you travel north up the West Coast, these are Dubai, Sharjah, Ajman, Umm Al Quwain and Ras Al Khaimah and, on the East Coast, Fujairah. They all play an important role in the UAE although none are as large or as powerful as the Abu Dhabi or Dubai emirates.

Ajman

The smallest of the seven emirates is Ajman, the centre of which lies about 160 km from Abu Dhabi. Ajman is not merely a coastal emirate, but also has two inland enclaves, one at Masfut on the edge of the Hajar Mountains and one at Manama in the interior between Sharjah and Fujairah. Ajman has one of the largest dhow building centres in the UAE, which offers fascinating insight into this traditional skill.

Investment in this small emirate is growing, with the opening of the Ajman Kempinsky Hotel & Resort and the popular shopping complex, Ajman City Centre. Outlets here include Carrefour hypermarket, Magic Planet amusement centre, many small shops and a six screen Cinestar cinema complex.

Dubai

Dubai is the second largest and most important of the emirates after Abu Dhabi. Dubai's wealth is founded on trade and although, like Abu Dhabi, it has discovered oil, its natural resources are not as great as those of its southern neighbour.

Originally a small fishing settlement based around a creek, Dubai was taken over by a branch of the Bani Yas tribe from the Liwa oasis in the south in 1830. The Maktoum family led the take over, and descendants of this family still rule the emirate.

This modern city has grown up around the large creek, which makes an excellent starting point for any exploration.

Dubai has a reputation in the Middle East for being a liberal and 'happening' place – it most certainly is the place to come for a good night out! It is also often described as the 'shopping capital of the Middle East' since it will keep a shopaholic with a healthy credit card amused for far longer than a weekend. In recent years Dubai has become a very popular tourist destination and hosts an exciting calendar of sporting events and festivals to encourage this.

Dubai Creek

South of the city on the road to Abu Dhabi is the largest manmade port in the world: Jebel Ali, and its famous free zone which houses a huge industrial complex.

Hatta

About 10 km from the border with Oman, but within the emirate of Dubai, lies the town of Hatta. Nestling at the foot of the Hajar Mountains, the town is the site of the oldest fort in the emirate (built in 1790), and there are several watchtowers on the surrounding hills.

The town has a sleepy, relaxed feel about it but beyond the ruins and the Heritage Village, there is little to see or do here. However, past the village and into the mountains are the Hatta Pools, where you can see deep, strangely shaped canyons carved out by rushing floodwater.

As you come to Hatta, left at the fort roundabout on the main Dubai-Oman road, is the Hatta Fort Hotel. It is a popular weekend destination for many, either for a meal, to enjoy the range of activities, or for a longer stay. Also en route to Hatta on the main road is the Big Red sand dune, boasting a height of over 100 metres. It's a popular spot to practise dune driving in 4 wheel drives or dune buggies, as well as sand skiing. Alternatively, take a walk to the top (it takes about 20 minutes), for a sense of achievement and a great view.

For further information on the area around Hatta, refer to the *Off-Road Explorer (UAE)* by Explorer Publishing.

See also: *Dune Buggies [p.177]; Sand Boarding [p.195]; Tour Operators [p.115].*

Hatta Heritage Village

Location → Hatta town · On the road to Hatta Pools	na
Hours → 08:00 - 17:00 Closed Fri am	
Web/email → na	Map Ref → UAE-D3

Hatta Heritage Village is a recreation of a traditional mountain village set in an oasis. Constructed around an old settlement, you can explore the narrow alleyways and learn about the conventional way of life in the mud and barasti houses. Besides a large central fort, further up the hill is the South Tower that overlooks the village. Beyond the children's playground is a falaj, a tranquil oasis of running water and shaded seating areas.

A house just opposite the entry to the village displays traditional products and handicrafts.

Ras Al Khaimah

The most northerly of the seven emirates, Ras Al Khaimah (RAK) is one of the most fertile and green areas in the UAE, with possibly the best natural scenery of any city in the country. It lies at the foot of the Hajar Mountains, which can be seen rising into the sky just outside the city. Some areas of the town are even built on slightly elevated land with a view — rare when compared to other cities in the UAE, which are as flat as the proverbial pancake!

Wadi Bih, RAK

Like all coastal towns in the region, it traditionally relied on a seafaring existence and had an important port for pearling, trading and fishing. It is really two towns; the old town (Ras Al Khaimah proper) and the newer business district across the creek (Al Nakheel). Visit the souk in the old town and the National Museum of Ras Al Khaimah, which is housed in an old fort, a former residence of the Sheikh.

The RAK Free Trade Zone is part of a five year development plan designed to accelerate economic growth in the emirate. A large shopping and leisure complex known as Manar Mall provides a one stop shop for everyday needs, a cinema complex, family entertainment centre and water sports area.

The town is quiet and relaxed and it is a good starting point for exploring the surrounding countryside and visiting the ancient sites of Ghalilah and Shimal. Alternatively, visit the hot springs at Khatt or the camel racetrack at Digdagga.

One town in the emirate, Masafi, is home of the country's favourite bottled spring water – the UAE's (far superior) answer to Evian.

RAK is the starting or finishing point of a spectacular trip through the mountains via Wadi Bih to Dibba on the East Coast and is also the entry point to the Mussandam Peninsula, Oman. Refer to the *Off-Road Explorer (UAE)* for further information on the trip through Wadi Bih, and also for exploring the Mussandam.

See also: *Wadi & Dune Bashing [p.200].*

Sharjah

Historically, Sharjah was one of the wealthiest towns in the region, with settlers earning their livelihood from fishing, pearling and trade, and to a lesser extent from agriculture and hunting. It is believed that the earliest settlements date back over 5,000 years. Today Sharjah is still a centre for trade and commerce, although Dubai has overshadowed its importance in this respect. The city grew around the creek or lagoon, which is still a prominent landmark in the modern city.

Sharjah is worth a visit, mainly for its various museums. In 1998, UNESCO named this emirate the cultural capital of the Arab world due to its commitment to art, culture, and preserving its traditional heritage. Opposite the Sharjah Natural History Museum, on the Al Dhaid road, past Sharjah Airport, a monument has been built to commemorate this award.

Sharjah Heritage Site

Sharjah is the only emirate with a coastline on both the Arabian Gulf and the Gulf of Oman. A visit from the city of Sharjah to its territory on the East Coast heads through the spectacular Hajar Mountains and takes 1½ - 2 hours (obviously depending on whether you're a speed demon or not). The towns of Dibba, Khorfakkan and Kalba are all part of Sharjah.

A useful guidebook to refer to for further information on this emirate is Sharjah The Guide. For a photographic tour of the stunning architecture of this emirate, pick up Sharjah's Architectural Splendour, published by Explorer Publishing.

Sharjah New Souk	
Location ➜ Nr Corniche · Sharjah	na
Hours ➜ 09:00 - 13:00 16:00 - 22:00 Closed Fri am	
Web/email ➜ na	Map Ref ➜ UAE-C2

Consisting of two low buildings running parallel to each other and connected by footbridges, Sharjah New Souk (or Central Souk) is a haven for bargain hunters. Although it is modern and functional inside, the exterior is intricately decorated and imaginatively built in an 'Arabian' style. Each building is covered yet open to the elements. Consisting of 600 shops, the ones upstairs sell furniture, carved wood, souvenirs and a fabulous range of carpets from a variety of countries while the shops downstairs sell modern items, such as clothing, small electrical goods, shoes, textiles, gold jewellery and toys.

Souk Al Arsah

Location → Nr Bank St · Sharjah | na
Hours → 09:00 - 13:00 16:30 - 21:00 Closed Fri am
Web/email → na   Map Ref → UAE-C2

This is one of Sharjah's oldest souks, which has been renovated in the style of a traditional market place with shells, coral, African wood and palm leaves. There are about 50 small shops set in a maze of peaceful alleyways, selling traditional silver jewellery, perfumes, spices, coffee pots and wedding chests, plus numerous other items, old and new.

Sharjah Creek

Sharjah is built around Khalid Lagoon, commonly known as the Creek, with a walkway around it known as the Sharjah Corniche. The Corniche is a popular spot for a stroll in the cool of the evening, especially with families, and there are various places for coffee along the way. In the middle of the Creek is a huge fountain, or jet of water, allegedly the second highest in the world.

From three points on the lagoon, small dhows can be hired for a trip around the Creek to see the lights of the city from the water. It is also a great photo opportunity during daylight hours. Prices are fixed and cost Dhs.30 for a 15 minute trip for a party of up to ten, while a tour of the lagoon to the bridge and back takes about 30 minutes and costs Dhs.60.

Majaz Canal

Over the last couple of years, an eighty million dirham project has linked the Khalid Lagoon with the Al Khan Lagoons and the Mamzar Park area via the new 1,000 metre long Majaz Canal.

The aim was to create a 'Little Italy' tourist attraction along the canal, complete with boat rides between the two lagoons. The development is in keeping with the Sharjah Government's desire to develop the tourism industry on a cultural and educational basis. Three bridges have been built over the canal near Khalid Lagoon, on Al Khan Road, and near Al Khan Lagoon as part of the project.

Al Dhaid

Al Dhaid is a green oasis town on the road from Sharjah to the East Coast. It is the second most important town in the Sharjah emirate and was once a favourite retreat from the deserts and coasts during the scorching summer months. Years ago, an extensive falaj (irrigation system) was built both above and below ground to irrigate the land. The area is fertile, and agricultural produce includes a wide range of fruit and vegetables from strawberries to broccoli and, of course, a large date crop.

On the outskirts of Al Dhaid, shoppers will find roadside stalls selling local pottery, carpets, fruit and vegetables.

During the winter months camel racing is held at the racetrack on the road to Mileiha.

Umm Al Quwain

Lying further north along the coast, between Ajman and Ras Al Khaimah, is the emirate of Umm Al Quwain. The town is based around a large lagoon or creek and has a long seafaring tradition of pearling and fishing. On a superficial level, not much has changed here over the years offering a glimpse of life in the UAE in earlier times. The emirate has six forts that still exist and a few old watchtowers around the town. Other than this, there's not much else to see or do in the town itself.

However, the lagoon with its mangroves and birdlife is a popular weekend spot for boat trips, windsurfing and other water sports, since it is sheltered and free of dangerous currents. Just north of Umm Al Quwain, the area near the Barracuda Hotel (and grey market liquor store) is a growing fun park area. Dreamland Aqua Park, UAQ Flying Club, UAQ Shooting Club and the opportunity to try karting and paintballing make this the 'activity centre' of the Northern Emirates. With more resorts and facilities planned, this area can only get better.

East Coast

Other options → **Weekend Breaks [p.129]**

A trip to the East Coast of the Emirates is well worth taking, even if you are only in the UAE for a short time. The coast can be reached in 1½ - 2 hours and the drive takes you through the rugged Hajar Mountains and down to the Gulf of Oman. Take the road through the desert to Al Dhaid and Masafi (source of the local bottled water). At Masafi, you can either drive north to Dibba and along the coast to Fujairah and Kalba then back to Masafi, or the other way round.

The mountains and the East Coast are popular for camping, barbecues and weekend breaks, as well as various sporting activities. Snorkelling is excellent even if you're close to the shore, and locations such as Snoopy Rock are always popular. In addition, the diving on this coastline is usually excellent, with plenty of flora and fauna to be seen on the coral reefs. Check out the *Underwater Explorer (UAE)* published by Explorer Publishing for further information.

Fans of off-roading will find the route to the East Coast interesting with its various diversions. Check out the *Off-Road Explorer (UAE)* for further information.

See also: *Camping [p.168]; Diving [p.173]; Snorkelling [p.197].*

Badiyah

Probably best known as the site of the oldest mosque in the UAE, Badiyah is roughly located about half way down the East Coast, north of Khorfakkan. This mosque stands next to the coast road and is made from gypsum, stone and mud bricks. Officially known as the Al Masjid Al Othmani, it is thought to date back 1,400 years to when it was built in the year 20 Hijra in the Islamic calendar, or 640 AD in the Roman calendar. Recently repaired and re-whitewashed, this small building is surrounded by a 1½ metre wall, which is still used for prayer, so non-Muslim visitors will have to be satisfied with photographs from outside. It is built into a low hillside with several ruined watchtowers on the hills behind.

The village of Badiyah itself is one of the oldest settlements on the East Coast and is believed to have been inhabited since 3000 BC.

Bithna

Set in the mountains about 12 km from Fujairah, the village of Bithna is notable chiefly for its fort and archaeological site. The fort once controlled the main pass through the mountains from east to west and is still very impressive, probably more so than the fort at Fujairah. It can be reached from the Fujairah-Sharjah road where the village of Bithna is signposted. The fort is through the village and wadi.

The archaeological site is known as the Long Chambered Tomb or the T-Shaped Tomb and was probably once a communal burial site. It was excavated in 1988 and its main period of use is thought to date from between 1350 and 300 BC, although the tomb itself is older. Fujairah Museum has a detailed display of the tomb that is worth visiting since the site itself is fenced off and covered against the elements. The tomb can be found by taking a right, and then left turn before the village, near the radio tower.

Dibba

Located at the northernmost point of the East Coast on the border with the Mussandam, Dibba is made up of three fishing villages. Unusually, each part comes under a different jurisdiction: Dibba al Hisn is Sharjah, Dibba Muhallab is Fujairah and Dibba Bayah is Oman. However, there is no sign of this when you visit the town, which is relaxed and friendly.

The area is very historical and there are various burial sites throughout the region. Rumour has it that a vast cemetery with over 10,000 headstones can still be seen (although we have yet to hear of anyone actually finding it!). This is the legacy of a great battle fought in 633 AD, when the Muslim armies of Caliph Abu Baker were sent to suppress a local rebellion and to re-conquer the Arabian Peninsula for Islam.

The Hajar Mountains provide a wonderful backdrop to the village, rising in places to over 1,800 metres. Dibba is the starting or finishing point for the stunning drive to the West Coast, through the mountains via Wadi Bih.

Tip: For the journey through Wadi Bih, a 4 wheel drive is pretty essential, since boulders carried by the floods often block the route. So either be prepared to rebuild the road, or to turn back!

See also: *Dhow Charters [p.120].*

Fujairah

Fujairah often seems to be best known as the youngest of the seven emirates, since it was part of Sharjah until 1952. However, there is a lot more to the only emirate located entirely on the East Coast. It is in a lovely area with golden beaches bordered by the Gulf of Oman on one side and the Hajar Mountains on the other. The town is a mix of old and new; worth visiting in particular is the old fort, which is reportedly about 300 years old and overlooks the atmospheric old town.

The surrounding hillsides are dotted with ancient forts and watchtowers, which add an air of mystery and charm. Off the coast, the seas and coral reefs make it a great spot for fishing, diving and water sports. It is also a good place for birdwatching during the spring and autumn migrations since it falls on the migratory route of birds from Africa to Central Asia.

The emirate has started to further encourage tourism by opening new hotels and providing even more recreational facilities. Since Fujairah is close to the mountains and many areas of natural beauty, it makes an excellent base from which to explore the countryside and see wadis, forts, waterfalls and even natural hot springs.

The Municipality (09 222 7000) and Fujairah Tourism Bureau (09 223 1436) have come up with an excellent tourism map. It includes great hill shading, roads, graded tracks, 4 wheel drive tracks, a decent co-ordinate system and places of interest. On the reverse side is a brief overview of each place of interest, combined with an overview of the city.

Kalba

If you go on an outing to the East Coast don't turn back at Fujairah, for just to the south lies the tip of the UAE's Indian Ocean coastline. Here you will find Kalba, which is part of the emirate of Sharjah and renowned for its mangrove forest and golden beaches. The village is a pretty but modern fishing village that has retained much of its charm.

A road through the mountains linking Kalba to Hatta has recently been completed, creating an interesting alternative to returning to Dubai on the Al Dhaid-Sharjah road.

Khor Kalba

South of the village of Kalba is Khor Kalba, set in a beautiful tidal estuary ('khor' is Arabic for creek). This is the most northerly mangrove forest in the world, the oldest in Arabia and considered to be a biological treasure ie, home to a variety of plant, marine and birdlife not found anywhere else in the UAE. If you are a birdwatcher or nature lover, try to spend a few days in this surprising and beautiful region of Arabia.

A proposal to make this a fully protected nature reserve has been made but it is still waiting Federal protection. The mangroves in this area grow due to the mix of saltwater from the sea and freshwater from the mountains, but they are receding due to excessive use of water from inland wells.

For birdwatchers, the area is especially good during the spring and autumn migrations where you will find species including the reef heron and the booted warbler. It is also home to the rare white-collared kingfisher, which breeds here and nowhere else in the world. There are believed to be only 55 pairs of these birds still in existence.

A canoe tour by Desert Rangers is an ideal opportunity to reach the heart of the reserve and

you can regularly see over a dozen kingfishers on a trip. If you're lucky, you might catch a glimpse of the region's endangered turtles, or a dugong, although sightings are more common when diving rather than from the shore or boat. The reserve is a unique area so treat it with respect — leave it as you would wish to find it.

See also: *Desert Rangers – Canoeing [p.169]; Birdwatching [p.118]; Falconry [p.121].*

Canoeing in Khor Kalba

Khorfakkan

Khorfakkan lies at the foot of the Hajar Mountains halfway down the East Coast between Dibba and Fujairah. It is a popular and charming town, set in a bay and flanked on either side by two headlands, hence its alternative name 'Creek of the Two Jaws'. A favourite weekend spot, it has an attractive corniche (waterfront) and beach and a new souk that sells the usual range of the exotic and the ordinary. There are plenty of things to do including fishing, water sports or a trip to Shark Island; alternatively, you can sit in the shade with a fruit juice and indulge in people watching.

Part of the emirate of Sharjah, it has an important modern port; ships discharging their cargo here can save a further 48 hour journey through the Strait of Hormuz to the West Coast. The old harbour nearby is an interesting contrast to the modern port.

Set in the mountains further inland is the Rifaisa Dam. Local legend has it that when the water is clear, a lost village can be seen at the bottom.

Wahala

This site is inland from Khor Kalba and is notable for a fort, which archaeologists judge to be over

3,000 years old. It is believed that the fort once protected the resources of the mangrove forests for the local population.

Al Hisn Fort

Location → Kalba, Nr Fujairah · East Coast	**09 277 4442**
Hours → 09:00 - 13:00 17:00 - 21:00 Closed Mon & Fri am	
Web/email → na	**Map Ref →** UAE-E2

As you drive along the coast road in Kalba town, you come to the restored house of Sheikh Sayed Al Qassimi, which overlooks the sea. Located at the end of a large grassy expanse, swings and small rides keep the children entertained while adults can peruse the town museum, housed on the opposite side of the road in Kalba's Al Hisn Fort. It includes a limited display of weapons and admission is free.

Note: *Ladies and children only on Wednesdays.*

Mussandam

Other options → **Weekend Breaks [p.129]**

The Mussandam Peninsula is the Omani enclave to the north of the UAE. It has only been opened to tourists relatively recently and is a beautiful, unspoilt region of Arabia. The capital is Khasab, a quaint fishing port largely unchanged by the modern world. The area is of great strategic importance since its coastline gives control of the main navigable stretch of the Strait of Hormuz, with Iran only 45 km across the water at the narrowest point. To the west is the Arabian Gulf and to the east, the Gulf of Oman.

The region is dominated by the Hajar Mountains, which run through the UAE and the rest of Oman. It is sometimes called the 'Norway of the Middle East', since the jagged mountain cliffs plunge directly into the sea and the coastline is littered with inlets and fjords. The views along the coast roads are stunning. Inland, the scenery is equally breathtaking, although to explore properly, a 4 wheel drive and a good head for heights are pretty indispensable! Just metres off the coast are beautiful coral beds with an amazing variety of sea life, including tropical fish, turtles, dolphins (a common sight), sharks occasionally, and on the eastern side, whales.

To reach the Mussandam from Abu Dhabi, follow the coast road north through Ras Al Khaimah. At the roundabout for Shaam, take the exit right and follow the road to the UAE exit post. The Omani

entry point is at Tibat, then basically follow the road until it runs out. Note that by car, non GCC Nationals can only enter and exit the Mussandam on the Ras Al Khaimah side of the peninsula, not at Dibba on the East Coast. There are UAE and Omani border posts, so the correct visas are required. Alternatively, it is possible to fly to Khasab from Dibba, although it takes longer than driving from Dubai and is more expensive.

Refer to the *Off-Road Explorer (UAE)* for further information on this fascinating part of Arabia.

Sultanate of Oman

Other options → **Weekend Breaks [p.129]**

The Sultanate of Oman is a friendly, laid back and very beautiful place to visit, especially after the hustle and bustle of Abu Dhabi. Visitors have two options – either to go east and into Oman proper, or north to visit the Omani enclave known as the Mussandam. Both areas can be visited by either plane or car.

If you are driving into Oman, there are two main border crossing points – at Hatta or through the Buraimi Oasis, near Al Ain. At both places your vehicle will be searched, so it is advisable not to include prohibited items (alcohol etc) in your luggage. The journey from Abu Dhabi to Muscat by car takes 4 - 5 hours (from Al Ain it is about 4 hours), although crossing the border at the start or end of a public holiday can sometimes be tediously slow with a 1 - 2 hour wait.

Flying to Muscat takes about 45 minutes. Daily flights by Gulf Air, British Airways and Oman Air cost between Dhs.600 - 900 (plus Dhs.250 tax), depending on the season.

The local currency is the Omani Riyal (referred to as RO) which is divided into 1,000 baisa (or baiza). The exchange rate is usually about Dhs.10 = RO.1.

Note that talking on handheld mobile telephones whilst driving is illegal in Oman, as is driving a dirty car (yes, seriously)!

Omani Visas

Visas for Oman are required for most nationalities, whether entering by air or road. Different regulations apply depending on your nationality and how long you want to stay in Oman. In general, a visit visa for Dhs.35 – 50 can be obtained upon arrival at the airport, or upon reaching the border crossing. Remember that regulations in this part of the world often change virtually overnight, so check details before you leave to avoid disappointment.

Turtle – Ras Al Jinz, Oman

It is a straightforward procedure to apply at the consulate in Abu Dhabi for a visit visa, though this will cost more than just arriving at the border. Alternatively, let your sponsor (hotel, tour operator, Omani company) do the paperwork for you. Certain nationalities in the UAE on a tourist visa may obtain an Omani tourist visa (without sponsorship) on arrival at Seeb International Airport for Dhs.50. If you wish to return to the UAE after your visit to Oman, you will need a new visa.

If you are a UAE resident, a visa can be obtained on arrival at the border for Dhs.35. British and American citizens with UAE residency may consider applying for a two year multiple entry visa (Dhs.100).

For the Mussandam, a standard visit visa is needed, either from the consulate or by applying at the border (if you fulfil the criteria).

WEEKEND BREAKS

Other options → Camping [p.168]
Out of the City [p.122]
Tours & Sightseeing [p.115]

Going away for the weekend is a great way to escape the hassles of the city and work. This can either be a 'do it yourself' break within the UAE or to Oman, or a special deal arranged through a travel agent to a destination such as Jordan, the Seychelles or Kish Island.

With distances in the UAE being relatively small, it's easy to be well away from home without having to drive for hours — just checking into a beach hotel minutes from your home will give the feeling of having entered another world. The alternative to staying in a hotel is to camp, and this is a very popular, well established pastime in the Emirates.

For people who feel like doing something a little different from the standard UAE breaks, just contact the main travel agents in Abu Dhabi for any special offers they might have on — how about a trip to Zanzibar, Bahrain or India? These offers are generally only available to GCC residents. The travel agents listed in the table on [p.115] are focused on people living in Abu Dhabi who want good advice, exciting itineraries and holidays that will not cost the earth. Last minute deals can often be found on the Internet (ie, www.emirates.com, www.dnata.com or www.arabia.msn.com).

If you decide to stay in a hotel and are booking with them direct, remember that (if asked) they will often give a discount on their 'rack' rate or published price. Quite often, you may stumble upon special promotions, particularly in the quieter summer months when there are some incredible bargains available at five star hotels. The cost of breakfast may or may not be included, so check when you book. Typically, for a weekend in the peak season or for corporate rates, expect a 30% discount off the rack rate. Off peak the discount can go as high as 60%.

For a list of places to stay, check out the Weekend Break table that lists standard room costs at hotels. However, as explained above, these may be discounted further. Before choosing a destination, you may like to refer to the information on the other emirates under Out of the City or the Sultanate of Oman. For more detailed information on the emirate of Dubai, refer to the *Dubai Explorer* by Explorer Publishing. For camping options, see the *Off-Road Explorer (UAE)*, and if you're a fan of the marine world, the *Underwater Explorer (UAE)* summarises 58 top UAE dive sites with suggested dive plans and detailed instructions.

Weekend Break Summary

United Arab Emirates (+971)

Abu Dhabi Emirate	Hotel	Phone	Email	Rate
Abu Dhabi[02]	Abu Dhabi Hilton	681 1900	auhhitw@emirates.net.ae	900 (+16%)
	Inter-Continental	666 6888	abudhabi@interconti.com	790(16%)
	Khalidia Palace	666 2470	kphauh@emirates.net.ae	550(+16%)
	Le Meridien	644 6666	meridien@emirates.net.ae	1300(+16%)
	Mafraq Hotel	582 2666	mafraq@emirates.net.ae	550(+16%)
	Sheraton Abu Dhabi	677 3333	sheraton@emirates.net.ae	750(+16%)
Al Ain[03]	Al Ain Hilton	768 6666	alhilton@emirates.net.ae	650(+16%)
	Inter-Continental	768 6686	alain@interconti.com	600(+16%)
Jazira[02]	Al Diar Jazira Beach	562 9100	reservations@jaziraresort.com	175(B)
Liwa[02]	Liwa Resthouse	882 2075	–	165(B)

Ajman Emirate

	Hotel	Phone	Email	Rate
Ajman[06]	Ajman Kempinski	745 1555	ajman.kempinski@kemp-aj.com	950(+20%)

Dubai Emirate

	Hotel	Phone	Email	Rate
Dubai[04]	Jumeirah Beach	348 0000	reservations@jumeriahbeachhotel.com	1,700(+20%)
	Ritz-Carlton Dubai	399 4000	rcdubai@emirates.net.ae	2,150
	Royal Mirage	399 9999	royalmirage@royalmiragedubai.com	1,225(+20%B)
Hatta[04]	Hatta Fort	852 3211	hfhhotel@emirates.net.ae	650(+20%)
Jebel Ali[04]	Jebel Ali Resort	883 6000	hoteluae@emirates.net.ae	918

East Coast Emirates

	Hotel	Phone	Email	Rate
Al Aqah[09]	Le Meridien	244 9000	reservations@lemeridien.alaqha.com	300(15%)
Fujairah[09]	Al Diar Siji	223 2000	sijihotl@emirates.net.ae	650(+16%)
	Fujairah Hilton	222 2411	shjhitwsal@hilton.com	725(+15%)
	Sandy Beach Motel	244 5555	sandybm@emirates.net.ae	385
Khorfakkan[09]	Oceanic Hotel	238 5111	oceanic2@emirates.net.ae	400(+15%)

Ras Al Khaimah Emirate

	Hotel	Phone	Email	Rate
RAK[07]	Al Hamra Fort	244 6666	hamfort@emirates.net.ae	700(B)
	Ras Al Khaimah Hotel	236 2999	rakhotel@emirates.net.ae	250(B)
	RAK Hilton	228 8888	rkhilton@emirates.net.ae	550

Umm Al Quwain Emirate

	Hotel	Phone	Email	Rate
UAQ[06]	Flamingo Beach Resort	765 1185	flaming1@emirates.net.ae	350

Sultanate of Oman (+968)

	Hotel	Phone	Email	Rate
Barka	Al Sawadi Resort	895 545	sales@alsawadibeach.com	230(+17%)
Khasab	Khasab	830 271	–	340
Muscat	Al Bustan Palace	799 666	albustan@interconti.com	1,290(+17%)
	Crowne Plaza	560 100	cpmct@omantel.net.om	580(+17%)
	Grand Hyatt Muscat	602 888	hyattmct@omantel.net.om	880(+17.4%)
	Holiday Inn Muscat	687 123	mcthinn@omantel.net.om	590(+17%)
	Inter-Continental	600 500	muscat@interconti.com	700(+17%)
	Mercure Al Falaj	702 311	accorsales@omanhotels.com	420(+17%)
	Radisson SAS	685 381	sales@mcdzh.rdsas.com	550(+17%)
	Sheraton Oman	799 899	sheraton@omantel.net.om	650(+17%)
Nizwa	Falaj Daris	410 500	fdhnizwa@omantel.net.om	295
Salalah	Salalah Hilton Resort	211 234	sllbc@omantel.net.om	660(+17%)
Sohar	Sohar Beach	841 111	soharhtl@omantel.net.om	350(+17%)
Sur	Sur Mercure	443 777	reservationssur@omanhotels.com	430(+17%)

Key Rack Rate = Price in dirhams of one double room; +xx% = plus tax; B = inclusive of breakfast.

Note The above prices are the hotel's peak season rack rates. Remember many hotels will offer a discount off the rack rate if asked!

THE TIDE'S CHANGING

A place to visit, a place to spend the day, a place to take you miles away. A landmark in shopping and entertainment, set on the sparkling waters of the Abu Dhabi breakwater.

مركز المارينا
MARINA MALL

Telephone: (+971 2) 6812310 Facsimile (+971 2) 6818668 Email : info@marinamall.ae

Shopping

Shopping

SHOPPING

Other options → Exploring [p.100]

Shopping in Abu Dhabi is cultural, entertaining and fun, and a very serious business indeed! However, this does not always translate into bargains galore in every store, leaving visitors often surprised and a little disappointed. Although prices on speciality goods in the region such as carpets, textiles and, of course, gold are extremely competitive, many imported goods are generally similar to any other major city in the world. The key to shopping like a pro is to bargain where possible since prices, especially in the souks, can drop substantially.

What this city does afford avid shoppers, however, is choice and innumerable ways to part with their money. Shopping addicts who want to flex their plastic further may enjoy a trip to Dubai, aka the 'Shopping Capital of the Middle East'. For more information, check out Explorer Publishing's *Dubai Explorer*. The following section provides information on all that is relevant for shoppers in Abu Dhabi — what to buy, where to buy it, and a few tips on how to stretch the mighty dirham.

Abu Dhabi's glitzy shopping malls, replete with world renowned shops and adequate parking, are covered in detail. The recent past has seen the shopping mall become a social centre for residents and visitors alike. Malls have given birth to a new breed of entertainment, totally equipped with air conditioning, a hotchpotch of nationalities and a vast selection of shops and activities to pass the time.

Refer to the coloured boxes for a list of the most popular brand names and where you can buy them. The intrepid shopper will certainly be able to track down some genuine bargains in the shopping malls and various areas of Abu Dhabi, including its souks (worth braving the heat for).

Consumers will quickly become aware of the numerous (and endless) promotions and raffles offered by the local radio and TV shows, the Abu Dhabi International Airport, and even the smallest, most insignificant of shopping malls. The majority of these don't even require you to buy a special ticket, but will simply hand them over with your till receipt. Great fun, especially if you win that Lexus!

All international brands including department stores, designer stores and car dealerships are in the UAE on an agency basis, mostly run by a few large National families such as Al Futtaim, Al Ghurair, Al Tayer and Al Nabooda.

Note: Traps for the unwary shopper do exist. Some of the international stores sell items at prices that are far more expensive than in their country of origin and at times, you can even see the original price tags. The price differential can go as high as 30%, so beware.

Refunds and Exchanges

Faulty goods are not usually refunded but can be exchanged at the shop of purchase, so always keep receipts and ask to see the manager if there is a problem. If, however, you have simply changed your mind about a recently purchased item, most retailers are not so obliging. Most will only exchange or give credit notes and very few will refund. You may also find that their policy changes for different items.

For any level of success, unwanted items being returned need to be untouched, unworn, unused and in their original packaging. Always check the refund and exchange policy when buying something, and always keep your receipt somewhere safe. You will find that most retailers get hot under the collar if you persist – just let them know that the customer is always right! As a last resort, appeal to their need for ongoing patronage by their customers. Still, if you really think you've been duped, here is some info that might be of help.

Consumer Rights

Unfortunately there are no laws, codes or regulations that protect consumers. In other words, this means the stores can do what they please. There is however an excerpt in the UAE Civil and Commercial code that states that the customer is entitled to recover the price which has been paid on faulty goods. But unless you are prepared to take the shop to court, a simple exchange will have to suffice.

If you are persistent and have a complaint about a purchased item but cannot get any assistance from the shopkeeper, the Emirates Society for Consumer Protection based in Sharjah (06 556 7333) should be able to help you.

Shipping

Shopping is a popular pastime for UAE residents, and even more so for the numerous visitors who come to shop their hearts out, especially during the Dubai Shopping Festival taking place in the neighbouring emirate. Exporting goods can be a tedious task, but there is certainly no shortage of shipping and cargo agencies that offer good value for money. The best plan of action is to contact an agency directly. You will find plenty of listings under 'shipping' in the Abu Dhabi Yellow Pages. Most companies operate globally and are quite reliable. For larger items such as the odd bits of furniture, many shippers will happily make room in containers booked by other customers who haven't quite filled them up – and they give good discounts while they're at it.

Quotes can vary quite dramatically, but to give an idea, the average cost per kilo to Australia is Dhs.95, to the UK, around Dhs.85, and to North America, Dhs.180. These prices are inclusive of handling and packing charges. You can expect to pay almost double for door to door service, but half if travelling by boat. You also have the option of sending the items by airmail, courier, or sea. For even larger shipments refer to New Residents [p.50].

How to Pay

You will have no problem exchanging money, withdrawing money or paying for goods. ATMs (otherwise known as automatic teller machines, service tills or cash points) are readily accessible. Most cards are accepted by the plethora of banks in Abu Dhabi which offer international access through CIRRUS or PLUS ATMs.

Credit cards, too, are widely accepted, the exception being small traders in the souks and local convenience stores. Accepted international credit cards include American Express, Visa, MasterCard and sometimes Diners Club. Discounting the high rates of interest you will have to pay, local banks reward their credit card users with a number of promotions, competitions and discounts. US currency is also widely accepted, even by the ubiquitous local store.

Since the dirham is pegged to the US dollar, the exchange rate offered is broadly the same throughout the Emirates. For the astute shopper though, the best bargains are secured by using the local currency. There are numerous money exchange bureaus in all major shopping areas. Being equipped with dirhams will make shopping a whole lot quicker, hassle free, and can potentially translate into some cash discounts for you.

See also: *New Residents {p.50]*

Bargaining

Other options → **Souks [p.161]**

Although bargaining is a somewhat alien way of doing business for many, it is a time honoured tradition in this part of the world. Vendors will often drop the price quite substantially for a cash sale, especially in the souks. So, relax, think something for 'nothing', and remember to take your time – this can be fun.

The key to bargaining is to state what you would be happy to pay for the item, and walk away if you don't get it for that. Always be polite and amiable, and never use rudeness or aggression as bargaining tools. Start with a customary greeting, and know the value of the item in negotiation; you can learn this by scouting around in other shops. Ask the shop assistant how much and when he tells you, look shocked, or at least indifferent. In the souk, a common rule is to initially offer half the quoted price.

Once you've negotiated, that's it – it's a verbal contract and you are expected to buy. Remember storekeepers are pros at this and have an instinct for a moment's weakness! Remember also that you don't have to buy if the price is not right. You can always walk away and return later. It is not uncommon for shop assistants to chase you out of the shop to secure a purchase. The consumer is the one with the power in the bargaining process – use it or lose it.

Away from the souks, bargaining is not common practice, although many stores offer a set discount, claiming that the price shown is 'before discount'. It's always worth asking if you can have money off, especially if you are paying by cash — if you don't ask, you don't get. Even pharmacies have a last price system whereby they will reduce what is shown on the price sticker, normally by ten percent.

WHAT & WHERE TO BUY

Abu Dhabi's stores sell an abundance of goods and you should have few problems finding what you need. The following section covers the main categories of products that can be bought in the city, from carpets and cars to electronics and gold, and where to buy them.

Alcohol

Other options → Liquor Licence [p.58]
On the Town [p.285]

Anyone over 21 years of age can purchase alcohol at licensed bars, restaurants, and some clubs for consumption on the premises. However, to buy alcohol or liquor for consumption at home requires a liquor licence – it's not just a case of popping into your local supermarket. Furthermore, only non-Muslim residents can apply for a liquor licence. For information on how to obtain a licence and the restrictions that apply, see [p.58] in the New Residents section. Residents who have a liquor licence from another emirate are not permitted to use it in Abu Dhabi.

Once you have gone through the trouble of acquiring a licence, it's easy enough to purchase alcohol from the special stores that are strategically scattered around the city. When you do get your licence, you may find that friends you never knew you had are angling to help you out on your trips to the liquor store! Although this may all sound very simple, there is one point to be aware of. When you get to the checkout, expect to pay 30% more than the marked price. The purchase of liquor attracts a hefty tax here.

African & Eastern Ltd	
Khalidiya	667 6041
Salam St	644 8685
Gray & Mackenzie Liquor Shop	
Khalifa St	612 3545
Mussaffah	554 3919
Old Mazda Road	676 5954
Spinneys Liquor	
Hamdan St	627 1090
Khalidiya St	681 2356
Al Ain	03 636 367
Your Shop	
Airport Road	444 9821
Al Ain Hilton	03 768 7017

There are however known ways of jumping the gun. There are a few 'hole in the wall' stores selling tax free alcohol to unlicensed patrons. These stores are easy to purchase from if you don't mind the trek. The Barracuda Beach Motel next to Dreamland Aqua Park in Umm Al Quwain is one of the most frequented. Similarly, there is another store opposite the Ajman Kempinski, which is quite literally a hole in the wall. Although this sounds like an easy option, you will find the selection not as comprehensive as the licensed outlets scattered throughout the cities. There is also a catch; it is illegal to transport alcohol over the border of an emirate and, in particular,

through Sharjah. Police often turn a blind eye to this followed practice, but if you get busted with booze in your car, we told you so!

Note that the Abu Dhabi authorities have a strict anti-drink driving stance. For further information refer to the booklet 'For Your Safety, be Aware of the Alcoholic Beverages Law' issued by the public relations department of the Abu Dhabi Police.

Al Ain has a liquor store in the Al Tawam Hospital (03 767 8948), but this facility can only be used by the hospital staff and is not open to outsiders, even if they have a valid liquor licence.

Arabian Souvenirs

Other options → Carpets [p.142]

For visitors and residents alike, many items from this part of the world make novel souvenirs, gifts or ornaments for the home. Historically, this was a Bedouin culture and possessions had to be practical and transportable, reflecting the nomadic lifestyle of the indigenous population. Prices and quality of traditional items vary enormously. The souks usually offer the best prices, but there is something to suit all budgets here.

Carpets are a favourite buy. Don't forget to take your time and see as many choices as possible, build up a rapport with the carpet seller, and haggle, haggle, haggle! Other items with a local theme include the coffeepot and cups (a symbol of Arabic hospitality), prayer beads (that look like worry beads), and wooden knick knacks such as dhows, falconry accoutrement and wooden canes. Genuine and old traditional items, such as Omani

wedding chests, are usually expensive and increasingly difficult to find in the UAE. However, modern 'antiqued' copies are widely available.

Traditional wooden doors are also sought after. These can be used as intended or hung against the wall as a piece of art. Alternatively, it's popular to have them turned into furniture, usually tables with a glass top, so the carving is visible and can be appreciated. The current ethnic trend is towards items from India or Oman and most of the furniture on sale today is from these countries.

Ancient looking rifles, muzzle loading guns and the functional and decorative 'khanjar' (a short, curved dagger in an elaborately wrought sheath) are also popular buys. However, if you're planning to take any such items back home as gifts or momentos, check first with your airline on procedures or you may just receive a rather hostile welcome from airport security.

Traditional wedding jewellery made of heavy silver and crafted into simply engraved (and extremely heavy) necklaces, bracelets, earrings and rings are coveted forms of historical art, especially as many of the larger pieces make excellent displays when mounted in a glass box frame.

Alternatively, if gold is more to your taste, then you are in the right country – there is an amazing choice of gold jewellery in the Emirates. Abu Dhabi's Central Market, also known as the Grand Souk, is well worth a visit, as is the Gold Souk in Dubai. The cost of workmanship is also very competitive, so you can tap the artist in you to create your own designs.

Once valued more highly than gold, the dried resin from the frankincense tree in southern Oman has

Arabian Souvenirs

been traded for centuries, and makes a charming gift, especially when bought with a small wooden chest and charcoal burner to give off its evocative scent. You will probably either love or hate the smell of incense and the heavy local perfumes, but they are great as authentic gifts that exude the culture of the Middle East. Oud is a popular and expensive oil used in many of the perfumes, while Myrrh and other sweet smelling mixtures are also sold. Ask to smell some already burning before deciding on your purchase.

Shisha or hubbly bubbly pipes are a fun item to have and can be bought along with flavoured tobacco, such as apple, strawberry and grape. Both functional and ornamental ones are available and some stores also sell a protective carrying case – handy if you are taking it into the desert or to the beach.

Where eatables are concerned, look out for delicious Lebanese sweets (usually made from pastry, honey, ground nuts and dates), or fresh dates in the homeland of the world's main producers of dates. Iranian caviar too, is widely available and good value for money, as it is sold without import duty or any value added tax.

Finally, there are the usual corny tourist souvenirs of the 'I heart Abu Dhabi' variety, fluffy camels, and sand pictures with glass panels that contain the seven different coloured sands of the seven different emirates (it's a wonder there's any sand left in the UAE). However, if you are tired of clichés and looking for a more upmarket and easily transported souvenir, it is worth picking up a good coffee table book such as *Images of Dubai and the UAE* by Explorer Publishing. This artistic, award winning photographic book, available in all good bookshops, offers a refreshing and insightful visual perspective of this part of the world.

Art

Other options → Art Classes [p.214]
Museums & Heritage [p.109]

While there's nowhere like the Tate Gallery or the Louvre in Abu Dhabi, there are a few art galleries that have interesting exhibitions of art and traditional Arabic artefacts, and then there's the Abu Dhabi Cultural Foundation, which hosts both local and international exhibitions. A free programme of events for the coming month is available from the foundation.

The Art Shop (667 8700) and Cornellian Gallery (666 0524) are more souvenir shop/galleries than true art galleries but are worth checking out.

Another place definitely worth a visit is the Sharjah Art Museum (06 551 1222) (refer to Museums & Heritage [p.109] for more information.

Art Supplies

Other options → Art Classes [p.214]
Art [p.139]
Museums & Heritage [p.109]

Creative types who like to dabble in arts and crafts can find tools of the trade at the following stores. If you're looking for anything specific, try contacting each individual store first before embarking on a wild goose chase.

Al Badia – Arts & Trading LLC	644 9020
All Prints	633 5853
Jarir Bookstore	673 3999
Mohammad Al Makhawi Est.	644 3141

Beach Wear

Other options → Clothes [p.143]

Since many residents spend their weekends either basking by the pool or catching some sporting action on the emirate's fabulous beaches, it is perhaps, not so surprising that people will often spend as much money on a set of swimming togs as they would on a suit for work.

The specialist beach wear boutiques stock everything from French and Italian designer wear to achingly hip Californian and Australian surfing labels, and generally, prices here are extremely high. Since there is no real 'off' season, these shops tend to have sales and discounts at strange times of the year. So if labels are crucial for your beach wear collection, it's worth asking to be put on a mailing list, thus being first in the queue to snap up the bargains.

The many sports shops in Abu Dhabi also stock a decent range of swimwear, but these veer towards no nonsense styles for competitive swimmers rather than catering to die hard beach babes. For those less bothered about making a fashion statement when they peel off on the beach, head for the department stores in the larger malls.

BHS, Woolworth's, Debenhams and Marks & Spencer all sell a good range of beach wear for women, men and children including all related

What & Where to Buy

Shopping

paraphernalia such as hats and beach bags, all at prices that won't break the bank.

Books

Other options → Libraries [p.220]
Second-hand Items [p.152]

A reasonable selection of English language books is sold in Abu Dhabi, covering a broad range of subjects from travel or computing to children's books, the latest best sellers, and coffee table books on and about the Emirates.

You are unlikely to find as extensive a range of books and bookshops as you would in your home country, although the number and size of outlets is increasing. Most of the larger hotels have small bookshops that offer a limited choice. You will also find that foreign newspapers and magazines, which are flown in regularly, are always much more expensive than at home. To all the males out there who enjoy perusing through racy blokes' mags, be warned – due to censorship laws in the UAE, pictures of semi-naked women are always disguised by a giant black pen mark.

Worth mentioning is the Jarir Bookstore, which claims it's more than just that. While this store has a selection of English and Arabic language books it is better known for having one of the best art and craft supply selections in town. They also stock stationery and office supplies, computers and accessories, school supplies, magazines, party goods, gifts and a very good selection of sensibly priced cards.

Al Mutanabbi	Old Airport Rd	634 0319
All Prints	Al Nasr St	633 8572
Book Corner	Liwa Centre,	631 5323
House of Prose Book Shop	Khalidiya St	665 6163
Jarir Bookstore	Meena Centre	673 3999
Spinneys	Nr Clock Tower R/A	621 2919
	Shk Zayed 1st St	681 2897
Al Marifa	Near Clock Tower R/A	03 663 221
The Box	Near Clock Tower R/A	03 643 754
University Book House	Nr Clock Tower R/A	03 764 3754

Another interesting (and cheaper) option is the House of Prose, Abu Dhabi's first and only second-hand bookstore. The store offers over 15,000 titles, comprising of a huge selection of fiction, non fiction, science fiction and children's books. They also buy and sell good quality English paperbacks.

Abela Superstore, Carrefour, Spinneys and the Co-op supermarkets at Manaseer and the Tourist Club areas also carry a decent selection of books and magazines.

There is a selection of bookshops tucked away in various parts of Abu Dhabi. The above list includes shops which stock a reasonable selection of European or English language books on a range of subjects, plus newspapers and magazines.

Cards & Stationery

Other options → Books [p.140]

Most supermarkets carry an ample supply of greeting cards, wrapping paper and stationery. However, there are a number of speciality stores to be found lurking amid the weaving and winding corridors of Abu Dhabi's streets and malls. It is at these places that you will find the best variety in Abu Dhabi, especially for cards, where they offer everything from Christmas and Easter to Mother's Day and Eid cards.

At the Stationery Store...

While postcards are a smashing bargain, greeting cards tend to be very expensive, especially those celebrating special occasions or holidays. Locally produced cards are much cheaper, more original, and often better quality – they can be found in most card shops and usually feature local artists' work.

Looking for wrapping paper? THE One and Woolworth's have some of the most unique and

certainly the most reasonable we've found. Similarly, Ikea sells gift wrapping paraphernalia at a fraction of the price of the more established card and gift wrap stores.

All Prints	Al Nasr Street	633 8572
Book Corner	Liwa Centre	631 5323
Gulf Greetings	Tourist Club area	644 9780
	Fatouh Al Khair Centre	621 5945
	Nr Co-Op, Khalifa St	626 3601

Carpets

Other options → Arabian Souvenirs [p.138]

Whether you are a regular buyer or just a novice, carpet shopping can be a fascinating experience. In Abu Dhabi, countries of origin for carpets range from Iran and Pakistan to China and Central Asia, and there is a truly exquisite array of designs and colours.

However, to ensure that you are buying the genuine article at a good price, it is advisable to learn a bit about carpets before making the final decision. A good place to start if you want to read up on the subject is Oriental Carpets: A Buyer's Guide. If possible, visit a number of shops to get a feel for price, quality and traditional designs, as well as the range available. As a very rough guide, the higher the number of knots per square inch, the higher the price and better the quality. Silk is more expensive than wool, and rugs from Iran are generally more valuable than the equivalent from Turkey or Kashmir. Check if it is machine or handmade (handmade ones are never quite perfect and the

pile is slightly uneven). Salesmen will happily offer plenty of advice, but don't let that influence your decision too much – your purchase should be based on what you want, at the price you want. Also, don't feel pressured into buying simply because the assistant has just unrolled over thirty carpets for you. Most importantly, do not forget to bargain; it's part of the game and expected in all

Al Radmani Persian Carpets	Opp All Prints	633 1238
Magic Carpets	Zakher Hotel	627 5882
Original Iranian Carpets	30th Street Corniche	681 1156
Persian Carpets	Rotana Mall	681 5900
Red Sea Handmade Carpets	Nr Al Noor Hosp, Khalifa St	626 6145

shops. Prices vary from a few hundred to many thousand dirhams, but are always negotiable.

A good starting point to see the wide range available in terms of price and quality, is the carpet souk at the Port end of Mina Road. Meena Souk (also known as Afghan Souk) is also well stocked. It is advisable to visit the more exclusive shops to compare quality and price. Most of the hotels have a fine quality carpet shop.

Cars

Other options → New Residents [p.50]

New residents are often pleasantly surprised to find that cars here are much cheaper than in their own country and, with competitive interest rates

Carpets

offered by banks and dealers, buying a new car isn't necessarily for an elite few. All the major car manufacturers are represented here and give good discounts close to the end of the year (when next year's model is due in the showroom).

Alternatively, the second-hand market is thriving with an abundance of used car dealerships. Airport Road is a good place to start. You'll find everything from barely used Porsches and Ferraris to 4x4's, ideal for some off-roading in the desert. Prices are never final so stand your ground if you're determined to clinch a deal; remember the dealer has paid its previous owner a fraction of the price he's attempting to claim from you.

For other good deals, check the newspapers, supermarket notice boards or Websites such as www.valueonwheels.com. It's a good idea to have the vehicle checked out by a reputable garage though, before you take the plunge and buy.

New Cars

Audi	Ali & Sons	677 9190
BMW	Abu Dhabi Motors	558 2400
Chevrolet	Al Otaibi	444 3333
Chrysler	Trading Enterprises	621 3400
Ford	Galadari Motors	677 3030
Galloper	Al Habtoor Royal Car	678 8400
Honda	Trading Enterprises	621 3400
Land Rover	Al Otaibi	444 3333
Lexus	Al Futtaim Motors	644 7888
Mercedes-Benz	Emirates Motor Co.	444 4000
Mitsubishi	Elite Motors	642 3686
Nissan	Al Masood	677 2000
Porsche	Ali & Sons	677 9190
Rolls Royce	Al Habtoor Royal Car	678 8400
Toyota	Al Futtaim Motors	644 7888
Volkswagen	Ali & Sons	677 9190
Volvo	Trading Enterprises	621 3400
Audi	Al Ain	03 721 0066
BMW	Al Ain	03 762 0022
Chevrolet	Al Ain	03 721 8888
Chrysler	Al Ain	03 721 1838
Ford	Al Ain	03 721 4775
Honda	Al Ain	03 721 1838
Land Rover	Al Ain	03 721 8888
Lexus	Al Ain	03 721 0888
Mercedes-Benz	Al Ain	03 721 7777
Mitsubishi	Al Ain	03 721 6252
Porsche	Al Ain	03 721 0066
Volkswagen	Al Ain	03 721 0066
Volvo	Al Ain	03 721 1838

Used Cars

Obaid Mohammed Trading	445 3961
Reem Auto Showroom	446 3343
Zahtrat Madeam Car Exhibition	445 1909
Al Ain Al Nuami Car Exhibition	03 765 6345
Al Yazreb	03 721 1833

Clothes

Other options → Beach Wear [p.139]
Shoes [p.152]

Followers of fashion will find everything from the priciest designer shops to up-to-the-minute boutiques to pile-it-high-sell-it-cheap bargain basements. Upmarket stores dedicated to designer names can mainly be found in the shopping malls and hotel arcades.

Most malls have a good selection of inexpensive quality clothing and there is now an increasing trend towards 'global' stores that sell the same clothing items the world over, turning over their stock every four to six weeks. Handily, they also show the retail price in each country on the tag, so it's quite satisfying to know that you are paying no more than anyone else is.

Benetton	Marina Mall	681 3320
BHS	Hamdan St	621 1242
Blue Marine	Salaam St	677 0236
Bugatti	Al Nasr St	665 4342
Can-Can	Hamdan Centre	621 1693
Emporio Armani	Corniche	681 4113
Esprit	Hamdan St	627 7600
Evans	Nr Emirates Hamdan St	639 2858
Fame	Nr Dana Plaza	665 4300
Guess	Hamdan St	627 7600
JC Penny	Abu Dhabi Mall	645 8400
Mango	Fatouh Al Khair Centre	621 3477
Marks & Spencers	Fatouh Al Khair Centre	621 3646
	Shk Zayed 1st St	665 3685
Monsoon	Fatouh Al Khair Centre	621 5069
Next	Najda St	621 9700
Oasis	Najda St	621 9700
Rodeo Drive	Khalifa St	626 4800
Sana Fashions	Najda St	631 6141
Splash	Tourist Club area	644 5565
BHS	Al Ain	03 766 8988
Evans	Al Ain Mall	03 766 0333
Next	Al Ain Mall	03 766 0333
Splash	Al Ain Mall	03 766 0333

What & Where to Buy

Shopping

An alternative to buying clothes off the rack is to have them custom-made by a tailor, and there are many places offering this service. They can make an item from a drawing or a photograph, or they can copy outfits perfectly, provided you leave the choice sample with them for a few days. If necessary, they will also advise on the amount of material you should buy. The finished result can be excellent and the price very reasonable. Word of mouth is the best method of finding a reliable, switched on tailor; otherwise, trial and error is the only way.

Clothes

Mass sales generally take place around August/September and January when stores get rid of the old stock and bring in the new. If you can bear to rummage, discounts of 70% aren't uncommon. Another excellent time for bargains is around the end of Ramadan when the Eid sales begin.

Computers

Other options → Electronics & Home
Appliances [p.144]

You should have few problems finding the right hardware and software to submerge yourself in the latest technology. Numerous outlets sell the latest merchandise.

If you are really serious about computers and the latest technology, it's worth driving into Dubai to check out GITEX – the biggest IT exhibition in the Middle East. Each year, around the middle of October, the exhibition halls at the Dubai World Trade Centre hold this exhibition, with every single computer company that you can think of, plus a few others, participating. There's also a GITEX Shopper held at the Airport Expo in Dubai, so when you've cruised the stands and decided what latest gizmo you can't live without, you can pop along and buy it with a good discount.

The UAE Government, together with the BSA (Business Software Alliance) is clamping down heavily on the sale of pirated software. As a result, most computer shops are reputable and offer the usual international guarantees.

However, if you have a legitimate problem with substandard computer equipment, and cannot gain a satisfactory outcome after complaining directly to the shop, the Consumer Protection Cell in the Department of Economic Development should be able to give practical assistance. This can include setting up and overseeing meetings between the two parties, implementing fines, and even arranging for the payment of refunds to be made at the Economic Department – this leaves 'dodgy' sales practices little room for manoeuvre.

Electronics & Home Appliances

Other options → Computers [p.144]

From well known to not-so-instantly-recognisable brands, Abu Dhabi's stores stock a reasonable selection of electronics and home appliances. Prices are often hyped as being lower than in many parts of the world, but check things out before leaving home, especially if you are out to buy a major item.

Like most goods, it pays to shop around for the best prices, although shops are generally fairly competitive due to the number of places offering the same or similar items. Again, bargaining is key and will reduce the price further.

Warranties, after sales service, delivery and installation should be finalised before making any purchase. If you intend on returning to your home country with an item, check that you are buying a model that will operate there (for example, manufacturers set the sound frequency on televisions differently in different parts of the world, so what works in Abu Dhabi won't necessarily work elsewhere). Alternatively, if you are happy buying second-hand electronics, check out the Classifieds sections of the local daily newspapers, advertising a range of items, often virtually as good as new. It may also be worth going to some of the 'garage' sales that are advertised by people who are usually returning to their home country and are selling off some of their unwanted possessions. You can buy something for nothing from departing expats; they usually sell at ridiculously low prices. Their main priority is often to get rid of everything as quickly as possible, regardless of how much money they lose. Remember, it's a buyer's market, and some great bargains can be found, making these options excellent for people who do not want to part with their hard earned cash.

Akai	Geco	443 6866
Black & Decker	Jashanmal	633 5569
Cost Less	Mina Mall	673 4848
Hitachi	Eros Electricals	633 6432
Jashanmal	Jashanmal	633 5569
JVC	Oasis Ent	621 7040
Kenwood	Jashanmal	633 5569
National	Jumbo Electronics	632 7001
Panasonic	Jumbo Electronics	632 7001
Pioneer	Bango Electronics	622 5272
Popular Brands	Yousaf Habib Al Yousaf	634 4553
Popular Brands	Carrefour	449 4300
Russell Hobbs	Jashanmal	633 5569
Salam Studios	Abu Dhabi Mall	679 2000
Samsung	Eros Electricals	633 6432
Sanyo	Al Futtaim	621 3577
Sharp	Cosmos	626 9398
Supra	Jumbo Electronics	679 0298
Sony	Jumbo Electronics	632 7001
Toshiba	Al Futtaim	673 3614
JVC	Al Ain	03 751 7238
Sanyo	Al Ain	03 764 1473
Supra	Al Ain	03 764 2898
Toshiba	Al Ain	03 751 7790

Eyewear

The strength of the sun in the Gulf means that for many people, sunglasses are their most important accessory. Consumers will find just about every brand of normal glasses and sunglasses imaginable, from designer names to designer rip offs and much more in between. While prices range from a few dirhams to many hundreds, it is best to buy sunglasses with a good quality lens. Make sure that they give 100% UVA and UVB protection, and are dark enough (and large enough) to protect the eye from the sun's glare.

Most of the larger shopping malls have an optician who can make up prescription lenses, offer a good range of glasses and contact lenses, and also give eye tests. These are free of charge in most optical

shops, as long as you order your glasses there or specify that the glasses are for driving. However, some places charge Dhs.20 - 50 for the eye test.

Flowers

Other options → Plant & Trees [p.152]

For those special occasions or for that special someone (or as a desperate last minute present), flowers make a beautiful gift. There is a reasonable selection of florists all over the city and places often sell dried flowers as well as fresh. Excellent flower arrangements can also be bought from Spinneys supermarkets. The local florists offer superb arrangements at very reasonable prices and their shops are worth a visit even if you don't intend on buying, as their skill and adeptness is well worth seeing first hand.

Flowers

If you are looking for florists who deliver internationally as well as locally, refer to the Abu Dhabi Yellow Pages. Interflora signs adorn windows of some local shops that offer international deliveries. Prices vary according to the type of arrangement and flowers you choose, but the minimum order for local delivery is usually Dhs.100 per bouquet

Flower House	Al Nasr	621 1647
Holland Flowers	Hamdan St	632 2636
Oleander	Salam St	677 3131
Green Garden	Al Ain	03 766 2428

What & Where to Buy

Shopping

Food

Other options → Health Food [p.148]

Abu Dhabi has a good range of stores and supermarkets that cater more than adequately to the city's multinational inhabitants. While there may be some speciality foods you cannot buy, most items are available.

Prices vary dramatically. Produce is imported from all over the world, and some items are double what they would cost in their country of origin. However, fresh foods, such as fruit and vegetables, can be amazingly cheap, especially if bought from fruit and vegetable marketplaces.

There are plenty of 'corner' shops in residential areas, good for a litre of milk and much more. Many accept orders over the phone for local home deliveries, saving you the walk. Popular food shops include the Abu Dhabi Co-operative, which has branches all over the city, while Al Ahlia Prisunic is often simply known as Prisunic. Alternatively, the souks are worth a visit, especially for fruit and vegetables.

Carrefour is a huge hypermarket and part of a large French chain. It sells everything from cheap shoes to toothpaste, as well as a good selection of fruit, vegetables and an excellent selection of fish and seafood. Other branches of Carrefour can be found in Ajman, Dubai, Al Ain, Sharjah and Ras Al Khaimah. If you are looking for a certain type of food, there are a number of speciality stores: for American food, try Choithrams, for Asian/Japanese and gourmet delicacies, head for Abela, for British and European, go to Spinneys, and for French

produce, look no further than Carrefour. Although pork is not included on the Arabic menu, the availability of this product is becoming more common. Spinneys has a designated pork section that is quite well-stocked.

Abela Superstore	Kailidiya	667 4575
Al Ahlia Prisunic	Beh Lamcy Dept. Store	681 1400
Abu Dhabi Co-operative Society	Corniche Road	633 7505
	Khalifa St.	626 4900
Carrefour	Nr Shk Zayed Stadium	449 4300
Choithrams	Khalidiya Road	666 0610
	Shk Zayed 2nd St.	676 5355
Emsons	Nr Le Meridien	676 8376
	Beh Sana	633 8653
Spinneys	Khalidiya	681 2897
	Airport Road	621 2919
Al Ahlia Prisunic	Al Khabeesi	03 763 4111
Choithrams	Main St.	03 765 6798
	Al Jimi	03 751 2227

Furniture & Household Items

Other options → Furnishing Accomodation [p.70]

Whether you need kitchenware, bathroom accessories, linens, towels, curtain rods, lampshades or furniture, you will find goods to suit every taste and budget. There are some excellent home furnishing stores in Abu Dhabi, but remember that in addition to the stores, many of

Furniture & Household Items

EXPLORE THE GREAT INDOORS

Armchairs, beds, candles, desks, easy chairs, fabrics, glassware, halogen lamps, kitchenware, lighting, mats, office furniture, plants, quilts, rugs, sofas, toys, venetian blinds, wall units....
IKEA stores literally cover the A to Z of good living without adding to your cost of living. We have over 12,000 inspiring, yet functional ideas for you to explore, so why not come and discover what best suits your lifestyle.

the supermarkets also sell kitchenware, a selection of linen etc.

2XL	Mina Zayed	673 0575
BHS	Hamdan Street	621 1242
Cane Craft	Tourist Club Area	678 4505
Carrefour	Airport Rd	449 4300
Eldiar	Khaladiya	666 2522
Gemaco	Airport Rd	633 9100
Grand Stores	Shk Zayed 1st St	631 2100
Home Centre	Najda St	626 2621
Hyssna	Tourist Club Area	644 7236
ID design	Najda St	671 2405
Marlin Furniture	Electra	677 4994
THE One	Khaladiya	681 6500

A number of expansive stores sell the latest styles in furniture. The larger: THE One, 2XL, Home Centre, Ikea and Homes R Us are a few of the many that offer the latest in home decor. Homes R Us takes up the whole top floor of Madinat Zayed Shopping Centre, describing themselves as the biggest home furnishing store in the UAE. Second-hand furniture can often be found through the classified pages in the newspapers or from supermarket noticeboards.

Hardware & DIY

Other options ➜ Outdoor Goods [p.151]

Whilst it is often easier and cheaper to get in 'a man who can' to tackle all those niggling domestic jobs, many still prefer to do-it-themselves. As a result of this demand, stores such as Ace Hardware have become better stocked with each passing year. Customised paints, glazes, special paint effect materials, electronic tools and hardware materials can all be easily obtained.

Ace Hardware	Mina Zayed	673 3174

Health Food

Other options ➜ Health Clubs [p.207]

Thanks to the health trend finally arriving in the UAE, specialist health food stores, and even regular pharmacies sell a range of supplements. The major supermarkets sell a somewhat limited range of organic and gluten free products, such as organic cornflakes, herbal teas, rice cakes, oat cakes, gluten free pasta etc. A small variety of herbal liver, kidney and blood cleansing products are available on the

market, as are some detoxifying products. Note that vitamins, minerals, supplements, and organic and health foods are expensive compared to back home, and the selection of brands, while improving, is still very limited.

Health Food & Vitamins

A number of sports shops offer products and supplements that are geared to sports performance or slimming. This area of nutrition is extremely well catered for, with many outlets packed to the brim with all sorts of shakes, meal replacement bars and performance enhancing supplements.

Jewellery, Watches & Gold

Other options ➜ Souks [p.161]

Jewellery found in the Emirates encompasses all styles; gaudy, beautiful, cheap, expensive, and the variety is unending. Gold is priced according to the international daily gold rate and available in 18, 21, 22 or 24 carats, in every form imaginable, from bracelets, rings and necklaces to gold ingots. Ingots of different sizes are available for investment or, if you prefer, to melt down and mould into a customised design. In addition to the weight price, a small charge is added for craftsmanship, which varies according to the intricacy of the design. The standards of workmanship can vary so if you are spending a lot of money, it is worth going to a more reputable store. Other than gold, silver jewellery from Oman is also available. Other varied forms of jewellery include cultured pearls from Japan, to classic, ethnic creations from India. The new souk at Madinat Zayed on 4th Street has many jewellers and houses some of the largest jewellery shops in the Gulf. The outlets in these areas cater more for

imagine yourself in a **home** where every **mood** is **young** and **naughty**.

it wasn't made to be, it just becomes so **with**

AMSTERDAM ZURICH GENEVA BRUXELLES LONDON MARSEILLE NICE TOULON AJACCIO RENNES BORDEAUX ABU DHABI SHARJAH

Arabic tastes, but there are a few shops listed below that sell styles more suited to European tastes.

Al Manara Jewellery	Hamdan St	627 5121
Damas Jewellery	Marina Mall	681 2391
Eastern Jewellery	Khalifa St	676 3958
Khalid Saleh Jewellers	Hamed Centre	632 1012
Khalifa Jewellery	Khalifa St	627 1268
Mansour Jewellery	Khalifa St	626 4260

When it comes to watches, the UAE is almost guaranteed to be able to supply whatever you are looking for. Prices range from a few dirham plastic cheapies to diamond studded watches costing many thousands of dirhams. Don't forget to check out the souks – here you can find all kinds of designs, for all ages and tastes. Besides housing the accredited agents for well-known brands (Swatch, Longines, Alfred Dunhill, Rolex, Omega, Tag, Breitling, Cartier etc), you can buy unknown cheaper brands. The Hamdan Centre is a good place to start – you'll find everything from the cheap and tacky to the exquisite and expensive.

Gold

Kids' Items

Other options → Places to Shop [p.154]
Support Groups [p.83]
Family Explorer

A variety of goods can be found in Abu Dhabi for children of all ages, from nursery equipment to the latest computer games, to mini designer fashions.

For younger children, it's even possible to hire specialised items, such as car seats or cots. Virtually every conceivable toy or game is available somewhere and you should have few problems whether buying old fashioned games or the latest fashionable 'must have' toys.

You may prefer to buy toys, especially for very young children, from more reputable shops that are less likely to sell substandard items. For a fuller picture on all that Abu Dhabi and Dubai have to offer families with children up to the age of 14 years, refer to the *Family Explorer* (formerly *Kids Explorer*). This offers invaluable information on everything from education and medical care to top venues for a birthday party, and both outdoor and indoor activities – perfect for when the temperatures soar.

Leather & Luggage

Good leather lasts forever. Imagination and artistry combine in a wide range of fine leather goods, from key rings, gloves or wallets, to handbags, shoes, suitcases etc. Many of the malls have expensive shops selling exclusive designer ranges. However, for more economical choices, the best place is the Hamdan Centre. There are several competitively priced shops selling leather goods and a range of suitcases, from cheap unknown brands to the well known, like Samsonite.

Grand Stores	Shk Zayed 1st St.	631 2100
Leather Palace	Liwa Centre	632 3340

Lingerie

Other options → Clothes [p.143]

Emirati ladies have a reputation for being one of the highest consumers of luxury lingerie in the world and, as testament to that, almost every mall houses a proliferation of frilly, frighteningly expensive lingerie boutiques.

Every designer name in lingerie is healthily represented, so if you are on the lookout for a few decent additions to a bridal trousseau, and money is no object, there surely can be few better places to shop.

Shopping — What & Where to Buy

However, if you veer towards function rather than glamour, there are several noteworthy alternatives. In the past year or so, lingerie chain La Senza has been opening up branches in shopping malls throughout the Emirates offering an extremely decent range of underwear and nightwear at affordable prices. Woolworth's stocks a good range of lingerie at excellent value. Marks & Spencer, of course, has a staunch following for its lingerie lines – but expect to pay heavily inflated prices for the privilege of buying the UK's favourite underwear in Abu Dhabi.

As long as you don't mind turning up at the cash till with your smalls nestling among the weekly shop, well regarded European lingerie labels are available in many supermarkets.

Medicine

Other options → General Medical Care [p.78]

There's no shortage of pharmacies or chemists in Abu Dhabi – these are indicated on shop signs by what looks like a snake wrapped around a cocktail glass. Remember to check the expiry date of medicine before purchasing it. Most pharmacies also carry a variety of beauty products, baby care items, sunscreens, perfumes etc.

In the Emirates you are able to buy prescription drugs over the counter. If you are certain what antibiotics or drug you need, it saves the expense and hassle of visiting a doctor, and pharmacists themselves are always quite happy to listen to symptoms and suggest a remedy.

Each emirate has at least one pharmacy open 24 hours a day – the location and phone numbers are listed in the daily newspapers. In addition, a Municipality emergency number (Abu Dhabi 02 677 7929; Al Ain 03 778 8888) will give the name and location of 24 hour pharmacies.

Music & Videos

Although the selection isn't as large or as up to date as in North America, Asia or Europe, you will find a number of audio and video stores selling the latest releases from all over the world. From famous international bands, Arabic or classical music, to Bollywood and Hollywood releases, Abu Dhabi caters for a variety of styles and tastes. However, CDs, DVD's and videos are only released once they have been screened (and censored, if appropriate) to ensure that they do not offend the country's moral code. Videos are in the PAL format and there are numerous video rental stores around the city – check one out in your area. Blank audio and videotapes are sold at major grocery stores. Rental prices range from Dhs.4 to Dhs.10 per video and around Dhs.10 (as well as a hefty deposit sometimes) per DVD.

Abela Video	Khaladiya	666 9962
Carrefour	Airport Rd	449 4300
Various	Hamdan Centre	na
Virgin Megastore	Abu Dhabi Mall	645 4858

Outdoor Goods

Other options → Camping [p.168]
Hardware & DIY [p.148]

Aside from the humidity, sand, and desert creepy crawlies, the UAE has a fascinating outdoor existence, and off-roading and camping are revered pastimes for many. A weekend away offers a peaceful escape from the hustle and bustle of the city, and there are virtually no limitations on where you can pitch your tent and light your fire. For most people, the lack of heat and humidity make the winter months the best time to go. However, if you choose your location carefully – at altitude or by the sea – the summer months aren't always completely unbearable. To get kitted with the basics for a night under the stars is fairly easy. However, if you are a more avid enthusiast and prefer to have specialised equipment, you'll have to either order it online or bring it from your home town.

Party Accessories

Other options → Party Organisers [p.230]

Most major supermarkets and stationery stores sell the basic party paraphernalia, and if you go to the more specialised shops, you'll find an even wider range. From cards, balloons, candles, table settings and room decorations to gift wrapping and fancy dress outfits, bouncy castles and entertainers, the choice for both children's and adults' parties is very comprehensive. Gray Mackenzie (02 612 3545) also offers a free of charge party service. Items should be returned within five days of payment of the deposit and a minimum breakage charge of Dhs.6 per glass will be deducted from the deposit and the balance refunded. A deposit of Dhs.500 will allow you use of

What & Where to Buy

Shopping

24 pint beer glasses, 24 wineglasses, 2 ice buckets, 2 waiter trays, 3 bar towels and 24 coasters.

| Balloon Lady, The | 04 344 1062 |
| Flying Elephant | 04 347 9170 |

Perfumes & Cosmetics

Other options → Souks [p.161]

Beauty in the Emirates is big business, and whether the temperature goes up or down, there's always a busy trade in perfumes and cosmetics. Just about every perfume in the world is available somewhere, and new fragrances are for sale almost as soon as they are launched in their country of origin.

For a more personalised fragrance, look out for the local perfumeries that are in every shopping area and a vital part of the locals' grooming ritual. Fragrances tend to combine a heady mix of aromatic Arabian oils which are individually blended – don't go overboard on application as one dab can last for days.

Ajmal Perfume Centre	Khalifa St	622 5394
Body Shop	Rotana Mall	681 4937
Grand Stores	Shk Zayed, 1st St	631 2100
Paris Gallery	Liwa Centre	631 7788
Best Perfume Store	Al Ain	03 764 3146

Plants & Trees

Other options → Flowers [p.145]

If you're lucky enough to have a garden, or even a bit of a balcony, it is definitely worth planting a few shrubs, trees or bedding plants in pots, all of which are good value for money. Having a garden full of foliage is great for keeping the sand at bay, and it's surprising how many varieties of plants can thrive in such arid conditions, although constant watering is vital. Be aware, the extra water will add substantially to your water bills, but hiring a gardener will most likely be cheaper than you imagined. If you can't be bothered to traipse around a nursery, all the larger supermarkets stock a good selection of indoor and outdoor plants, but expect to pay a few dirhams more for convenience.

Plants & Trees

Second-hand Items

For buying or selling second-hand items, such as furniture, cookers etc, remember to check out the Classifieds section of the local newspapers (as well as the Abu Dhabi sections of the Dubai-based papers), or the notice boards at the various supermarkets.

Shoes

Other options → Beach Wear [p.139]
Clothes [p.143]

Whether your penchant is for Doc Martins, flip flops or kitten-heeled mules, shoes come in as many shapes and sizes as there are feet. A wide range of styles is available, from high fashion to comfortable casual wear, in a variety of colours, materials and sizes.

Training shoes tend to be more reasonably priced here than elsewhere, although addicts may find that their favourite styles are often one season behind.

Florsheim	BHS	621 1242
Italian Shoes	Hamdan Centre	632 3169
K Corner	Nr Hamdan Centre	621 0939
Milano Shoes	Hamdan Centre	633 4749
Milano Shoes	Najda St	621 9700
Shoe Mart	Madinat Zayed	634 6461
Shoe Mart	Al Ain	03 766 6526

What & Where to Buy

Shopping

Sporting Goods

Other options → *Underwater Explorer (UAE)*
Off-Road Explorer (UAE)

Abu Dhabi is a great location for a variety of sports, from the more common ones, such as tennis, sailing, golf or football, to more unusual activities like sand skiing. Try the general sports shops listed below for items like squash racquets or sports clothing. You can also find specialist sports shops around the city, and unless yours is an unusual sport in the Emirates or you require a more specialised piece of equipment, you should have little difficulty finding what you require.

*See Also: **Cycling** (Carrefour); **Diving** (see dive centres); **Golf** (Sun & Sand Sports); **Ice Hockey & Ice Skating** (Hamdan Centre, Abu Dhabi ice rink, Al Ain Mall ice rink); **Off-road** (The Off Road Zone); **Snorkelling** (dive centres, Carrefour, Masaoods); **Water skiing** (Masaoods).*

Emirates Sports Stores	Madinat Zayed	632 5540
London Sports	Hamdan Centre	632 9783
Sun & Sand Sports	Hamdan Centre	674 6299
Gulf Sea Sports	Al Ain	03 765 539

Sporting Goods

Tailoring & Embroidery

Other options → Arabian Souvenirs [p.138]
Textiles [p.153]
Souks [p.161]

With the number of textile shops in Abu Dhabi, it's well worth buying some fabric and having items made up to your specification – whether it's curtains, cushions or an almost designer suit, most items are possible.

When trying a tailor for the first time, it is advisable to order only one item to check the quality of the work. Tailors can copy a pattern that you supply, or copy from an original item if you can leave it with them for a few days. Most tailors have a range of pattern books inhouse that you can browse through; alternatively check out a bookstore for pattern books. Even cuttings from magazines can be used as the basis for a design.

The tailor will also advise on how many metres of material are needed (buy a little extra to be on the safe side). Most tailors provide the notions such as buttons, shoulder pads, cotton and zips. Confirm the price (obviously the more complex the pattern, the higher the price) before committing to having it made, and make sure that it includes the cost of the lining, if appropriate.

A good tailor should tack it all together so that you can have a trying on session before the final stitching. When it is finished, try it on again. Don't be bashful about asking them to put something right if you are not completely happy.

In addition to the numerous tailors, there are specialist embroidery shops catering mainly for the heavily decorated Arabic version of the Western style white wedding dress. Embroidery can create a wonderful effect, especially for a special occasion. However, this intricate work will obviously greatly increase the cost of your item.

Textiles

Other options → Arabian Souvenirs [p.138]
Tailoring & Embroidery [p.153]
Souks [p.161]

The shops in the New Souk are a treasure trove of textiles, colours, textures and weaves from all over the world. Shimmering threads adorn thin voile and broderie anglaise, satin and silk tempt, and velvets jostle with peach skin, although good, drill cottons are still difficult to find. Serge and wool worsted simply beg to be made into classy gent's suits and taken to colder climes. Shop around as the choice is virtually unlimited and prices are negotiable. Look out for any sales, occurring quite frequently in this area.

Cairo Textiles	New Souk	622 4567
Paris Textiles	New Souk	622 5030
Rivoli Textiles	Hamdan St	679 2996

What & Where to Buy

Shopping

PLACES TO SHOP

The following section covers the three main Abu Dhabi and Al Ain malls plus the numerous additional smaller shopping malls, as well as a variety of souqs.

Shopping Malls

The attractive, and often imaginatively designed, modern shopping malls are one of the highlights of shopping here. They are generally spacious and fully air conditioned, offering a great escape from the often searing heat of the city. Here you will find virtually every kind of store that you can imagine, from supermarkets or card shops, to clothes emporiums and specialist perfume shops. However, the popular malls are more than just a place to buy goods, for in the evenings and especially the weekends, a lively, social buzz ensues as people window shop, meet friends, eat out and people watch as they sip coffee.

During Eid and festive occasions, the larger malls are venues for special events such as dancing or magic shows. These performances are always popular and involve acts from all around the world. The malls also feature numerous raffles during these months – the prize for the lucky few is usually a car.

Most malls have a food court, offering a variety of cuisine, from the ubiquitous hamburger, to Arabic meze, Italian or Mexican food. Some malls also have children's play areas, arcade games and cinemas, and most have convenient, extensive and free parking. The following are the more popular malls in Abu Dhabi and Al Ain.

Abu Dhabi Mall

Marina Mall

Main Shopping Malls

Abu Dhabi Mall

Location → Nr Beach Rotana Hotel · Al Meena | **645 4858**
Hours → 10:00 - 22:00 10:00 - 23:00 Thu   Closed Fri am
Web/email → na   Map Ref → 4-B4

A very 'happening' mall in Abu Dhabi, this new four storey, fully air conditioned mall is also one of the largest in the UAE. It houses over 200 retail outlets selling everything from affordable fashion wear to exclusive designer apparel, fancy gifts and accessories, electronics, videos, jewellery, shoes and much more. Some of these outlets are well known international and local retail names. It's no surprise that the mall's daily visitor count exceeds 26,000.

You know that full emphasis has been given to the shopper's convenience if you have 3,000 covered parking spaces and over 15 elevators providing direct access to every level. You'll find a restaurant or coffee shop on every floor in addition to a spacious food court featuring fast food favourites and an Italian style pizzeria. For movie lovers, Century Cinemas on the third floor boasts a nine screen cineplex with 800 seats. You will find the popular children's theme park, Toy Town on the third level – an ideal choice for children's parties given the considerable variety of rides and electronic games.

Abu Dhabi Mall

Places to Shop

Shopping

Books, Cards & Gifts
Book Gallery
Carlton Cards
Gulf Greetings

Cinema
Century Cinemas

Clothes
Austin Reed
Bershka
Betty Barclay
Blue Marine
Bossini
Docker's
Esprit
Evans
Gant
GFF Studio
Giordano
Guess
Hang Ten
Kenzo
La Senza
Levi's
Mango
Massimo Dutti
Max Mara
Morgan
Motivi
Next
Promod
Pull & Bear
Springfield
Triumph
U2
XOXO

Department Stores
Grand Stores
Jashanmal
JC Penny
Salam Studio & Stores

Electronics
Axiom Telecom
Bang & Olufsen

Eyewear
Al Jaber Optical Centre
Yateem Optician

Food
Auntie Anne's
Baskin Robbins
Café Du Roi
Cinnabon
Costa
Fujiyama
Gerard Coffee Shop
Hatam
Hediard
Il Firno Italiano
Manchow Wok
Moka Café
Starbucks
Subway

Furniture & Household
Applewoods
Descamps
Fretti
Home One
Sara

Hypermarket
Abu Dhabi Co-op

Jewellery & Gold
Alfred Dunhill
Al Futtaim Jewellery
Bvlgari
Cartier
Chopard
Claire's Accessories
Damas Jewellery
Mont Blanc
Paco Rabanne
Tanagra (Allied)

Kids' Stuff
A II Z
Adams
Early Learning Centre
La Senza Girl
Lapin House
Mothercare
Next
Osh Kosh & Colour 4 Kids
Premaman

Medicine/Health & Nutrition
GNC
Holland & Barrett
Nutrition Zone

Music & Videos
Virgin Megastore

Perfumes & Cosmetics
Body Shop
Crabtree & Evelyn
L'Occitane
Mac
Paris Gallery
Red Earth

Services
Al Ansari Exchange
National Bank of Abu Dhabi
UAE Exchange

Shoes
Aldo
BASS
Ecco
Florsheim
Furla
Maria Pino
Milano
Nine West
Salamander
Stuart Weitzman & Moreshi

Sporting Goods
Mega Sports

Watches
Omega
Rivoli
Swatch
The Watch House

Al Ain Mall

Location → Al Qwaitat St · Al Ain | **03 766 0333**
Hours → 10:00 - 22:00 10:00 - 24:00 Wed - Thu, 14:00 - 24:00 Fri
Web/email → www.alainmall.org | Map Ref → 15-C3

The Al Ain Mall is a haven for shoppers seeking refuge from the harsh desert heat. Covering three floors, this modern and bright building contains over 100,000 square metres of shopping and entertainment fun. Offering everything from tailoring to telecom, along with several anchor stores such as Spinneys, Home Centre and Paris Gallery, there's more than enough to tempt even the choosiest of shoppers to loosen their purse strings.

If shopping is not on the agenda, the family entertainment centre is a good option. Spread over 3,700 square metres, a 12 lane bowling alley and four cinemas are guaranteed to amuse adults and children alike. The indoor ice skating rink located on the ground floor keeps the youngsters busy while parents watch their antics from above. Al Ain's only destination mall also sports a small food court and covered parking on the ground floor for 1,000 cars.

Al Ain Mall

Books, Cards & Gifts
Carrefour
Gulf Greetings
Lifestyle

Cinema
Al Ain Mall Grand Cineplex

Clothes
Etam
Evans
Gasoline
Giordano
Hang Ten
Liz Claiborne
MEXX
Naf Naf
Next
River Island
Splash
Tiffany
Vid Rio

Department Stores
Grand Stores

Electronics
Jumbo Electronics
Oman Coast Studio

Eyewear
Al Ain Optical
Badie Optical
Yateem Optician

Food
Aunti Anne's
Baskin Robbins
Burger King
Café Du Roi
China Wall
Dubai Mughal Restaurant
Gloria Jean's Coffees
Hardees
Jabal Al Quds
KFC
La Cabana
Pizza Hut
Sombrero
Starbucks
Subway
Sweet Factory

Furniture & Household
Designer Furniture
Grand Stores
Home Centre
Life Style
Roma Gallery

Jewellery & Gold
Al Mandoos Jewellery
Al Sayegh Jewellery
Damas Jewellery
Dar Al Zain Jewellery
Mont Blanc
Oriental Stores

Kids' Stuff
Baby Shop
Banati
Cuts R Us
Early Learning Centre
East House
Magic Centre
Mother Care
Naf Naf
Toy Magic
Tweety Saloon

Lingerie
Cloud Nine
Nayomi

Medicine/Health & Nutrition
Al Manara Pharmacy

Music & Videos
Classic Audio & Video

Perfumes & Cosmetics
Al Haramain Perfumes
Al Rasasi Perfumes
Arabian Oud
Grand Stores
MAC Cosmetics
Make Up For Ever
Mikyaji
Paris Gallery
YAS Perfumes

Services
Al Ansari Exchange
Dubai Islamic Bank
National Bank of Abu Dhabi

Shoes
Cesare Paciotti
Milano
Stone N String

Sporting Goods
Alfa Sports

Supermarket
Spinneys

Watches
Rivoli
Swatch

Marina Mall

Location ➜ Breakwater · Breakwater | **681 8300**
Hours ➜ 10:00 - 22:00 10:00 - 23:00 Wed - Thu, 14:00 - 22:00 Fri
Web/email ➜ marinamall@emirates.net.ae Map Ref ➜ 10-B4

Situated on the Breakwater, well away from the hustle and bustle of the city, the spacious Marina Mall provides a breath of fresh sea air to its shoppers. Laid out underneath its impressive tented roof, 160 local and international retail outlets keep visitors happily entertained night and day. Major retailers such as Plug-Ins, Woolworth's and Sun and Sand Sports are located amidst a host of international fashion outlets and a number of smaller boutique style shops. Pier Import, a home furnishing store packed with unusual goodies, is well visited, along with the ever popular Ikea store that spreads over two levels. The basement level is dominated by the Carrefour hypermarket.

Three course restaurants, fast food outlets and coffee shops look after the needs of even the most exhausted shopper. Do watch out for the mall wide sales, beginning from 15th January to 28th February.

Shoppers will find some of the best bargains in town, and plenty of parking space allows you to freely indulge in some serious retail therapy.

This mall also scores high on entertainment. Cinestar has a nine screen complex, bringing the latest international releases, while Foton World provides excitement and fun for all. The fountain near the main entrance has choreographed musical interludes – it always attracts an admiring crowd and creates a good rendezvous spot.

Marina Mall

Books, Cards & Gifts
Al Salsabeel Flowers & Gifts
Arabian Oud
Carrefour
Gulf Greetings
Mont Blanc
Scarabee
Tiffany & Co.

Cinema
CineStar

Clothes
Bebe
British India
Can Can
ELLE
Gasoline
Giordano
Hang Ten
Indigo Nation
Kookai
Levis
MEXX
Promod
Springfield
Stradivarius
Studio R
Timberland
Truworths
United Colours of Benetton
Waipai
Young Designers
 Emporium
Zara

Department Stores
Woolworths

Electronics
Carrefour
MEGASTAR
Plug-ins
Radio Shack

Eyewear
Grand Optics
Grand Sunglasses
Optical Centre
Rivoli
Yateem Optician

Food
Baskin Robbins
Burger King
Dunkin Donuts
El Torito
Fuddruckers
Gerard Café
Gloria Jean's Coffees
Hatam
London Dairy
Popeye's
Starbucks Coffee
Sweet Factory
Tandoori Inn
Yin Yang

Furniture & Household
Carrefour
Chen One
IKEA
Pier Import
Woolworths

Hypermarket
Carrefour

Jewellery & Gold
Al Futtaim Jewellery
Bvlgari
Damas Jewellery

Kids' Stuff
A II Z
Early Learning Centre
Euro Hobbies
Foton World
Kid's Land Salon
Lapin House
Naf Naf
Neck & Neck
Ovo
Toy Magic
Woolworths
Zara

Leather & Luggage
Salamander

Lingerie
Cloud Nine
Silhouettes
Wolford
Women's Secret

Medicine/Health & Nutrition
Bin Sina Pharmacy

Perfumes & Cosmetics
Areej
Body Shop
Lush

Services
Abu Dhabi Commercial Bank
Al Ansari Exchange
Marina Laundry
National Bank of Abu Dhabi
Photo Magic
Smoker's Centre

Shoes
ALDO
Bata
Cesare Paciotti
Hush Puppies
Salamander
VIA SPIGA

Sporting Goods
Alfa Sports
Sports Link
Studio R
Sun & Sand Sports

Watches
Hour Choice
Oriental Stores
Rivoli
Rolex
Swatch
Tiffany & Co.
Watch House

Other Shopping Malls

Abu Dhabi Co-operative Society Complex

Location → Nr Le Meridien Htl · Shk Zayed 1st St | 644 0808
Hours → 08:00 - 24:00
Web/email → na   Map Ref → 4-B4

This older shopping centre has a hum about it in the evenings, on weekends, and when there's a raffle draw on. While the name remains, the Abu Dhabi Co-op has moved across the street to the newer Abu Dhabi Mall. The Complex's main draws now are the Landmark Group stores: Splash, packed to the brim with trendy, inexpensive fashions, Shoe Mart, with its tremendous range of reasonably priced shoes, and Lifestyles, one of the best stores in town for funky gift items. Other small shops range from computer suppliers to ladies' fashion outlets.

Abu Dhabi Cooperative Society

Al Ahlia Prisunic

Location → Nr Dana Plaza · Al Khalidiyah | 681 2997
Hours → 08:00 - 24:00
Web/email → na   Map Ref → 9-D1

This is a real one stop shop with a little bit of everything. There are some gems, like the Herb and Honey Centre which also sells a range of natural healing products, and a curio shop on the ground floor selling a well made and well priced range of household effects. There is also a

reasonable variety of clothes shops for the whole family and a good balance of individual boutiques stocking some unusual lines in women's fashion. There's also a lively and interesting café, which has a steady stream of patrons.

Al Falah Plaza

Location → Nr Nat Bank of Abu Dhabi · Al Falah St | 642 5800
Hours → See timings below
Web/email → na   Map Ref → 5-A3

Situated on Old Passport Road near Habib Bank, Al Falah Plaza is arguably one of the cheapest shopping centres in the capital. The Plaza stocks a wide variety of products ranging from costume jewellery to coffee makers, complemented by a well supplied ground floor supermarket. If you seek designer labels, this is not the place, but when it comes to household essentials, the Plaza is a one stop shop. Added features include a music store, pharmacy, fast food restaurant and café.

Timings: Supermarket: 09.00 – 23.30
           Stores: Sat – Thurs 09:00 – 14:00 16:30 – 23:00;
           Fri: 09:00 – 23:30

Al Hana Shopping Centre

Location → Opp Eldiar · Corniche Rd West | 681 6823
Hours → 07:00 - 24:00
Web/email → na   Map Ref → 9-E2

Fronted by exclusive designer stores, the Al Hana Shopping Centre is a haven for the well heeled as the range is very selective. Occupying prime space opposite the Abu Dhabi Corniche, the centre also boasts a large music store and a shop for grooming products. A café on the ground floor offers a view of the waterfront – an ideal spot to enjoy a refreshing brew when the weather cools.

Al Hosn Plaza

Location → Sheraton Bld · Shk Zayed 1st St | 667 5555
Hours → 09:00 - 14:00 17:00 - 22:00 Closed Fri am
Web/email → na   Map Ref → 9-B1

Sporting a bright, breezy interior, this mall hosts a range of brand name shops such as Mexx, Clarks and Calvin Klein, plus an eclectic range of small shops selling jewellery and lingerie and other quality goods. The second-hand bookshop, House of Prose, is located on the first floor and the Mezzanine floor houses a useful business centre.

Al Jernain Center

Location ➜ Nr. Al Hosn Plaza · Shk Zayed 1st St |na
Hours ➜ 09:00 - 23:30
Web/email ➜ na   Map Ref ➜ 9-B1

Amongst outlets such as Betty Barclay and Simba Kids, there are several clothing stores, a pharmacy and a sewing machine shop. If you're looking for the famous and upmarket Bateel, this mall boasts a branch. Bateel is a useful gift shop, known for its high quality dates from Saudi Arabia, but the store also stocks biscuits, chocolates and variously filled dates.

Al Muhairy Centre

Location ➜ Opp Cult Foundation · Shk Zayed 1st St |632 2228
Hours ➜ 10:00 - 13:30 16:30 - 22:00 16:00 - 22:00 Fri
Web/email ➜ www.almuhairycentre.com   Map Ref ➜ 8-E1

This centre has not really taken off yet. Spacious and bright, the shops are mainly aimed at Arab clientele. The ground and first floor have a selection of ladies' and men's wear shops including Boss. The main attraction, however, seems to be Fun World, a haven for youngsters with a great range of rides and games. This venue is ideal for kids' parties with sand art, water paints, a toddlers' playground, an educational zone and a noisy range of electronic games, simulators and rides. A children friendly hair salon and an educational toyshop within the mall are also worth checking out.

City Centre

Location ➜ Opp Nat Bk of Bahrain · Shk Hamdan St |627 7770
Hours ➜ 08:00 - 13:00 17:00 - 20:00 Closed Fri am
Web/email ➜ na   Map Ref ➜ 8-C2

This affordable, spirited mall contains lots and lots of clothes shops, plus sports shops and numerous other watch stores, electronics stores etc. A good music shop sells the latest sounds on most formats. Unlike the one in Dubai, and with no affiliation, this City Centre is not the most buzzing of places. It does, however, have its own café.

Dana Plaza

Location ➜ Nr Le Meridien Htl · Shk Zayed 1st St |665 1333
Hours ➜ 10:00 - 13:00 17:00 - 23:30 Closed Fri am
Web/email ➜ na   Map Ref ➜ 9-C1

Dana Plaza has a large range of good quality outlets selling everything from cosmetics and stationery to household goods, linen and fashions for the whole family. For discounts, head towards the third floor, or settle down for a break with a nice aromatic brew in the coffee shop on the ground floor.

Fotouh Al Khair Centre

Location ➜ Nr Etisalat · Shk Rashid B Saeed Al Makt St |621 1133
Hours ➜ 10:00 - 22:00 Closed Fri am
Web/email ➜ fotouhkc@emirates.net.ae   Map Ref ➜ 8-E1

Spacious, bright and airy, this two storey mall is popular all round, especially with youngsters, as many of their favourite shops are here. Marks & Spencer has a huge outlet here, spreading over two floors, which now includes a food section stocking many favourite items. Other well known stores are Wallis, Monsoon, Mango, Adams, Nine West, Carlton Cards and The Early Learning Centre. On the first floor, a popular and busy French restaurant, the Café de la Paix, is an ideal place for a reviving cuppa or lunch. Watch out for the parking though; underground parking costs Dhs.5 per hour and the reserved parking out front is for ladies and families only.

Fotouh Al Khair Centre

Hamdan Centre

Location ➜ Nr Novotel Centre Htl · Shk Hamdan St | na
Hours ➜ 10:00 - 13:30 17:00 - 22:30 Closed Fri am
Web/email ➜ na   Map Ref ➜ 8-C2

Located right in the heart of the city, the Hamdan Centre is still one of the most vibrant and low priced shopping complexes around. This long established mall has sporting goods, leatherware and suitcases, fashion boutiques, regional handicrafts, a pharmacy, and various shoe shops. This place is ideal for off-the-wall purchases and souvenir T-shirts besides being home to the multiplex Al Massa Cinema.

Khalifa Centre

Location ➜ Nr Abu Dhabi Coop · Tourist Club Area | na
Hours ➜ 08:30 - 13:30 16:30 - 22:30 Closed Fri am
Web/email ➜ na   Map Ref ➜ 4-B4

A trip to the Khalifa Centre is a must for anyone seeking Arabic souvenirs. This somewhat ethnic mall has two levels teeming with craft shops that sell products ranging from perfumed oils and incense burners to finely crafted Gulf silverware. It is also possible to buy Persian and Baluchi carpets here. The outlets include an Arabic music store, a restaurant and an ice cream parlour serving popular Arabic flavours.

Liwa Centre

Location ➜ Nr Novotel Centre Htl · Shk Hamdan St | 632 0344
Hours ➜ 09:30 - 13:30 16:30 - 18:30 09:00 - 24:00 Thu Closed Fri
Web/email ➜ na   Map Ref ➜ 8-D2

Jewellery stores, clothes outlets, plus top makeup and perfume brands are all available here. Situated on Sheikh Hamdan Street near the souk, this centre owes much of its appeal to a vibrant food court on the second level. For a relaxing evening, head to the coffee shop, which remains open until midnight.

Lulu Centre

Location ➜ Al Salam St | 677 9786
Hours ➜ 09:00 - 13:00 16:30 - 22:30 Fri Closed Fri am
Web/email ➜ emkegroup@emirates.net.ae   Map Ref ➜ 8-A2

Here's a place that sells everything under the sun! The mall offers quality products at some of the best prices in town, from electrical goods and stationery to cosmetics and travel apparel – you name it, they have it. There's a decent range of equipment for the sports enthusiast, as well as a well stocked toy section for the tiny tots. Clothing sections cater to all, also offering casuals and a range of suits for men. If you visit the basement of the smaller branch on Sheikh Hamdan Street, you will be pleasantly surprised to see beautiful sari materials at very reasonable prices.

Madinat Zayed Shopping & Gold Centre

Location ➜ Nr Main Post Office · East Rd | 631 8555
Hours ➜ 10:00 - 23:00 Closed Fri am
Web/email ➜ na   Map Ref ➜ 5-A4

Reputed to be one of the largest shopping complexes in the Middle East, this mall fits in about 400 shops offering toys, shoes, electronics, watches, phones, optics, pharmacies, clothes – the list goes on and on.

The Madinat Zayed Gold Centre is adjacent to the main shopping centre and includes some of the finest foreign and regional jewellers. Innumerable outlets sell exquisite gold items and other forms of jewellery, pearls and diamonds. The first floor has a huge home furnishing store, Homes R Us, which is worth checking out.

Should you want keep the kids happily occupied while you exercise your plastic, there's a supervised toddlers play area with an electronic tag system alerting the supervisor every time the little monster tries to go walkabout. For somewhat older children, an arcade centre provides the latest games

Mina Centre

Location ➜ Nr Toys R Us · Al Meena | 673 4848
Hours ➜ 10:00 - 22:00
Web/email ➜ na   Map Ref ➜ 7-B4

This huge shopping centre is another recent addition to Abu Dhabi's shopping scene. The first floor has an enormous Co-op (open every day 08:00 - 24:00), and three new shops have recently opened here: 2XL, Jarir Bookstore and Cost Less Electronics. 2XL is a French home furnishings store offering colourful, modern, reasonably priced furniture and home accessories. Jarir Bookstore sells much, much more than books, and Cost Less Electronic's name is pretty self explanatory. The outer area of the Mina Centre has various amusements for children and even a crazy golf game.

MultiBrand

Location ➜ Jct Hamdan & Najda St · Madinat Zayed | **621 9700**
Hours ➜ 10:00 - 22:00 17:00 - 22:00 Fri
Web/email ➜ mbrand@emirates.net.ae   Map Ref ➜ 8-B2

Commonly known as 'The Next Shop', this large open plan store houses a range of popular, well known shops to suit the whole family. From Mothercare that specialises in baby wear and accessories, and Claire's, a haven full of 'must haves' for the girls (this is where you get your leopard skin or fluffy pink steering wheel cover!), to Next and Oasis, displaying UK fashion – it's all under one roof. For more sedate fashion styles, visit the American chain Liz Claiborne, or be chic with Milano shoes.

Rotana Mall

Location ➜ Nr Al Ahlia Prisunic · Shk Zayed 1st St | na
Hours ➜ 09:00 - 13:00 16:00 - 22:00 Closed Fri am
Web/email ➜ na   Map Ref ➜ 9-D1

A stone's throw from the Abu Dhabi Corniche, this mall is the ideal place to shop for quality furnishings, including carpets and souvenir antiques. The more unusual items available, such as decorative Arabic pottery and brilliantly patterned wall hangings, can be found in some of the mall's more general trading outlets. The Body Shop, an all time favourite store, with its range of makeup and skincare products, is tucked amidst top of the range clothes and footwear for men and women.

Souks

Other options ➜ Abu Dhabi Areas [p.100]

Souk is the Arabic word for market or place where any kind of goods are bought or exchanged. Dhows from the Far East, China, Ceylon and India would discharge their cargoes, and the goods would be haggled over in the souks adjacent to the docks. Souks were very much a centre for life here, providing a place to meet friends and socialise outside of the family. Over the years the items on sale have changed dramatically from spices, silks and perfumes to include electronic goods and the latest kitsch consumer trends.

Traditionally, the souks were a maze of shady alleyways, with small shops opening on to the paths. Nowadays most of these have been replaced by large, air conditioned centres. Although Abu Dhabi's souks aren't as fascinating as others in the Arab world, such as Fes in Morocco or Mutrah in Oman, they are worth a visit for their bustling atmosphere, eclectic variety of goods, and the traditional way of doing business.

Abu Dhabi's main souk area stretches from Sheikh Hamdan Street almost to the Corniche. Some of the souks have porters who will carry your goods and follow you around for a few dirhams (agree on a price though, before they start).

Fish Market

Location ➜ Nr Dhow Harbour · Al Meena | na
Hours ➜ See timings below
Web/email ➜ na   Map Ref ➜ 7-C4

The heady smell of salt water, fresh seafood and the holler of wizened looking, middle men haggling over the price of 50 kg of squid at a bulk fish sale at 04:30, may not be ideal after a night on the town – but it is unforgettable. The wholesale market winds down by about 06:30 and then the squabbling over the best price for the choicest lobster continues over smaller quantities as the daily market begins. If you do trawl around this hive of activity, wear shoes that are not too precious. The market is located in the port area and is run by the Fisherman's Co-operative.

Fish, Meat & Produce Souk

Location ➜ Btn Al Istigal/Al Nasr St · Al Markaziyah | na
Hours ➜ See timings below
Web/email ➜ na   Map Ref ➜ 8-E2

Not for the squeamish, this fish, meat, vegetable and fruit souk can usually be located by simply following your nose! Situated between Al Nasr and Istiglal Streets, prices here are often lower than in supermarkets. Even then, it is advisable to go early, preferably before 08:00, for the best selection. It is operated by the Abu Dhabi Municipality and everything is sold by the kilo, so build up an appetite!

Places to Shop

Shopping

Iranian Souk

Location ➜ Nr Al Meena Carpet Market · Al Meena | na
Hours ➜ 08:00 - 23:00
Web/email ➜ na   Map Ref ➜ 7-B4

Barges and dhows arrive every three days from Iran laden with the good, the bad and the garish! Plastic framed pictures and household goods can be found, along with exotic carpets and bedspreads. There is also an attractive range of metalware and unbelievably cheap terracotta urns, assorted glassware and cane work. The goods are laid out under awnings – don't expect air conditioning – and the traders are friendly and ready to offer agreeable prices. Located in the port area, the market is just a couple of minutes' walk from the fish market and dhow wharfage. Bear in mind that photography is not allowed.

Meena Souk

Location ➜ Al Meena Rd · Al Meena | na
Hours ➜ 09:00 - 22:00
Web/email ➜ na   Map Ref ➜ 7-C4

Located on the right side of Meena Road, just before you enter the main port area, it is also known as the Afghan Souk, since it sells a range of 'oriental' carpets. When buying any, however, be aware that most of these are machine made copies of traditional designs with a scattering of better quality handmade items and some tribal handmade carpets. Other than carpets, a reasonable selection of plastic and kitchen goods are also on offer.

Mwaifa Souk

Location ➜ Nr Jebel R/A, Shk Khalfia B Zayed St · Al Mutarad | na
Hours ➜ 10:00 - 22:00
Web/email ➜ na   Map Ref ➜ 14-D3

This modern, purpose-built souk houses a variety of shops, including a branch of Choithrams, Shoe Mart, a bakery, butcher, baby shop and a toy shop, all placed in a long central strip. It even boasts a small snooker outlet. However, if the choice seems somewhat limiting, the souk faces a busy dual carriageway with additional souk buildings on the other side. Over there, you can find a variety of outlets, including tailors and a branch of the Body Shop.

Shopping Malls – Contact Information		
Mall Name	**Tel**	**Map Ref**
Abela Superstore	667 4675	9-C1
Abu Dhabi Co-operative Society Complex	644 0808	4-B4
Abu Dhabi Mall	645 4858	4-B4
Al Ahlia Prisunic	681 2997	9-D1
Al Falah Plaza	642 5800	5-A3
Al Hana Shopping Centre	681 6823	9-E2
Al Hosn Plaza	667 5555	9-C1
Al Jernain Center	na	9-B1
Al Muhairy Centre	632 2228	8-E1
City Centre	627 7770	8-C2
Dana Plaza	665 1333	9-C1
Fotouh Al Khair Centre	621 1133	8-E1
Hamdan Centre	na	8-C2
Khalifa Centre	na	4-B4
Lamcy Department Store	681 4500	9-D1
Liwa Centre	632 0344	8-D2
Lulu Centre	677 9786	8-A2
Madinat Zayed Shopping & Gold Centre	631 8555	5-A4
Marina Mall	681 8300	10-B4
Mina Centre	673 4848	7-B4
MultiBrand	621 9700	8-B2
Rotana Mall	na	9-D1
Al Ain Mall	03 766 0333	15-C3
Al Falah Plaza	03 766 2200	15-B3
Al Jimi Shopping Centre	03 763 1185	12-E3

The Leading Annual Lifestyle Guidebook to Dubai

Comprehensive, fun and easy to use, this book covers everything worth knowing about Dubai and where to do it. Meticulously updated annually, this is the most in-depth, practical and accurate coverage around. This insiders' guide to what's hot and what's not is ideal for residents, short term visitors, business people and tourists, and is an essential resource for anyone exploring this vibrant and surprising city.

- General information & UAE overview
- Resident tips & advice
- New, informative business section
- 450 independent restaurant, bar & cafe reviews
- Exploring – museums, heritage, parks & beaches
- Shopping – what to buy & where to buy it
- Activities – sports, leisure, clubs & kids
- 30 fully referenced photographic maps + a pull out city map

Available from leading bookstores, hotels, supermarkets or directly from Explorer Publishing

Explorer Publishing & Distribution • Dubai Media City • Building 2 • Office 502 • PO Box 34275 • Dubai • UAE
Phone (+971 4) 391 8060 Fax (+971 4) 391 8062 Email info@Explorer-Publishing.com Web www.Explorer-Publishing.com

EXPLORER
www.Explorer-Publishing.com

Insiders' City Guides • Photography Books • Activity Guidebooks • Commissioned Publications • Distribution

Offering Only
The Most Fertile Trips

Sunshine Tours presents intriguing
desert adventures. Experience a
romantic safari under the stars with
a traditional Arabic feast, belly
dancing and camel riding. Or try an
overnight safari. Go sand-skiing. Try
wadi-bashing. Along the way, see
beautiful mountains and landscape,
swim in fresh water pools and find
a spot in the oasis for lunch. Meet
Bedouin tribesmen or explorer the
Liwa dunes, one of the largest sand
deserts in the world. Take your pick.
Whether you prefer sandy gravel
tracks, dried up riverbeds or lush green
oasis, this is one desert storm that
shouldn't be missed.

Sunshine Tours
Feel the Pulse of the Emirates
A DIVISION OF THE ABU DHABI NATIONAL HOTELS

To book your tour, call us on 971 2 444 9914.
Tours can also be booked via the Sunshine Tours
representative at your hotel.
Website: www.adnh.com

Activities

EXPLORER

Activities

ACTIVITIES

Other options ➜ Exploring [p.100]
Going Out [p.234]

It might not seem readily apparent, but life in Abu Dhabi is not all shopping malls, restaurants, and 5 star hotels. No matter what season, visitors and residents alike will discover a variety of engaging activities to fulfil almost any interest or hobby. Warm winters provide the perfect environment for a variety of outdoor activities, while a host of diversions are available to take your mind off the extreme heat and humidity of the summer. From ice skating to pottery lessons or dance classes, the fun doesn't have to stop when the tarmac starts melting! However, it's surprising what can actually be done in the heat of the summer, and even in the hottest months you can find dedicated enthusiasts sailing or playing golf when it's 48° C!

Land access is far less of a problem than in many expats' home countries, so it can be easy travelling into the wilderness of the mountains or onto remote beaches. Between Abu Dhabi and Jebel Ali Hotel, however, it is illegal to do certain activities on the beaches, such as 4 wheel driving, horse riding, fishing or water sports. This may not seem to be rigorously enforced in the quieter areas, but is still against the law if you're caught.

Sometimes word of mouth is the best way to learn about your favourite hobby so, if it's not listed here, ask around and you may well find that trainspotting really does go on.

As usual, we welcome your suggestions as to what to include or change in the book next year. If you belong to any club, organisation, or group; however, small, large, official or unofficial — we'd like to hear from you. Log on to our Website (*www.explorer-publishing.com*) and send us your comments and details via the *Reader Profile Survey*.

SPORTS

The warm winters in the Emirates provide the perfect environment for athletes and outdoor enthusiasts, making it hard to imagine that there is a sport or activity that isn't being practised at some point in the year.

Traditional favourites such as tennis, golf (on beautifully manicured courses), aerobics, rugby, cricket and hashing abound, but there are also more radical pursuits such as skydiving, rock climbing, mountain biking and caving.

With the proximity of the warm Gulf waters, it is no surprise that a variety of water sports are available. Scuba diving is probably the most popular, while less organised but still prevalent ways to have fun getting wet include sailing, surfing, water skiing, and a rising interest in the unconventional sport of kiteboarding.

Bear in mind that while the Gulf waters often seem tranquil and harmless, there are dangers such as stingrays and jellyfish. Strong currents and riptides can also be a hazard for the unwary. At beach parks, pay attention to the lifeguard's flag (if it's red, stay on the beach!), and if you're at one of the unguarded public beaches take greater care.

One of the most popular pastimes is getting out into the wilderness. As you spend more time in the area, and the weather cools, you too will feel the lure of the desert, the dramatic wadis and the uncompromising mountains. If you enjoy camping, hiking, wadi and dune bashing, or any combination of these, we suggest you check out the *Off-Road Explorer (UAE)* published by Explorer Publishing. Included in the guide are stunning photographs and detailed satellite imagery of many routes and hikes – ideal for discovering the best of the UAE's scenery. Apart from the detailed maps, the handy guide also has GPS co-ordinates, photos and information on flora and fauna, and 20 off-road routes to explore. It really is the UAE's definitive outdoor guide!

As you read on, under each sport the entries for the different cities have been listed separately for further clarity, with Abu Dhabi first followed by Al Ain.

For information on where to buy sports equipment, refer to Sporting Goods [p.153].

Aerobics

Other options → Dance Classes [p.215]
Health Clubs [p.207]

The Abu Dhabi aerobic scene is a paradise for everyone obsessed with throwing their legs and arms around or pumping some heavy weights to funky music. Seriously, you will have a good choice of classes. Check with your desired club for timetables and bookings, as they can get crowded. You can either join one of the health clubs, buy a voucher for ten aerobic sessions for about Dhs.200, or turn up as and when you want. Prices per class are between Dhs.20 - 30.

Archery

There are currently no archery clubs in the Abu Dhabi emirate. However, enthusiasts may wish to visit the small and informal Dubai Archery Group in Dubai (04 344 2591), or the Shooting Club in Ras Al Khaimah (07 236 3622). For more information, consult the Sports section of the *Dubai Explorer*.

Hatta Fort Hotel	
Location → Hatta Fort Hotel · Hatta	04 852 3211
Hours → Timings on request	
Web/email → www.dutcohotels.com	Map Ref → UAE-D3

The Hatta Fort Hotel's archery range is 25 metres long and has eight standard target stands. The recurve bow, which is curved forward at the ends and straightens out when the bow is drawn, is suitable for adults and children over the age of ten years. Archery fans can enter the hotel's annual archery competition and the Dubai Archery Club holds its annual archery tournament here.

Hotel residents can try archery for a nominal fee of Dhs.10, while visitors are charged Dhs.30 for 30 minutes. Professional assistance is available for this surprisingly challenging sport.

Sports

Activities

Badminton

Other options ➔ Sporting Goods [p.153]

Badminton Club

Location ➔ Club, The · Al Meena | 673 1111
Hours ➔ Sat - Wed 19:15
Web/email ➔ www.the-club.com   Map Ref ➔ 7-A2

This small section within The Club has two social evenings a week, lasting until late. In the past, they've played league matches against opposing teams in Abu Dhabi, although this is only possible when the quality and numbers of players permit. Note that to join the Badminton Club, membership of The Club is first required – contact them for further details. They welcome players of any standard, so turn up and join in.

Basketball

Other options ➔ Sporting Goods [p.153]

Al Ain Men's College

Location ➔ Al Ain Men's College · Al Ain | 03 782 0888
Hours ➔ Timings on request
Web/email ➔ na   Map Ref ➔ 17-B2

A variety of sporting and adventurous outdoor activities are offered here, but mainly for college members. The inaugural AAMC basketball tournament got off to a successful start in 2003; teams wishing to play in next year's tournament should contact the college for further details. David Jens, the Physical Education Director, can be contacted for information on local basketball, soccer and volleyball teams, either for arranging fixtures or information on joining a team.

Bowling

Abu Dhabi Tourist Club

Location ➔ Nr Le Meridien Htl · Tourist Club Area | 672 3400
Hours ➔ 08:00 - 24:00
Web/email ➔ adclub@emirates.net.ae   Map Ref ➔ 7-D1

Located in the grounds of the Tourist Club, the bowling alley is in a separate building to the main facilities, on the left as you approach along the main walkway. This is a 12 lane centre and is popular with Nationals and expats alike, especially in the evenings and also in the summer months when the heat drives everyone indoors. The layout is simple, with no frills, although soft drinks and snacks are available.

Costs: *Dhs.7 for one game; Dhs.3 for shoe rental. Take your own socks, or buy them for Dhs.4.*

Khalifa International Bowling Centre

Location ➔ Nr Zayed Sports Complex · Abu Dhabi | 403 4648
Hours ➔ 12:00 - 24:00 Thu 10:00 - 24:00 Fri 14:00 - 24:00
Web/email ➔ na   Map Ref ➔ 2-B1

This state-of-the-art bowling centre boasts 40 lanes and is apparently one of the most modern bowling alleys in the world. The fee for playing one game is Dhs.7, shoe hire is Dhs.2 and the billiard table costs Dhs.15 for one hour.

Camping

Other options ➔ Outdoor Goods [p.151]
Tours & Sightseeing [p.115]
Weekend Breaks [p.129]

With the weather rarely anything other than sunny coupled with spectacular locations in various parts of the country, the UAE is a great place for camping. For most people, the best time to go is between October and April, as in the summer it can get unbearably hot sleeping outside. Choose between the peace and stillness of the desert or camp among the wadis and mountains, next to trickling streams in picturesque oases. Good campsites can be found only short distances from tarmac roads, so a 4 WD is not necessarily required.

In general, very little rain and warm temperatures mean you can camp with much less equipment and preparation than in other countries. This can be the perfect introduction for first timers or families with children of any age, although a certain amount of care is needed to avoid the occasional bug.

Note Although the UAE has a low rainfall, care should be taken in and near wadis during the winter months for flash floods (remember it may be raining in the mountains miles from where you are and when it rains, boy, does it rain!).

For most people a basic amount of equipment will suffice. This may include:

- Tent (to avoid creepy crawlies/rare rain shower)
- Lightweight sleeping bag (or light blankets and sheets)

Sports

Activities

- Thin mattress (or air bed)
- Torches and spare batteries (a head torch is a useful investment)
- Cool box (to avoid food spoiling/away from insects)
- Water (always take too much)
- Food and drink
- Camping stove, firewood or BBQ and charcoal (if preferred)
- Matches!
- Insect repellent and antihistamine cream
- First aid kit (including any personal medication)
- Sun protection (hats, sunglasses, sunscreen, long sleeves)
- Jumper/warm clothing for cooler evenings
- Spade
- Toilet rolls
- Rubbish bags (ensure you leave nothing behind)
- Navigation equipment (maps, compass, Global Positioning System (GPS))

For the adventurous with a 4 WD, there are endless possibilities for camping in remote locations among some of the best scenery in the UAE. The many locations in the Hajar Mountains (in the north near Ras Al Khaimah or east and south near Hatta or Al Ain), and the huge sand dunes of Liwa in the south provide very different areas, each requiring some serious off-road driving to reach, but offering the real wilderness camping experience.

For more information on places to visit, refer to the *Off-Road Explorer (UAE)*.

Canoeing

Other options → Tour Operators [p.115]
Outdoor Goods [p.151]
Kayaking [p.188]

For those interested in getting up close to the marine and bird life of the UAE, or for a slightly different sport that provides access to hidden places, canoeing is an enjoyable and revealing activity.

Areas for good canoeing include Khor Kalba Nature Reserve, the coastal lagoons of Umm Al Quwain, between the new and old towns of Ras Al Khaimah, north of Ras Al Khaimah before Ramsis and through the mangrove covered islands off the north coast of Abu Dhabi. Many of these areas are on their way to becoming protected reserves, so treat them with respect. Some adventurous kayakers occasionally visit the Mussandam in sea touring canoes. Here it is possible to visit secluded bays and view the spectacular rocky coastline, with its fjord like inlets and towering 1,000 metre cliffs.

For further information, refer to the *Off-Road Explorer (UAE)* and the Hatta to Kalba route.

See also: *Khor Kalba [p.127]*.

Al Jazira Hotel and Resort

Location → Btn Abu Dhabi & Dubai · Ghantoot Area | 562 9100
Hours → Timings on request
Web/email → na   Map Ref → na

Located halfway between Abu Dhabi and Dubai, the water sports facilities at Al Jazira Hotel and Resort rarely get too crowded. A small number of one and two man canoes are available and these are ideal for beginners. Anyone from youngsters up (as long as they're big enough to hold the paddles) can try this sport, either for 30 minutes (Dhs.30) or for an hour (Dhs.60). The resort provides life jackets, paddles and basic instruction.

Since this activity is offered by the leisure club, there's a day entry fee Dhs.50 for an adult and Dhs.30 for children, unless you are a club member, a guest of a member or resident of the hotel.

Desert Rangers

Location → Shk Zayed Rd · Dubai | 04 3402408
Hours → 09:00 - 18:00 Closed Fri (office)
Web/email → www.desertrangers.com   Map Ref → UAE-C2

Desert Rangers offers trips through the mangroves of the unique nature reserve at Khor Kalba on the East Coast in 2 - 3 seat Canadian canoes. Initial instruction is followed by hands on practice to develop skills and confidence, then paddle through the mangrove lagoon and experience the unique scenery and abundant wildlife found nowhere else in the UAE. Enjoy the tranquillity and beauty; all you can hear is the lap of the water and the clicking of crabs' claws.

A guide accompanies you and the cost per person is Dhs.300. Only a basic level of fitness is needed and it is suitable for all ages.

Palm Beach Leisure Club

Location → Al Diar Gulf Htl · Al Maqtaa | 441 4777
Hours → na
Web/email → www.aldiarhotels.com   Map Ref → 1-D3

A small number of open canoes are available for hire for paddling around the calm waters off the

Sports

Activities

club's beach. Suitable for children and adults alike, this activity is offered by the leisure club. So unless you are a club member, a guest of a member or resident of the hotel, you will have to pay the day entry charge . Canoes are available from 09:00 to sunset.

Costs: *Dhs.40 for 60 minutes; Dhs.20 for 30 minutes.*

Canoeing in Khor Kalba

Caving

Other options → Out of the City [p.122]

The caving network in the Hajar Mountains is extensive and much of it has still to be explored and mapped. As in any region, caving varies from the fairly safe to the extremely dangerous. Even with an experienced leader, it's not for the casual tourist or the poorly equipped.

Some of the best caves are near Al Ain, the Jebel Hafeet area and in the Hajar Mountains just past Buraimi, near the Omani border. The underground passages and caves have spectacular displays of curtains, stalagmites and stalactites, as well as pretty gypsum flowers and wool sparkling – all unimaginably fragile, so don't touch! Unfortunately, there are no companies offering guided tours; caving is limited to unofficial groups of dedicated cavers who plumb the depths on a regular basis.

The Hajar Mountain range continues into the Sultanate of Oman, where it is even higher and more impressive. In Oman the range includes what is believed to be the second largest cave system in the world, as well as *Majlis Al Jinn Cave*,

the second largest known chamber in the world. However, entering isn't for the fainthearted since it starts with a 160 metre free abseil from the entrance in the roof!

It is important to understand the dangers of going underground and the precautions that must be taken. Take at least two torches each and enough spare batteries and bulbs – someone will always drop a torch or one may fail. Other equipment includes: a couple of litres of water (at least), a hard hat and long sleeved overall to protect you from sharp rocks or knee and elbow pads, basic first aid kit and twine to mark less obvious parts of the route (remember to take it, and any other rubbish, with you when you leave). In addition, never wander off alone and don't break any of the rock formations to take away as souvenirs.

Check the weather forecast or the local meteorological office to find out about recent rainfalls. Flash floods occur regularly at certain times of the year.

Warning: *No mountain rescue services exist, therefore anyone venturing into the mountains should be reasonably experienced or with someone who knows the area. Tell someone who is not going with you where you are going and when you will be back. Tragedies have occurred in the past.*

Climbing

Other options → Health Clubs [p.207]
Out of the City [p.122]
Mountaineering [p.192]
Hiking [p.184]

Despite the shattered appearance of most of the mountains in the UAE, there is excellent rock climbing in a number of locations, particularly in Ras Al Khaimah, Dibba and Hatta. In addition there are some really good crags around Al Ain/Buraimi and the area near the border with Oman including the infamous 'Wonderwall'. By choosing venues carefully, it's possible to climb all year round – even in midsummer with daytime air temperatures approaching 50°C.

The earliest recorded rock climbs were made in the southeast near Al Ain/Buraimi in the late 1970's and, apart from some climbing in the Ras Al Khaimah area, little seems to have been recorded until the mid 1990's. Since then, a small but active group of climbers has been pioneering new routes and discovering a number of major new climbing areas (a guidebook is currently under preparation).

To date more than 200 routes have been climbed and named. These vary from short outcrop routes

Sports

Activities

to difficult and sustained mountain routes of alpine proportions, which have more than their share of loose rock. New routes are generally climbed 'on sight', with traditional protection.

At the top...

Most routes are in the higher grades – ranging from (British) Very Severe, up to extreme grades (E5). Due to the nature of the rock, some climbs can feel more difficult than their technical grade would suggest. However, there are some excellent easier routes for new climbers, especially in Wadi Bih and Wadi Kham Shamsi. Many routes, even in the easier grades, are serious propositions with loose rock, poor belays and difficult descents, often by abseil, making them unsuitable for total novices.

Sports climbing is starting to appear, with some areas being bolted where protection would otherwise be impossible. Some of the hardest routes in the country are currently being developed by serious climbers from Abu Dhabi and Dubai.

For further information on climbs around Buraimi and in the Hajar Mountains in Oman refer to the guidebook Rock Climbing in Oman by RA McDonald (Apex Publishing 1993, London/Oman). Despite being several years old, it gives a comprehensive overview of the most frequented climbing sites and provides plenty of practical information. Few new routes have been opened or documented since the book was published.

Pyramids	
Location ➜ Wafi City · Umm Hurair · Dubai	04 324 0000
Hours ➜ Timings on request	
Web/email ➜ www.pyramidsdubai.com	Map Ref ➜ UAE-C2

This indoor rock climbing wall is currently the only one in the Emirates and is definitely worth a visit. Some climbers make the trip from Abu Dhabi just to climb here, especially in the summer when it's too hot outside. There's a varied set of walls for climbing routes and bouldering, along with a safety mat covering the base of the wall. Qualified instructors are available several times a week to provide lessons for enthusiasts of all ages and fitness levels.

For more information, consult the Sports section of the *Dubai Explorer*.

Crab Hunting

Lama Desert Tours	
Location ➜ Al Khaleej Rd · Deira · Dubai	04 273 2240
Hours ➜ Timings on request	
Web/email ➜ na	Map Ref ➜ UAE-C2

This is a more unusual tour of the Emirates. Leaving from Dubai at 16:00 by coach, you head to Umm Al Quwain where you are offered a light dinner before heading out by boat to hunt crabs. This is followed by a BBQ buffet dinner, where your catch of the day is served boiled or grilled, then at 23:00 you head back to Dubai. A minimum of six people is required for the tour to go ahead and the charge per person is Dhs.220. For further information, call the above number, 04 273 1007 or 050 453 3168.

Cricket

Other options ➜ Sporting Goods [p.153]
UAE Annual Events [p.42]

With the large numbers of enthusiastic fans from all over the world, especially from India, Pakistan and Sri Lanka, cricket seems to lead even football as the most popular sport in Abu Dhabi! Car parks, rough land and grassy parks all sprout stumps at weekends and evenings, when a mix of ages come out to play. Many organisations field their own cricket teams for inter-company competitions and it's also very popular in schools. Coaching is available.

Sports

Activities

Major international matches are held regularly in the Emirates, especially at the ground in Sharjah, where it's possible to see some of the world's best teams and to get the chance to cheer your own side on.

Abu Dhabi Cricket Council	
Location → Salam Street · Abu Dhabi	645 9790
Hours → 08:00 - 13:30 19:00 - 22:00 Closed Fri	
Web/email → na	Map Ref → 4-C4

Affiliated to the Emirates Cricket Board, the council was set up in 1988 to promote and run cricket affairs in the emirate. It organises various inter-company matches, 7 aside games and annual competitions throughout the year, including the annual Abu Dhabi Duty Free Tournament, which has been running for over ten years. There are currently 45 local clubs registered, with over 1,000 players of all nationalities. If you want to play cricket, the council should be able to put you in contact with a suitable club.

The council is currently building a new international stadium next to Abu Dhabi Golf Club on Channel Street. Completion is due by summer 2003.

Al Ain Cricket Association	
Location → Nr Al Ain Hilton · Al Khatem St	050 623 1590
Hours → Timings on request	
Web/email → atansari@emirates.net.ae	Map Ref → 15-D4

Al Ain Cricket Association (ACA) is the oldest cricketing body in the UAE and has been running cricket affairs in Al Ain since April 1989. Until last year, the association had five grounds, but recent plans to beautify Al Ain have deprived them of two (although space has been allocated for at least nine new grounds). The season starts in September with the ACA Winter League, followed by the Jinnah Cup and Nehru Cup, and ends with the Summer League in May.

Currently there are sixteen teams (both seniors and juniors) and the association has over 300 resident players from all nationalities. Coaching is available.

Contact: *Dr Ahmad Tariq Ansari (050 623 1590).*

Cycling

Other options → Mountain Biking [p.191]
Sporting Goods [p.153]
Out of the City [p.122]

Abu Dhabi, and the Emirates in general, are not the most bike friendly of places, but there are plenty of areas to ride, and exploring where you can go and what there is to see is a great way to get to know the city.

There are quieter areas with fewer cars and some roads have wide footpaths providing traffic free routes for biking around town. However, riding in traffic requires a lot of care and attention, as in any country, but more so in the Middle East. Drivers vastly underestimate the speed cyclists are capable of and don't allow enough room, or time for them – be especially careful at junctions and roundabouts. Although helmets are not legally required, serious consideration should be given to wearing one.

Outside the city, the roads are fairly flat and boring until you near the mountains. Jebel Hafeet near Al Ain, the Hatta area of the Hajar Mountains and the central area in the mountains near Masafi down to the coast at either Fujairah or Dibba offer interesting paved roads with better views. The new road from Hatta through the mountains to Kalba on the East Coast is probably one of the most scenic routes in the country.

Clubs and groups of cyclists generally ride on weekends, early mornings and evenings when the roads are slightly quieter.

Desert Driving Courses

Other options → Wadi & Dune Bashing [p.200]

For those who would like to master the art of manoeuvring a 4 wheel drive vehicle over rolling sand dunes, several organisations offer a full day course accompanied by professional drivers. Both individual and group tuition per vehicle is available. Picnic lunch and soft drinks may be included. Participants are expected to bring their own 4 wheel drive, alternatively you can hire a vehicle at an additional cost. Expect to pay around Dhs.200 - 300 for the day, depending on the programme.

Learning what not to do...

Desert Rangers

Location ➔ Shk Zayed Rd · Dubai | 04 340 2408
Hours ➔ 09:00 - 18:00 Closed Fri (office)
Web/email ➔ www.desertrangers.com   Map Ref ➔ UAE-C2

Desert Rangers in Dubai offer lessons for anyone wanting to learn how to handle a car in the desert. If you are just starting, introductory days teach you the basics of venturing off-road, including how to negotiate easy dunes, how to avoid getting stuck and how to get out when you do! Advanced days involve guided drives to more challenging areas of the desert where you can learn how to get yourself out of bigger trouble.

Courses are available for individuals or groups and since programmes are flexible, they can be combined with barbecues and other activities to make your ideal day.

Jeep UAE Off-Road Driving Academy

Location ➔Various locations | 04 268 5758
Hours ➔ Timings on request
Web/email ➔ na   Map Ref ➔ na

Jeep owners wanting to discover the do anything, go anywhere nature of their vehicle can take a specialised full day driving course. Although aimed at novice desert drivers, it can serve as a valuable refresher course for those who have driven off-road previously.

You'll learn the full range of your Jeep's capabilities in a controlled desert environment. The course

consists of four modules: know your vehicle, 4x4 systems and selection, deflation; ascent, descent and approach angles, speed and gear selection, stopping in sand; vehicle recovery and towing, use of low ratio gears, digging out your vehicle; and orientation, convoy driving, rules for sand driving. Courses are not available during the summer.

Cost: *Dhs.280 for you and a friend, but strictly for Jeeps and their owners. New Jeep customers are offered this course free.*

Sunshine Tours

Location ➔ Abu Dhabi National Htls Co. · Airport Rd | 444 9914
Hours ➔ Timings on request
Web/email ➔ adnh.com   Map Ref ➔ 2-B2

Dune driving courses, either using a 4 wheel drive or sand buggies, are organised by Sunshine Tours. Courses are available for a half or full day, for beginners or the more advanced, and are conducted by experienced instructors. The beginners' course includes soft drinks, while on the advanced course there's a barbecue dinner provided in the desert.

The company also arranges water sports activities, island trips and wadi bashing. For further information, contact Mr Kazem.

Diving

Other options ➔ Snorkelling [p.197]

The waters around the UAE are rich in a variety of marine and coral life that make diving here a fascinating sport and paradise for water babes. It's possible to dive all year round in the warm seas and the waters are relatively undisturbed and unpolluted. As well as exotic fish, such as clownfish and seahorses, it's possible to see spotted eagle rays, moray eels, small sharks, barracuda, stingrays, sea turtles, and much more.

Experienced divers, intermediates and people wishing to learn how to dive are well catered for by a plethora of companies in the UAE. These offer all levels of courses, starting from an introductory dive to instructor level and technical diving, under the different international training organisations, such as CMAS, PADI, NAUI, IANTD, HAS etc.

The UAE is fortunate to have two coastlines; to the west, covering Abu Dhabi, Dubai, Sharjah etc, and on the East Coast, covering Fujairah, Khorfakkan and Dibba. Most of the wrecks are on the western

Sports

Activities

coast, while the beautiful flora and fauna of coral reefs can be seen to the east.

Many good dive sites are easily accessible from Abu Dhabi, including wreck or deep water dives, reef dives and shallower dives for the less experienced. Destinations include Coral Garden and Cement Barge for shallow dives (up to 8 metres). While deeper dives (18 metres plus) for the more experienced are at Hannan, MS Jazim and MS Lion City. On most dives you can see a variety of marine life and corals, occasionally turtles and even sharks. The 18 year old Breakwater should make a good training dive, once the Corniche extension is completed. Visibility ranges from 10 - 25 metres.

In addition, most scuba schools organise trips to the area north of the UAE, known as the Mussandam, which is an enclave of the Sultanate of Oman. Often described as the 'Norway of the Middle East', it offers some of the most spectacular and virgin dive sites in the region. Here sheer wall dives with strong currents and clear waters make it a thrilling experience for advanced divers, while the huge bays, calm waters and shallow reefs offer easier dives for the less experienced. Visibility ranges from 10 - 35 metres. Note that you are not allowed to take your own tanks across the border, but must rent from one of the dive centres there.

Alternatively, from Dibba on the East Coast, fast boats take divers up the coast for 5 - 75 km. The cost, for what is normally a two dive trip, ranges between Dhs.150 - 500. During the winter, whale sharks are sometimes sighted and dolphins normally ride the bow waves of boats.

Diving

For further information on diving in the UAE and the Mussandam, refer to the *Underwater Explorer (UAE)*. For more general information on Dubai and the Sultanate of Oman refer to the *Dubai Explorer* published by Explorer Publishing.

See also: *The Mussandam – Sultanate of Oman [p.128].*

7 Seas Divers	
Location → Nr Khorfakkan Souk · Khorfakkan	09 238 7400
Hours → 08:00 - 20:00	
Web/email → www.7seasdivers.com	Map Ref → UAE-E2

This PADI (Professional Association of Diving Instructor) 5 star IDC dive centre offers daily day and night diving trips to a variety of sites in Khorfakkan, Lima Rock and to the Mussandam in Oman. Training is given from beginner to instructor level and lessons can be given in Arabic, English, French, German or Russian. Facilities include four boats and the centre also arranges equipment sale, rental and servicing from their base close to Mashreq Bank and the Khorfakkan Souk.

The company can arrange accommodation, transport and visas for visitors to the UAE. They have an office at the Oceanic Hotel, as well as in Khorfakkan.

Abu Dhabi Sub Aqua Club	
Location → Al Meena Zayed · Abu Dhabi	673 1111
Hours → Timings on request	
Web/email → www.adsac.co.ae	Map Ref → 7-A2

Formed in 1975, this lively club has around 100 members, including about 20 who are instructor standard. The club is an official overseas branch of the British Sub Aqua Club (BSAC), so safety standards are high, and a range of training courses are regularly held for all standards of diver. Dives are on Thursdays and Fridays and trips aren't only local, but also to Dubai, Sharjah, the East Coast and the Mussandam. The club has two boats based in Abu Dhabi and one near Khorfakkan, where they rent a villa.

On the social side, the club meets every Monday evening at The Club. Note that to join the Sub Aqua Club, membership of The Club is first required. For further information please call The Club.

Sports

Activities

Al Jazira Diving Centre

Location ➜ Al Diar Jazira · Abu Dhabi |562 9100
Hours ➜ 09:00 - 18:00
Web/email ➜ na   Map Ref ➜ UAE-B3

Located halfway between Abu Dhabi and Dubai, this dive centre is under German management and teaching is according to the International Standards of Recreational Diving SS and CMA. On offer are a variety of programmes – from discovery to advanced courses, such as night diving. The open watercourse leads to a licence allowing you to scuba dive anywhere in the world, and they also offer a bubble maker course for kids aged 8 - 12 years.

For more information, contact Irmgard Mackenbrock, Recreation Manager (050 476 3436) or simply drop in and blow some bubbles with Irmgard and her crew.

Blue Dolphin Company LLC

Location ➜ Htl Inter-Continental · Bainuna St |666 9392
Hours ➜ 08:00 - 19:00
Web/email ➜ www.interconti.com   Map Ref ➜ 10-C1

This company offers a range of PADI dive training, from 'open water' and 'advanced open water diver' to 'rescue diver' and 'divemaster'. They also have a number of specialities such as 'wreck diver' and 'night diver'. Their 'discover scuba' involves an hour in the classroom and swimming pool and is a basic introduction to scuba diving, alternatively their slightly more advanced 'discover local diving' takes half a day and includes a session in the sea. Certified divers can take full day dive trips on Thursdays and Fridays. Classes can be given in Arabic, French or English and all equipment is provided.

Prices: *Range from Dhs.100 for 'discover diver' in the pool, to Dhs.1,000 for 'rescue diver' and Dhs.2,000 for 'divemaster'.*

Emirates Diving Association

Location ➜ Heritage & Diving Village |04 393 9390
Hours ➜ Sat - Wed 08:30-13:00 17:00-21:00
Web/email ➜ www.emiratesdiving.com   Map Ref ➜ UAE-C2

The main aim of this group is to conserve, protect and restore the UAE's marine resources by understanding and promoting the marine environment and environmental diving. They do this in a variety of ways including promoting research on the marine environment and by holding the annual 'clean up dive' and 'beach clean up' campaigns. In the future, Emirates Diving Association hopes to establish a marine park using the artificial reefs technique, which tries to create coral reefs, as well as having monitoring stations for research purposes. Contact them for more information on diving in the UAE.

Golden Boats

Location ➜ Nr Central Bank Bld · Al Bateen |666 9119
Hours ➜ Timings on request
Web/email ➜ golbomat@emirates.net.ae   Map Ref ➜ 10-C1

Golden Boats offer diving trips for certified divers and scuba courses for the beginners with a qualified instructor. Courses are run at flexible times and are available for adults and children aged between 8 - 12 years.

It takes about ten minutes by boat from Abu Dhabi to reach the island. A variety of water sports are offered, including fishing, water skiing and wind surfing, banana ski and paddleboats, and dhow island cruises for groups of minimum 20 people.

Activities are available at four centres: Le Meridien Abu Dhabi, Khalidia Palace Hotel, Raha Beach Centre and Marine Sports Club Centre.

Thurs 20:00 - 01:00, Arabic theme Night Party for Dhs.150.

Fri 10:00 - 17:30, Family Day, Dhs.100 (adults) & Dhs.50 (kids between 6 - 12 years).

Sandy Beach Dive Centre

Location ➜ Next to Sandy Beach Htl · Fujairah |09 244 5050
Hours ➜ 08:00 - 18:00
Web/email ➜ www.sandybm.com   Map Ref ➜ UAE-E2

This dive centre is now managed by the Sandy Beach Hotel and offers a qualified and dynamic team of dive instructors and support staff. It's open all year round for diving, accommodation and a retail outlet that stocks the latest diving gear (products from Scubapro, Ikelite and Uwatec, to name a few).

Their famous house reef, Snoopy Island, is alive with hard corals and marine life and is excellent for both snorkelling and scuba diving. The more adventurous can take a trip on one of the dive boats that depart daily to sites around Fujairah and Khorfakkan. Trips to the Mussandam (Oman) offer fascinating dives for the more experienced.

Sports

Activities

Boat timings: *09:30, 12:00, 02:30.*

Location: *Al Aqqah, Fujairah – halfway between Dibba and Khorfakkan.*

Scuba 2000

Location ➜ Al Badiyah Beach · Fujairah	**09 238 8477**
Hours ➜ 09:00 - 19:00	
Web/email ➜ www.scuba2000uae.com	Map Ref ➜ UAE-E2

This East Coast dive centre is open all year and provides daily trips to dive sites on both the Dibba and Khorfakkan sides. All sites are easily accessible by boat from the centre; in particular, Snoopy and Sharque islands provide excellent diving and snorkelling, with an abundance of colourful fish, coral, turtles and barracuda.

The standard courses are available for everyone from beginners to advanced divers. The centre has one fully qualified PADI instructor and an experienced diver is on hand if a buddy is needed. The resort has a large, secluded beach nestling among palm groves, and also hires out jet skis, canoes and pedal boats.

Costs: *Range from Dhs.250 for discover scuba; Dhs.1,500 for open water; Dhs.800 for advanced.*

Location: *On the beach halfway between Dibba and Khorfakkan. After Al Badidya Mosque on your left, turn right and follow the signs.*

Scuba International

Location ➜ Fujairah Int Marine Club · Fujairah	**09 222 0060**
Hours ➜ 10:00 - 19:00	
Web/email ➜ www.scubainternational.net	Map Ref ➜ UAE-E2

The first diving college in Arabia, Scuba International offers facilities for both divers and non divers, from recreational dive charters and diver training (PADI, DSAT and TDI), to RYA sanctioned boat handling courses, chamber operating courses, instructor courses or water sports and dive vacation bookings. Two wrecks provide the ideal opportunity for first time and experienced divers. The 'discover scuba' dive costs Dhs.250.

The college is purpose built to cater to divers' needs, and offers accommodation nearby in Fujairah's hotels with a pool, beach, restaurant and bar; an onsite pool will be completed by December 2003. It operates a recompression chamber with on call chamber staff that is able to treat any diving emergency 24 hours a day.

Sharjah Dive Club

Location ➜ Shj Wanderers · Sharjah	**050 636 6802**
Hours ➜ na	
Web/email ➜ www.sharjahwanderers.com	Map Ref ➜ UAE-C2

Sharjah Dive Club is a main member section of the Sharjah Wanderers Sports Club (SWSC). So, in addition to an energetic and friendly diving club, members get the benefit of the sports and social activities of SWSC.

The diving club is a full member of the British Sub Aqua Club (BSAC branch number 406), and follows its training, certification and diving practices. The clubhouse facilities include a training room, social area, equipment room, compressors, dive gear for hire, two dive boats and on site pool facilities. Club night is every Tuesday from 20:30 until late, with diving every Thursday and Friday, weather permitting.

Sirenia

Location ➜ Tourist Club Area	**645 4512**
Hours ➜ Timings on request	
Web/email ➜ veryan@emirates.net.ae	Map Ref ➜ 4-B3

Veryan Pappin is the main PADI master instructor for Sirenia. He has eight years experience of diving in the UAE and will complete dive training from beginner to assistant instructor. Also available are a variety of specialities from 'night diving', 'wreck diving', 'deep diving', 'enriched air', 'naturalist', 'drift diving' and 'search and recovery diving'. He also undertakes underwater photographic surveys, installation inspections and marine environmental impact assessments. For further details, contact Veryan on the above number or 050 6134 583.

Dune Buggy Riding

Exhilarating and fun, dune buggies are not particularly environmentally sound, but are surprisingly addictive.

Every Friday, the area around the 'Big Red' sand dune on the Dubai - Hatta Road is transformed into a circus arena for off-road lovers. Future Motor Sports, along with about four other companies, rent off-road quad bikes and karts, which are available to drive (without a licence) in fenced off areas. Alternatively, if you're in the area on a

Sports

Activities

Friday, hang around to be entertained by the sight of locals driving their Nissan Patrols on two wheels!

Buggy addicts could also contact the tour operators [p.115], since many of them offer the chance to try dune buggies as part of their desert safaris. Remember, if you fall when you go up and over a dune, these things are heavy!

Al Badayer Motorcycles Rental

Location → Hatta Rd · Hatta Rd | 050 636 1787
Hours → 09:00 - 18:00
Web/email → na   Map Ref → UAE-D3

Also called quad bikes, dune buggies are great fun and extremely exhilarating. Al Badayer Motorcycles Rental has buggies that range in power from 50 or 80cc to 250cc – watch out for the 250 if it's your first time! Prices vary from Dhs.80 - 200 per hour. For further details, contact Ahmed Sallam on the above number.

Desert Rangers

Location → Jct 2, Shk Zayed Rd · Dubai | 04 340 2408
Hours → 09:00 - 18:00   Closed Fri (office)
Web/email → www.desertrangers.com   Map Ref → UAE-C2

Having been given a helmet and a brief talk on safety, you are led to the course to familiarise yourself with the dune buggy. Designed and built in the UK, they are safe and lots of fun. There are single and two seat buggies, allowing ten people to be on the course at one time. It's possible to run relays of participants at intervals of 10 - 15 minutes. All activities are closely monitored by experienced Rangers.

A half day dune buggy safari costs Dhs.350 per person and leaves in the morning or afternoon.

Fishing

Other options → Boat & Yacht Charters [p.119]

Fishing has become increasingly popular in recent years, and this is one of the reasons why the Government has introduced regulations to protect the fish stocks off the coast of the UAE. Nevertheless, you can still fish if you have the right papers or by chartering a licensed tour guide.

September through to April is the most productive season, although it's still possible to catch sailfish and queenfish in the summer months. Other commonly caught fish include shari, tuna, kingfish,

dorado or jacks. The more adventurous with cash to spare may consider deep sea fishing or trawling. Alternatively, the truly competitive may like to enter the annual international fishing competition arranged by the Abu Dhabi International Marine Sports Club (02 681 5566).

Al Dhafra

Location → Al Dhafra · Al Meena | 673 2266
Hours → 12:30 - 16:00   19:00 - 24:00
Web/email → www.aldhafra.net   Map Ref → 7-C4

How about a fishing trip with a difference? Al Dhafra has four traditional wooden Arabic dhows, which can be chartered for fishing (if required the company will supply food for an extra cost). Most clients take their own fishing equipment, since there's only a limited amount on board. Prices start at Dhs.150 per hour for hire of the smallest dhow, *Al Tawash*, which takes up to ten people.

Al Jazira Hotel and Resort

Location → Btn Abu Dhabi & Dubai · Ghantoot Area | 562 9100
Hours → Timings on request
Web/email → na   Map Ref → na

Since the waters of the Gulf are full of an interesting variety of marine life, nearly all resorts and hotels provide fishing facilities. Al Jazira is one of the less expensive options, and quieter too, situated between Abu Dhabi and Dubai. Two choices are available: either a half day (4 hours for Dhs.400) or a full day (8 hours, for Dhs.800) fishing trip. Alternatively, rent snorkelling gear for Dhs.50 for a glimpse of the colourful world underwater.

Beach Rotana Hotel & Towers

Location → Nr Gulf Optical Centre · Tourist Club Area | 644 3000
Hours → Timings on request
Web/email → www.rotana.com   Map Ref → 4-B3

The hotel's boat is available for hire for fishing or cruising the Gulf. The driver will suggest different locations depending on the season, but with hundreds of small islands just off the coast, good fishing and scenery is guaranteed.

Bookings should be made 24 hours in advance and a deposit of Dhs.100 is required. Trips, including equipment, cost Dhs.500 (for three hours) for boat hire for a maximum of four people (Dhs.175 per

Sports

Activities

extra hour). Alternatively, try a cruise of the Corniche for Dhs.125 or Dhs.75 per person. Refreshments and snacks can be provided.

Blue Dolphin Company LLC

Location → Htl Inter-Continental · Bainuna St | 666 9392
Hours → 08:00 - 13:00 16:00 - 19:00   Closed Fri
Web/email → www.interconti.com   Map Ref → 10-C1

Experience the thrill of the chase from Blue Dolphin's fully equipped Barracuda boats. Departure is anytime, although early morning (about 6 am) is recommended since the sea is calmer and the fish 'easier' to catch. Instruction is offered for the novice line fisherman – be prepared to catch hammour, shari, barracuda, tuna and sailfish, if you're lucky!

Trawling (when the boat moves slowly through the water with the line trailing behind) is also available. This method of fishing is better for catching medium size and larger fish, but instruction is not offered. The 31 ft motorboats take a maximum of seven people and have shady areas on deck. The company also offers dhow cruises.

Prices: *Dhs.800 for a minimum four hour charter; Dhs.250 on an hourly basis (two hour minimum). Includes water and soft drinks.*

Bounty Charters

Location →Various locations | 04 348 3042
Hours → Timings on request
Web/email → na   Map Ref → na

Bounty Charters is a fully equipped 36 ft Yamaha Sea Spirit game fishing boat captained by Richard Forrester, an experienced game fisherman from South Africa.

Fishing charters can be tailor made to your needs, whether you want a full day trying for the challenging sailfish, or a half day trawling or bottom fishing for the wide variety of fish found in the Gulf. There's also night fishing or charters of 3 - 5 days to the Mussandam Peninsula (book in advance, since planning takes 7 - 10 days). For prices and more details contact Richard on the above number or (050 658 8951).

Le Meridien Abu Dhabi

Location → Le Meridien · Tourist Club Area | 644 6666
Hours → na
Web/email → www.forte.com   Map Ref → 7-D1

At Le Meridien, the choice of what to do is not easy, as more or less everything to do with fishing or cruising is offered. You can fish in the early morning for four hours (Dhs.220 - 275), race among the islands off Abu Dhabi in a speedboat or simply dream away the hours lying on the deck of a traditional dhow. Island camping is also an option for those who enjoy the wilderness; a full day, including snacks and BBQ, costs Dhs.195 per head.

Oceanic Hotel

Location → Beach Rd, Khorfakkan · East Coast | 09 238 5111
Hours → na
Web/email → www.oceanichotel.com   Map Ref → UAE-E2

Round off a trip to the East Coast with a sunset fishing trip. Set off in a speedboat to the local fisherman's favourite fishing spot (apparently a catch is virtually guaranteed). Then watch the sunset as you return to the hotel. The catch can be cooked by the hotel chef who will prepare it according to your taste. All equipment is supplied.

Cost: *Dhs.600 for a maximum of five people from 15:00 - 19:00.*

Palms Resort

Location → Sheraton Abu Dhabi · Corniche Rd East | 677 3333
Hours → 07:30 - 22:30
Web/email → sheraton@emirates.net.ae   Map Ref → 8-A3

Expeditions are run from the resort for deep sea fishing, with definite catches of hammour, shari and barracuda, even for total beginners. Everything is provided, including refreshments and experienced guides to ensure every trip is a success.

Special charters can be arranged on request. Alternatively, join the sunrise fishing trip (06:00 - 09:00) or sunset trip (14:00 - 17:00 and 15:00 - 18:00).

Prices: *Dhs.480 per three hour trip, plus Dhs.100 per hour extra.*

Sports

Activities

Soul of Stars

Location → Le Meridien Mina · Al Sufouh	050 694 2960
Hours → Timings on request	
Web/email → na	Map Ref → UAE-B2

Soul of Stars, a traditional 65 ft clipper, can be hired for deep sea fishing trips for groups of 1 - 25 people. The charge per person is Dhs.250 for four hours or Dhs.300 for six hours, minimum six people (trips include soft drinks and light snacks).

Every Thursday at 18:00 the boat departs for a two night fishing/sailing trip to the Mussandam, returning on Saturday morning at 07:00 (price Dhs.1,700 per person, full board, including Omani permit). The boat can also be hired for private parties for up to 35 people, and during the week there are two hour morning and sunset cruises (Dhs.175 per person, including unlimited soft drinks and snacks). Skipper and crew are provided.

Flying

Other options → Helicopter Tours [p.121]
Plane Tours [p.121]

At present there are no private flying clubs available in the Abu Dhabi or Al Ain area. However, those keen to learn can travel north to learn in Dubai, Umm Al Quwain or Fujairah on the East Coast. A variety of courses and qualifications are offered. Those with a private pilot's licence can contact the Dubai Flying Association (04 299 5227), while at Umm Al Quwain Flying Club the brave can not only fly, but can also try skydiving, parachuting or microlighting.

See the Sports section of the *Dubai Explorer* for further details.

Fujairah Aviation Centre

Location → Fujairah Int Airport · Fujairah	09 222 4747
Hours → Timings on request	
Web/email → www.fujairahaviationcentre.com	Map Ref → UAE-E2

High calibre instructors and accreditation as a flying school from the Civil Aviation Authorities in the UAE and UK are backed by facilities that include twin and single engine training aircraft, an instrument flight simulator and a workshop for repairs. Training is offered for the private pilot's licence, commercial pilot's licence, instrument rating and multi-engine rating. Trial lessons and gift vouchers are available. English is the language of civil aviation, so pupils must be conversant in written and oral English.

Costs: *Trial flying lessons Dhs.240 per half hour, Dhs.480 per hour. Ground training Dhs.50 per hour, flight training Dhs.400 per hour.*

Flight training for the new Cessna 172S is Dhs.480 per hour, the Cessna 172P Dhs.400 per hour, and twin engine Dhs.1,200 per hour.

Umm Al Quwain Aeroclub

Location → 17 km North of UAQ on RAK Rd · UAQ	06 768 1447
Hours → See timings below	
Web/email → www.uaqaeroclub.com	Map Ref → UAE-C1

This was the first sports aviation club in the Middle East, providing opportunities for aviation enthusiasts to fly and train throughout the year at excellent rates. Activities include flying, skydiving, skydive boogies, paramotors and helicopter training. The modern facilities include a variety of small aircraft, two runways, eight spacious hangars with engineering services, pilot's shop and a briefing room.

The club also offers sightseeing tours by Cessna aircraft (Dhs.300 per 30 minutes for three people, plus pilot; or 10 minute tours for Dhs.50 per person). For longer flights, a plane with a professional pilot can be hired for Dhs.600 per hour. A trip by air is the perfect way to view the beautiful lagoons and beaches of UAQ.

Location: *16 km along the road from UAQ roundabout heading in the direction of Ras Al Khaimah, before Dreamland Aqua Park and opposite UAQ Shooting Club, on the left hand side of the road... just look for the big aeroplane by the sea.*

Timings: *08:30 - 17:30 winter; 09:00 - 19:00 summer.*

Football

Other options → Sporting Goods [p.153]

Like most places on the planet, you don't have to travel far to have a game of football in the Emirates. On evenings and at weekends, parks, beaches and any open areas seem to attract a game, generally with a mix of nationalities taking part. Even villages in the countryside usually have a group knocking a ball around on the local sand and rock pitch – see if you can join in, or join a more formal club.

Sports

Activities

Abu Dhabi Fianna GAA

Location → Various locations   **605 2477**
Hours → 20:00 - 22:00
Web/email → www.abudhabifianna.com   Map Ref → na

The club is open to men and women of all nationalities, with Gaelic football and hurling played each week. No previous experience is required for participation. Training is normally twice a week for two hours and they also enter a number of tournaments each year in Abu Dhabi, Al Ain, Bahrain and Dubai.

The social side of the club is just as important as the athletic, and meetings are held in the clubhouse or at Heroes Diner at the Crowne Plaza Hotel after training sessions.

Contact: *For more information, call Neil Creedon (050 445 7813).*

Abu Dhabi Nomads Club

Location → Various locations · Abu Dhabi   **672 4900**
Hours → Timings on request
Web/email → dshields@zadco.co.ae   Map Ref → 1-D3

Abu Dhabi Nomads Football Club was formed by the amalgamation of Abu Dhabi Football Club and Abu Dhabi Strollers to allow expats to continue to play football. There's no formal registration at present, although as moves are afoot to enter the club in the competitive league, a membership fee may be introduced. The club trains and plays at Al Jazira Sports Club on Monday evenings. Although membership is currently at full capacity, they are always looking for new players of a good standard.

Contact: *Alan Groves, Chairman (698 9246); David Shields, Secretary (050 446 8795).*

Golf

Other options → **UAE Annual Events [p.42]**

The UAE is quite rightly known as *the* golf destination in the Gulf, with excellent year round facilities and many important tournaments being held here. Courses are either fully grassed or brown (sand) courses, or a mixture of the two.

Abu Dhabi is home to a variety of local tournaments held on an annual or monthly basis, such as the regular *Abu Dhabi Duty Free Medal*. While on the international scene in Dubai,

Emirates Golf Club and Dubai Creek Golf & Yacht Club are hosts to the *Dubai Desert Classic*, which is part of the European PGA (Professional Golf Association) Tour.

Golf

Abu Dhabi Golf & Equestrian Club

Location → Nr Immigration Office · Al Mushrif   **445 9600**
Hours → 06:00 - 22:00
Web/email → na   Map Ref → 3-D3

The golf club is located within the racetrack of the Abu Dhabi Equestrian Club and the two clubs are closely linked. The par 70 course, totalling 3,145 yards for the front nine and 3,220 yards for the back nine, boasts what could be the largest par 5 hole in the world.

During the racing season, the course and driving range close two hours before the first race. Competitions are held each Friday and the Junior Golf Academy for 8 - 14 year olds currently offers an eight week teaching programme for Dhs.300. The clubhouse overlooks the course and features a restaurant, spike bar, lounge area, function rooms, barbecue terrace and a fully stocked pro-shop.

Prices: *Visitors: Green fees 18 holes Dhs.230; 9 holes Dhs.140. Cart hire Dhs.40 (18 holes); Dhs.25 (9 holes). Range balls: Members Dhs.10 per bucket; non members Dhs.20.*

Sports

Activities

Abu Dhabi Golf Club by Sheraton

Location → Umm Al Nar St |558 8990
Hours → 06:00 - 24:00
Web/email → www.adgolfsheraton.com   Map Ref → 1-A1

Although quite a way out of the city, the trip here should be worth it, especially considering the very reasonably priced golf lessons. The excellent facilities include two 18 hole par 72 grass courses, a driving range, special putting and pitching greens with plenty of room to practice and a golf academy with state-of-the-art training facilities. Additional facilities include restaurants, a pro shop, gym, swimming pool, spa and tennis courts (coaching available). Junior golf lessons are held every Thursday, 16:00 - 17:00, and cost only Dhs.15 per child, including equipment. A variety of membership schemes are on offer, including family, individual and corporate.

Al Ain Golf Club

Location → See below |03 768 6808
Hours → Timings on request
Web/email → jimross@emirates.net.ae   Map Ref → 15-E4

Al Ain Golf Club was formed in 1991 by a few dedicated volunteers. The original course was on a disused rubbish dump, but in 1994 sufficient land became available to build a proper golf course. Now there's an 18 hole sand course, with browns, a clubhouse and a floodlit driving range.

The club is part of the United Arab Emirates Golf Association, which in turn is affiliated to the Royal & Ancient Golf Club of St Andrews, Scotland. This means that handicaps gained on the Al Ain course are valid internationally. Visitors are welcome with prior notice.

Location: *Past the Inter-Continental Hotel, on the right hand side of the road on the way to Oman.*

Al Ghazal Golf Club

Location → Nr Abu Dhabi Int Airport · Abu Dhabi |575 8040
Hours → 08:00 - 20:00
Web/email → golfclub@emirates.net.ae   Map Ref → na

Abu Dhabi's first purpose built 18 hole sand golf course, driving range and academy opened adjacent to the capital's airport in 1997. Situated two minutes from the main passenger terminal, anyone can play here, including transit passengers

with a few hours to kill. Airlines can arrange free 96 hour passenger transit visas for travellers passing through the airport who want to play golf or use the facilities.

The club has a clubhouse with restaurant, terrace, health club, swimming pool and tennis courts, and the course follows the natural contours of the land, with the first 9 holes being dictated by a 1,000 year old well.

Prices: *Green fees for 18 holes Dhs.100 - 120; club hire Dhs.40 - 100; half hour lesson before playing Dhs.85 - 95.*

Hilton Al Ain Golf Club

Location → Hilton Al Ain · Al Ain |03 768 6666
Hours → 08:00 - 22:30
Web/email → www.hilton.com   Map Ref → 15-C4

This par 3 course was the first grass course to be built in the Abu Dhabi emirate. The average distance of each hole is about 80 yards, but although short in length, it can play tough! The course has nearly 30 bunkers and with very small quick greens, it tests even the most accomplished of golfers.

The club is open to non members and tuition is available with the resident golf pro, Kevin Duplessis, who also teaches at the Al Ain Golf Club driving range. Club hire is available and prices start at Dhs.30 for a half set. The clubhouse is not just for golfers – they use the Hiltonia Sports Bar for meetings and presentations.

Rotana Junior Golf League

Location → Golf & Equestrian Club · Al Mushrif |445 9600
Hours → 06:00 - 22:30
Web/email → na   Map Ref → 3-D3

When it comes to starting golf, the younger the better is the answer and kids in Abu Dhabi can learn as a member of the Rotana Junior Golf League. Run by the Junior Golf Academy at Abu Dhabi Golf & Equestrian Club, the season runs from September to April. Golf has a reputation for being an expensive sport, but daily fees are not unreasonable: membership is Dhs.100, plus Dhs.30 for a 3 hole or Dhs.40 for a 9 hole tournament (including refreshments, lunch and a T-shirt). Equipment rental is also possible. Tournaments are held on Thursday mornings and pre-tournament coaching sessions are offered on

Wednesdays at 16:00 for Dhs.20. The Club is open from 06:00 – 22:30 daily.

UAE Golf Association

Location → Creek Golf Club · Dubai
Hours → 09:00 - 17:00   Closed Fri
Web/email → www.ugagolf.com

| 04 295 6440

Map Ref → UAE-C2

Overseen by the Ministry of Youth and Education and affiliated to the Royal and Ancient Golf Club of St Andrews in the UK, this non profit making organisation is the governing body for amateur golf in the UAE. Its aims are to make golf more accessible in the UAE for everyone from juniors to the national team. Members receive certain benefits, including reduced green and lesson fees, plus privileged prices on merchandise and golfers' insurance.

Subject to availability, a handicap can be attained according to CONGU (Council of National Union of Golf) or LGU (Ladies Golf Union) for Dhs.100. Regular golf days are organised for these UGA handicap scheme members and these count as qualifying competitions for fixing handicaps.

Membership: *Starts at Dhs.200 for affiliate membership.*

Hang Gliding

Other options → Flying [p.180]

Hashing

Other options → Pubs [p.290]

The Hash House Harriers is a worldwide family of social running clubs, the aim being not to win (which is actually frowned on), but to be there and take part. It was started in Kuala Lumpur in 1938 and is now the largest running organisation in the world, with members in over 180 countries, in approximately 1,600 chapters.

Hashing consists of following a course laid out by a couple of 'hares'. Running, jogging or walking are acceptable and the courses are varied and often cross country. Hashing is a fun way to keep fit and meet new people, since clubs are invariably very sociable and the running is not competitive.

While it was in Malaysia that the sport first took off, its roots can be traced to the British cross country sport of 'hare and hounds', and also probably to

similar activities in other parts of the world. In the 1930s, British servicemen in Malaysia were stationed at the Royal Selonger Club, which was known as the 'hash house' due to the quality of its food. After a particularly festive weekend, a hare and hound paper chase was suggested, and so the hash began.

Abu Dhabi Island Hash House Harriers

Location → Various locations
Hours → Mon – one hour before sunset
Web/email → www.geocities.com/auh4/index.html

| 404 8325

Map Ref → na

Founded in 1979, Abu Dhabi Island Hash House Harriers (or AUH4) has now completed over 1,250 runs. Sometimes referred to as the Family Hash, they welcome all ages. If you think you need the drinking capacity of an elephant and the running ability of Sebastian Coe to join a Hash, think again. Sprint, run, walk or hobble; it's up to you to do as much as you like. They welcome runners but also have plenty of walkers.

After the run, there's a social gathering, which includes food. It's excellent value at Dhs.30 for members, Dhs.40 for non members. Social activities are also organised, including quiz nights, desert drives and camps, parties and, of course, the annual black-tie ball.

Contacts: *For further details visit the Website, contact Barry on the above number, or call Chris Lewis (050 667 0887) or Frankie Wilkes (050 616 2694).*

Abu Dhabi Mainland Hash House Harriers

Location →Various locations
Hours → 16:30 Winter, 17:30 Summer
Web/email → na

| 665 5893

Map Ref → na

Founded by dog lovers Cameron Knight, John Kearns and Gordon Clarke in December 1980 (hence the sniffing dog logo), the Mainland Hash (HHH) usually meets off island – allow about 45 minutes by car to reach the usual sites. This HHH has the reputation of making participants sit on a block of ice (occasionally, to be fair). This hash provides food and beverages in return for a contribution, and entertains participants via a Religious Advisor (RA), hence the ice.

Email David Treasure for further details; dtreasure @adma.co.ae

Al Ain Hash House Harriers

Location → Various locations | 050 618 3102
Hours → Winter 17:30, Summer 18:00
Web/email → na Map Ref → na

Started in April 1984, this hash has run over 900 times, with no break, despite rain, lightning and the occasional near hurricane! The runs vary in difficulty and generally last 20 - 40 minutes. Runners get a good workout and the 'knitting circle', which strolls along behind, enjoys a good chat and a walk. There are occasional torchlight runs after dark, plus hashes are held to celebrate various special days. The hash hosts the annual Nash Hash on UAE National Day with an overnight camp for local hashers and visitors. Refreshments are supplied on alternate meetings, but runners bring their own food etc. This is a family affair that welcomes people of all ages.

Contacts: *Gerry McGuire (050 618 3102) or Garry Bluff (fax 03 762 5093).*

WASP Hash House Harriers

Location → Various locations | na
Hours → Meet on Sat
Web/email → na Map Ref → na

The Wasp Hash House Harriers (Wasp H3) is a relatively small kennel (hive?) that caters more for the hasher without a mobility problem as opposed to the perambulating version. However, everyone is welcome, from walkers to runners, children or adults.

Members meet about an hour before sunset at a pre-arranged location on the island, generally anywhere between the Corniche and the ice rink. Runs last 40 - 70 minutes and afterwards a short circle is held for announcements etc, and the hash toast, before moving to the hare's house for refreshments. Wasp H3 operates a 'bring your own' for drinks, but food is provided.

Contact: *Alan Ettridge (050 662 9154).*

Charges: *Dhs.10 run only; Dhs.15 includes food.*

Hiking

Other options → Outdoor Goods [p.151]
Climbing [p.170]
Mountaineering [p.192]
Out of the City [p.122]

Although the area around Abu Dhabi island is fairly flat and uninspiring for hiking, a 90 minute drive will take you to very different surroundings, ideal for hiking and far removed from the sprawling, hectic city. The nearest place to reach from the city is the foothills of the Hajar Mountains – 'hajar' is Arabic for rock. Here the lovely purple coloured mountains and wadis offer peace and tranquillity. The terrain is heavily shattered and eroded due to the harsh climate, but there are many good trails, ranging from short easy walks to longer treks over difficult terrain.

Once near the mountains, explore turnings you like the look of – along most are numerous paths, wadis and scaleable hills. Good areas include anywhere near Al Ain, many places in Wadi Bih (the mountainous route from Ras Al Khaimah to Dibba) or the mountains near the East Coast. The mountains here do not disappoint and the further off the beaten track you get, the more likely you are to find interesting villages where the people live much as they have for centuries.

Many of the paths follow centuries old Bedouin and Shihuh trails. However, information is presently limited and word of mouth is probably the best option for finding good trails. For short-term visitors especially, who have little time or local knowledge, an organised guided tour can be a good option. The best season for walking is in the winter months, October - March/April, since the mix of sun, humidity and altitude in summer can be exhausting.

As with any trip into the UAE 'outback', take sensible precautions. Tell someone where you're going and when you should be back, take a map and compass or GPS and stout walking boots (for the loose rock). The sun during the day is fierce, so cover up, but at night temperatures can drop surprisingly. Take food for energy, suncream and most importantly loads of water.

Refer also to the *Off-Road Explorer (UAE)* published by Explorer Publishing. Apart from striking satellite images of routes to explore, there are details of interesting hikes with tracks superimposed on photographs. This is a handy manual and includes information on health and safety, flora and fauna, GPS co-ordinates, and so on. One of the most important warnings is to be especially careful in wadis (dry riverbeds) during the wet season, as dangerous flash floods can flood a wadi in seconds.

Contacts: *Useful contacts willing to advise like minded people are: Dubai, Alistair MacKenzie (Alistair@Explorer-Publishing.com); Ras Al Khaimah, John Gregory (050 647 7120).*

Sports

Activities

Desert Rangers

Location → Jct 2, Shk Zayed Rd · Dubai | 04 340 2408
Hours → 09:00 - 18:00 Closed Fri (office)
Web/email → www.desertrangers.com | Map Ref → UAE-C2

This Dubai based company offers hikes in the majestic mountains of the UAE with an experienced guide. A variety of routes can be taken to suit the group's age and level of fitness. Locations include Fujairah, Dibba, Masafi, Ras Al Khaimah and Al Ain. For more information consult the *Dubai Explorer*.

Cost: *Dhs.275 per person.*

Hiking Frontiers

Location → Various locations | na
Hours → na
Web/email → na | Map Ref → na

A sister club to Biking Frontiers with pretty much the same outdoor loving members, this group is involved in hiking around the UAE and Oman. They're a diverse bunch of active hikers and bikers, both male and female, who either meet on Friday mornings, or head out camping on Thursday evening and hike Friday.

The typical hiking season is from October through to March. Main requirements are that you are enthusiastic, have proper walking boots, carry enough water and are reasonably fit. You are responsible for your own safety and ensuring that you don't exceed your own capabilities. If you are interested in meeting a fun bunch of like minded people, or in knowing a bit more, email Alistair Mackenzie at Alistair@Explorer-Publishing.com.

Hockey

Other options → Ice Hockey [p.186]

Abu Dhabi Hockey Club

Location → Various locations | 674 4410
Hours → Timings on request
Web/email → na | Map Ref → na

Abu Dhabi Hockey Club (ADHOC) was formed in 1994 by Veryan Pappin (Club President), a former member of the England hockey team that won the gold medal at the Seoul Olympics. Various other club members have also played for their national teams in England, India, Pakistan and Scotland.

The club takes part in various tournaments held each year in Abu Dhabi, Dubai and Sharjah and has been winners or runners up quite a few times. The club is usually able to field men's, women's and mixed teams, depending on what tournament is being played. They also run a mini hockey league. Contact Manish (674 4410 or 050 621 0534) for further details.

Horse Riding

Other options → UAE Annual Events [p.42]
Horse Racing [p.45]
Polo [p.193]

Horses are of great significance in this part of the world, both in historical and modern terms and, despite its size, the UAE has a wealth of equine talent. Recreational riding is extremely well supported, and most stables offer quality horses for hacking in the desert or rides along the beach.

Horse racing is also extremely popular. In March each year, Dubai hosts the world's richest horse race, the US$6 million Dubai World Cup, which is one of the events on the UAE's social calendar.

Abu Dhabi Equestrian Club

Location → Nr Immigration Office · Al Mushrif | 445 5500
Hours → Timings on request
Web/email → na | Map Ref → 3 D3

Following a Dhs.20 million project to update the facilities at Abu Dhabi Equestrian Club in 1995, the club offers excellent horse racing and show jumping grounds. There is also a very active riding club, which currently has 100 horses suitable for all levels of riders. The school offers comprehensive instruction from beginner to jumping, endurance desert riding and stable management courses. Instructors are mainly European with relevant qualifications and lessons can be taught in English, French or German. A sample price is Dhs.50 for a one hour lesson with 6 - 10 people. Members only.

Sports

Activities

Hurling

Abu Dhabi Fianna GAA

Location → Various locations
Hours → 20:00 - 22:00
Web/email → www.abudhabifianna.com

| 605 2477

Map Ref → na

Not taken very seriously among the locals, the game still rates high with them in the entertainment arena and they are quite amused to watch. Despite this, the association is thriving in the UAE and the Gulf since its inception in 1993. Now, every three months or so, groups throughout the area meet for a weekend competition of hurling and Gaelic football (see also Football [p.180]).

In Abu Dhabi, there are about 50 members and meetings are held twice a week on Monday and Wednesday evening. Ladies' football and camogie are also thriving with many social activities. Players hail from all over and everyone's welcome; whatever your standard or knowledge of the games, you'll receive a warm Irish welcome.

Contact: *For more information, call Neil Creedon (050 445 7813).*

Ice Hockey

Abu Dhabi Falcons Ice Hockey

Location → Abu Dhabi Ice Rink · Abu Dhabi
Hours → Thu, Fri & Sun
Web/email → www.abufalcons.com

| 698 6666

Map Ref → 2-A1

This non-profit organisation is dedicated to the development of youth ice hockey in a fun and safe environment. Formally established in 1996, the club has grown steadily over the years. For the 2002 - 03 season it has 75 players from 16 countries split into four divisions (novice, juniors, intermediates and seniors). Practices are on Thursday and Friday mornings, and Sunday evenings at Abu Dhabi's Olympic sized rink.

The club has an internal youth league with three teams and participates in local tournaments. Each year, the club holds a hockey camp with professional coaches flown in from Canada. Both boys and girls are welcome to join.

Contacts: *Interested players should consult the club's Website or contact Vincent Saubestre, Club President, on the above number.*

Al Ain Youth Ice Hockey Teams

Location → Hili Fun City · Hili
Hours → na
Web/email → david.smicer@hct.ac.ae

| 03 705 5561

Map Ref → 13-C1

The Al Ain Youth Ice Hockey Teams formally came into being in late January 1998. The official team name is the Al Ain Vipers, with four youth teams split according to age (under 8s, under 10s, under 13s and under 17s). There's also a well-established adult league. All players are required to register on the team lists.

The season runs from September to May, with a break for Ramadan. Both boys and girls are welcome and team aims are equal ice time for all players in the spirit of fair play. Many nationalities are represented, including non traditional hockey nations, and new players are always welcome. There's an annual registration fee.

Contact: *Team President, David Smicer (03 782 1039/050 448 1967 or work 03 705 5561).*

Ice Skating

Abu Dhabi Ice Rink

Location → Zayed Sport City ·
Hours → See timings below
Web/email → na

| 444 8458

Map Ref → 2-A1

Abu Dhabi Ice Rink offers a fun couple of hours, especially in the summer months to escape the heat. As well as ice skating, the rink has a variety of other facilities available including bumper cars, video cars, video games, billiard tables and a fast food restaurant. They can also accommodate group visits and have a birthday hall and Arabic tent.

Two instructors offer lessons for all levels of ability – fees vary depending on the size of the group and length of lesson. A membership system operates which includes free entry and skating; fees are reasonable. Skates can be hired or you can take your own.

Entrance: *Dhs.5 per person (children below three years are free); skate hire Dhs.10 per person (for one session). Skate sharpening Dhs.15 per pair.*

Timings: *Split into 4 sessions from 10:00 - 12:00, 12:30 - 14:30, 15:00 - 17:00 & 17:30 - 19:30*

Wed, Thurs & Fri: Last session at 20:00 - 22:00

Sat and Sun: Last session at 15:00 - 17:00.

Sports

Activities

Hili Fun City & Ice Rink

Location → Mohammed Bin Khalifa St · Hili
Hours → See timings below
Web/email → www.hilton.com
03 784 5542

Map Ref → 13-B1

Opened in 1985 by HH Sheikh Tahnoon Bin Mohammed Al Nahyan, Hili Fun City is one of the largest amusement parks in the Gulf. The ice rink is located on the eastern side of the park at a separate entrance with a mammoth 60x30 metre ice rink seating 3,000 spectators. Besides public skating sessions, there are ice hockey and ice skating tournaments throughout the year with a show on ice during the Al Ain Festival.

Timings: *Winter: 16:00 - 22:00 Sun - Wed & 9:00 - 22:00 Thurs, Fri and public holidays.*

Summer: *17:00 - 23:00 Sun - Wed & 9:00 - 23:00 Thurs, Fri and public holidays.*

Tues. & Wed. are ladies and children only.

Jet Skiing

Other options → Beach Clubs [p.203]
Beaches [p.114]
Water Skiing [p.203]
Wakeboarding [p.202]

Al Jazira Hotel and Resort

Location → Btn Abu Dhabi & Dubai · Ghantoot Area
Hours → Timings on request
Web/email → na
562 9100

Map Ref → na

If you've not tried it before, think of jet skiing as rather like riding a Harley Davidson, but on water, so it's a bit more exciting. Safety is the top priority: you are connected to the machine by a safety chord, which stops the engine once it's disconnected ie, when you fall off. This, and wearing a life jacket, helps prevent accidents. Starting at Dhs.50 for 15 minutes of adrenalin rush (speeds of 40 kmph are possible), this fun is not cheap.

Karting

Leisure Games Centre

Location → Nr AUH Tourist Club · Tourist Club Area
Hours → See timings below
Web/email → na
679 3330

Map Ref → 7-D1

This is one of the few opportunities to try this popular sport in Abu Dhabi. The track has several features, including an electronic circuit timer, two hairpin bends, a U-turn and straights where you can reach speeds of up to 50 kmph. Safety is top priority and training is provided each week, targeting different age groups, from 7 - 50 year olds. The karts are fitted with two stroke engines (200cc, 250cc and 390cc). All equipment is supplied and over recent months the track, facilities and equipment have been substantially upgraded. The club is also involved in organising endurance and 24 hour races.

They can handle group bookings and corporate days out – larger numbers get a good discount, and it's one way to practice some crazy driving before taking to Abu Dhabi's roads!

Cost: *Dhs.30 for 10 minutes on the track. If you find yourself hooked on the sport, you can buy your own kart for Dhs.9,000.*

Timings: *Weekdays 09:00 - 12:00 & 17:00 - 24:00; Wed, Thu & Fri 09:00 - 12:00 & 16:00 - 01:00.*

Kayaking

Other options → Tours & Sightseeing [p.115]
Canoeing[p.169]

Beach Hut, The

Location → Sandy Beach Motel · East Coast
Hours → Timings on request
Web/email → www.sandybm.com
09 244 5050

Map Ref → na

The Beach Hut offers a variety of water sports equipment. For those who just want to paddle out to Snoopy Island to explore, there are kayaks for hire at Dhs.30 an hour. You can also try windsurfing, and diving and snorkelling equipment is available for rent or sale.

Kitesurfing

Kitesurfing is a fast growing new sport that's gaining loads of publicity, partly because it's so extreme. It's not windsurfing, it's not wakeboarding, it's not surfing and it's not kite flying, but instead is a fusion of all these disciplines with other influences to create the wildest new water sport in years.

Arabian Gulf Kite Club, The

Location → Various locations
Hours → Timings on request
Web/email → www.fatimasport.com
04 880 1010

Map Ref → na

Along with mountain board kiting, power kiting, display kiting and kite buggies, this new club offers

Sports

Activities

the chance to try kitesurfing; an up and coming extreme sport that involves flying across the water harnessed to a kite and a small windsurfing board. The only downfall is that you have to be fit to even attempt it. A popular meeting place for kitesurfers is in Dubai on the beach between the University of Wollongong and Umm Suqeim Clinic, off Jumeira Beach Road.

Equipment sale and training courses are available and the club recommends equipment by Naish, Flexifoil and Peter Lynn for use in Arabian Gulf conditions. For further details, contact Fatima Sports (050 455 5216).

Martial Arts

Abu Dhabi Shotokan Karate Club

Location ➜ Hiltonia · Corniche Rd West | 667 3840
Hours ➜ na
Web/email ➜ na   Map Ref ➜ 10-C2

Learn this ancient form of karate under the guidance of 5th dan Mahmoud Tillawi. He teaches to all levels of ability, and also offers coaching in swimming, general fitness and judo. Lessons are held all over Abu Dhabi at various times. Contact the above number for further details.

Baroudy's Sports Club

Location ➜ Golden Tower · Corniche | 626 8122
Hours ➜ 09:00 - 21:00   Closed Fri
Web/email ➜ tbaroudy@hotmail.com   Map Ref ➜ na

This martial arts club teaches taekwondo, which embraces the traditional beliefs of honour, integrity, loyalty and compassion and is both a sport and an art. The meaning of the word is 'tae', to strike with the foot; 'kwon', to destroy with the hand or fist; and 'do', way or method.

It teaches self defence, as well as improving physical fitness, mental discipline, self control, concentration, timing and emotional calmness. The art develops a sense of responsibility for one's self and others, and it is now an Olympic event. The club also runs a children's summer camp. Contact Tony Baroudy on the above number or call 050 621 4399.

Emirates Sports Centre

Location ➜ Nr Abu Dhabi Int Htl · Tourist Club Area | 676 6757
Hours ➜ 09:00 - 13:00 & 16:00 - 21:30   Closed Fri
Web/email ➜ naseema@adma.co.ae   Map Ref ➜ 8-A1

At Emirates Sports Centre sessions in karate and kung fu are available. Lessons are conducted by experienced instructors and there are separate classes for ladies, children and girls. They also arrange for grading sessions and certificates are issued from their international headquarters in Malaysia to successful candidates. Contact Mr P.M. Hamid on the above number for further details.

Costs: *Admission Dhs.50. Monthly fees: Dhs.100 for two lessons per week; Dhs.140 for three lessons per week; Dhs.175 for four lessons per week; Dhs.200 for five lessons; Dhs.250 for six lessons. Karate uniform Dhs.60; kung fu uniform Dhs.75. Transport within Abu Dhabi city Dhs.30.*

Freddie Alfaro Aikido

Location ➜ Hiltonia Beach Club · Corniche Rd | 050 617 4596
Hours ➜ Timings on request
Web/email ➜ na   Map Ref ➜ 10-C2

Aikido literally means harmony and love with the spirit of the universe – 'ai', to come together and harmonise; 'ki', spirit, the inner power; 'do', the way. Its uniqueness as a martial art lies in its awareness of a deep sense of harmony with all creation. Therefore training is not only designed to defend oneself, but to bring the assailant under control without inflicting injury. In fact, Aikido rejects all forms of violence and competition.

Learn the ancient skills with black belt Sensei Freddie Alfaro. For further details, contact the above number or 681 2922 / 692 4218.

Kung Fu Health Centre

Location ➜ Airport Rd | 632 5109
Hours ➜ 08:00 - 13:00   16:00 - 22:00   Fri 17:00 - 21:00
Web/email ➜ luhuiming@hotmail.com   Map Ref ➜ 8-A1

This centre is a member of the Asian Martial Arts Association and teaches Shaolin kung fu. The focus is on basic Shaolin arts including; Shaolin fist, stick play, knife play, swordplay, spear play and southern fists. The aim is to strengthen physique, improve health and strengthen will power. Courses are run by coach Lu Hui-Ming, and for ladies and children there's an experienced female coach, who was an army championship

Sports

Activities

winner in China. She teaches Tai Chi, lady Shaolin, self defence and varieties of kung fu, as well as aerobics and offers help with slimming.

Please note: *The Kung Fu Health Centre may change its name. However, at the time of printing, this new name had yet to be decided.*

Oriental Karate & Kobudo Club

Location → Tourist Club Area	**677 1611**
Hours → Timings on request	
Web/email → orientalkarate.com	Map Ref → 7-D1

The chief instructor at this club is Sensei Ali Mohammed who's a 5th dan in karate and a 4th dan in kobudo martial arts. He offers separate sessions for adults and children at all levels of age and ability. Lessons are held at various places around Abu Dhabi, call the above number, or the following centres: Madinat Zayed (634 5080); Airport Road (445 7375); Khalifa Street (627 3808); Tourist Club area (677 8878).

Price: *Monthly fee Dhs.100 per person for classes twice a week. Transport is available within Abu Dhabi island for children.*

UAE Wrestling Association

Location → Various locations	**050 563 3332**
Hours → Timings on request	
Web/email → www.adcombat.com	Map Ref → na

Previously known as Abu Dhabi Combat Club, this association is headed by HE Mohammed bin Thaloob Al Darare. While the club now focuses on freestyle wrestling, classes in kickboxing, wrestling judo and Brazilian ju-jitsu are still offered.

Wadokai Karate Club

Location → Various locations	**050 643 2945**
Hours → Timings on request	
Web/email → na	Map Ref → na

Wadokai karate is a Japanese style of karate developed by Master Hironori Ohtsuka. The emphasis is on speed and evasion and only light contact is allowed. 'Wa' means peace or harmony, 'do' means way and 'kai' means school.

Any age can train from six years up, and training is built up gradually and carefully. It's affiliated to clubs from around the world and grades are officially recognised and conducted. Classes are held throughout the week, with different timings for children, ladies and men or mixed sessions.

Costs: *Adults Dhs.20 for members (Dhs.25 for non members); children Dhs.15 for members (Dhs.20 for non members).*

Locations: *Abu Dhabi – National Institute of Karate Do; Al Ain – Hotel Inter-Continental and the Al Ain English Speaking School.*

Mini Golf

Other options → Golf [p.181]
Kids' Stuff [p.226]

Hatta Fort Hotel

Location → Hatta Fort Hotel · Hatta	**04 852 3211**
Hours → Timings on request	
Web/email → www.dutcohotels.com	Map Ref → UAE-D3

With a background of lovely views of the Hajar Mountains, Hatta Fort offers a choice of mini golf or a 9 hole cross country fun golf course. The mini course is American style crazy golf and lies mostly in the shade of the trees below the hotel. The charge for two people is Dhs.25. The 9 hole course can be played for Dhs.35 per person, per round (including clubs and balls). Each hole is par 3, ranging from 68 to 173 yards. Golf instruction and lessons are available.

Entrance fees: *Day visitors on Fridays and public holidays purchase a voucher at the entry gate (Dhs.40 for adults, Dhs.20 for children), which is redeemable against hotel facilities.*

Moto-Cross

Abu Dhabi MX Club

Location → Various locations	**634 5527**
Hours → Timings on request	
Web/email → na	Map Ref → na

Started in 1983, the Abu Dhabi Motor-Cross Club organises moto-cross racing and other related informal off-road motorcycling events. The racing programme, in concert with the UAE Championship, the Umm Al Quwain Championship and the UAE Off-Road Championship, runs from October to March. Training continues throughout the year and includes off-road Enduro riding, covering distances of 30 - 200 km.

MX race classes are organised in Umm Al Quwain and Dubai for all skill levels, and both boys and girls are welcome to join. Enthusiastic beginners can initially borrow a bike, helmet etc, although availability may be limited depending on the day.

Sports

Activities

For further information, contact Klaus Schwingenschloegl (050 612 4614).

Membership: *Annual; Dhs.350 family, Dhs.250 individual; plus Dhs.60 per race day.*

Motorcycling

Other options → Driving Licence [p.55]

Al Ramool Motorcycle Rental

Location → The Big Red Dunes Area · Hatta Rd | 050 453 4401
Hours → 08:30 - 18:30
Web/email → na | Map Ref → UAE-D3

Al Ramool offers LT50, LT80, 125cc, 350cc and 620cc motorcycles for rent. Crash helmets are provided for safety and prices range from Dhs.20 - 100 for 30 minutes. The company offers a variety of tailor made packages – contact Mohammad Ali Rashed (050 453 3033) for further details.

Mountain Biking

Other options → Cycling [p.172]
Out of the City [p.122]

Contrary to the initial perception of the Emirates, the interior has a lot to offer outdoor enthusiasts, especially mountain bikers. The 'outback' is rarely visited, but on a mountain bike it's possible to see the most remote places that are inaccessible even by 4 wheel drive.

The best areas are north of Abu Dhabi and are definitely worth the journey, as the variety of rides

Mountain Biking

will satisfy even the most hardcore biker. There's a good range of terrain, from super technical rocky trails, in areas like Fili and Siji, to mountain routes like Wadi Bih, which climb to over 1,000 metres and can be descended in minutes. The riding is mainly rocky, technical and challenging. There are many tracks to follow and, if you look hard, some interesting singletrack can be found.

However, be prepared and be sensible – the sun is strong, you will need far more water than you think and it's easy to get lost. Plus falling off on this rocky terrain can be extremely painful.

For further information on mountain biking in the UAE, including details of possible routes, refer to the *Off-Road Explorer (UAE)* published by Explorer Publishing.

Biking Frontiers

Location → Various locations | 050 450 9401
Hours → See timings below
Web/email → www.bikingfrontiers.com | Map Ref → na

So you're a mountain biking fan? If you don't mind thrashing yourself over seriously rocky trails, through wadis and like getting lost once in a while... then give Biking Frontiers a call. Mainly based in Dubai, they are a fairly serious group of riders, but any competent mountain bikers are welcome. Your own bike, helmets and proper gear are essential. Rides are every Friday, and sometimes Saturdays, as well as weekday city rides in the evenings. They're usually out for 4 - 5 hours and in the saddle for 3 - 3½, with the occasional giant ride.

The group also enjoys camping, hiking and barbecues, so if you're into mountain biking or the outdoors in general, contact Paul on the above number or Pete (050 450 9401).

Departure times: *Vary. Winter (November - March) usually 10:30 - 12:30. Summer usually 14:30 - 15:30.*

Meeting point: *Usually the car park at the World Trade Centre, Dubai.*

Desert Rangers

Location → Jct 2 · Shk Zayed Rd · Dubai | 04 340 2408
Hours → 09:00 - 18:00 Closed Fri (office)
Web/email → www.desertrangers.com | Map Ref → UAE-C2

Whether you're a fanatical biker craving challenging terrain or a complete beginner preferring a gentler introduction to the delights of off-road biking, Desert Rangers will determine a

Sports

Activities

suitable route depending on your requirements and group size. The company is one of only a few outward-bound leisure companies to specialise in more unusual activities in the UAE.

The price of Dhs.300 per person is inclusive of bike, helmet, guide, pick up, drop off and soft drinks.

Mountaineering

Other options → Out of the City [p.122]
Climbing [p.170]

The area immediately surrounding Abu Dhabi is mostly flat sandy desert; however, there are regions inland that are a paradise for the more adventurous mountain walker. In the far north, the Ru'us Al Jibal Mountains contain the highest peaks in the area, at over 2,000 metres. To the east, the impressive Hajar Mountains form the border between the UAE and Oman, stretching from the Mussandam Peninsula north of Ras Al Khaimah, to the Empty Quarter desert, several hundred kilometres to the south.

The terrain is heavily eroded and shattered due to the harsh climate, and trips range from short easy walks leading to spectacular viewpoints, to all day treks over difficult terrain, with some major mountaineering routes on faces of Alpine proportions. Many of the routes follow centuries old Bedouin and Shihuh trails through the mountains and a few are still used today to access more remote settlements. Some of the terrain is incredible and one can only wonder at the skills of the hardy mountain people who pioneered the trails.

Battered photocopies of a guide written in the mid 1980s exist, and this may form the basis of a dedicated climbing and mountaineering book at some point.

Heat and humidity mean that serious mountain walking is best between the months of November and April. For further information on possible routes for mountaineering in the UAE, refer to the *Off-Road Explorer (UAE)*, published by Explorer Publishing.

Warning: *No mountain rescue services exist, therefore anyone venturing into mountains should be reasonably experienced, or be with some one who knows the area. Tragedies have occurred in the past.*

Contacts willing to advise like minded people are: Alistair MacKenzie (Alistair@Explorer-Publishing.com) (Dubai).

Netball

Abu Dhabi Netball Club

Location → Club, The · Al Meena | 673 1111
Hours → Timings on request
Web/email → www.the-club.com | Map Ref → 7-A2

Netball was first played in Abu Dhabi in 1976 when Linda Taylor, an ex England International Captain, started at the Al Khubairat school. The sport developed from playing on sand courts and car parks to the formation of the formal Abu Dhabi Downs League in 1980. The league has developed into a strong competitive side in the Gulf and with a membership of 85 registered players, netball is a fast growing sport in Abu Dhabi. The official season runs from November to April and team practice as well as league games are played at The Club on Tuesday evenings. Membership of The Club is not required to play netball.

There's an annual Dhs.100 registration fee. Anybody interested in playing should contact Natali Hoffman (050 536 3821).

Paintballing

Other options → Shooting [p.196]

At present there's nowhere in Abu Dhabi to cover friends or relatives in paint! However, addicts can always make the trip north since this fun activity is available in Dubai – see the *Dubai Explorer*.

Pursuit Games

Location → WonderLand · Umm Hurair · Dubai | 04 324 1222
Hours → Timings on request
Web/email → wonderld@emirates.net.ae | Map Ref → UAE-C2

This is great for teenagers and adults; get a crowd together and they'll quickly be divided into teams by the experts, who give a thorough safety demonstration before equipping everyone with overalls, 'Darth Vader' type facemasks and special guns equipped with paintballs. Stalk your enemies and get them before they get you! For further information, contact Kaz (050 651 4583).

Cost: *Dhs.70 for a typical two hour game with 100 paintballs, gun and gas. An extra 100 paintballs costs Dhs.50.*

Sports

Activities

Parachuting

At present this exciting sport is not available in the Abu Dhabi emirate. However, those willing to travel can contact Umm Al Quwain Flying Club (06 768 1447) or refer to the *Dubai Explorer*.

Paragliding

Other options → Skydiving [p.196]
Flying [p.180]

To try this in the UAE you will have to travel to Umm Al Quwain Flying Club in the Northern Emirates (06 768 1447), since it is not available in Abu Dhabi. Also refer to the *Dubai Explorer*.

Polo

Other options → Horse Riding [p.185]

Ghantoot Polo & Racing Club

Location → On Shk Zayed Rd towards Dubai	562 9050
Hours → Timings on request	
Web/email → na	Map Ref → na

With six floodlit polo fields, a 2,000 seat racing grandstand, tennis courts, swimming pool, gym, sauna and restaurant, this club has first class facilities for all the family to enjoy. Membership is available and non members are welcome to dine at the restaurant or to watch the regular polo matches. The polo season starts in October and continues until the end of April. The calendar is full with regular chukka tournaments and high profile international games. The quality of play and horses is high, and spectators are always welcome. Ghantoot also hosts race meetings in December and April.

Location: *Ghantoot is located halfway between Dubai and Abu Dhabi, near Al Jazira Hotel and Resort.*

Rally Driving

Other options → UAE Desert Challenge [p.46];
Desert Rallies [p.44]

Emirates Motor Sports Federation

Location → Nr Aviation Club · Al Garhoud · Dubai	04 282 7111
Hours → Timings on request Closed Thu, Fri	
Web/email → www.emsf.org.ae	Map Ref → UAE-C2

Emirates Motor Sports Federation is the sanctioning authority for all motor sports and motoring events in the UAE. The EMSF actively promotes motor sports by supporting its member clubs. It also organises a variety of events throughout the year; including the UAE Rally Championship (a six round championship that starts with the Peace Rally in January and ends with the National Day Rally in November); the Emirates Autocross Championship (an eight round championship with approximately one race every month); plus a variety of non competitive events (such as Classic Car Shows and the popular RoadStar Safety Campaigns). The federation also sanctions a variety of motoring events, such as the popular Gulf News Fun Drive.

Roller Blading

Other options → Parks [p.111]
Beaches [p.114]
Sporting Goods [p.153]

Great fun and great exercise, this sport is for adults and children alike. Look for areas with few people and enough slopes and turns to make it interesting – and to increase your skills and balance. In Abu Dhabi the Corniche and Breakwater make a good long paved area and taking in the view is a bonus (although present construction hampers this somewhat). Take care though, it does get busy in the cool of the evenings. Prepare for the inevitable falls with helmets and knee, elbow and wrist pads, just in case.

Rugby

Other options → UAE Annual Events [p.42]
Sporting Goods [p.153]

Abu Dhabi Rugby Football Club

Location → Madinat Zayed · Abu Dhabi	050 662 3069
Hours → See timings below	
Web/email → na	Map Ref → 7-A2

This club was founded in 1970 and is affiliated to the Arabian Gulf Rugby Football Union. There are presently over 100 members.

All teams take part in various tournaments in the Emirates or around the Gulf, and in the past there were various overseas tours. The ladies' team, established in 1994, were 1999 Gulf League Champions. The mini section is probably the most successful in the Gulf with over 200 kids turning up to the weekly training session. Games are

Sports

Activities

currently played on a grass pitch at the Military Stadium, with after match activities taking place at the Crowne Plaza Hotel. A yearly subscription goes towards the cost of running the club. All standards of players or non players are welcome.

Contacts: *Aubrey Roberts, Club Captain (050 662 3069); Clare Shryane, Ladies Coach (050 626 1661); Riaan Smuts, for minis and youth (050 536 3718).*

Training: *Seniors 19:00 Sunday and Wednesday (September through to May); minis 18:00 Wednesdays. On Wednesdays there's rugby club night at Heroes Diner, Crowne Plaza Hotel from 21:00 onwards.*

Al Ain Amblers Rugby Club

Location ➜ Htl Inter-Continental · Al Khubeirah | **050 623 0941**
Hours ➜ Timings on request
Web/email ➜ na   Map Ref ➜ 15-E4

Al Ain Amblers Rugby Club was formed in early 1981 by expats who enjoyed the playing and social activities of Rugby Union. Over the years the club has had all standards of players, and now has many Arabic speaking players. The club plays in the Emirates League, playing home games at the Al Ain Inter-Continental Hotel. Plans for 2003 include starting a youth and mini section for children aged 10 - 16. For further details, contact the Club Chairman on the above number.

Dubai Exiles Rugby Club

Location ➜ Al Awir Rd · Dubai | **04 333 1198**
Hours ➜ Timings on request
Web/email ➜ na   Map Ref ➜ UAE-C2

Definitely Dubai's serious rugby club, the Exiles is the Emirates' oldest and best established bastion of the sport. Training sessions are scheduled throughout the week with the 1st and 2nd XVs meeting on Sundays and Wednesdays and veterans on Tuesdays and Saturdays. There's also training for children (mini's) on Mondays and Wednesdays. The 1st XV play in the Arabian Gulf First Division and the 2nds in the Emirates League, so there's plenty of regional travel and competition. There are matches most Friday afternoons and some Wednesdays.

The Exiles also host the annual Dubai International Rugby Sevens tournament, which attracts international teams from all the major rugby playing nations. The club also provides facilities for the Emirates Football League, and clubhouse facilities are available for hire.

Running

Other options ➜ UAE Annual Events [p.42]

For over half the year, the weather couldn't be better for running in the Emirates, while in the summer, despite the high temperatures and humidity, you'll find dedicated runners out pounding the miles all over the UAE. In the hottest months, the evenings and especially, the early mornings , are the best times to be out.

Clubs and informal groups meet regularly to run together, with some runs being competitive or training runs for the variety of events organised throughout the year. Regular, short distance races are held, as well as a variety of biathlons, triathlons and hashes, which provide a reasonably full and varied schedule. The epic Wadi Bih Run is one of the favourite competitions where teams of five run the 70 km from Ras Al Khaimah on the west coast to Dibba on the east, over mountains topping out at over 1,000 metres. Backed by a support vehicle, runners take turns on different stages and this event, held annually, attracts up to 300 participants. The Abu Dhabi Marathon is another popular event as is the Jebel Hafeet Road Race arranged by the Al Ain Hilton.

Contacts: *Wadi Bih race, John Gregory (050 647 7120).*

Abu Dhabi Striders

Location ➜Various locations | **050 441 4886**
Hours ➜ Wed 18:00
Web/email ➜ na   Map Ref ➜ na

Abu Dhabi Striders was formed in late 1983 by regular runners who were looking for fellow enthusiasts. Members are from all walks of life, with many nationalities and standards of fitness. At each training session a choice of 3, 5, 8, 10 and 15 km courses are marked out. Everybody predicts the time for their chosen distance and then walks/runs without a watch, but against the clock. Those closest to their predictions win a prize.

Each year they organise a 10 km half marathon and full marathon, and enter races in other parts of the UAE. The club has won the Wadi Bih relay race. They also organise various social events.

Contacts: *Ash (050 692 8601); Steve Reay on the above number, (050 441 4886) or fax (645 6320). Steve will fax a map to those interested.*

Sports

Activities

Al Ain Road Runners

Location → Htl Inter-Continental · Al Khubeirah | 050 618 3702
Hours → Sat, Tue & Wed
Web/email → www.interconti.com   Map Ref → 15-E4

Al Ain Road Runners are generally runners/hashers who want to do a 'bit more'. They have two routes at each training session, one for the jogger of about 5 km and one for the more serious runner. Running is on a mixture of roads and cross country tracks. The times of meetings vary according to the time of year. Runs on Tuesday are longer at 15 km. All are welcome.

Sailing

Other options → UAE Annual Events [p.42]
Boat & Yacht Charters [p.119]

Sailing is a popular pastime in Abu Dhabi and in winter the temperatures are perfect for water sports, while in summer you can escape some of the scorching heat on land. Membership of the sailing clubs allows you use of the leisure facilities, to join in the activities, hire sailing and water sports equipment and moor or store your boat (always an extra cost).

Many companies will take you out on a cruise, either for a couple of hours or for a full day, for pleasure or for fishing. You can also charter your own boat for periods ranging from one morning to several weeks.

Abu Dhabi Catamaran Association

Location → Abu Dhabi Corniche · | 443 5339
Hours → Timings on request
Web/email → na   Map Ref → 8-B2

This small but keen sailing club caters to the multihull boat sailor in Abu Dhabi. The high sailing speeds combined with the robust construction of the catamaran makes it an ideal craft for sailing in the Gulf.

Regular races are held every alternate Thursday afternoon throughout the year, and also, at times, on Friday. Racing can be very exciting regardless of prior experience and members are encouraged to compete.

The association offers advice to prospective owners, access to spare parts, tools, and lots of friendly 'know how' to all sailor levels. In addition,

there's a social club with many racing get togethers and outings. Membership fees are reasonable and new members are always welcome.

Contact: *Commodore Kingsley Ashford-Brown on the above number*

Abu Dhabi Sailing Club

Location → Club, The · Al Meena | 673 1111
Hours → Mon & Thu
Web/email → www.the-club.com   Map Ref → 7-A2

Founded over 30 years ago by a group of enthusiastic sailors employed by local oil companies, Abu Dhabi Sailing Club is now a sub section of The Club and ADSC members must also be members of The Club.

The club supports three fleets (Kestrels, Lasers and Laser II), and boats are syndicated to members who qualify as helms. They are then responsible for its maintenance and seaworthiness. The water off The Club provides a mixture of flat water and strong tides. Organised races are held on most Monday and Thursday afternoons, while Fridays are generally for cruising.

The annual fee for membership of the sub section is Dhs.950. Contact Carol Milne (621 7394).

Sand Boarding/Skiing

Other options → Tour Operators [p.115]

The big dunes at Liwa, some of which are more than 300 metres high, are a wonderful place to try this exciting and unusual sport. OK, so it's rather like skiing through sludge, but it can be great fun! Find yourself some big dunes and feel the 'rush' of the wind as you take a slow, jerky ride down the sandy slopes. It's a quick sport to learn and it doesn't hurt when you fall.

The boards are usually standard snowboards, but as the sand is quite hard on them, they often can't be used for anything else afterwards. Some sports stores sell 'sand boards', which are cheaper and more basic snowboards. As an alternative for children, a plastic sledge or something similar is enough to give a lot of fun.

All the major tour companies offer tours to ski the highest dunes and give basic instruction on how to stay up, how to surf and how to fall properly! This can be available either as part of another tour or as a dedicated sand boarding tour. A half day sand boarding tour costs Dhs.175 - 200.

Sports

Activities

Shooting

Other options ➜ Paintballing [p.192]

At present there are no shooting clubs in Abu Dhabi for expats to join, so your best bet is to head north to Dubai, Ras Al Khaimah or Umm Al Quwain for some target practice.

Hatta Fort Hotel

Location ➜ Hatta Fort Hotel · Hatta	04 852 3211
Hours ➜ Timings on request	
Web/email ➜ www.dutcohotels.com	Map Ref ➜ UAE-D3

Clay pigeon shooting is one of the many activities offered at Hatta Fort Hotel, which is about two and a half hours' drive from Abu Dhabi. More frequently visited as an overnight retreat from the hustle and bustle of the cities, Hatta Fort has a variety of sports, plus the added attraction of superb food and beverage facilities, including a Friday barbie for Dhs.85 net.

> **Cost:** *Dhs.95 for 25 shots. Day visitors on Fridays and public holidays purchase a voucher at the entry gate (Dhs.40 for adults, Dhs.20 for children), which is redeemable against hotel facilities.*

Jebel Ali Shooting Club

Location ➜ Nr Jebel Ali Htl · Jebel Ali	04 883 6555
Hours ➜ 13:00 - 22:00 Closed Tue	
Web/email ➜ www.jebelalihotel.com	Map Ref ➜ UAE-B3

The Jebel Ali Shooting Club welcomes members and non members alike. Shooting is done in clay on five different floodlit ranges from Skeet to Ball Trap, American Trap, Olympic Trap and Sporting, as well as on the indoor 25 metre computerised pistol range. Instructors are available for comprehensive lessons in either pistol or clay shooting.

> **Prices:** *Lessons for non members – Dhs.100 (clay shooting), Dhs.75 (pistol shooting); lessons for members – Dhs.75 (clay shooting), Dhs.50 (pistol shooting).*
>
> *The club is currently closed for renovation.*

Ras Al Khaimah Shooting Club

Location ➜ Al Dehes · 20 min from RAK Airport	07 236 3622
Hours ➜ 15:00 - 20:00	
Web/email ➜ na	Map Ref ➜ UAE-D1

This club welcomes anyone interested in learning to shoot any type of gun, from 9mm pistols to shotguns and long rifles. There are a variety of ranges, some air conditioned and indoors such as the 50 metre rifle range, while others are outdoors, like the 200 metre rifle range. Archery is also available. A canteen sells snacks and soft drinks, and the club is open on Mondays for women and children only.

Skydiving

Other options ➜ Paragliding [p.193]
Hang Gliding [p.183]

Umm Al Quwain Aeroclub

Location ➜ See below	06 768 1447
Hours ➜ 09:00 - 17:30	
Web/email ➜ www.uaqaeroclub.com	Map Ref ➜ UAE-C1

In addition to flying paramotors and microlights, Umm Al Quwain Aeroclub dropzone operates as a skydive school and boogie centre. You can enjoy an eight level AFF (Accelerated Free Fall) parachute course (price Dhs.5,200; Dhs.200 is refundable) and train for your international parachute licence. Alternatively, if you are curious to know what jumping out of a plane feels like, try a tandem jump with an instructor from 12,000 feet for Dhs.720. Special rates are available for practice jumps for professional teams and skydivers from all around the world are welcome.

> **Location:** *16 km along the road from UAQ roundabout heading in the direction of Ras Al Khaimah, before Dreamland Aqua Park and opposite UAQ Shooting Club, on the left hand side of the road… just look for the hangars and the big plane by the sea!*

Snooker

Abu Dhabi Snooker Centre

Location ➜ Sedar Bld · Khalidiya	633 3300
Hours ➜ 09:00 - 24:00 Fri 15:00 - 24:00	
Web/email ➜ mmgroup@emirates.net.ae	Map Ref ➜ 9-A1

This is the first snooker hall to have opened in Abu Dhabi and is currently open to anyone wishing to play, although a membership scheme may eventually come into operation. There are eight full sized BBL Monarch tables imported from the UK and available in two different rooms. Prices are Dhs.25 for downstairs or Dhs.30 for the upstairs tables, for one hour's play. Pre-booking is advisable.

Abu Dhabi Snooker League

Location → Club, The · Al Meena **621 3983**
Hours → Tue 19:30
Web/email → www.the-club.com   Map Ref → 7-A2

The snooker section holds a weekly event called the 'Snooker Scene' on Tuesday evenings, which is open to both members and their guests. This is the night when snooker enthusiasts gather for a fun evening, playing either singles or doubles through to midnight.

A snooker league exists for club members, and tournaments are arranged throughout the autumn, winter and spring months for those interested in competition play. The Club snooker room has three full size tables. Waiter service is available from the main bar.

For further details contact snooker section Chairman, David Dorrington (681 1127).

Note: *Membership of The Club is required to play here.*

Snooker

Shooters

Location → Htl Inter-Continental · Al Khubeirah **03 768 6686**
Hours → 18:00 - 01:00
Web/email → www.interconti.com   Map Ref → 15-E4

Shooters is home to four pool tables and a snooker table for anyone who wants to brush up on their skills. Refreshments and light snacks are available and the club aims to be closely associated with other pool and snooker clubs around the country.

Snorkelling

Other options → Diving [p.173]

A mask and snorkel is a great way to see the varied underwater life of the Gulf or the East Coast, where it is especially good. On the Gulf of Oman coast, popular places include Snoopy Island, near the Sandy Beach Motel, Dibba. There are also good spots further north, such as the beach north of Dibba village, where the coast is rocky and there's coral close to the shore.

Most hotels or dive centres rent equipment; snorkel, mask and fins. Costs vary greatly, so shop around.

Check out the *Underwater Explorer (UAE)* for further information on where and how to go snorkelling in the UAE.

Beach Hut, The

Location → Sandy Beach Motel · East Coast **09 244 5050**
Hours → Timings on request
Web/email → www.sandybm.com   Map Ref → na

For those who want an exhilarating snorkelling experience, this East Coast venue is the only way to go. Snoopy Island, the 'house' reef, is just off their private beach and is an excellent site to enjoy the underwater world. Equipment is available for sale, alternatively rent a full set for the day for Dhs.50. You can also try kayaks or windsurfing.

Blue Dolphin Company LLC

Location → Htl Inter-Continental · Bainuna St **666 9392**
Hours → 08:00 - 13:00 16:00 - 19:00 Closed Fri
Web/email → www.interconti.com   Map Ref → 10-C1

Snorkel equipment can be hired for Dhs.50 per set for 24 hours. Alternatively, for Dhs.500 the company will take you to an interesting snorkelling area, such as off Ras Al Ghurb Island. This covers boat hire and equipment for a 1 - 1½ hour trip for about five people. Snorkel equipment can also be hired for their dhow trips. Timings are available on request.

Sports

Activities

Oceanic Hotel

Location → Beach Rd, Khorfakkan · East Coast	**09 238 5111**
Hours → 09:00 - 17:00	
Web/email → www.oceanichotel.com	Map Ref → UAE-E2

An ideal place for snorkelling, the East Coast boasts beautiful clear waters and plenty of fish and coral. The Oceanic Hotel offers a boat ride to Sharque Island and provides snorkelling gear for Dhs.60, alternatively snorkel and swim from the hotel beach to Hidden Beach. Equipment hire is Dhs.30 for one hour. These prices apply to hotel residents; visitors will also have to pay an entrance fee of Dhs.45 per adult and Dhs.25 per child. When you've had enough of the beach and water, enjoy the hotel's Spa Ayurveda.

Scuba 2000

Location → Al Badiyah Beach · Fujairah	**09 238 8477**
Hours → 09:00 - 19:00	
Web/email → www.scuba2000uae.com	Map Ref → UAE-E2

This East Coast centre offers snorkelling either directly from the beach or with a boat ride, usually to Snoopy and Sharque Islands, or Al Badiyah Rock. Snorkelling trips to these destinations cost Dhs.50, inclusive of fins, mask, snorkel and boots. The centre also has other water sports facilities, including diving, jet skis, pedal boats and canoes.

Softball

Abu Dhabi Softball League

Location → Various locations	**na**
Hours → Timings on request	
Web/email → na	Map Ref → 3-B2

Established in 1990, Abu Dhabi Softball League (ADSL) has grown rapidly in size from a mere 50 players to over 250. Derived from baseball, America's number one sport, softball has proved tremendously popular in Abu Dhabi, not only for Americans but for all expats. Softball games in Abu Dhabi are held over the weekends and played on the College fields, which have been donated to the league. ADSL has eight men's and four ladies' teams and occasionally holds co-ed games, which are very popular and always a great

success. The league also participates in international tournaments.

Contact: *Commissioner, Don Larson (050 621 7532).*

Squash

Other options → Health Clubs [p.207]

Courts are for hire mainly through the hotel sports clubs and private clubs. The squash league provides the best opportunities for competitive playing and meeting new players.

Abu Dhabi Squash League

Location → Various locations	**622 4292**
Hours → Wed 18:30	
Web/email → na	Map Ref → na

Run under the auspices of the Abu Dhabi Squash Rackets Association, the league has been going for over 20 years. There are five divisions with seven or eight teams in each division. Several tournaments are run throughout the year and teams meet on Wednesdays at a variety of venues (clubs, hotels, oil company facilities). The squash season runs from October - April, with a break for Christmas and Ramadan, and finishes with a dinner dance and presentations.

There's no minimum or maximum age eligibility, but a reasonable level of play is required. Annual membership is Dhs.750 per team of seven players. Contact Chairman Medhat Al Hammami (050 622 4292).

Swimming

Other options → Beaches [p.114]
Health Clubs [p.207]

Abu Dhabi's location on the Arabian Gulf means easy access to water that's relatively clean and a pleasant temperature for most of the year. During the three hottest months of the summer, the water near the beach is often hotter than a bath!

Most hotels have swimming pools that are open for use by the public for a day entrance fee. This charge varies, but ranges from Dhs.50 - 60 weekdays and Dhs.75 - 100 at weekends. Swimming lessons are available; expect to pay Dhs.50 - 70 for 30 minutes private tuition. The pools are usually cooled for the summer months.

Swimming off the beaches is possible, whether it's a public beach or beach club or park. Remember to be modest in your choice of costume and, on the East Coast of the UAE, keep an eye out for jellyfish etc.

Warning: *When swimming in the sea do not underestimate the strength of the tides and currents. Even on the safest looking beaches, rip tides have been known to carry people out to sea. In 1999, 100 people drowned off the UAE's coast, due in part to the combination of strong rip tides and lack of swimming ability.*

Table Tennis

Other options ➜ Health Clubs [p.207]

Please refer to the list of beach, health and sports clubs. Most offer at least one table tennis table.

Tennis

Other options ➜ Health Clubs [p.207]
Dubai Tennis Open [p.45]

Tennis is well provided for in Abu Dhabi, with courts available for use by the public in hotels or in private organisations solely for their members. Many courts have floodlighting to allow play in the evenings – the coolest time of the day, and about the only time you'll want to play outside in the summer. Prices for hiring courts vary between Dhs.25 - 50 weekdays, but you may be charged as much as Dhs.100 at weekends. Group or individual coaching is widely available.

For those interested in professional tennis, Dubai has firmly established itself on the international tennis circuit with the US$1,000,000 *Dubai Duty Free Tennis Open*, held in the middle of February each year at Dubai Tennis Stadium. For further information, check out the *Dubai Explorer*.

Dubai Tennis Academy	
Location ➜ American University, Dxb · Al Sufouh	050 655 6152
Hours ➜ Timings on request	
Web/email ➜ na	Map Ref ➜ UAE-C2

Dubai Tennis Academy offers professional coaching year round for aspiring players of all ages and abilities. All coaches are USPTA (United States Professional Tennis Association) qualified professionals. The academy is a worldwide agent for the Florida based Bollettieri Sports Academy (BSA) and organises international tennis clinics with BSA coaches to tie in with major tournaments on the pro tennis circuit. Plans for 2003 include clinics in

Dubai, Melbourne, New Zealand, Sydney and Singapore. The academy's full time adult and junior programmes include private lessons, group clinics, competitions and ladies' tennis mornings. They also offer school holiday sports camps for children.

Tennis

Triathlon

Other options ➜ Running [p.194]
Swimming [p.198]
Cycling [p.172]

There are a fair number of triathlon enthusiasts in the Emirates and, through the winter season from about October to April, there's quite a busy calendar of triathlons, biathlons and aquathons held in Abu Dhabi and Dubai.

Abu Dhabi Triathlon Club	
Location ➜ Various locations	na
Hours ➜ Timings on request	
Web/email ➜ www.geocities.com/abudhabitri	Map Ref ➜ na

The Abu Dhabi Triathlon Club is an informal but well-represented group of people who train and race together. Some of the group are experienced and able athletes, some are beginners looking to complete their first triathlon, and others just enjoy the social aspect of having someone to chat to while running.

Sports

Activities

Thanks to the efforts of a secret emailer, everyone is kept in the loop with regular training and event updates. Enthusiasts can find groups of people training every day of the week, and newcomers are welcome. Anyone interested in joining or being added to the regular email list should send an email to the tri club.

Wadi & Dune Bashing

With vast areas of rarely visited wilderness to explore, wadi and dune bashing are among the most popular pastimes in the UAE. The wadis, the mountains, the desert and the African 'savannah-like' plains offer a variety of challenging driving.

Dune or desert driving is possibly the toughest challenge for car and driver, but probably the most fun, while in the mountains and wadis the driving is relatively straightforward. Wadis are (usually dry) gullies that follow the course of seasonal rivers and are carved through the rock by rushing floodwater.

If you're going seriously off-road, it's always advisable to travel with at least two vehicles. If anything goes wrong, you'll be glad of an extra pair of hands or a tow. Driving in the mountains and wadis just requires common sense and quick thinking about the choice of gears for the hills and river crossings. But if you're trying desert driving for the first time, go with someone who has experience, since driving on sand needs very different skills to other surfaces. Caution should be the watchword, especially when you're learning – don't tackle anything you're not sure of, even if someone else has done it. A steady approach is usually the best, using low gears and 4 wheel drive to keep your speed under control.

One point about the word 'bashing' — while a popular term for this form of entertainment, it can be misleading. Most, if not all, of your journey off-road should be on existing tracks to protect the environment from further damage. Try to avoid the temptation to create new tracks across virgin countryside. Although much of the UAE 'outback' may look devoid of life, there is a surprising variety of flora and fauna that exists in a delicate balance.

For further information and tips on driving off-road, including stunning satellite imagery with 20 superimposed routes, detailed route descriptions and striking photos, refer to the *Off-Road Explorer (UAE)* published by Explorer Publishing. This also includes a useful Off-Road Directory.

If you want to venture into the wilderness, but don't want to organise it yourself, contact the tour companies; all offer a range of desert and mountain safaris. See Tour Operators [p.115].

If you don't have a 4 wheel drive, one can be hired from most car hire companies. See Car Rental Agencies [p.34].

Dune bashing

OffRoad Emirates

Location → Nr BHS Bld · Shk Hamdan St	**633 3232**
Hours → 08:00 - 13:00 16:00 - 19:00 Closed Fri	
Web/email → www.offroademirates.com	Map Ref → 8-A1

Founded in 1986, OffRoad Emirates specialises in trips throughout the UAE, Oman and Iran for individuals or small groups. The trips suit those with a sense of adventure and cultural and historical interest.

The company organises exclusive entry to the wildlife sanctuaries located east and west of Liwa Oasis, where visitors can view gazelle, oryx and other indigenous wildlife. They also offer guided trips to the Rub Al Khali desert by 4 wheel drive (this can be arranged in your own 4 WD). Camping equipment is provided, along with meals, and trips are tailor made to your requirements, lasting from a weekend to extensive touring in Oman or Iran for up to 26 days. Contact George Duncan.

Sports

Activities

Wakeboarding

Other options → Beaches [p.114]
Jet Skiing [p.188]
Water Skiing [p.203]

Al Jazira Hotel and Resort

Location → Btn Abu Dhabi & Dubai · Ghantoot Area | 562 9100
Hours → Timings on request
Web/email → na   Map Ref → na

It looks easy on telly, but your first try will definitely end up in a fun, but disastrous mess! The Jazira resort, with its secluded artificially constructed bay, new equipment and instructors is a great spot to learn without looking like a complete loser. The idea is similar to snowboarding, or water skiing with one ski. Try to keep your body under control and your legs more or less straight, creating resistance against the water. Once you've figured the basics out, addiction might follow. Ten minutes, including a driver, costs around Dhs.50.

Water Parks

Other options → Amusement Parks [p.230]

Currently, Abu Dhabi doesn't have a water park; however, a family trip to Dreamland Aqua Park in Umm Al Quwain can be worthwhile, as well as being excellent value for money. For further information on water parks, refer to the *Dubai Explorer*.

Dreamland Aqua Park

Location → 17 km North of UAQ on RAK Rd · UAQ | 06 768 1888
Hours → 10:00 - 20:00
Web/email → www.dreamlanduae.com   Map Ref → UAE-C1

Located in Umm Al Quwain, Dreamland Aqua Park brings you the excitement of four million gallons of fresh water, over 60 acres of grounds and 25 aquatic and non aquatic attractions. It is one of the largest aqua parks in the world – a truly unique experience for any resident or visitor to the Middle East.

Dreamland combines the best water rides with lush green lawns (pleasant for relaxing). Alternatively, visit the amusement centre or the 400 metre go-kart track (available without a Dreamland pass). All the excitement may make you hungry... food stalls and restaurants offer a variety of cuisine; you can even relax and cool down at the jacuzzi bar.

Entrance fees: *A visit here is excellent value for money; adults Dhs.40; children Dhs.20.*

Opening hours: *Change according to the season. Fridays and public holidays are for families; season pass holders or pre-booked groups only.*

SplashLand

Location → WonderLand · Umm Hurair · Dubai | 04 324 1222
Hours → 10:00 - 20:00   Closed Sun
Web/email → wonderld@emirates.net.ae   Map Ref → UAE-C2

Yet another water park located in Dubai, SplashLand is part of the WonderLand Theme & Water Park experience. Try any of the nine water rides, relax by the pool and sunbathe or eat at one of the restaurants. There's an adult swimming pool plus a children's activity pool, with slides, bridges and water cannons. Lockers and changing rooms are available.

See also: *WonderLand Theme & Water Park [p.230].*

Timings: *Change seasonally, so check before leaving home to avoid disappointment.*

Wild Wadi Water Park

Location → Umm Suqeim · Dubai | 04 348 4444
Hours → 11:00 - 21:00
Web/email → www.wildwadi.com   Map Ref → UAE-C2

Wonderfully named, Wild Wadi in Dubai is one of the world's most advanced water adventure theme parks. Spread over 12 acres, it's based around the adventures of Juha, a mythical friend of Sinbad. The park offers a variety of water rides, ranging from the relaxing to the downright terrifying! For the young and young at heart, this stunning park offers a day of unforgettable fun.

Entrance fees: *Adults Dhs.99; children Dhs.80.*

Lifeguards patrol all water areas and rides are regulated by height restrictions for those under 1.1 metres. To safeguard your wallet, you are given a wrist credit card – what you don't spend is refunded when you leave.

Sports

Activities

Water Skiing

Other options ➔ Beach Clubs [p.203]
Jet Skiing [p.188]
Wakeboarding [p.202]

Al Jazira Hotel and Resort

Location ➔ Btn Abu Dhabi & Dubai · Ghantoot Area | **562 9100**
Hours ➔ Timings on request
Web/email ➔ na   Map Ref ➔ na

Fascinated by the thought of doing dazzling acrobatics on water, but don't want to be seen trying it at your club? Drive up to Al Jazira (ideal of you're one of those people who divide their life between the capital and Dubai) for the perfect opportunity to escape and maybe learn how to ride the water professionally (coaching is on the programme, you'll be relieved to hear!).

Costs: *Water skiing and wakeboarding Dhs.50 for 10 minutes. Five coaching sessions plus one free, Dhs.400*

BEACH, HEALTH & SPORTS CLUBS

Relaxation junkies and keep fit fans should have no problem finding facilities that suit them from among Abu Dhabi's excellent range of beach, health, golf and sports clubs.

To help distinguish between the various facilities available, they have been categorised as follows:

- Health clubs generally offer workout facilities: machines, weights etc, plus classes varying from aerobics to yoga.
- Beach clubs are similar to health clubs, but with the added bonus of beach access.
- Sports clubs have similar facilities to health clubs, but also offer additional activities such as swimming, tennis and squash.
- Golf clubs, obviously offer golf, although many have additional facilities such as a swimming pool, tennis courts or a gym.

Neighbourhood gyms also exist in Abu Dhabi. Many of these are filled with 'serious' workout fanatics (lots of beefy men in vests!) and the facilities can be older and dated. Prices, however, are generally a fraction of health club membership fees.

Although built on an island, you'll have difficulties finding a good public beach in the capital. The best option is to join one of the beach clubs to swim, play sports and laze in the sun in relative peace and quiet. The beach clubs in particular are very popular with families at weekends and can get rather busy. Combined with excellent food and beverage outlets, it's not surprising that these are popular destinations for the day.

Most places offer membership schemes and these usually prove the best value for money, if the place is used regularly. If you're part of a couple or a family you'll get the best bargain, as your charges can be almost the same as a single person would pay.

Before becoming a member somewhere have a good look around at what's on offer. It really is worth taking the time to do this since once you've signed a membership contract it can be difficult to get out of (nothing is more irritating than paying loads of money to join a club and then wishing you'd joined the one down the road!). Most of the clubs allow day entry to non members for a fee. At weekends, many offer a Friday brunch or barbecue and the price includes use of the leisure facilities, as well as food.

Refer to the Club Facilities Table [p.209] for details of the various clubs in Abu Dhabi, including membership rates and facilities.

Beach Clubs

Other options ➔ Health Clubs [p.207]

Abu Dhabi Marina "The Yacht Club"

Location ➔ Nr Le Meridien Htl · Tourist Club Area | **644 0300**
Hours ➔ Timings on request
Web/email ➔ www.abudhabimarina.com   Map Ref ➔ 4-B4

Squeezed between the giant Abu Dhabi Mall and Le Meridien Hotel, this club is often simply associated with the Colosseum nightclub or Alamo, but it's actually a leisure venue with its own private beach and marina. An attractive courtyard surrounds a large, deep swimming pool; perfect for doing lengths. A second smaller pool complements the children's play area. Surrounded by artificial rocks, small waterfalls, sun loungers and an Arabic tent, it's easy to relax after a busy day.

Squash and tennis courts can be used by full members or you can join on a cheaper membership that excludes these activities. Unfortunately, the gym is rather small and with dated equipment, although the range is varied.

Costs: *Non members daily entrance Dhs.50; peak times Dhs.100.*

Abu Dhabi Tourist Club

Location → Nr Le Meridien Htl · Tourist Club Area | **672 3400**
Hours → 08:00 - 24:00
Web/email → adclub@emirates.net.ae   Map Ref → 7-D1

Established in 1972, this club offers a range of activities for all ages. From water sports and children's play areas to a bowling alley, library, food outlets and Internet café, the club is a virtual hive of activity.

Water sports include water skiing, swimming and windsurfing from the large beach. Tuition is available. There are also marina facilities for members' boats, and boat hire. Other activities include football (the pitch is floodlit), badminton, tennis, volleyball, basketball and table tennis. Martial arts are also offered with coaching for both adults and children. There's even a billiard and snooker room, and a theatre for children's events and stage shows.

Al Diar Jazira Beach Resort

Location → Al Diar Jazira Htl · Abu Dhabi | **562 9100**
Hours → 09:00 - 18:00 Thu & Fri 09:00 - 19:00
Web/email → jazbeach@emirates.net.ae   Map Ref → na

If you want to get out of Abu Dhabi for a while, this could be the ideal destination since there's enough here to entertain the family for the whole day.

A small private beach lines the spectacular bay beneath the hotel, and borders a manmade canal. The beach is home to the water sports centre where you can jet ski, windsurf, sail, fish, scuba dive etc, and there's no problem with tides and surf. There's also a swimming pool with plenty of places to relax, a children's play area and 9 holes of crazy golf. Good health club facilities include squash and tennis courts, basketball, table tennis and a gym with views over the gardens down to the canal.

Every Friday sees a beach party (11:00 - 17:00; the Dhs.25 entrance fee is redeemable at Dalma Restaurant) with free camel rides along the beach.

Club, The

Location → Club, The · Al Meena | **673 1111**
Hours → 08:00 - 01:00 Fri 08:00 - 24:00
Web/email → www.the-club.com   Map Ref → 7-A2

Over a quarter of a century ago, the basis of what was to become The Club was formed, but even today the aims remain the same; to provide a social, sporting and cultural centre for expats in Abu Dhabi.

Sports and leisure facilities are extensive: as well as the pool and beach, there's diving, sailing, tennis, squash, badminton, snooker, exercise classes, children's activities, swimming lessons, laundry and a library. A new gym complex is due for completion in the summer/autumn 2003. Various food and drink outlets include a family room, top deck bar, pool bar and a sports bar, and the club hosts a variety of quality entertainment, including concerts and the Jongleurs Comedy Club.

While devoid of 5 star luxury, this functional, family orientated club makes up for this by the friendly atmosphere, wide variety of activities and facilities, and reasonable prices. It's a private members facility and cannot be accessed by non members, unless accompanied by a member.

Health Spa & Leisure Club

Location → Le Meridien · Tourist Club Area | **697 4254**
Hours → 09:00 - 22:00
Web/email → spa@meridien-abudhabi.co.ae   Map Ref → 7-D1

Extensive renovations transformed the facilities at Le Meridien. The landscaped area around the three swimming pools provides a relaxing, 'get away from it all' atmosphere. There's a small, clean sandy beach, and an area of sea marked off for safe swimming. Palm trees and sunshades provide respite from the sun and waiter service is on hand to bring you refreshments.

Offshore, visitors can enjoy a range of water sports, including windsurfing, diving and fishing. The energetic can enjoy the excellent gym facilities, various exercise classes, tennis, squash, beach volleyball, basketball and, of course, the swimming pools. Then perhaps take the advice of the friendly staff to choose between over 30 treatments at the spa. There's something here for everyone.

Costs: *Daily Dhs.215 for use of all facilities; Dhs.90 for gym only. Women only times apply to the gym, spa and squash – check to avoid disappointment.*

Hiltonia Beach Club

Location → Hilton Abu Dhabi · Corniche Rd West | **681 1900**
Hours → 08:00 - 20:30
Web/email → www.hilton.com   Map Ref → 10-C2

After undergoing a long reconstruction programme, this beach club opened in 2001. One

Best Beach in Abu Dhabi

"RO-RO" Chinese Restaurant   "Le Jardin" International Restaurant   "Arirang" Korean Restaurant

Chalet   "Argila" Oriental Restaurant   Rooms

120 rooms and Chalets all with sea view and balconies situated only 5 KM from the city centre.
Seven Food Outlets including 24 hours room service.
Temperature controlled swimming pool and 2 children's pools.
Extensive water sport facilities including Jet Ski & Dhow.
New health club with modern equipment, 2700m^2 of children's Fun Park with video games.
Visa assistance & airport transfers.

KHALIDIA PALACE HOTEL فندق الخالدية بالإس
Abu Dhabi أبـوظبـي

Tel.: 02-6662470 Fax: 02-6660411
E-Mail: kphauh@emirates.net.ae Website: www.khalidiapalacehotel.co.ae

of the highlights here is the amount of space on the beach with lots of sun loungers and a scenic view over the Breakwater and Lulu Island. Activities include windsurfing, sailing, water skiing, fishing trips, a six hole pitch and putt, golf green and volleyball. The large pool has a swim up bar and children have two separate pools (one with a slide). There's also a garden area with palms for shade and more sun loungers. There are plans of moving the gym from the main hotel to the beach club in July/August 2003.

Food outlets include Coconut Bay BBQ and the open air Vasco's. A large terrace with a built in stage is used for special events and concerts.

Hiltonia Beach Club

Palm Beach Leisure Club

Location → Al Diar Gulf Htl · Al Maqtaa | **441 4777**
Hours → 09:00 till sunset
Web/email → www.aldiarhotels.com   Map Ref → 1-D3

Family orientated and with large grassy grounds interspersed with palms, this aptly named leisure club is ideal for those living in the outer areas of the city. The swimming pool is a delight for both swimmers and observers, as it has a walkover bridge and a fountain. Cool down by the pool bar, or in another pool with a large waterslide. Apart from the beach, there's also a play area especially for younger children.

The busy gym has the usual range of equipment for cardiovascular or strength training. As befits a complex this size, several areas serve refreshments

and there's a barbecue on Friday afternoons with accompanying live music. This club is also the site for an annual raft race competition.

Activities: Water skiing, kneeboarding, banana and tube rides (all cost Dhs.35 for 10 minutes); surfing, canoeing (both Dhs.40 per hour); sailing (Dhs.65 per hour). The club also has four tennis courts, two squash courts (instruction available), table tennis and snooker.

Palms Resort

Location → Sheraton Abu Dhabi · Corniche Rd East | **677 3333**
Hours → 07:30 - 22:30
Web/email → sheraton@emirates.net.ae   Map Ref → 8-A3

With a central location, Palms Resort is one of the older and more established beach resorts in Abu Dhabi. It recently underwent renovation and the small beach overlooking the sea and Lulu Island now offers a busy view of construction. The spacious and large modern gym has windows overlooking the beach and offers a good choice of classes. There's also a swimming pool, children's pool, play area and activity club.

Even when busy, the club maintains a relaxed and exclusive atmosphere, with friendly and helpful staff. Activities range from sailing and windsurfing to water skiing, catamaran, fishing, island and sightseeing cruises, banana rides, tennis, squash and table tennis.

Sadiyat Island Beach Resthouse

Location → Tourist Club · Tourist Club Area | **672 3400**
Hours → See timings below
Web/email → na   Map Ref → 7-D1

Managed by the Abu Dhabi Tourist Club, this resort is a short boat ride away from Abu Dhabi. It has a long pristine beach and offers a variety of water sports. Less energetic activities, such as backgammon or snooker, are catered for in the entertainment hall (ideal for escaping the summer heat). There are 14 chalets offering accommodation for overnight stays, plus a bar and restaurant that offer a mixture of international cuisine.

Timings: On Fridays, a boat leaves at 09:00 and 11:00 from the Tourist Club, returning at 16:00 in the winter and 16:00 and 18:00 in the summer (check timings). The trip takes 15 minutes by speedboat and the cost is Dhs.60, which includes lunch. On other days of the week, 24 hour advance booking is required to reach the island and this is only available to families or larger groups.

Beach, Health & Sports Clubs

Activities

Other options → Beach Clubs [p.203]
Sports Clubs [p.212]
Sporting Goods [p.153]
UAE Annual Events [p.42]

Abu Dhabi Health & Fitness Club

Location → Golf & Equestrian Club · Al Mushrif | 443 6333
Hours → 08:30 - 22:00
Web/email → www.adhfc.com   Map Ref → 3-D3

There's no excuse not to exercise when you consider the glitzy, luxurious surroundings at what must be Abu Dhabi's most opulent health club. The palatial exterior is easily matched by the quality and range of facilities and activities on offer inside, and it's all being extended to create a small Wild Wadi water park.

This 'sports heaven' includes two extensively equipped gyms (one for VIPs and one for the masses), squash, volleyball and tennis courts, 2 lane bowling alley (Dhs.60 per hour), exercise classes, crèche, and much more.   Regular competitions and tuition programmes are held and coaching is available in tennis, horse riding and swimming. Outside there's an excellent swimming pool. Although the club has no beach, the outside jacuzzi, plunge pool and dining area (excellent food and service) make the club an ideal destination for a lazy afternoon.

Cost: *Daily guest rate: Dhs.100 for use of all facilities; Dhs.50 for use of pool and gym only.*

Women only: *Monday and Wednesday 08:00 - 11:00.*

Bodylines

Location → Al Ain Rotana Htl · Zayed Bin Sultan St | 03 751 5111
Hours → 08:00 - 22:00
Web/email → www.britishcouncil.org/uae   Map Ref → 14-E4

Set in landscaped gardens with a relaxing atmosphere and friendly staff, this health club could entertain the whole family. Facilities include squash and tennis courts, and a gym with well-maintained equipment. The male and female changing rooms have their own sauna and steam room, and massage and aerobics are also offered.

The gym overlooks the green courtyard with a large swimming pool set in attractive and cosy surroundings with plenty of places to relax. A

separate swimming pool with a roof keeps children occupied and under good supervision. Drinks and refreshments are available from the pool bar.

Entrance fees: *Non members, weekends, adults Dhs.75, children Dhs.50; non members, weekdays, adults Dhs.50, children Dhs.30.*

Dhabi Health Club

Location → Al Ain Palace Hotel · Corniche Rd East | 679 4777
Hours → 08:00 - 22:00 Fri 08:00 - 19:00
Web/email → aphsales@emirates.net.ae   Map Ref → 8-B3

This health club is attached to the Al Ain Palace Hotel, but the complex is shared with guests of the Abu Dhabi Grand hotel. Facilities include a gym, squash courts, mixed sauna, steam room, jacuzzi, exercise room and beauty parlour (some amenities have allocated ladies' and gents' periods). While the facilities are functional, they are perhaps not as glitzy as at other health clubs.

Outside, the new swimming pool is due for completion in June/July 2003.   Private beach facilities are available at Lulu Island, directly opposite the hotel. Many of the staff are old hands and all are friendly and helpful. Parking can be difficult.

Membership: *Club membership is available for periods ranging from one month to a full year. Daily rate: Dhs.40 per adult, Dhs.20 per child (Dhs.60/30 weekends and public holidays).*

Falcon Health Club, The

Location → Tourist Club · Tourist Club Area | 672 3400
Hours → 08:00 - 24:00
Web/email → na   Map Ref → 7-D1

As part of the Abu Dhabi Tourist Club, the Falcon Health Club offers a gym and small health spa. The gym is small but functional and personal trainers are available to offer specialised advice (if you can hear them over the music!). A large aerobics studio offers a variety of classes, including aerobics, ballet and karate. There's also tennis, badminton, basketball, bowling, a swimming pool and a beach.

The club has the feel of a government run leisure centre. Facilities are clean, extensive and in good order, but are dated and the service is limited. However, day entrance and membership fees are lower than for a hotel health club, making it good value. Opening times are sometimes restricted to men or women on different days – check before you go.

Beach, Health & Sports Clubs

Activities

Club Membership Rates

Club Name	Location	Membership Rates				
		Male	Female	Couple	Family	Non Members (peak)
Beach Clubs & Spas						
Abu Dhabi Marina & Yacht Club	Nr Le Meridien Htl, Tourist Club Area	4200	2500	5500	250+	50
Abu Dhabi Tourist Club	Nr Le Meridien Htl, Tourist Club Area	On req.	On req.	On req.	On req.	–
Beach Club, Rotana*	Nr Le Meridien Htl, Tourist Club Area	Not Available at time of printing				
Beach Club, The, Khalidia						
Full Membership	Khalidia Palace Hotel	3800	2800	5000	800	25+
Beach		2850	2100	3750	801	–
Tennis		1500	1500	na	1500	–
Club, The*	Al Meena Port	1550	1400	na	2950	25+
Health Spa and Leisure Club						
Gold	Le Meridien Hotel	8000	6000	10000	10000	35+
Silver		6000	4000	8000	8000	–
Health Club only		4500	3500	na	na	125
Hiltonia Beach & Sports Club	Hilton Abu Dhabi Corniche Rd West	6100	4200	8900	9980	40+
Sports Club Only		3000	2500	3560	4000	30+
Palm Beach Leisure Club	Al Diar Gulf Hotel & Resort	4000	3000	5800	7000	50+
Palms Resort						
Diamond	Sheraton Abu Dhabi Resort & Towers	8500	4900	10500	On Req.	50+
Emerald		6500	3750	8000	On Req.	50+
Sadiyat Island Beach Resthouse	Tourist Club	1800	1800	na	2000	20
Jazira						
Al Diar Jazira Beach Resort	Between Dubai & Abu Dhabi Road	1500	1500	2000	2500	50
Health Clubs						
Abu Dhabi Health & Fitness Club	Abu Dhabi Golf & Equestrian Club					
Gold		8000	6000	8000	10000	25+
Silver		4000	3000	4000	6000	
Abu Dhabi Ladies Club	Near Khalidia Palace Hotel	na	3500	na	7000	–
Dhabi Health Club	Al Ain Palace Hotel	2400	1800		3400	20+
Falcon Health Club	Abu Dhabi Tourist Club	2000	2000	na	na	30
Flex Fitness	Shk. Rashid Bin Saeed Al Maktoum St	1890	1790	2980	na	40
Inter-Fitness, Abu Dhabi						
Gold	Hotel Intercontinental	6000	4500	9000	11000	50+
Silver		4000	3000	7500	9000	50+
Le Club Health & Fitness	Millenium Hotel	2500	2500	5000	na	0-60
Powerfit Executive Fitness Centre	Crowne Plaza	3499	2499	4099	5099	35+
Sands Hotel Fitness Club	Sands Hotel	1500	1200	1900	2200	30
Skyline Health Club	Hilton Baynunah Tower	3000	2000	2800	2800	60
Viking Health Club	Sheraton Residence, Abu Dhabi	2500	2000	3500	4000	30+
Al Ain						
Bodylines	Al Ain Rotana Hotel	2300	1650	2750	250+	75
Hiltonia Resort & Aquatic Club	Hilton	2300	2300	2800	3000	20+
Inter-Fitness, Al Ain	Hotel Intercontinental	3000	2500	3500	150+	90

* Currently under renovations, due for completion in August 2003. Please phone the hotel for more details.

Beach, Health & Sports Clubs

Activities

Club Facilities

Club Name	Gym						Activity				Relaxation				
	Treadmills	Exercise bikes	Step machines	Rowing machines	Free weights	Resistance machines	Tennis courts	Swimming Pool	Squash courts	Aerobics/Dance Exercise	Massage	Sauna	Jacuzzi	Plunge pool	Steam room
Beach Clubs & Spas															
Abu Dhabi Marina & Yacht Club	1	1	1	–	✔	2	3FL	2	2	–	–	–	–	–	–
Abu Dhabi Tourist Club	6	5	3	2	✔	10	6FL	2	–	–	✔	✔	✔	–	✔
Beach Club, Rotana*	✔	✔	✔	✔	✔	✔	3	2	2	✔	✔	✔	✔	–	✔
Beach Club, The, Khalidia	9	2	2	1	✔	8	1FL	3	–	✔	✔	2	✔	–	✔
Club, The*	8	6	3	3	✔	10	4FL	1	2	✔	✔	✔	✔	✔	✔
Health Spa and Leisure Club	5	4	2	2	✔	16	2FL	2	2	✔	✔	✔	✔	✔	✔
Hiltonia Beach & Sports Club	✔	✔	✔	✔	✔	✔	2FL	2	1	✔	✔	✔	✔	✔	✔
Palm Beach Leisure Club	6	3	3	2	✔	30	4FL	1	2	✔	✔	✔	✔	✔	✔
Palms Resort	8	4	2	2	✔	25	2FL	3	2	✔	✔	✔	✔	✔	✔
Jazira															
Al Diar Jazira Beach Resort	1	2	1	1	✔	–	2Fl	2	1	–	✔	✔	✔	–	✔
Health Clubs															
Abu Dhabi Health & Fitness Club	7	10	6	2	✔	6	4FL	2	2	✔	✔	✔	✔	✔	✔
Abu Dhabi Ladies Club	5	3	2	2	✔	11	2FL	2	–	✔	✔	✔	✔	✔	✔
Dhabi Health Club	4	6	2	1	✔	15	–	✔	2	✔	✔	✔	✔	✔	✔
Falcon Health Club	6	5	3	2	✔	10	6FL	1	–	✔	✔	✔	✔	–	✔
Flex Fitness	6	5	3	2	✔	35	–	–	–	✔	–	✔	–	–	✔
Inter-Fitness, Abu Dhabi	9	6	3	2	✔	13	4FL	1	1	✔	✔	✔	✔	✔	✔
Le Club Health & Fitness	2	3	1	0	✔	1	–	1	–	–	✔	✔	–	–	✔
Powerfit Executive Fitness Centre	5	6	2	1	✔	17	–	✔	–	–	✔	✔	✔	–	✔
Skyline Health Club	3	2	1	1	✔	9	–	1	–	✔	✔	✔	–	–	✔
Viking Health Club	3	3	1	–	✔	8	–	1	–	✔	✔	✔	–	–	✔
Al Ain															
Bodylines	3	2	1	1	✔	15	2FL	2	2	✔	✔	✔	✔	–	✔
Hiltonia Resort & Aquatic Club	5	6	5	2	✔	1	4FL	3	2	✔	✔	✔	✔	–	✔
Inter-Fitness, Al Ain	5	4	2	2	✔	1	4FL	3	2	✔	✔	✔	✔	✔	✔

*Currently under renovations, due for completion in August 2003. Please phone the hotel for more details.

Le Meridien Gym

Flex Fitness

Location → Shk Rashid B Saeed Al Makt St | 621 3300
Hours → Sat - Thu 09:00 - 22:00 Fri 15:00 - 20:00
Web/email → flexfit@emirates.net.ae | Map Ref → 3-C4

Workout heaven – no frills, but every piece of equipment you can imagine! Flex Fitness is one of a growing band of fitness clubs that are independent of a hotel. Facilities include a large gym, cardio theatre (with TVs, personal remote controls and headphones), studio classes, small ladies' gym, jacuzzi, steam room, massage, Internet facility, café and crèche, plus reciprocal membership with their club in Dubai. Train your hardest by hiring a personal trainer for Dhs.100 for members (Dhs.130 non members).

With its personal touch and very reasonable membership rates, Flex Fitness is a great alternative to the more expensive and generally less focused hotel gyms.

Hiltonia Resort & Aquatic Club

Location → Hilton Al Ain · Al Ain | 03 768 6666
Hours → 08:00 - 22:00
Web/email → www.hilton.com | Map Ref → 15-D4

Situated in beautiful landscaped gardens, this is one of the best destinations in Al Ain for working out or spending a day by the pool. The health club offers an excellent range of facilities, including tennis and squash courts, a gym, 25 metre lap pool (excellent for undisturbed, length swimming), aerobics studio and an all grass, 9 hole par three golf course. However, if you feel in need of a little more leisure, the pool complex is a relaxing and tranquil environment. There's plenty of space to lounge by the pool, which also has a swim-up bar, water slide and water play area. Add to this, saunas, jacuzzis and steam rooms, as well as excellent food outlets or poolside service, and you're set for the day!

> **Timings:** The health club is open until 22:00 each evening, but the adult pool closes at 20:30 and the kids' pool at 18:00 winter, 19:00 summer.

Hiltonia Sports Club, The

Location → Hilton Abu Dhabi · Corniche Rd West | 681 1900
Hours → Check for timings
Web/email → www.hilton.com | Map Ref → 10-C2

While some facilities at Hiltonia will remain in the hotel, the sports club will be located next to the beach club (previously the sports club was in the hotel with the beach club across the street). Due for completion in August 2003, this club promises all the latest equipment and facilities, including a spa and a crèche, and should please any fitness enthusiast.

Tennis and squash facilities will remain in the hotel. Tennis coaching is available and Hiltonia is one of the venues for the Abu Dhabi Squash League. Instruction is excellent, offering professional advice and training tips.

Inter-Fitness, Abu Dhabi

Location → Htl Inter-Continental · Bainuna St | 666 6888
Hours → 06:00 - 23:00
Web/email → www.intercontinental.com | Map Ref → 10-C1

The main attraction here is the fantastic view over the marina and sea from the pool, beach and gym. The gym is spacious and airy with floor to ceiling windows and a welcoming atmosphere (and of course the lovely view), but the range of machines is limited. There's also a separate ladies' gym (again limited equipment), squash courts and pools. Membership is currently at 500+.

Inter-Fitness Abu Dhabi

Inter-Fitness, Al Ain

Location → Htl Inter-Continental · Al Khubeirah | 03 768 6666
Hours → 08:00 - 22:00
Web/email → www.interconti.com | Map Ref → 15-E4

Inter-Fitness offers the best facilities in Al Ain for a good workout, as the gym is very well equipped, clean and airy. For more exercise, try one of the classes – aerobics, martial arts or even line dancing are on offer, then brave the squash courts before relaxing in the sauna, jacuzzi or steam room. In the pleasant landscaped grounds of the hotel are four tennis courts (floodlit for evening use), and two swimming pools. One is an Olympic size pool which is good for length swimming and there's also a leisure pool with a bar and relaxation area.

Le Club Health & Fitness

Location → Millenium Hotel · Khalifa Bin Zayed St | 626 2700
Hours → 07:00 - 22:00
Web/email → www.millenniumhotels.com   Map Ref → 8-B2

At Le Club, they claim that relaxation is at the top of the agenda. This new club is about a year old and is rarely crowded – patrons are mainly hotel guests, plus a few outside members. The gym is rather small, but there's an instructor there all day if you have any queries about how to use the equipment. Membership comes with a 10% discount at all Millennium restaurants.

Nautilus Equipment

Powerfit Gym

Location → Crowne Plaza · Shk Hamdan St | 621 0000
Hours → 05:30 - 23:00
Web/email → abu-dhabi.crowneplaza.com   Map Ref → 8-C1

Located on the top two floors of the hotel, the general atmosphere here is of friendly, unhurried calm. On the roof the tranquil 'Acropolis' swimming pool is complemented by a jacuzzi, an area for sunbathing and a pool bar. Group and individual swimming lessons are available.

One floor down, the small fitness studio is functional and modern, and there's a new cardio room. Personal training programmes are available and the view of Abu Dhabi through the surrounding picture windows is stunning. You can also book various massage treatments; all come highly recommended. Membership numbers are limited to avoid the frenetic atmosphere evident in other oversubscribed gyms.

Swimming pool: *Open 07:00 - 22:00; closes slightly earlier on Thursday and Friday.*

Sands Hotel Fitness Club

Location → Sands Hotel · Shk Zayed 2nd St | 633 5335
Hours → 08:00 - 22:00
Web/email → na   Map Ref → 8-C1

You'll get a bit of a workout on the stairs up to this health club after leaving the elevator on the 16th floor. If you live around the corner from the hotel and don't need to be inspired by your surroundings, then this gym could suit you. The workout space is on the small side, but cardio machines and free weights are available, plus refreshments from the fridge beside the counter. There's a sauna to relax you after a tough session. Alternatively, head for the pool – its main feature is that it's on the roof, but again it's small. Use of the Abu Dhabi Tourist Club is included in the membership.

Skyline Health Club

Location → Baynunah Tower · Corniche Rd West | 632 7777
Hours → 07:00 - 22:00
Web/email → na   Map Ref → 9-A2

This club is probably in the most impressive location in Abu Dhabi, offering an amazing view over the Corniche and the city from the 29th floor. The fitness machines are arranged by the windows, so you can run, step or pump iron while enjoying the vista. The only disadvantage is that the gym is rather small and lacks some machines, which leads to overcrowding.

Other facilities include sauna and steam room, plus an indoor swimming pool (rarely crowded and also with a gorgeous view). Various classes include salsa, kickboxing, yoga and Tae Boe, as well as swimming lessons and massage, while if you want a tan, climb the stairs to the sundeck on the 31st floor.

Costs: *Daily Dhs.35; weekends Dhs.60.*

Viking Health Club

Location → Sheraton Residence · Shk Zayed 1st St | **666 6220**
Hours → 07:00 - 22:30
Web/email → sherresi@emirates.net.ae   Map Ref → 9-B1

Opened in 1997, this health club is suited to gym users who simply want to get on with their daily fix of exercise. The small complex offers a swimming pool, gym, steam room and sauna, various fitness classes and swimming lessons. The gym is well equipped with the latest Nautilus machines, but the choice of free weights is limited. The room is light and airy with a superb view over the Corniche. The swimming pool on the roof also has wonderful views, although it's not designed for the serious swimmer.

While it doesn't offer any unique features, this club is not overused and offers a comfortable 'get away from it all feel', especially on weekdays.

Sports Clubs

Other options → Beach Clubs [p.203]
Health Clubs [p.207]

Abu Dhabi Ladies Club

Location → Nr Ladies Beach · Al Ras Al Akhdar | **666 2228**
Hours → 10:00 - 22:00 Sat 12:00 - 20:00
Web/email → na   Map Ref → 10-E4

Located near the Corniche on private grounds, this spacious and opulent club provides a unique concept in entertainment, sports, fitness and leisure. Exclusively for ladies and children, the staff everywhere – be it in the fitness centre, restaurants, tennis courts, educational centre, or anywhere inside the club – are all females. Members have total freedom and privacy to enjoy all the facilities.

Membership is predominately Arabic, but all nationalities are welcome. Besides the usual health and fitness facilities including basketball and volleyball courts, the Abu Dhabi Ladies Club also offers a wide variety of children's activities as well as a nursery, a library and computer facilities, arts and crafts classes, and the famous Cleopatra's Spa offering every kind of treatment imaginable.

Without a member, non members on their own may only attend swimming, dance and aerobic classes. Boys only under the age of 7 are permitted (entry is free)

Membership fees: *3 months - Dhs.1500, 6 months - Dhs.2500, 1 year - Dhs.3500.*

LEISURE

Long term visitors or residents will find that although the choice of activities in Abu Dhabi is not huge, the range is constantly changing and growing. The following section covers a variety of pleasurable and interesting activities for your leisure time, from educational classes and the environment to language schools or the performing arts, such as music and dance, and much more in between. Whatever your leisure and pleasure, there's a good chance someone in town is willing to provide it.

Beauty Salons

Other options → Beauty Training [p.215]
Perfumes & Cosmetics [p.152]

Beauty is big business in the UAE! Abu Dhabi has a huge variety of salons to visit, offering every type of treatment imaginable. Shoppers can find a range of products (including everything from Paul Bryan and Toni & Guy). Services range from manicures to pedicures, waxing to henna, to the latest cuts and styles. Salons here are really popular and busy at night, especially for weddings and important occasions/functions. As can be expected, the quality and range of treatments vary greatly, so trial and error or word of mouth is probably the best way of finding a good salon.

Salons are mostly filled with a multitude of cultures. The alternative to visiting one is to have the stylist come to your home. Stylists in the city are female, barring hotels that have both male and female. Independent salons are good for privacy as men are not permitted inside and the windows are blocked out from nosy pedestrians.

There are also numerous small salons focusing on the Arabic female clientele. Their distinguishable characteristic is henna design service – look out for a decorated hand on the signs in shop windows. The traditional practice of painting henna on hands and feet, especially

Leisure

Activities

for weddings or special occasions, is still very popular with the national population. The intricate brown patterns fade after 2 - 3 weeks. A design on the ankle or shoulder can make a great memento of your visit to the Emirates and costs only about Dhs.30.

Bridge

Al Ain Bridge Club

Location ➜ Htl Inter-Continental · Al Khubeirah | 03 768 6686
Hours ➜ Mon 20:00
Web/email ➜ www.interconti.com   Map Ref ➜ 15-E4

Al Ain Bridge Club holds weekly duplicate sessions in a relaxed, congenial atmosphere. Beginners are welcome, although to take part in the duplicate session, you should be able to cope with basic bidding and play. They may hold beginners' lessons, if there is sufficient interest.

A charge of Dhs.10 per night is payable to the hotel, which covers hire of the room and tea, coffee and water. Members may order food or drinks at standard prices. Whatever your standard of play, go along for a social night out and meet others with a similar interest. Contact Carl Haigh (050 743 0133) for further details.

Chess

Abu Dhabi Chess & Culture Club

Location ➜ Behind Islamic Bank · Madinat Zayed | 633 1110
Hours ➜ 17:00 - 23:00
Web/email ➜ www.abudhabichess.com   Map Ref ➜ 7-D1

The interest in chess is part of an overall interest in developing all aspects of sport and culture in the country. Abu Dhabi Chess & Culture Club was opened in 1979 and has since participated in many activities, both locally and internationally. Since its inception, the club has sponsored many tournaments and competitions, and enrolled new members from all age groups, who now total about 800. The club also collaborates with other clubs in the country. All are welcome.

Darts

Abu Dhabi Darts League

Location ➜ Khalifa Bin Zayed St | 050 641 705
Hours ➜ Sun 8:30
Web/email ➜ www.kgbdart.com   Map Ref ➜ 8-C2

Darts has been enjoyed in Abu Dhabi for well over 20 years. It was first played in people's homes, but as Abu Dhabi grew, darts moved to the hotels and then to The (British) Club, where tournaments were held in the car park to accommodate the many entrants. Darts today is played in the hotels, to be enjoyed either as a player or a spectator.

All communities are represented in the league and all levels of players are accepted. There are now 12 teams registered playing at eight outlets every Sunday night from 21:00. Anyone interested should contact Chairman Sam Murtada (050 641 7050).

Drama Groups

Abu Dhabi Dramatic Society (ADDS)

Location ➜ Club, The · Al Meena | 681 1127
Hours ➜ Timings on request
Web/email ➜ www.a-d-d-s.org   Map Ref ➜ 7-A2

Formed many years ago, ADDS is an easygoing group of individuals from all walks of life. Every year they perform a pantomime that is usually a sell-out. This is a good time for those who are a little shy to come on stage and hide as part of the Chorus. For the more serious, there are other productions throughout the year. No experience is necessary and, even if you don't fancy acting, there's always plenty to do behind the scenes.

It costs nothing to join, but you do have to be a member of The Club (although you don't have to be a member to watch an ADDS performance).

Leisure

Activities

Health Spas

Other options → Health Clubs [p.207]
Massage [p.214]

Health Spa & Leisure Club

Location → Le Meridien · Tourist Club Area | 697 4254
Hours → 09:00 - 22:00
Web/email → spa@meridien-abudhabi.co.ae   Map Ref → 7-D1

For the ultimate in stress relief and personal pampering, a trip to one of the capitals longest established spas is a must. Treatments range from a session in the aquamedic pool with its carefully positioned, powerful jets of water for soothing away aches and pains, to a relaxing massage. If you're brave, try a stimulating seaweed wrap, before plunging into the temperature controlled pools of the Turkish bath. More medicinal treatments, such as 'pressotherapy' for lymphatic drainage, are available, as are facials and other cosmetic applications. After a session of pampering, use the other facilities on offer – gym, beach or eat at one of the food outlets. A real treat for body and mind.

Massage

Other options → Health Spas [p.214]
Health Clubs [p.207]

Probably the ultimate way to pamper and unwind is by having a massage. Whether it's a regular weekly treat or to get over a particularly trying time at work, it's sure to relax and soothe. Prices and standards vary, so shop around until you find someone that suits you. The cost for a full body massage ranges from Dhs.100 - 220 for one hour of heaven!

Meditation & Reiki

Other options → Support Groups [p.83]

Reiki and meditation are excellent for creating a sense of calm and well being. While meditation can be performed at home with only basic knowledge, reiki is a healing technique based on the belief that energy can be channelled into the patient by means of touch. Translated as 'universal life force energy', reiki can, like meditation, emotionally cleanse, physically invigorate and leave you more focused.

EXPAND YOUR HORIZONS

Other options → Education [p.83]
Support Groups [p.83]

Since you've come all this way, why not take that course in Arabic that you've always dreamed of or one of the many other languages available. Abu Dhabi has a surprising range of extracurricular activities for the eternal student, from painting classes or dance lessons to special interest groups; learning opportunities are abundant and flexible enough to fit your schedule. Go on, make the time!

Art Classes

Other options → Art [p.139]
Art Supplies [p.139]

Cultural Foundation

Location → Opp New Etisalat · Shk Zayed 2nd St | 619 5280
Hours → 08:00 - 14:00 & 17:00 - 21:00
Web/email → www.cultural.org.ae   Map Ref → 9-A1

The Cultural Foundation has a thriving and popular Art Workshop, which attracts both adults and children. Classes include silk painting, watercolours, oils, ceramics, sculpture, Arabic calligraphy etc. With so many options, all that is needed is time and the willingness to learn. The classes, which are open to everyone, are held throughout the week and some of the finished art, especially the sculptures produced by students are good enough to be featured at exhibitions.

Timings: *07:30 - 14:30 & 17:00 - 20:00; Thurs. 09:00 - 12:00 & 17:00 - 20:00; Fri. 17:00 - 20:00*

Abu Dhabi Cultural Foundation

Ladies Art Group, The

Location → Cultural Foundation · Shk Zayed 2nd St | 619 5313
Hours → na
Web/email → na   Map Ref → 9-A1

Started in 1997, this group meets once a week to paint. Members' abilities range from complete beginners to trained experts and the latter are always on hand to give advice. They paint in all mediums; watercolours, acrylics, oils and pastels, and usually provide their own materials, although basic supplies are available for beginners. Workshops are occasionally organised for introducing new mediums or techniques and the group exhibits annually in the Delma Corner of the Cultural Foundation. Various nationalities make up the membership and anyone is welcome to join whatever their level of artistic ability.

Contact: *Call the Delma Cafe at the Cultural Foundation for more information.*

Beauty Training

Cleopatra & Steiner Beauty Training Centre

Location → Wafi Residence · Umm Hurair · Dubai | 04 324 0250
Hours → 08:30 - 20:00
Web/email → www.cleopatrasteiner.com   Map Ref → UAE-C2

Based in Dubai, this is the Middle East's first internationally endorsed beauty and holistic training centre. A wide variety of topics are available, from basic make up and teenage grooming to advanced facial treatments and aromatherapy.

The centre provides opportunities for beginners or those pursuing their hobby, as well as those wishing to build on existing qualifications. Lasting from 12 to 250 hours, the courses can help develop career opportunities in beauty salons, sales and consultancy, marketing and management and assist self employed therapists. On completion, participants are awarded an internationally recognised diploma. For successful students, there may be employment opportunities within the organisation.

Dance Classes

Other options → Music Lessons [p.220]
Singing Lessons [p.221]

Sociable, great fun and excellent exercise for all ages and standards, dance has a universal appeal that breaks down barriers and inhibitions (sometimes). As well as the following organisations that are dedicated to dance, some health clubs, restaurants and bars hold weekly sessions in flamenco, salsa, samba, jazz dance, ballroom, and so on. In addition, some health clubs offer dance based aerobic classes that are good fun and surprisingly energetic.

Al Ain Contemporary Dance Ensemble

Location → Various locations | 03 76 2 3 720
Hours → Timings on request
Web/email → www.geocities.com/dance_uae   Map Ref → na

Al Ain Contemporary Dance Ensemble is run by Valmae Ypinazar, a qualified teacher who started teaching dance in Australia in 1986. Tap and modern classes are taught, and RAD classical ballet is offered from pre primary through to intermediate levels. Classes are available in all styles for students aged 5 years and over. There is also an adult ballet class. The emphasis at the Dance Ensemble is on technical development, enjoyment and performance skills. Contact Valmae for further details on 050 449 0643.

Location: *Classes are held at either the Inter-Continental Hotel or the Hilton Hotel in Al Ain.*

American Arabian Gulf Squares

Location →Various locations | 445 2490
Hours → Timings on request
Web/email → na   Map Ref → na

If you can commit yourself once a week and you like to dance, this friendly square dancing group in Abu Dhabi might be just for you. The steps are easy to learn, it's excellent exercise and it's enjoyable. Beginners are taught with the help of

Expand Your Horizons

Activities

experienced dancers and there's a separate session for the advanced group. Originally from America, square dancing has spread all over the world, with many clubs in Europe and Asia (where it's extremely popular). At present it's free to join. For more information on timings and classes, call Denise Smith.

Tap Dancing

Location ➜ Corniche Social Club · Abu Dhabi |642 1777
Hours ➜ Thu 10:00 - 12:00
Web/email ➜ na   Map Ref ➜ 8-A3

If your children want to tap dance over the parquet floor like Fred Astair, then these classes will be for them (lessons for adults are also available, if your feet can't stop moving). The teacher, Louisa al Rumaithi, instructs children from age four and upwards. Lessons last 30 or 45 minutes, depending on age.

Cost: *Dhs.25 per session.*

Dog Training

Other options ➜ Pets [p.71]

Dog Training Classes

Location ➜ Various locations |04 347 2592
Hours ➜ Timings on request
Web/email ➜ na   Map Ref ➜ na

OK, so we all yearn to complete the happy family picture – the kids, the parents and the beautiful dog. But so often that harmonious picture is shattered as the four legged mutt crashes onto the domestic scene. No need to give up in despair, and no need for Rover to rule the roost. Training can change an impossible dog into a wonderful family companion, but it takes patience and understanding.

For details of group or individual dog training classes, contact Anne (04 347 2592/050 655 8925). Training for deaf dogs is also provided.

Environmental Groups

Other options ➜ Environment [p.12]

Over the last few years, environmental issues have gradually become more important in the UAE;

however, as is always the case, far more needs to be done by all sections of the community.

Leading the way, HH Sheikh Mohammed bin Rashid Al Maktoum, Crown Prince of Dubai, has established a prestigious international environmental award in honour of HH Sheikh Zayed bin Sultan Al Nahyan, President of the UAE. The award, which was first presented in 1998, goes to an individual or organisation for distinguished work carried out on behalf of the environment.

On an everyday level there are increasing numbers of glass and plastic recycling points around the city, most notably outside Spinneys supermarkets. The Khaleej Times sponsors bins for collecting newspapers for recycling; these are easily spotted at a variety of locations, but mainly outside shopping centres. In addition, the Government is gradually taking action with school educational programmes and general awareness campaigns, plus the development of a number of conservation areas, such as Sir Bani Yas Island and on the East Coast, Khor Kalba Nature Reserve. However, overall, there seems to be very little done to persuade the average person to be more active environmentally, for instance by encouraging the use of unleaded petrol or by reducing littering.

If you want to do something more active, contact one of the environmental groups that operate in the Emirates. These range from the Emirates Environmental Group and the flagship Arabian Leopard Trust to Feline and K9 Friends. They always need volunteers and funds. Go on, do your bit!

Abu Dhabi Emirates Natural History Group

Location ➜ Various locations |604 3313
Hours ➜ Timings on request
Web/email ➜ www.arabianwildlife.com/main.htm   Map Ref ➜ na

From small beginnings over 20 years ago, this group has grown in size to a very respectable 600 members, based in Abu Dhabi, Al Ain and Dubai.

The Abu Dhabi group meets every first and third Tuesday of the month for an evening lecture on any aspect of natural history, from astronomy or archaeology to botany or zoology. The group also meets regularly for outdoor excursions – anything from a local half day trip to weekends along the East Coast. As well as being fun, these trips are an opportunity to learn more about the natural world from good field naturalists.

New members are always welcome; membership is Dhs.100. Call Steve James (050 611 8846) for further details.

Al Ain Emirates Natural History Group

Location → Htl Inter-Continental · Al Khubeirah | 050 533 0579
Hours → Timings on request
Web/email → enhg.4t.com/index.html   Map Ref → 15-E4

Interested in the environment and natural history? Join the Al Ain branch of the Emirates Natural History Group. Meetings take place every second and fourth Tuesday of the month, when there's also the opportunity to use their library. Talks last 1 - 1½ hours and are on topics as varied as the sky at night, UAE medicinal plants, Bedouin food or the Mussandam. Field trips are organised every weekend and cover everything from trips to archaeological sites, nature walks, museum visits or camping. In addition, they hold an annual photographic competition and the winning pictures illustrate their calendar.

Annual membership: *Dhs.80 family; Dhs.50 individuals; Dhs.10 non members per meeting.*

Contact: *Brien Holmes (050 533 0579).*

Emirates Environmental Group

Location → Various locations | 04 331 8100
Hours → Timings on request
Web/email → www.eeg-uae.com   Map Ref → na

This is a voluntary, non governmental organisation devoted to protecting the environment through education, action programmes and community involvement. The group started in September 1991 and has since grown considerably. Its membership includes everyone from individuals to corporate members and schools.

Activities include regular free evening lectures with speakers on environmental topics and special events such as recycling collections and clean-up campaigns. It publishes a free bilingual, biannual newsletter with a circulation of 20,000, plus a monthly newsletter for its members. Volunteers are always needed.

For further information, phone, fax (04 332 8500) or visit their Website.

Annual membership: *Adults Dhs.50; students Dhs.10 - 25. Corporate membership is also available.*

Feline Friends

Location → Various locations | 673 2696
Hours → 19:30 last Tue of the month
Web/email → felinefriendsuae.com   Map Ref → na

This non-profit organisation of volunteers of all nationalities aims to: care for sick and injured street cats and kittens; rescue abandoned pet cats and foster them until permanent homes can be found; control the local street cat population humanely by sterilisation, rather than by poisoning; and encourage responsible animal ownership and care. Sponsors and donations are always needed (from money to tins of food), plus volunteers for various fundraising activities. Volunteers are also needed during holidays to visit the cat homes to feed them on a daily basis.

At the monthly meetings, members plan various practical projects to aid the plight of cats in the UAE – everyone is welcome and the entrance fee is a can of food.

K9 Friends

Location → Various locations | 04 347 4611
Hours → 09:00 - 13:00 Closed Fri
Web/email → na   Map Ref → na

Started in 1989 and staffed by volunteers, K9 Friends has many aims, including the provision of a re-homing service for stray and abandoned dogs. It promotes responsible dog ownership and the importance of dog training, as well as encouraging a neutering programme to help control the population of stray dogs. The group also gives talks in schools on correct dog care and offers emergency aid to sick and injured dogs.

K9 Friends seeks to place strays in permanent homes and there is a constant need for foster homes to care for and assess dogs until a permanent home is found. A shelter in Al Quoz, Dubai houses around 60 dogs and is always full. Volunteers are always needed.

Expand Your Horizons

Activities

Gardening

Other options → Plant & Trees [p.152]

Flower & Garden Group

Location → Various locations | 445 6622
Hours → Timings on request
Web/email → na   Map Ref → na

This group was established in 1994 with the aim of creating environmental awareness and promoting individual gardening in the Gulf by planting seeds, flowering plants and trees. The group provides a learning environment for its members, who are encouraged to participate in the ongoing process of keeping Abu Dhabi green.

General meetings are held once a month at different places, and there are also various workshops and field trips throughout the year, as well as exhibits by floral artists. They welcome new members and are open to ideas or suggestions to further develop the group. Additional contact numbers are 621 7781 and 050 622 3701.

Language Schools

Other options → Education [p.83]

Alliance Française

Location → Choithram Bld · Khalidiya | 666 6232
Hours → 09:00 - 13:00 16:00 - 20:30 Thu 09:00 - 13:30 Closed Fri
Web/email → na   Map Ref → 8-C2

Alliance Française is a non-profit organisation supported by the French Embassy to promote French language and culture throughout the world. Started in Paris in 1883, it's the world's largest French teaching association with 1,135 schools in 138 countries.

The Abu Dhabi branch was established in 1974 and aims to widen access to the French language and culture, to encourage education, cultural exchange and friendly dialogue between countries. In addition to language courses, the centre provides information on France. The organisation also sponsors a number of cultural events (concerts, plays, ballets etc) each year. Their monthly brochure details upcoming events.

American Language Center

Location → Opp Hamdan Centre · Shk Hamdan St | 627 2779
Hours → 08:00 - 13:00 17:00 - 21:00 Thu 09:00 - 13:00 Closed Fri
Web/email → alc@emirates.net.ae   Map Ref → 8-C2

Approved to operate by the Abu Dhabi Ministry of Education, the American Language Center runs various English courses each month. Courses include TOEFL preparation and all levels of general or specialised English teaching. There are separate classes for ladies, with classes tailor-made to suit student requirements. They also run a summer school for children in the summer months.

Berlitz

Location → Opp Burger King · Khalidiya | 667 2287
Hours → 08:00 - 20:00 Closed Fri
Web/email → berlitz@emirates.net.ae   Map Ref → 9-D1

For more than a century, Berlitz has been operating worldwide and the 'Berlitz method' has helped more than 41 million people to acquire a new language. The Abu Dhabi branch is the first franchise in the Arab world. A variety of courses are offered and they can be customised to fit specific requirements, such as 'English for banking' or 'technical English'. Instruction is in private or small groups and there are morning classes for ladies and special children's classes (minimum age four years).

Additional training includes translation and interpretation, self-teaching audio and videotapes, books, interactive CD-ROM and travel related guides in both print and new media.

British Council

Location → Al Nasr St, nr Indian Embassy · Khalidiya | 665 9300
Hours → 08:30 - 13:30 16:30 - 19:00 Closed Thu & Fri
Web/email → www.britishcouncil.org/uae   Map Ref → 8-B2

The British Council's purpose is to promote cultural, scientific, technological and educational co-operation between the UK and other countries. It does this in various ways, including operating a range of English language courses and providing advice on opportunities for further education in Britain. The Teaching Centre also runs Arabic courses and the CELTA teacher training programme. The council arranges British examinations on behalf of all accredited British examining bodies.

In addition, the British Council promotes cultural events and traditional and contemporary arts through exhibitions, performances, talks and workshops. British Council centres are also located in Dubai, Sharjah and Ras Al Khaimah.

Circolo Italiano Culturale E Ricreativo – CICER

Location ➜ Italian Embassy · Al Manasir | 665 8033
Hours ➜ Timings on request
Web/email ➜ www.italian-embassy.org.ae   Map Ref ➜ na

Formed in 1989, CICER has a thriving membership of about 100 people and offers a variety of social activities, from outdoor visits to occasional exhibitions and concerts. For those interested in learning Italian, language lessons are offered privately by some members of the Italian community. These can be from beginner to advanced levels, and can be taken individually or in groups (maximum of six people per class). Contact Loredana Frizzi on the above number for information on fees and timings.

Working closely with the Italian Embassy, the association also offers members the use of a small Italian library, plus a video library with over 2,000 Italian movies. Other benefits include use of the facilities at the Khalidiya Palace Hotel.

ELS Language Center

Location ➜ Nr. Sheraton Residence · Al Khalidiyah | 666 9225
Hours ➜ 08:30 - 13:30 16:30 - 19:30 Closed Thu, Fri
Web/email ➜ www.els.com   Map Ref ➜ 9-D1

Since opening their first language centre in Washington DC more than 30 years ago, ELS has grown into one of America's largest intensive English programmes. Today, they teach more than 140,000 students each year within a network of more than 100 schools on five continents.

In the UAE, ELS teaches individual students, businesses and government departments. The intensive English programme focuses on practical English, featuring grammar, conversation, reading and writing, and gives access to the multimedia lab. The courses are open to anyone. Ladies only classes are also offered.

The teachers are native English speakers, and they all possess a TEFL (Teach English as a Foreign Language) certificate. The centre also provides educational counselling to assist individuals who are considering studying abroad.

ELS Language Center, Al Ain

Location ➜ Hamdan B Zayed St · Al Jimi Khabisi | 03 762 3468
Hours ➜ 08:30 - 13:30 16:00 - 21:30 Thu 09:00 - 13:00 Closed Fri
Web/email ➜ www.ELS.com   Map Ref ➜ 12-E4

For information on this school, see the entry under ELS Language Centers, Abu Dhabi.

German School, The

Location ➜ 32 Sultan Bin Zayed St · Al Markaziyah | 666 8668
Hours ➜ 08:00 - 13:15 Closed Thu & Fri
Web/email ➜ DSAD1976@emirates.net.ae   Map Ref ➜ 8-E1

The German School Abu Dhabi offers German language courses for adults at all levels of competence. Qualified German teachers run the courses and, for language training, the classes are all in the evenings. It also offers a German education for children from Kindergarten to Grade 10.

International English Inst. for Language Stud

Location ➜ Opp Bus Station, Defence St · Abu Dhabi | 642 2407
Hours ➜ 09:00 - 13:00 17:00 - 21:00 Closed Thu & Fri
Web/email ➜ na   Map Ref ➜ 3-B4

The International English Institute for Language Studies offers a range of language courses to suit all requirements and levels of ability. Whether you are a student aiming to improve your skills in English, planning to study in an English speaking country, a frequent traveller abroad or need to improve your business English, there will be a course for you. However, it's not just English that is covered: the institute also offers lessons in French, Spanish, Italian and German. Classes are designed to develop your confidence to interact in another language and programmes run morning or afternoon. Separate classes are available for children over 7 years old and for ladies.

Expand Your Horizons

Activities

Libraries

Other options ➜ Books [p.140]
Second-hand Items [p.152]

Alliance Française

Location ➜ Choithram Bld · Khalidiya | 666 6232
Hours ➜ 09:00 - 13:00 16:00 - 20:30 Thu 09:00 - 13:30 Closed Fri
Web/email ➜ na   Map Ref ➜ 8-C2

The Alliance Française has a multimedia library comprising more than 12,000 books (including reference, fiction, poetry, history, travel, local interest), 2,500 videos (ranging from documentaries to fiction and children's films), 200 CD-ROMs (educational, information, games), textbooks and 800 CDs, as well as a selection of French newspapers and magazines. New material is released every month.

Everybody is welcome to use the library, although a membership fee is required if you want to check out material, (membership is available for one month, six months or one year). Students of the Alliance Française are entitled to a 50% discount on yearly membership fees.

Club, The

Location ➜ Club, The · Al Meena | 673 1111
Hours ➜ See timings below
Web/email ➜ www.the-club.com   Map Ref ➜ 7-A2

A library is one of the many facilities offered by this organisation; however, note that to enjoy the excellent selection of fiction and non-fiction titles, you will first have to become a member of The Club. The latest best sellers from the UK and US are ordered on a regular basis and a large variety of paperbacks, reference books and a children's section ensure that most individuals are well catered for. A CD-ROM section is also featured. The Internet facility in the library may be booked in advance or taken 'on spec'.

Timings: *Sat, Sun, Tue & Wed 11:00 - 19:00; Mon 11:00 - 21:00; Thu 10:00 - 18:00; Fri closed.*

Cultural Foundation

Location ➜ Opp New Etisalat · Shk Zayed 2nd St | 619 5280
Hours ➜ See timings below
Web/email ➜ www.cultural.org.ae   Map Ref ➜ 9-A1

Located in the main complex of the Cultural Foundation, the National Library is responsible for collecting, keeping and organising all national literary information. It is made up of three separate halls – a main reading hall with private research chambers as well as a periodical hall, the Gulf library hall, and the audiovisuals hall equipped with modern, highly advanced audiovisual equipment.

The library was built to hold a staggering two million titles. At present, it has approximately 422,000 Arabic volumes and 75,000 English volumes, in addition to 700 Arabic periodicals and 500 English periodicals. New items are being added regularly. The library also has an Internet section, which can be used for a moderate fee. Hence it is very popular with the students.

Timings: *08:00 - 14:00 & 17:00 - 21:00; Thurs. 09:00 - 12:00 & 17:00 - 20:00; Fri. 17:00 - 20:00*

Daly Community Library

Location ➜ St Andrews Centre · Al Mushrif | 446 4752
Hours ➜ See timings below
Web/email ➜ na   Map Ref ➜ 3-C3

Daly Community Library was opened in 1978 and now has nearly 7,000 books, covering fiction and non-fiction for adults and children. Books are ordered from the UK and new publications, including best sellers, are added each month. It's a subscription library and is open to anyone.

Subscriptions: *Adults Dhs.100 annually, plus Dhs.75 initial joining fee; children (under 14) Dhs.50 annually, plus Dhs.40 initial joining fee.*

Timings: *Wednesdays 12:00 - 14:00 & 17:00 - 18:30; Thursdays 11:00 - 13:30; Sundays 15:30 - 19:30.*

Music Lessons

Other options ➜ Singing Lessons [p.221]
Dance Classes [p.215]

Beethoven Institute of Music

Location ➜ Nr. Clock Tower & Fish Market · Al Nasr St | 632 7588
Hours ➜ Timings on request
Web/email ➜ na   Map Ref ➜ 8-E2

Started in 1984, this was one of the first music institutes in the UAE. Proprietor and director Stan D'Souza comes from a family of musicians and his daughter Shahnaz has inherited his musical talent, while his wife runs the institute. On offer are lessons in the piano, organ, guitar and drums. The emphasis is on quality teaching and playing, which is also interesting and enjoyable. Children can start as young as six and summer courses are also held.

Expand Your Horizons

Activities

The family owns Beethoven Musical Instruments, Abu Dhabi and Mozart Musical Instruments, Dubai. For further details, call the above number or 633 9195/050 641 2530.

Royal Music Academy

Location → Nr Eldorado Cinema · Elektra Street | 674 8070
Hours → 09:00 - 12:00 16:00 - 21:00 Closed Fri
Web/email → vinsylauh@hotmail.com · · · · · Map Ref → 8-B1

The motto of the Royal Music Academy is 'devote time, promote talent' and already there are 200 or so students learning under the guidance of qualified teachers. The aim is to ready the young musicians for exams by the Trinity College, London, as well as preparing them for live performances. Instruments include the guitar, drums, violin, piano and keyboards and the aim is to add more instruments to the Academy's repertoire. Watercolour, pencil drawing and dance classes are offered to bring out the best in creativity.

The academy also conducts summer camps for children during holidays; activities include swimming, ice skating, arts and crafts, painting and camping.

Nature Reserves

Sir Bani Yas Island

Location → From Meena Zayed Port · Abu Dhabi | na
Hours → na
Web/email → na · · · · · Map Ref → na

Located just 9 km off Jebel Dhanna headland, some 170 km west of Abu Dhabi, this private island is owned by President HH Sheikh Zayed bin Sultan al Nahyan. It was established as a breeding and conservation reserve for indigenous UAE animals and desert animals from the Middle East and Africa. The animals, such as the Arabian wolf and oryx, are kept in large breeding pens, while other species, such as gazelles, giraffes, rhea and wild sheep, roam wild over the island. Priority is given to breeding endangered species like the Arabian tahr, one of the region's rarest creatures. The island is also a good stopping off point for migrating birds in the spring and autumn, encouraged no doubt by the tree planting programme.

In addition, some 36 archaeological sites have been identified on the island, including a Nestorian monastery and church dating to the 6-7th centuries AD.

Outside visitors are allowed to visit the island, but only on a prearranged basis and then as organised groups (such as school children or with the Emirates Natural History Group). Groups are usually transferred by hydrofoil from Meena Zayed Port and taken around the island by bus. The overnight stay is in comfortable, but fairly basic portakabins and all food is provided.

The island is run by the Environment and Wildlife Management (EWM) department of the President's Private Office. Bona fide groups, societies and school parties can contact the EWM or PO Box 77, Abu Dhabi for further information.

Pottery

Abu Dhabi Pottery

Location → 16th St, Nr Khalidiya Garden · Khalidiya | 666 7079
Hours → 09:00 - 13:00 16:30 - 20:30 Closed Fri
Web/email → na · · · · · Map Ref → 9-D1

For those fascinated by clay, pottery classes are available for adults and children (aged five and up). Try hand building and wheel techniques and look out for special holiday classes for children. Everything is done under the supervision of friendly staff, except the glazing since toxic materials are involved. The company can also provide the entertainment at a child's birthday party (minimum eight children, maximum twenty). The Dhs.35 charge, plus Dhs.50 for the clay, glazing and firing per child are worth it for the novelty factor alone.

Cost: *Dhs.240 per month for four sessions, plus clay and firing fee.*

Singing Lessons

Other options → Music Lessons [p.220]

Abu Dhabi Choral Group

Location → St Andrew's Church · Al Mushrif | 681 2340
Hours → Tue 20:00
Web/email → na · · · · · Map Ref → 3-C3

This community choir is open to anyone interested in singing. They are all amateurs and at present have 73 members, representing 12 different nationalities. Annual productions include a Christmas concert in December, a concert in February for Valentines Day and a musical in May. The main feature in 2002 was a performance of HMS Pinafore.

It's a non-profit making organisation and when possible, once production expenses are covered, a charitable donation is made. The group is accompanied by the Festival Orchestra of Abu Dhabi. If you would like to know more, contact Marcia Jeiroudi.

Social Groups

Other options → Support Groups [p.83]

With its cosmopolitan population, it's not surprising that Abu Dhabi has a large number of social and cultural groups. These are sometimes linked to an embassy or business group and can be an excellent way of meeting like-minded people. However, if your particular interest or background is not covered, now is the perfect opportunity to challenge your organisational skills and start something new – there'll always be someone out there who'll join in. Refer also to the Business Section [p.92].

Abu Dhabi Ladies

Location → Various locations	667 3024
Hours → Wed 10:00 - 12:00	
Web/email → na	Map Ref → 8-D3

Abu Dhabi Ladies (previously known as the Abu Dhabi Ladies Association) offers a range of social activities and support to expat women of all ages and nationalities, whether they've just arrived or been here for years. They're a non-profit group run by volunteers, and meet every Wednesday for a coffee morning between 10:00 – 12:00. For just Dhs.10, non members can attend to get a better feel before deciding to join. The group also runs various activities on an informal basis, plus there's always someone to lend an ear or give advice to new arrivals. The group sends out a monthly newsletter with information on activities in Abu Dhabi.

Membership: *250 people, ladies only. Annual subscription Dhs.40.*

Contacts: *Angie Cummings (050 621 6213) or Audrey Clarke (050 443 8472).*

Abu Dhabi Mums

Location → Various locations	448 2562
Hours → Timings on request	
Web/email → na	Map Ref → na

Abu Dhabi Mums was formed in January 1994 as a social meeting group for mums with pre-school children under the age of five. The original group started with four members, but since then has grown to an average of 230 members each year. It's a non-profitable voluntary organisation, run with the purpose of providing informal support and activities for both parents and children. Various events and group meetings are organised throughout the year and it is open to anyone in Abu Dhabi who is expecting or has children up to the age of five years. For further information, contact Revi.

Abu Dhabi St George's Society

Location → Various locations	44 5 6 403
Hours → Timings on request	
Web/email → http://rssg-auh.cjb.net/	Map Ref → na

This society has been active in Abu Dhabi for over 20 years and has a hardcore group of longstanding members, along with regular intakes of newcomers. They hold events on a regular basis and annually commemorate Trafalgar Day and St George's Day with formal dinners and host a New Year's Eve Ball. Other events include car treasure hunts, quizzes, Ramadan curry night etc. Proceeds raised at events are distributed to UK charities each year.

Membership is open to all English families, and associate membership to any individuals supporting the objectives of the society.

Contact: *For further information, email the secretary, Steve Wiltshire, or visit the Website.*

Al Ain Caledonian Society

Location → Various locations	03 721 6718
Hours → Timings on request	
Web/email → na	Map Ref → na

Formed in 1989, this society encourages friendly relations among Scottish people and their families resident in Al Ain and fosters relations between Scots and other nationalities in the district. They also promote Scottish culture and traditions in an appropriate manner and of course celebrate St. Andrew's Day and Burns Night. The Scottish

Country Dance Team also provides demonstrations at the main social events. One of the main purposes of the society is to raise funds for charity and over the years donations have been made to the Royal Erskine Hospital and the RNLI in Scotland. They currently have 70 members. Contact Stuart Walker (050 663 6485).

Membership: *By nomination. Annual subscription Dhs.60. Ordinary membership is for those born in Scotland of Scottish ancestry and their spouses. Associate membership is granted to non Scots.*

Meeting once a month at the Inter-Continental Hotel Al Ain at 19:30.

Al Ain Irish Society

Location ➜ Various locations | 050 663 2721
Hours ➜ Once a month
Web/email ➜ na   Map Ref ➜ na

Celebrating the Irish is something that Al Ain has enjoyed for over 17 years. St Patrick's Day, March 17, is the date of the Irish Ball and during the year the society is active with a number of events, such as a welcome back get together in September or a sunset buffet during Ramadan. Irish dancing classes are taught and in past years there have been Gaelic language classes for children. The annual Rose of Tralee competition held in Dubai is supported and members also participate in the Gulf Gaelic Athletic Association Tournament – with plenty of craic after the hard work on the pitch.

Membership is open to anyone with an interest in Irish culture. At present, there's no membership fee.

For further information, contact President, Jerome McCormack on the above number.

Al Ain St George's Society

Location ➜ Various locations | 03 767 1723
Hours ➜ Timings on request
Web/email ➜ na   Map Ref ➜ na

Al Ain St George's Society was founded in November 1996 by Annie Lawton and Sue Aiken. The first St George's Night Ball was held at the Al Ain Hilton on, appropriately, St George's Day, Wednesday 23 April 1997. The ball was a great success, with entertainment provided by the Morris Dancing Group, formed by Phil Iddison, and John Kennedy who sang some traditional English songs, accompanying himself on accordion and guitar. All those interested in English culture or way of life or just in meeting new faces should contact Sue Aiken on the above number for further details about the society.

American University of Beirut Alumni Associat

Location ➜ TNT Bld · Khalifa Bin Zayed St | 679 5633
Hours ➜ Timings on request
Web/email ➜ www.aubalumni.org   Map Ref ➜ na

This association was formed in 1986 with the objective of increasing awareness of the American University of Beirut and its academic role in the Middle East region, and to raise funds for scholarships for needy students. The Abu Dhabi branch is active throughout the year, organising events such as concerts, lectures, days out, 'Layali Ramadan', fundraising dinners and the Alumni Spring Ball. The group currently has more than 700 graduates living in the Abu Dhabi emirate. To join, or for more information, call the above number or contact PO Box 71518, Abu Dhabi.

American University of Beirut Alumni Associat

Location ➜ Various locations | 03 767 7444
Hours ➜ Timings on request
Web/email ➜ www.aubalumni.org   Map Ref ➜ na

For AUB alumni based in Al Ain, information about the group can be obtained from Antoinette Yzbeck on the above number. See the entry under Abu Dhabi for further details.

American Women's Network

Location ➜ Various locations | 050 642 7180
Hours ➜ na
Web/email ➜ na   Map Ref ➜ na

The goal of this informal group of women is to offer an informative, warm and welcoming atmosphere to newcomers. They meet on the first Saturday of every month, alternating mornings and evenings, and offer monthly programmes covering a variety of interests.

Although the group is primarily for Americans, they welcome women with links to America. There is a basic annual fee of Dhs.40, plus extra for the cost of additional activities. Whether you want to keep in touch with your community or meet new friends, you'll be welcome. Contact Renee Nearpass (050 642 7180) or Sharon Moynihan (634 8417).

Expand Your Horizons

Activities

Club des Femmes Francophones

Location ➜ Novotel Centre Hotel · Shk Hamdan St | 633 3555
Hours ➜ Sat & Tue 11:00 - 13:00
Web/email ➜ novoad@emirates.net.ae   Map Ref ➜ 8-D2

The Club des Femmes Francophones was created by volunteers in 1987. Nowadays there are approximately 200 members, representing 26 different nationalities. The objective of the association is the exchange of different cultures and traditions among all French speaking ladies. The association is apolitical and non religious. One of the main aims of the club is to introduce members to the culture and traditions of the UAE, and the group is part of the Emirati Women's Association. There are also many regular activities throughout the year, such as bowling, silk painting, yoga, badminton, bridge and scrabble.

South African Group Abu Dhabi, The

Location ➜ Various locations | 445 4034
Hours ➜ Timings on request
Web/email ➜ www.sagroupuae.com   Map Ref ➜ na

Catering to South Africans in Abu Dhabi and Al Ain, this group organises various events for the community, including dinner and dances as well as barbecues and desert trips. The Afrikaans Christian Children's Group meets at the Evangelical Church at 19:00 every Monday evening, while a newsletter sent out every month updates the South Africans in the region of all scheduled events. For more information, email them at abudhabi@sagroupuae.com.

St Andrews Society of Abu Dhabi

Location ➜ St Andrews Centre · Al Mushrif | 050 443 5175
Hours ➜ Timings on request
Web/email ➜ na   Map Ref ➜ 3-C3

This well-established group of expat Scots, who are joined by more than a few 'foreigners', enjoy getting together for social gatherings and other Scottish cultural activities. The society holds three main functions annually: the St Andrew's Ball in November, the Burns' Supper in January and the Chieftain's Ball in May, which is also used as a fundraising event for various charities in the UAE and Scotland. The annual general meeting is held in September, when a new committee is elected. Membership is open to any resident of the UAE for

a nominal fee of Dhs.50 per year, and everyone is welcome. Write to the society at PO Box 59451, Abu Dhabi for more information.

St David's Society

Location ➜ Various locations | 677 9751
Hours ➜ Timings on request
Web/email ➜ na   Map Ref ➜ na

St David's Society is the youngest of the British tribal societies, formed only in 1992 by some enthusiastic Welsh expats. It has grown in strength ever since and has a current membership of over 120. A regular newsletter keeps members informed of events held each month (except August), such as quiz evenings, dhow trips, weekend breaks or social gatherings. The highlight of the year is the annual ball, held on the Thursday closest to the national day, 1 March.

Membership is open to all Welsh people or anybody having an association with Wales, however distant. Associate membership is also available.

Contacts: *President, Peter Stevens (050 614 5191); Vice President, Peter Rhydderch (050 622 1832).*

Annual fees: *Dhs.50 per person (not exceeding Dhs.100 per family).*

Wine Tasting

African & Eastern (N.E.) Ltd

Location ➜ Al Salam St | 631 2300
Hours ➜ 10:00 - 13:00 16:00 - 20:30
Web/email ➜ na   Map Ref ➜ na

African & Eastern arrange tastings from time to time. To take part you will need a liquor licence. Call Timothy Broughton on the above number if you would like to add your name to the database for the next event.

Gray MacKenzie Liquor Shop

Location ➜ Opp Le Meridien Htl · Al Khalifa St | 627 3131
Hours ➜ Timings on request
Web/email ➜ na   Map Ref ➜ na

Gray MacKenzie arranges occasional tastings on an ad hoc basis. To paticipate, all you need is a liquor licence. Call the customer service line on the above number for further details.

شركة كري مكنزي وشركاه
أبوظبي المحدودة (ذ.م.م)

Gray Mackenzie & Partners
Abu Dhabi Limited Co. (L.L.C.)

P.O. Box 247, Abu Dhabi
United Arab Emirates
Telephone: 02-6767672
Customer Service: 02-6783930
Facsimile: 02-6767678

Retail Outlets:

Khalifa Street	02-6123545	Tourist Club Area	02-6765954

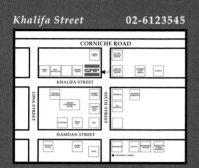

More of the *World's Finest*
Brands than any other,
with the *service* and
offers to match

Mussaffah   02-5543919

KIDS' STUFF

Other options ➔ Education [p.83]

As each year passes, activities for kids in Abu Dhabi grow in number and quality and while not as lively an experience as its neighbour Dubai, the capital has much to offer the under 14s. Many activities are organised through the schools and hotels, sports, health and beach clubs, and cultural and social groups.

For pre-school ages, the choices are limited, but try some of the social groups or churches. However, once school has started, the options improve for the 4 to 14 age group. There are generally a variety of after-school activities on offer, such as sports, music or art and crafts. However, for older teens there appears to be a lack of any organised youth or social clubs, although again the schools and some of the churches are active.

The hotels often have events and activities for children – ask to be added to their mailing lists and check the daily newspapers. Some have special kids' clubs (generally for members only, but some are open to outsiders), with activities such as treasure hunts, fishing trips and sandcastle competitions etc. Contact the individual hotels for further information. Additionally in the hotter months, some organisations run summer camps, which offer a variety of activities from arts and crafts to sport, in a safe and supervised environment.

Dubai has a much wider range of options for a family day out, so head north for a change of scene – for information on family life in Abu Dhabi and the Northern Emirates, refer to the *Family Explorer (Dubai & Abu Dhabi)* published by Explorer Publishing.

Children's City	
Location ➔ Creekside Park · Dubai	**04 334 0808**
Hours ➔ 09:00 - 22:00 Fri 16:00 - 22:00	
Web/email ➔ www.childrencity.ae	Map Ref ➔ UAE-C2

Opened in 2002, Children's City is an educational project providing kids with their own learning zone and amusement facilities by providing hands-on experiences of the theoretical subjects that they learn at school. Children's City is aimed at 5-12 year olds, although items of interest are included for toddlers and teenagers. Highlights include a planetarium with a 180 degree screen and a mock-up of the front of an aircraft in the flying gallery.

Club, The	
Location ➔ Club, The · Al Meena	**673 1111**
Hours ➔ 08:00 - 01:00 Fri 08:00 - 24:00	
Web/email ➔ www.the-club.com	Map Ref ➔ 7-A2

The Club is a very British institution and a truly old establishment with its foundation in 1962. The family membership is annual and you have to be a member to involve your kids in the wide variety of activities offered for younger members of all ages, organised by the Activities Co-ordinator. These may include sports, games, fun in the pool, organised trips and Easter/summer camps. Swimming and tennis coaching can be arranged. Two shaded baby pools are located on the beach for under fives, complemented by a variety of play and climbing equipment. The family room has an adjoining outside play area that is open for families to eat and drink from noon until 20:30.

Cultural Foundation	
Location ➔ Opp New Etisalat · Shk Zayed 2nd St	**619 5280**
Hours ➔ 08:00 - 14:00 17:00 - 21:00	
Web/email ➔ www.cultural.org.ae	Map Ref ➔ 9-A1

The Cultural Foundation is a non-profit organisation offering numerous activities and facilities for everyone in the capital. The monthly changing schedule offers various activities for children and adults, such as computer lessons, painting and an introduction to the work of the library. In addition, there's a cinema, plus various exhibitions, theatre performances and lectures held throughout the year. As the programme changes quite often, it's advisable to check their website or call the above number to find out what's going on.

Futurekids	
Location ➔ Abu Dhabi	**632 3325**
Hours ➔ na	
Web/email ➔ na	Map Ref ➔ na

Futurekids is an international franchise company committed to bringing computer mastery to children and adults. It was established in 1983 in America and has since expanded to over 2,000 locations in more than 60 countries. Futurekids believes that children learn best in an exciting and co-operative environment where the computer is used as a highly effective learning tool and a medium for creative self-expression.

Classes and curricula are carefully designed for each age level from 3 years and above, along with adult classes. Groups consist of 4 - 8 students per instructor, depending on the ages. Lessons are offered all year round, after school hours, mornings, evenings and on weekends. They also offer camps and special interest groups for children.

The teachers attend a three month training programme before they start teaching their own classes. All of them have good practical technological experience and enjoy working with children, so much so that sometimes it's difficult to determine who's enjoying the classes more – the teachers or the students!

At the moment, Futurekids is only operating out of Dubai. For further information, call 04 331 8248 or 04 331 2425.

Gymboree Play & Music

Location → Khalidia Palace Htl · Khalidiya | 665 8882
Hours → 08:00 - 18:00 Closed Fri
Web/email → www.gymboree.com Map Ref → 10-E2

This is an upmarket pre-school children's amusement centre, designed to create an educational and fun interaction between parents and their offspring (this means parents have to invest some quality time here). Depending on age, there are various classes and programmes scheduled – the music lessons are very popular and you can even bring babies as young as six months. Theme parties and birthday parties can also be arranged.

The centre is spacious, clean and bright (everything in the facility is imported from the USA), and the friendly staff not only undergo intensive training, but also have child-orientated backgrounds.

Cost: Dhs.55 for 45 minutes; monthly memberships are available.

Kids Play

Location → Toys 'R' Us · Salahuddin Rd, Deira | 673 2332
Hours → 10:00 - 22:00
Web/email → na Map Ref → 7-B4

This is quite the ultimate play experience for kids, combined with shopping as it is attached to Toys 'R' Us. The centre is designed by fitness experts from the UK, using the latest and safest, indoor soft play equipment for children under 14 years. The area includes a monorail, a padded play area with whirlpools filled with balls, climbing frames, slides, monkey climb, mountain climb etc. A smaller area is more suited for kids under three. The staff is friendly and helpful and if your kids need some 'petrol' before continuing playing, there's a café serving chips and pizzas. It sometimes gets a bit too crowded, but is still a good option to amuse your children or for celebrating a birthday in one of the function rooms.

Entrance: Toddlers age 1 - 4, Dhs.10; 4 years and above, Dhs.15 for unlimited time.

Sahara Leisure Centre

Location → Sahara Residence · Shk Zayed 2nd St | 631 5152
Hours → 09:00 - 23:00 Fri 10:00 - 13:00 16:00 - 21:00
Web/email → na Map Ref → 8-C1

This centre specialises in courses for children, ranging from art workshops, martial arts and ballet to modern dance. Other facilities include a small soft-play area, slide, ball pool, small library, computer games and a small café serving juices and sweets. They also run a birthday party service.

Pay per session (Dhs.25) or on a monthly basis. Monthly prices for classes twice a week, such as ballet and judo, start at Dhs.200, while art workshops and various other activities are offered for Dhs.20 - 75 per session.

Shooting Stars

Location → Jumeirah Rd · Dubai | 04 344 7407
Hours → Timings on request
Web/email → na Map Ref → UAE-C2

Shooting Stars is an adventure video production company that produces keepsake videos of children in imaginative situations. Using the latest digital technology, they can turn children into the stars of their own video adventure: a popular choice is 'My Arabian adventure' (the background tape is filmed in the dunes at Hatta). A unique and rather unusual gift to send back to the grandparents. For more information contact the above number or 050 798 8209.

St Andrews Playgroup

Location → St Andrews Church · Al Mushrif	67 3 3 130
Hours → Sat, Mon & Wed 10:00 - 12:00	
Web/email → na	Map Ref → 3-C3

This is a great place for mums to meet other mums and to have a chat while keeping an eye on their children. The group is for newborn to pre-school children and it's especially good for new people in town. The hall is equipped with suitable toys and at the end of each session everyone sits in a circle and sings nursery rhymes (a great hit with all the tots), before helping to tidy up. Some mums turn up early to help clean the toys and organise the room – volunteers are always welcome.

Cost: *each session is Dhs.15; this includes tea/coffee for parents and juice and biscuits for children.*

Amusement Centres

Foton World

Location → Marina Mall · Breakwater	681 5526
Hours → 10:00 - 23:00	
Web/email → na	Map Ref → 10-B4

A big range of computer and video games, carousels and other funfair facilities awaits you on the second floor of the mall. Foton World is not a 'learning through playing' centre, but a typical high tech amusement outlet – a good option for keeping your kids busy while you shop (if you decide to spend some 'quality' time here with your youngsters, don't forget to take your earplugs!).

Entry is free, but tokens are needed for the games. A wristband is available for Dhs.35, which allows the player an unlimited number of rides.

Fun Island

Location → Al Jernain Centre · Shk Zayed 1st St	665 9009
Hours → 10:00 - 22:00 Fri 16:00 - 22:00	
Web/email → na	Map Ref → 9-B1

Fun Island caters mostly to kids under five with a large area of soft play facilities: tube slides, ball ponds, hanging ropes and cruiser rollers. Other areas include a Lego room, birthday party room and space for computer games for older children. Birthday party packages are provided to suit different budgets and tastes, but the pizzeria and fried chicken from the nearby coffee shop will be enough to get any child's eyes sparkling. Space for parents to have a break is unfortunately limited.

Entrance: *Dhs.15 per child, no time limit.*

Fun World

Location → Opp Cultural Foundation · Al Hosn	632 2255
Hours → 10:00 - 13:30 16:30 - 23:00 Fri 15:00 - 23:00	
Web/email → na	Map Ref → 9-A1

Situated in one of the newest shopping malls and covering almost an entire floor, Fun World has a more educational approach than some amusement centres. It offers computer games that are intended to encourage kids to draw, paint, puzzle, thread beads and create sand art. Plus, there's a soft-play area for the youngest generation, a coffee shop and children's hairdresser all on the same floor.

Paying for this fun means either buying separate tokens or a wristband for Dhs.20, which allows unlimited use of the facilities. Restrictions are based on height.

Toy Town

Location → Abu Dhabi Mall · Al Meena	645 5567
Hours → 09:30 - 23:00 Fri 15:00 - 22:00	
Web/email → toytown@emirates.net.ae	Map Ref → 4-B4

Opened in summer 2002, Toy Town is already a facility that kids don't want to miss – you could find it's a struggle to get your offspring to leave! Spread over 4,000 square metres on the upper floor of the mall, this well designed playground transports you to the jungle. Look out for a gigantic spider climbing up the wall, a rubber snake hiding under some stones or a model gorilla. Other facilities include a water slide, bumper cars, Wild West train, roller coaster, plus virtual, laser and video games.

Costs range between Dhs.2 - 15, plus slight variations depending on the season and time.

Something to reveal?

Then let us know!

Whether it's an idea, a correction, an opinion or simply a recommendation, we want to hear from you. Log on and become part of the Explorer Community. Let your opinions be heard, viewed, compiled and printed...

www.explorer-publishing.com

Amusement Parks

Other options → Water Parks [p.202]

Hili Fun City & Ice Rink

Location → Mohammed Bin Khalifa St · Hili | 03 784 5542
Hours → 16:00 - 22:00 09:00 - 22:00 Closed Sat
Web/email → www.hilton.com   Map Ref → 13-B1

The Hili Fun City gives you a chance to go to the moon in a space ship, experience the thrill of a giant roller coaster or tour in style with your very own stagecoach. Opened since 1985, it's still the largest amusement park in the Gulf and covers a total area of 86 hectors. Entertainment options include thrilling rides from runaway trains to alien encounters, which can be enjoyed by people of all age groups. For the first timers, the Road Train is a good place to start. Hop on for an overview of the entire city and its attractions; this will help you decide which rides you want to try first. In addition, there's an Olympic size (60m x 30m) ice rink located on the eastern side of the City.

Fast food is available at the main restaurant and all other types of food can be arranged by special order. A BBQ food outlet also operates in the afternoon hours for those craving grilled food.

Rides are paid for by tokens issued with the entry tickets and no ride is more than four tokens.

Timings: *Winter: 16:00 - 22:00 Sun - Wed & 9:00 - 22:00 Thurs, Fri and public holidays. Tues & Wed are women and children only. Closed Sat.*

Summer: *17:00 - 23:00 Sun - Wed & 9:00 - 23:00 Thurs, Fri and public holidays.*

WonderLand Theme & Water Park

Location → Umm Hurair · Dubai | 04 324 3222
Hours → 15:00 - 21:00 Thu & Fri 12:00 - 21:00 Closed Sun
Web/email → www.wonderlanduae.com   Map Ref → UAE-C2

A trip to WonderLand is worth the drive to Dubai to experience the numerous exhilarating attractions, thrilling rides and games. Facilities include wet and dry rides, go-karting, paintballing, an air conditioned family entertainment centre with a soft play area, video and skill games, bumper cars and food outlets, to name but a few.

Timings change seasonally, plus there are days for ladies, families and schools only, so check opening hours before you leave the house. For further information, refer to the *Dubai Explorer*.

Crazy Golf

Other options → Golf (Sports)

Al Diar Gulf Hotel & Resort

Location → Al Diar Gulf Htl · Al Maqtaa | 441 4777
Hours → 09:00 - 22:00
Web/email → www.aldiarhotels.com   Map Ref → 1-D3

A nine hole obstacle course is available at the Gulf Hotel for all budding Nick Faldos! Cost is Dhs.5 for 30 minutes of play.

Party Organisers

Flying Elephant

Location → Jct 3, Shk Zayed Rd · Dubai | 04 347 9170
Hours → Timings on request
Web/email → www.flyingelephantuae.com   Map Ref → UAE-C2

With over six years experience of planning and providing entertainment, ranging from birthday parties for two children to corporate events for 4,000 staff, the team at Flying Elephant pretty much has it covered! What's on offer ranges from product launches and team building to children's parties and entertainment, balloon decorations, corporate theme decorations and clowns, and much more. They can supply professional entertainment with a fine eye to detail and are always interested in new ideas from customers, so if you want to hand over the whole party or would simply like some advice on what to do, they'll be happy to have a chat.

Gymboree

Share
the dream.

All within the walls of an Arabian fort, a stunning lobby…
exquisitely refurbished restaurants designed for warm memories.
So cruise the world with us…. Touch Italy with its irresistible
cuisine… linger into Mexico where the spices take over; sail to the
Mediterranean to feel lover's paradise while enjoying the
best seafood. One step above join the fusion of Eastern and
Western flavours all day long. To make it different, hop into Great
Britain to quench your thirst. End your gourmet journey in Cuba
to explore the aroma of rolled cigars, tantalizing grand piano
music and personalized service.

Call 00971-2-677.33.33 or your travel planner.
Visit sheraton.com. Best rates, guaranteed.

منتجع وبرج شيراتون ابوظبي
Sheraton Abu Dhabi
RESORT & TOWERS

See for yourself

Going Out

EXPLORER

Going Out – Eating Out / On the Town

GOING OUT

If you're going out and about in Abu Dhabi, you will come across a surprising variety of places to go and things to do. It may not be quite the buzzing city found in other parts of the world, but Abu Dhabi offers enough choice to keep even the most ardent socialite happy.

The following section has been divided into two; the city's numerous restaurants are listed under Eating Out [p.234], while bars, pubs, nightclubs and any 'cultural' entertainment, such as theatre, cinema and comedy clubs, are listed under On the Town [p.285].

Eating Out

Eating out is extremely popular across all segments of the Abu Dhabi community. Along with offering the chance to enjoy delectable cuisine from around the world, it also gives the opportunity to exchange news or argue the merits of anything, from a foreign leader to the latest movie.

Cosmopolitan and bustling, Abu Dhabi has an excellent variety of restaurants. From Moroccan to Mediterranean, Indian to Italian and everything in between, there really is something to suit every taste and budget. Most places open early in the evening at around 19:00, but generally aren't busy until about 21:00. In addition to dining out, dining in with takeaway is also very popular, to the extent that you may wonder if anyone in Abu Dhabi knows how to cook!

Most of Abu Dhabi's restaurants are in hotels. However, there are a number of independent restaurants throughout town, some of which are licensed. Options are diverse, from a choice of Emirati food in an authentic, ancient village setting, to seafood on a floating dhow! Also remember that there are many independent restaurants around town that are superb and shouldn't be ignored just because they are unlicensed.

Quite a few restaurants specialise in more than one style of cuisine; for instance, an Indian restaurant

Going Out

may also serve Thai and Chinese food. In addition, many places promote theme nights with different types of cuisine or ingredients, such as Italian or seafood, allowing you to sample some truly international cuisine. The choice of what you can eat is thus, dramatically increased. Many restaurants have weekly buffet nights when you can eat, and sometimes drink, as much as you like for a great value, all inclusive price.

Drinks

Although Abu Dhabi is among the more liberal states in the GCC, alcohol is only available in licensed restaurants and bars that are within hotels plus a select few non hotel outlets, such as golf clubs and some government owned establishments. There are certain exceptions to this rule, such as the outlets in the Abu Dhabi Marina & Yacht Club and The Club.

The mark up can often be considerable – it's not unknown for a Dhs.20 bottle of indifferent wine to be charged at Dhs.100 plus. While most independent restaurants cannot serve alcohol, don't let that put you off since the food is often just as good, and sometimes better.

Like alcohol, a bottle of house water can also be outrageously marked up, especially for premium brands. Imported water can be charged at up to Dhs.30 a bottle and if you object to this, we suggest you send it back and ask for a local bottled water (but not tap water). A standard one litre bottle of water usually costs Dhs.1.50 in a supermarket, and is in no way inferior to imported brands.

See also: *Alcohol [p.139]*

Hygiene

The municipality regularly checks outlets on good standards of hygiene. They are strict on warning places to improve and, when necessary, closing them down. So rest assured, whatever you're consuming from the 'tatty' little shawarma shop by the side of the road is safe and you're unlikely to get food poisoning. Indeed, you'll probably have an excellent cheap and atmospheric meal.

Tax & Service Charges

On top of the basic bill, there is a 15 - 16% service charge, which is incorporated into the customers'

bill, but often indicated as being in addition to a price with a ++. This information has to be indicated somewhere on the menu. It is still unclear as to whether the latter charge is actually passed on to staff or whether it can be withheld for poor service, but when in doubt, give the servers a break.

Tipping

Tipping is another grey area, but following the standard rule of 10% will not be out of line. It's not necessarily expected, but will be appreciated. Few waiters seem to realise that there's a direct correlation between good service and the size of the tip!

Independent Reviews

We undertake independent reviews of all restaurants and bars that we include in this book. All the outlets mentioned have been visited by our freelance reporters and the views expressed are our own. The aim is to give a clear, realistic and, as far as possible, unbiased view (that we are permitted to print!). However, if we have unwittingly led you astray, please do let us know. We appreciate all feedback, positive, negative and otherwise. Please email, phone, fax, or snail mail a letter. Your comments are never ignored.

Ratings

Rating restaurants is always a highly subjective business. We asked our reviewers to summarise their experiences (see the bottom of each entry) in terms of Food, Service, Venue and Value. They were also asked to compare the restaurant with other venues in the category and in the same price range. In other words, you may notice that a local cafe has the same summary rating as a premium gourmet restaurant. This is not to say that they are equal. It's just a way to gauge the standard of restaurants that are similarly styled and priced to each other. We hope this will help you make informed choices regardless of your taste or budget.

Each rating is out of four – one blue dot means poor, two means acceptable, three means good and four means fab:

Food ●●●● Service ●●●● Venue ●●●● Value ●●●●

Venues scheduled to open later in 2003 received 'na' ratings:

Food – na Service – na Venue – na Value – na

Restaurant Listing Structure

With over 200 specially selected outlets in Abu Dhabi and Al Ain, the choice can seem daunting. Listed alphabetically by region, then country or commonly known style of cuisine, this section hopes to add to your dining experience by giving as much information as possible on the individual outlets. For an 'at a glance' clarification of this listing, refer to the index at the beginning of this section.

As with all good, simple rules, there are exceptions. Restaurants in the international category usually serve such a variety of food that it is impossible to pin them down to one section. For example, a restaurant that specialises in cooking seafood in styles from all over the world will be found in the Seafood section, while a Thai restaurant that cooks a lot of fish, Thai style, will still be listed under Thai. Make sense? We hope so!

Where a restaurant specialises in more than one type of cuisine, the review appears under the main category.

In order to avoid any confusion concerning a particular restaurant's listing, any non-English names retain their prefix (ie, Al, Le, La and El) in their alphabetical placement, while English names are listed by actual titles, ignoring prefixes such as 'The'. Bon appetit!

Privilege Cards

The table shows a list of privilege or discount cards for use at various establishments. These cards are basically offered to encourage you to return as often as possible. Generally, they can be used at a number of restaurants, so you won't get bored, and most offer incredible discounts and other added benefits, making them excellent value for money.

Icons – Quick Reference

For an explanation of the various symbols or icons listed against the individual reviews, refer to the Quick Reference Explorer Icons table.

Quick Reference Explorer Icons	
🍴	Explorer Recommended!
100	Meal for 2. Average price ± Dhs.25 (3 courses per person)
🚫	NO Credit Cards Accepted
🎸	Live Band
🍷	Alcohol Available
😊	Have a Happy Hour
�:	Will Deliver
👶	Kids Welcome
📞	Reservations Recommended
👔	Dress Smartly
⛱	Outside Terrace
Ⓥ	Vegetarian Dishes

The prices indicated are calculated as the cost of a starter, main course and dessert for one person. This includes any relevant taxes, but excludes the cost of drinks. Another good cost indication is the restaurant location (in a hotel or not), type of cuisine, whether the outlet is licensed etc. The

Privilege Cards			
Hotel/Company	**Includes**	**Phone**	**Cost**
Crowne Plaza	Inter-Continental Abu Dhabi	621 0000	Gold 699 Platinum 899
Hilton Hotels	Hilton Abu Dhabi, Hilton Corniche, Hilton Baynunah, Hilton Al Ain	681 1900	795
Inter-Continental Hotels	Hotel Inter-Continental Abu Dhabi, Hotel Inter-Continental Al Ain	666 6888	Gold 640 Platinum 895
Rotana Hotels	Al Ain Rotana, Al Maha Rotana, Beach Rotana Hotel & Towers	671 2365	Gold 630 Platinum 895
Sands Hotel	La Piazza Restaurant (30 Lunches)	633 5335	1,150
Sheraton	-	677 3333	Gold 740 Classic 595
Hilton Hotels	Hilton Abu Dhabi, Hilton Corniche, Hilton Baynunah, Hilton Al Ain	03 7686666	795
Inter-Continental Hotels	Hotel Inter-Continental Abu Dhabi, Hotel Inter-Continental Al Ain	03 7686686	895

Dhs.150 icon indicates that an average meal should cost anywhere between Dhs.125 to Dhs.175, ie Dhs.150 ± 25.

Vegetarian Food

Vegetarians may be pleasantly surprised by the range and variety of veggie cuisine that can be found in restaurants in Abu Dhabi. Although the main course of Arabic food is dominated by meat, the staggering range of meze, which are often vegetarian, and the general affection for fresh vegetables should offer enough variety to satisfy even the most ravenous herbivore. A word of warning: if you are strict veggie, confirm that your meal is completely meat free. Some restaurants cook their 'vegetarian' selection with animal fat or on the same grill as the meat dishes.

Nowadays, most outlets offer at least one or two veggie dishes. However, if you want a little more variety, choices include the numerous Indian vegetarian restaurants, which cater for the large number of Indians who are vegetarian by religion. These offer so many styles of cooking and such a range of tasty dishes that Indian cuisine is hard to beat for vegetarians. Other highlights include loads of excellent Italian, Mexican, Far Eastern and International restaurants all over the city.

RESTAURANTS

American

Other options → **American Bars [p.286]**
Steakhouses [p.271]
Tex-Mex [p.271]

49er's The Gold Rush

Location → Al Diar Dana Hotel · Tourist Club Area | **645 8000**
Hours → 12:00 - 02:30 Thu - Fri 12:00 - 03:30
Web/email → www.sfcgroup.com   **Map Ref →** 4-B4

Showcasing panoramic views over the marina, 49ers provides a full evening of entertainment, with dining, live music and dancing till late. Part of an American steakhouse chain, they offer an impressive variety of good quality, reasonably priced imported beef, lamb and chicken, alongside locally caught fish, prawns and lobster. Your selection is charcoal grilled, and the food charged according to weight; veggie options are limited. Service is friendly and attentive, and the dining area separate from the bar/dance floor, allowing for peace while you eat. **LB**

Theme nights: *Saturday – Ladies Night; Sunday – Hoteliers Night; Monday – Steak Night, Tuesday and Wednesday – Ladies Night; Friday – Sports Night.*

Food ●●○○ Service ●●●○ Venue ●○○○ Value ●●●○

Chili's

Location → Grand Al Mariah Cineplex · Umm Al Nar St | **671 6300**
Hours → 11:00 - 24:00 Fri 13:30 - 24:00
Web/email → www.chilis.com   **Map Ref →** 8-B2

  100

Chilis attracts a clientele of a wide variety of nationalities who know they will be attended to by enthusiastic and efficient wait staff. The atmosphere is open and friendly, and the time of day and week will dictate how busy you'll find it. Their extensive Tex-Mex menu is bursting with dishes to tantalise the taste buds, and the dessert menu is not to be missed! Although the prices may seem a little on the more expensive side, satisfaction is almost guaranteed. **MSG**

Food ●●●○ Service ●●●○ Venue ●●●○ Value ●●○○

Fuddruckers

Location → Marina Mall · Breakwater | **681 8160**
Hours → 08:00 - 24:00 Fri 08:00 - 24:00
Web/email → fudafsab@emirates.net.ae   **Map Ref →** 10-B4

   50

At Fuddruckers, you'll find the food is what you may expect from a chain restaurant in a mall. But this American chain may just serve the best hamburgers in town. You get to order them the way you want, and then add toppings from a small relish bar, which also doubles as a salad bar. The menu is limited and the place can sometimes be noisy with families and sounds coming from a private party room in the rear. Good value for fresh, quick meals. **EF**

Food ●●●○ Service ●●●○ Venue ●●●○ Value ●●●○

Restaurants

Going Out

Heroes Diner

Location → Crowne Plaza · Shk Hamdan St | **621 0000**
Hours → 12:00 - 01:00 Tue, Thu & Fri 12:00 - 02:30
Web/email → www.crowneplaza.com   **Map Ref** → 8-C1

This bar dominated style venue does not deter its staff from providing efficient service and rather large portions of American/Tex-Mex/pub grub style dishes that more than satisfy a grumbling tummy! Large screens playing a wide variety of sports events (F1 motor racing, football, golf, tennis etc) draw a steady stream of regular clientele. The weekends tend to be busier, which converts the music to more foreground rather than back! A quiet romantic venue, Heroes is not. The place does offer a reasonable meal in a bustling atmosphere followed by dancing, which is a good way to start the weekend. **MSG**

Food ●●●○ Service ●●●● Venue ●●●○ Value ●●●○

Rock Bottom Café

Location → Al Diar Capitol Hotel · Mina Road | **677 7655**
Hours → 11:30 - 15:30 19:00 - 23:30 Thu 19:00 - 24:00
Web/email → www.rockbottomcafe.com   **Map Ref** → 7-E2

Capitalising on the winning formula established in Dubai, the Rock Bottom has taken Abu Dhabi by storm. Loud, raucous, busy, and serving good (if heavy) food, this bar has stirred up the island's nightlife. The cover band is particularly good, the prices reasonable, the staff friendly, and the clientele happy. Dancing ensues most nights after the crowd is sufficiently inebriated but many prefer the earlier, more congenial hours when the bar is chummy and more akin to a pub. Nevertheless, a great concept and well executed. **CB**

Food ●●●○ Service ●●●○ Venue ●●●● Value ●●●○

Americas

This is a cuisine for meat lovers with offering prime quality meat especially flown in from the States to be cooked to your preferred temperature. Desserts vary widely, but often the old favourites like Mississippi mud pie, apple pie or chocolate cake with lashings of ice cream can be found somewhere on the menu. The usually hearty fare has more emphasis on the size of portions and can make dainty eaters cringe with disbelief. Often main courses come with chips, but most restaurants will offer alternatives, such as a baked potato or salad for those concerned about their arteries.

Check out the following varieties in cuisine:

American, Mexican & Tex-Mex, and Steakhouses

TGI Friday's

Location → Opp Le Meridien Hotel · Tourist Club Area | **674 4500**
Hours → 11:00 - 01:00
Web/email → na   **Map Ref** → 7-E1

This popular international chain offers the same atmosphere in its Abu Dhabi outlet as you would find in any other TGI Friday worldwide. Dark wood and stained glass are predominant in the décor and the food is delicious, requiring a hearty appetite. The cuisine leans heavily towards calorific American fare with strong Tex-Mex bias, and the menu includes everything from appetisers, speciality salads, pasta and ribs to enormous burgers and sizzling Fajitas. Portions are huge, so try and leave room for the tantalising sinful desserts! A great family venue, particularly Friday (special family day). **MM**

Food ●●○○ Service ●●●○ Venue ●●●○ Value ●●●●

Arabic/Lebanese

Other options → **Dinner Cruises [p.274]**
Persian [p.266]

Al Aris Restaurant & Grill

Location → Al Salam St · Opp Abu Dhabi Com Bank | **645 5503**
Hours → 08:00 - 01:30
Web/email → na   **Map Ref** → 8-A1

One of the many casual shawarma/Lebanese restaurants in town, Al Aris distinguishes itself with particularly friendly service and especially garlicky shawarma. Conveniently located on Salam Street, this venue is a good choice for the ubiquitous juices, grills or Arabic meze. The small, undistinguished outdoor seating area is an added bonus for pedestrians who want a brief nosh on a pleasant evening. Recommended is the 'shawarma chicken fatta' served in yoghurt with pine nuts and chickpeas. Great for takeaways too. **CB**

Food ●●●○ Service ●●○○ Venue ●●○○ Value ●●●●

Top Arabic

Al Areesh	Min Zaman
Al Dana	Shamyat
Marakesh	

Restaurants

Going Out

Al Atlal

Location ➜ Sands Hotel · Shk Zayed 2nd St | **633 5335**
Hours ➜ 20:00 - 24:00
Web/email ➜ www.sands-hotel.com   **Map Ref** ➜ 8-C1

For an enjoyable, good value, Arabic meal, Al Atlal Lebanese Restaurant is a great option. Although the menu is slightly limited, the various traditional dishes on offer are enjoyable, and if you have a particular favourite, the chef will prepare it for you. Quiet early on, Al Atlal heats up around 23:00 when the band and the authentic Lebanese experience begins. Book ahead if you plan to eat late. Their friendly, attentive service, combined with excellent food make for a guaranteed good evening out. (MSG)

Food ●●●○   Service ●●●○   Venue ●●○○   Value ●●●○

Al Atlal

Al Birkeh

Location ➜ Le Meridien · Tourist Club Area | **644 0666**
Hours ➜ 12:00 - 15:00   19:30 - 02:30
Web/email ➜ www.forte.com   **Map Ref** ➜ 7-D1

A Lebanese restaurant that serves up a traditional experience ie, fresh, tasty and plentiful food portions, sometimes stand offish service, a bellydancer and accompanying live music. Typical of most venues of this sort, arriving before 22:00 will find you in an almost deserted eatery; we recommend you make a night of the set menu and lively atmosphere and go with a group of friends. Pace yourself over the evening – remember there's always more food to come! (PG)

Food ●●●●   Service ●●●○   Venue ●●●○   Value ●●●○

Al Dana

Location ➜ Htl Inter-Continental · Bainuna St | **667 3098**
Hours ➜ 12:00 - 16:00   20:00 - 02:30
Web/email ➜ www.intercontinental.com   **Map Ref** ➜ 10-C1

An authentic Lebanese experience, complete with a bellydancer and live music, the popular Al Dana serves up a sumptuous feast to diners. The set menu will more than satisfy the most ravenous and the most discerning alike. Carnivores are more catered to than veggies, though the latter will still find plenty to choose from amongst the 20 assorted meze that are placed at the table shortly after your arrival (à la carte is also available). The service is wonderful, but watch out for the pricey service charges! (PG)

Food ●●●●   Service ●●●●   Venue ●●●○   Value ●●●○

Al Diwan

Location ➜ Next to Itihad Bank · Shk Khalifa St | **03 764 4445**
Hours ➜ 09:00 - 01:00   Closed Fri am
Web/email ➜ na   **Map Ref** ➜ 15-A3

This new restaurant on Khalifa Street takes both décor and menu variety up a notch or three. Its red carpet entry leads into a light, contemporary interior of plush seats, booths and private rooms. Most of the trade is takeout; reservations are unnecessary. The menu covers a range of Lebanese, Iranian and seafood dishes, but also includes an Italian and continental selection. Dishes are served with Arabic and fresh-from-the-oven Iranian breads, and preceded by generous meze. Portions are large, prices are small, and the service good. (AP)

Food ●●●○   Service ●●●○   Venue ●●●○   Value ●●●○

Al Mawal

Location ➜ Hilton Abu Dhabi · Corniche Rd West | **681 2773**
Hours ➜ 12:30 - 15:30   19:30 - 02:30
Web/email ➜ www.hilton.com   **Map Ref** ➜ 10-C2

Al Mawal is well known not only for its authentic Lebanese food but also for its great Arabic entertainment. Arrive in time to chat and enjoy the fabulous Dhs.125 set menu which includes an awesome amount of delicious traditional meze, meats, and desserts, as at 23:00, the loud live Arabic music begins followed by exotic bellydancing. Don't be too charmed by the sensuous movements of the dancers, or you might be chosen to get up and join in!

Food ●●●○ Service ●●●○ Venue ●●●○ Value ●●●●

Al Qasr Restaurant & Grill

Location → Opp Beach Rotana Htl · Tourist Club Area | 644 9933
Hours → 10:00 - 24:00
Web/email → www.aplace2eat.com   Map Ref → 4-B4

Al Qasr is an inexpensive, understated, but very fine Lebanese restaurant. It gets crowded and noisy late because they usually have a belly dancer, so if you're looking for a quiet dinner, make sure you're there early. All portions are large, and quite tasty, so if you're not feeling ravenous, you might think about sharing. They also have a lovely Friday brunch that's about half the price of most of the other places in town. **EF**

Food ●●●● Service ●●●○ Venue ●●●○ Value ●●●●

Al Rousha

Location → Opp Navigate T Club · Tourist Club Area | 627 2637
Hours → 12:00 - 01:00
Web/email → None   Map Ref → 8-C2

This bright, spacious restaurant is a good place to relax and enjoy a barbecued mixed grill without working up a sweat! The enormous table space allows you to sample a whole range of meze without feeling cramped. Service is excellent and attentive, while the background music is pleasant and relaxing. Language barriers are broken by the talented staff who speaks five European languages. The restaurant attracts a mixed expat community, including a large Lebanese quota making the atmosphere cosmopolitan and warm.

Food ●●●○ Service ●●●○ Venue ●●●○ Value ●●●○

Argila

Location → Khalidia Palace Htl · Khalidiyah | 666 2470
Hours → 13:00 - 02:00
Web/email → khalidiapalacehotel.co.ae   Map Ref → 10-E2

Located in one of the city's older hotels, Argila will give you a taste of local cuisine in the open air, or to the sounds of a local band in the large function room adjacent. Buzzing with mostly Arab and local families, this somewhat shabby restaurant offers

kids plenty of space to run around – till the early hours. Five private cabanas are available to rent for a meal or shisha, each with a TV. The cuisine is good, simple Lebanese and Egyptian fare, served by polite staff. **AF**

Food ●●○○ Service ●●○○ Venue ●○○○ Value ●●○○

Middle Eastern

There is no one distinct Middle Eastern or Arabic cuisine. It is instead, a blend of many styles of cooking from the region. Thus an Arabic meal will usually include a mix of dishes from countries as far afield as Morocco or Egypt to Lebanon and Iran. In Abu Dhabi, modern Arabic cuisine almost invariably means Lebanese food. Typical ingredients include beef, lamb, chicken, rice, nuts (mainly pistachios), dates, yoghurt and a range of seafood and spices. The cuisine is excellent for meat eaters and vegetarians alike.

A popular starter is a selection of dishes known as 'meze' (or mezzeh), which is often a meal in its own right. It is a variety of appetisers served with flat bread, a green salad and 'radioactive' pickles. Dishes can include 'humous' (ground chickpeas, oil and garlic), 'tabouleh' (parsley and cracked wheat salad, with tomato), 'fatoush' (lettuce, tomatoes and grilled Arabic bread), and 'fattayer' (small, usually hot, pastries filled with spinach and cottage cheese).

Charcoal grilling is a popular cooking method and traditionally dishes are cooked with many spices including ginger, nutmeg and cinnamon. An authentic local dish is 'khouzi' (whole lamb, traditionally wrapped in banana leaves, buried in the sand and roasted, then served on a bed of rice mixed with nuts), which is most often available at Ramadan for the evening meal at the end of the day's fast ('Iftar'). It would also have been served at the 'mansaf'; the traditional, formal Bedouin dinner, where various dishes would have been placed on the floor in the centre of a ring of seated guests. Other typical dishes include 'kibbeh' (deep-fried balls of mince, pine nuts and bulgar (cracked wheat), and a variety of kebabs. Seafood is widely available and local varieties of fish include hammour (a type of grouper), chanad (mackerel), beyah (mullet) and wahar, which are often grilled over hot coals or baked in an oven.

Meals end with Lebanese sweets, which are delicious, but very sweet. The most widely known is 'baklava' (filo pastry layered with honey and nuts) and 'umm Ali' (mother of Ali), which is a rich, creamy dessert with layers of milk, bread, raisins and nuts - an exotic bread and butter pudding. Check out the following variety in cuisine:

Arabic/Lebanese, Egyptian, Emirati, Moroccan, Persian and Turkish

Golden Beach Café & Restaurant (Floating Rest.)

Location ➜ Bateen Area, Dhow Harbour · Al Bateen | **666 6331**
Hours ➜ 13:00 - 01:00
Web/email ➜ na   Map Ref ➜ 6-E3

Walk the gangplank. Pass the fish tanks (and your dinner). Board the ageing dhow and enter the dining hall decorated with fading photographs of Abu Dhabi's elite. You have beamed back to well frayed Arabian old world charm. Efficient, prompt service quickly lays before you an array of meze. Yet, the best is to come; lightly spiced prawns, surprisingly tender calamari in garlic butter sauce, succulent hammour, and lobster to die for. This meal is why you walked the plank. **DG**

Food ●●●○ Service ●●●○ Venue ●●●● Value ●●○○

L'Auberge

Location ➜ Nr Corniche Residence Htl · Al Markaziyah | **627 3070**
Hours ➜ 12:00 - 16:00 19:00 - 24:00
Web/email ➜ na   Map Ref ➜ 8-C2

This upmarket Lebanese restaurant has built an excellent reputation over the 26 years of service in Abu Dhabi. The modern, chic and bright surroundings should suit the trendiest of clientele who can relax in comfortable high back chairs and enjoy the quality Arabic and Lebanese cuisine. The menu is extensive and the staff is attentive and courteous. With nearby offices in its vicinity, the place is quite busy and popular for business lunches. Although rather more expensive than most, prior reservations here are recommended, but parking, as always in Abu Dhabi, can be a problem. Outside catering and home delivery are available. **AML**

Food ●●●○ Service ●●○○ Venue ●●●○ Value ●●●○

Las Palmas Complex

Location ➜ Layali Zman · Corniche Rd East | **627 4555**
Hours ➜ 08:00 - 03:00
Web/email ➜ na   Map Ref ➜ 8-D3

This unexpectedly sprawling complex consists of a 24 hour coffee shop, Café La Fayette; an Arabic tent, Layali Zaman; and the Beach Castle restaurant. It's a great place for groups of friends or families to enjoy atmospheric and relaxed surroundings, and the Arabic band which plays on Wednesdays and Thursdays. The extensive menu has mainly Arabic, Lebanese, Italian and continental cuisine (wonderful fresh fruit juices). A daily dish is offered for a nominal price and there's a buffet at 13:30 every Friday. Shisha is available until 03:00 each day. **AML**

Food ●●○○ Service ●●●○ Venue ●●●○ Value ●●●○

Lebanese Flower

Location ➜ Nr Choithrams · Khalidiyah | **665 8700**
Hours ➜ 07:00 - 02:00
Web/email ➜ na   Map Ref ➜ 9-B1

Offering no nonsense peasant cooking, food preparation and authenticity are taken very seriously indeed. Clean and simple décor with pleasant and efficient service, the restaurant also offers a great variety from an extensive menu (prices range from Dhs.8 - 30). Grilled meats and seafood, roasted chicken and falafel are among the favourites and must be accompanied with their fresh juices. Be prepared to stand in a long takeaway line for the shawarma and famous 'meal deal' – Dhs.30 includes a whole rotisserie chicken, fries, Arabic bread, humous and pickles. **EF**

Food ●●●○ Service ●●●○ Venue ●●○○ Value ●●●●

Marroush

Location ➜ Nr Chamber of Commerce · Corniche Rd | **621 4434**
Hours ➜ 07:00 - 01:00
Web/email ➜ na   Map Ref ➜ 8-E3

The owners of Marroush claim that this was the first and most famous Lebanese restaurant in Abu Dhabi. Judging by the clientele, it is indeed very popular, both for take away or eating in. Fresh meze are placed promptly at your table while you choose a main. Starters consist of the usual Lebanese fare; the falafel are moist and possibly the tastiest in Abu Dhabi. The shish tawook and fillet of hammour are also recommended. The food is wholesome and inexpensive with a starter costing Dhs.15 and main courses Dhs.17. The staff is friendly and efficient, and the outdoor terrace is a suitable venue in cooler weather. **MM**

Food ●●●○ Service ●●●○ Venue ●●●○ Value ●●●○

Restaurants

Going Out

Min Zaman

Location → Al Ain Rotana · Zayed Bin Sultan St | **03 754 5111**
Hours → 18:00 - 02:30 Wed & Thu 18:00 - 03:30
Web/email → na   **Map Ref** → 15-A3

Open 'from eight till late'; rest assured you would be granted your fill of delicious Lebanese food, local culture and exotic entertainment. Things don't really get going until after 23:00 when the crowd, mostly local, starts to filter in, and a live band and bellydancing kick off. A set menu featuring cold and hot meze, entrees and dessert will no doubt leave you adequately full. A reasonable variety of wines and spirits are on offer and the 'arak' is recommended for the adventurous, after which, you can kick back with a shisha and allow yourself to be entertained!
Food ●●●● Service ●●●○ Venue ●●●● Value ●●●●

Shamyat

Location → Nr Regency Htl · Al Salam St | **671 2600**
Hours → 09:00 - 24:00   Closed Fri am
Web/email → na   **Map Ref** → 8-B2

Water trickling down the stone wall, orange trees, twittering birds, the traditional bread maker – these are just some of the things that entrance the first time visitor to this Syrian restaurant. However, it's the excellent value for money and the quality and freshness of the food that brings back its regular clientele. Prepare yourself for a reasonably priced feast served by knowledgeable staff who are happy to share their culinary heritage. This place is busy everyday and very popular with families; great for introducing visitors to Arabic food.
Food ●●●○ Service ●●●○ Venue ●●●● Value ●●●●

Bam Bu

Tarboush Lebanon

Location → Opp Liwa Centre · Shk Hamdan St | **626 0700**
Hours → 08:00 - 01:00
Web/email → na   **Map Ref** → 8-D2

In a cosy, relaxed and comfortable atmosphere, simple Lebanese dishes are cooked well, pleasantly presented and reasonably priced. On offer is a full range of typical cuisine and 'sagi' is the speciality. 'Plate of the day' is an exciting promotion (five or more dishes including dessert for Dhs.18). Alternatively, choose from the menu or follow the manager's recommendation. End the meal with a relaxing cup of mint tea. Overall exceptional value for money; a visit is highly recommended.
Food ●●●○ Service ●●●○ Venue ●●●○ Value ●●●●

Chinese

Other options → **Thai [p.272]**

Bam Bu

Location → Marina & Yacht Club · Tourist Club Area | **645 6373**
Hours → 12:00 - 15:00 17:00 - 24:00   Closed Fri am
Web/email → www.abudhabimarina.com   **Map Ref** → 4-B4

Entering this restaurant across a bridge, you are immediately filled with a sense of calm. Comfortable seating is arranged overlooking a peaceful marina, service is prompt, efficient and friendly, and there is an extensive range of mouth watering food for all tastes. Pancakes filled with crispy duck melt in your mouth. Delicious deep-fried ice cream proves a grand finale to an outstanding meal. The all inclusive Dhs.95 offer of unlimited food and alcohol is excellent value for money.
Food ●●●● Service ●●●● Venue ●●●● Value ●●●●

Top Asian Subcontinent

Maharaja	Foodlands
Tanjore	

Restaurants

Going Out

Golden Tower

Location → Nr Madinat Zyd Sh Complex · Madinat Zyd | **631 1766**
Hours → 12:00 - 15:00 18:30 - 24:00
Web/email → na   Map Ref → 5-B4

 50

Greetings at this restaurant are without ceremony. You will be directed upstairs to the square dining room that comprises eight tables and an uninspiring décor – hanging lanterns and Chinese tiles are a charming minimum effort for an oriental touch. The varied and large menu offers 141 savoury dishes to choose from, 14 of these being soup! The 'hot and sour soup' and spring roll starters are good, but watch out for the unpredictable main course. Be smart and let the waiters help you choose. Desserts mostly include lychee. Take away is popular and orders over Dhs.100 are delivered free of charge. **AML**

Food ●●○○ Service ●●○○ Venue ●●○○ Value ●●●○

Grand Shanghai

Location → Int Rotana Inn · Shk Hamdan St | **677 9900**
Hours → 12:00 - 24:00   Closed Sat
Web/email → www.rotana.com   Map Ref → 8-A1

100

Grand Shanghai is an odd dimly lit room that seats about 20. It's spartanly decorated and has a huge bar. The crowd manning the dartboard in the corner is noisy. Service is friendly, though clumsy, but the food is good. Venture away from the classics and try the jellyfish salad. Then substitute an expensive Peking duck for some tasty honey roasted chicken. And round off with a helping of fried bananas that feeds a table. Eat them hot and come back for more, despite the odd surroundings. **FVB**

Food ●●●○ Service ●●○○ Venue ●○○○ Value ●●●○

Hot Plate

Location → Nr Shoe Mart · Madinat Zayed | **634 4696**
Hours → 12:00 - 15:00 18:30 - 24:00
Web/email → na   Map Ref → 5-B4

100

Hot Plate offers some of the best home delivered Chinese food; portions are generous and deliveries arrive hot. If you eat in, you'll find that a lot of effort has been made with the décor, but although intimate, atmosphere is not a strong point. The quality of food varies at times, and

includes the usual range of Chinese dishes, with hot and sour soup and spring rolls for starters, while for main courses, the special fried rice and Singapore noodles are excellent. For takeaway this place is a gem. **AF**

*Other locations: **Meena Road (02 676 5488); Mussafah (02 552 1277)**.*

Food ●●●○ Service ●●○○ Venue ●●○○ Value ●●●○

Imperial Chinese Restaurant

Location → Sands Hotel · Shk Zayed 2nd St | **633 5335**
Hours → 13:00 - 16:00 19:30 - 02:00
Web/email → www.sands-hotel.com   Map Ref → 8-C1

100

In a crowded category, this licensed Chinese venue rates a visit. A longstanding favourite with expats, the restaurant has particularly good ambience. Although dripping with rather campy décor, the live strolling musicians and the staff is authentic Chinese. The menu is surprisingly good with endless dumplings/wontons/spring rolls etc. However, avoid the banal familiar dishes and sample the jellyfish salad, crispy duck pancakes, or 'special' (pork) ribs. The tasting shows promise, so build up a hearty appetite. For serious Chinese fare and a delightfully unpretentious atmosphere, the Imperial Chinese ranks highly. **CB**

Food ●●●○ Service ●●●○ Venue ●●●○ Value ●●●○

Imperial Chinese

Kawloon Chinese

Location ➜ Nr Khalidiyah Tower · Khalidiyah | 634 3436
Hours ➜ 12:00 - 15:00 18:00 - 23:00
Web/email ➜ na   Map Ref ➜ 9-B1

A Chinese restaurant in non Oriental surroundings, Western music plays in the background and there's not a chopstick in sight! The restaurant has a main area seating about 50 with several booths for smaller groups. A full main menu offers an extensive range in pseudo oriental cuisine but a limited choice in dessert. Pros of the place include clean and hygienic surroundings and quick and efficient service – a choice spot for tasty yet inexpensive food. Additional services include take away, free home delivery and outside catering. **GK**
Food ●●○○ Service ●●●○ Venue ●●●○ Value ●●○○

Mandarin

Location ➜ Al Ain Palace Hotel · Corniche Rd East | 679 5288
Hours ➜ 12:30 - 15:30 19:00 - 24:00
Web/email ➜ aphsales@emirates.net.ae   Map Ref ➜ 8-B3

More exclusive than your normal Chinese menu, don't expect to see 'chow mien' or 'chop suey' listed. Oriental décor and a pleasant ambience greet as you cross the bridge over a pond. Choose to sit inside, or outdoors on a terrace overlooking the hotel swimming pool (reservations are recommended for the latter). Prompt service delivers delicious food with more than adequate portions. The steamed dumplings or the paper wrapped chicken is highly recommended and the sweets range from 'birds nest in syrup', ice cream to a good fruit salad. **RP**
Food – na Service – na Venue – na Value – na

Oasis Chinese Restaurant

Location ➜ Opp Abu D Dental Clinic · Madinat Zayed | 635 1545
Hours ➜ 12:30 - 15:30 18:30 - 24:00
Web/email ➜ na   Map Ref ➜ 5-B4

Although Oasis is probably better known for its home delivery service, it's an ideal restaurant for taking the family for a cheap and cheerful Chinese. The décor is 'typically' Chinese in both of the branches on either side of town. There's a choice of seating upstairs in comfortable booths or at tables for four downstairs. The extensive menu offers all the usual favourites and large portions of tasty food ensure that diners get good value for money. Service is quick and efficient. **MM**
Food ●●○○ Service ●●●○ Venue ●●○○ Value ●●●○

Panda Panda Chinese Restaurant

Location ➜ Nr Jashanmal · Ist Istiglal St | 633 9300
Hours ➜ 12:30 - 16:00 19:00 - 24:00 Fri 01:30 - 16:00
Web/email ➜ panda@emirates.net.ae   Map Ref ➜ 8-E2

A bright and clean outlet offering standard Chinese fare in a modern ambience (the interior accommodates just enough artefacts to confirm cuisine intent). Extremely generous portions of mouthwatering cuisine, served by friendly and quick staff, are both delicious and fresh. An extensive menu offers a large seafood selection and plenty of vegetarian options. Prices may seem high but remember – one main dish feeds two! A good option for the family. Parking at the front is a problem, but there is ample space behind the restaurant. **LB**
Food ●●●○ Service ●●●○ Venue ●●●○ Value ●●○○

Top Far East

Bam Bu	**Panda Panda**
Bonsai	**The Royal Orchid**
Imperial Chinese	

Restaurant China

Location ➜ Novotel Centre Hotel · Shk Hamdan St | 632 5661
Hours ➜ 12:00 - 15:30 19:00 - 23:30
Web/email ➜ novoad@emirates.net.ae   Map Ref ➜ 8-D2

Over the top Chinese décor is meant to complement well-prepared Chinese dishes covering the country's provincial cuisine. Friendly attentive staff will help you with menu choices and have an impressive ability of memorising the regulars! The food is mouthwatering and the portions large. A meal can be pricey, depending on your choice, but do include stuffed mushrooms with your starter. The Peking Duck and Beef Kung-Pao are recommended – avoid the little black chillies! Finding a parking space can be like winning the lottery – so get a taxi, or walk. **LB**
Food ●●○○ Service ●●●○ Venue ●●●○ Value ●●○○

Ro-Ro

Location ➜ Khalidia Palace Htl · Khalidiyah | **666 3936**
Hours ➜ 11:00 - 15:30 19:00 - 23:30
Web/email ➜ khalidiapalacehotel.co.ae   Map Ref ➜ 10-E2

Somewhat unimaginative, takeaway style Chinese food is served in a clean but uncoordinated outlet. The choice in wine is extremely limited and at the budget end of the scale, but the service is prompt with good value for money. A little extra effort would add considerable value both to the food and to steering customers back to this outpost. Access and parking is good, but the overall deal does not come to par with local competition. Recommended for late night refugees only. **LB**

Food ●○○○ Service ●●○○ Venue ●●○○ Value ●○○○

Talk of the Town

Location ➜ Nr Blue Tower · Khalifa Street | **627 4308**
Hours ➜ 09:00 - 01:00
Web/email ➜ na   Map Ref ➜ 8-D2

This outlet is well known throughout the region for cheap and cheerful food. Items are freshly cooked (with the exception of the white goo soup that is a complimentary offering while you wait for your order). Popular with all nationalities, the premises are presentable and the menu very extensive. **AF**

Food ●●●○ Service ●●●○ Venue ●●○○ Value ●●●●

Emirati

Other options ➜ **Arabic/Lebanese [p.238]**

Al Areesh

Location ➜ Al Dhafra · Al Meena | **673 2266**
Hours ➜ 12:00 - 16:00 19:00 - 24:00
Web/email ➜ www.aldhafra.net   Map Ref ➜ 7-C4

 150

Al Areesh Restaurant doesn't look promising from outside, but once inside, you'll feel you're on a desert island – and it's a food paradise. The food is fresh, plentiful, reasonably priced and beautifully presented, buffet style, on a small dhow in the centre of the restaurant. Your waiter will escort you to the buffet where you

can choose seafood and meat items you want prepared. Be sure to order an Al Areesh Cocktail. Private rooms with majlis style, floor seating are available for a more authentic Emirati experience. **AML**

Food ●●●● Service ●●●○ Venue ●●●● Value ●●●●

Al Safina Dhow Restaurant

Location ➜ Breakwater · Al Ras Al Akhdar | **681 6085**
Hours ➜ 12:00 - 15:30 19:00 - 22:00
Web/email ➜ na   Map Ref ➜ 10-A4

The fabulous views of the Abu Dhabi Corniche from this converted dhow donated by Sheikh Zayed make this an ideal venue for tourists and residents alike to enjoy local specialities such as hammour, prawns, chicken and lamb dishes. The attentive staff is knowledgeable about the à la carte menu, and are keen to make suggestions. The grilled specialities are attractively served on a unique heated copper tureen. The number of Emiratis dining here must say something for the quality of the cuisine. **MM**

Food ●●●○ Service ●●●○ Venue ●●●○ Value ●●●○

Al Safina

Local Cafe & Restaurant

Location → Breakwater · Al Ras Al Akhdar | **681 6211**
Hours → 10:30 - 15:30 19:00 - 23:00
Web/email → na Map Ref → 10-B4

Enjoy good Arabic cuisine at one of the most picturesque venues in Abu Dhabi. Enter a fortified stone watchtower into an Arabic 'village' with a stunning view of the Corniche. Tables line the edge of the Breakwater, or choose the more private seating inside small wooden shelters. Drinks include coffee or Moroccan tea and delicious fruit cocktails; you can further enhance the mood with an aromatic shisha. A daily evening buffet of meze and salads, meat and fish, served with rice and vegetables, is tasty and tempts you back for more. Don't forget to leave room for dessert. **MM**

Food ●●●○ Service ●●●○ Venue ●●●● Value ●●●●

Far Eastern

Other options → **Chinese [p.242]**
Japanese [p.260]
Thai [p.272]

Wok, The

Location → Htl Inter-Continental · Al Khubeirah | **03 768 6686**
Hours → 12:30 - 15:00 19:30 - 23:00 Closed Fri
Web/email → www.interconti.com Map Ref → 15-E4

Far Eastern cuisine cooked to near perfection describes a meal at the Wok. Set on the ground floor of the hotel, the restaurant offers a choice of eating indoors or al fresco as the venue spills over landscaped gardens and the poolside. A highly skilled chef blends fine food with eastern spices, delivering an array of flavours and wonderful tastes. Coupled with charming and friendly table service, the scene is set for a relaxing and unforgettable dining experience. Worth more than one visit. **GW**

Food ●●●● Service ●●●● Venue ●●●○ Value ●●●○

Wok, The

Location → Crowne Plaza · Shk Hamdan St | **621 0000**
Hours → 12:30 - 15:30 18:30 - 24:00
Web/email → www.crowneplaza.com Map Ref → 8-C1

Authentic wood and wicker furnishings fill this cosy Thai restaurant and a descriptive menu takes away the guesswork from exotic names. Soup from Singapore, sushi from Japan, different types of Thai salads and Pacific Rim entrees can be complemented with a choice from the wine and beverage list, which is modest but adequate. The desserts are positively mouthwatering; the hot ginger chocolate fondue with bananas and vanilla ice cream is recommended. With its diversity of cuisine and various preparation methods, The Wok ensures your return again and again till you exhaust the menu. **DW**

Food ●●○○ Service ●●●○ Venue ●●○○ Value ●●●○

Fish & Chips

Other options → **Pubs [p.290]**
Seafood [p.268]
International [p.252]

Chippie, The

Location → Marina & Yacht Club · Tourist Club Area | **644 0300**
Hours → 18:00 - 02:30
Web/email → na Map Ref → 4-B4

This is the only place in Abu Dhabi where you can indulge in a fish supper from sheets of salt and vinegar soaked paper. The concept is the same as a traditional local chippie, except for the quality of the food, which is excellent; the batter is crisp and the chips succulent and moreish. The menu offers the traditional selections, together with the usual idiosyncratic accompaniments, such as chip butties. Seating is available for eating in, plus there's a small bar. **AF**

Food ●●●○ Service ●●●○ Venue ●●●○ Value ●●●○

French

La Brasserie

Location → Le Meridien · Tourist Club Area | **644 6666**
Hours → 12:30 - 16:00 19:00 - 24:00
Web/email → www.forte.com Map Ref → 7-D1

La Brasserie is an elegant French/international outlet facing onto Le Meridien's popular 'culinary village'. Inside it's spacious and well lit (the terrace offers a little more seclusion). An impressive à la carte and buffet are available throughout the day, served with wines from a

Restaurants

Going Out

variety of countries. The food is well presented and popular nights are Mondays for seafood and Fridays for the barbecue. During the cooler months, it's worth taking a seat on the terrace to enjoy the communal buzz from the surrounding outlets. **AF**

Food ●●●○ Service ●●○○ Venue ●●○○ Value ●●○○

Le Beaujolais

Location → Novotel Centre Hotel · Shk Hamdan St | **633 3555**
Hours → 12:00 - 01:00
Web/email → novoad@emirates.net.ae   Map Ref → 8-D2

  100

To sample a wide selection of French wines in an atmosphere of energetic cosmopolitan chat and bon ami, Le Beaujolais is your venue. The well presented standard menu caters for international tastes at a reasonable cost. Additional choice, for a price, comes from the regularly changing and more flamboyant French cuisine promotions, which give an option for more refined dining. The décor is tastefully pseudo French and relaxing. Buzzing every night of the week, Le Beaujolais is definitely for those who prefer people to posing – well worth the trip. **AF**

Food ●●●○ Service ●●●○ Venue ●●●○ Value ●●●○

Le Bistrot

Location → Le Meridien · Tourist Club Area | **644 6666**
Hours → 12:30 - 15:00 19:00 - 23:30   Closed Sat
Web/email → www.forte.com   Map Ref → 7-D1

  100

For people watching and fine French wine and cuisine, head for the terrace of Le Bistro. Located in the heart of Le Meridien 'culinary village', the restaurant is close to the buzz of the other outlets but retains an intimacy of its own, helped by abundant foliage. The food is good and well presented and the wine list extensive. Although Le Bistro has its own wine bar, it's more likely that people will head here to enjoy a quiet meal served by polite and attentive staff. **AF**

Food ●●●○ Service ●●○○ Venue ●●○○ Value ●●●○

Le Bistrot

Le Rabelais

Location → Novotel Centre Hotel · Shk Hamdan St | **633 3555**
Hours → 12:30 - 15:00 19:30 - 24:00
Web/email → novoad@emirates.net.ae   Map Ref → 8-D2

150

At Le Rabelais fine French international dining is offered in an intimate environment; ideal for that special occasion or business meal. The professional bustle in the unobtrusive show kitchen provides a pleasant diversion and dishes, which include complimentary entrée and sweets, are superbly presented. Special fixed price meals are available, as well as a Dhs.120 à la carte menu in the evening and a business lunch deal for Dhs.80. Weekend evenings and the special fondue on a Saturday are generally busy and reservations are recommended. **AF**

Food ●●●● Service ●●●○ Venue ●●●○ Value ●●●○

Top European	
Amalfi	Le Rabelais
Brauhaus	Prego's
Chequers	Teplancha
La Mamma	Vasco's

Going Out   Restaurants

Fusion

Other options → **International [p.252]**

90 Degrees

Location → Htl Inter-Continental · Bainuna St | **693 5214**
Hours → 12:00 - 15:30 19:00 - 24:00
Web/email → abudhabi@interconti.com Map Ref → 10-C1

'Minimalist' best describes the deliberately understated interior of this popular restaurant. Whether you choose to dine indoors, or out on the terrace overlooking the marina, allow plenty of time to peruse the menu. The eclectic range of Mediterranean cuisine is diverse enough to be a conversation piece in itself! Friendly professional staff waits nearby and a varied, well priced menu and wine at quaffing prices ensures that you don't just dine here on special occasions, but make it your regular rendezvous spot. Worth mentioning is the lunchtime special for Dhs.75, which includes a three course meal and soft drinks. GK

Food ●●●○ Service ●●●○ Venue ●●●○ Value ●●○○

90 Degrees

Top Al Fresco

90 Degrees	Vasco's
Meridien Village	Il Paradiso

Flavours

Location → Sheraton Abu Dhabi · Corniche Rd East | **677 3333**
Hours → 06:00 - 24:00
Web/email → www.sheraton.com Map Ref → 8-A3

With a possible June opening date, this fusion restaurant will offer daylong dining from three show kitchens in an innovative setting overlooking pools and lush gardens. It will be aimed at all ages and cultures and will offer weekly speciality nights plus a bar. RP

Food – na Service – na Venue – na Value – na

German

Brauhaus

Location → Beach Rotana · Tourist Club Area | **644 3000**
Hours → 12:00 - 01:00
Web/email → beach.hotel@rotana.com Map Ref → 4-B3

This indoor/outdoor German venue at the back of the older section of the Beach Rotana Hotel offers substantial meals in an atmospheric pub style outlet. The main focus is on pork, sausages and veal, but there's a wide ranging menu covering most tastes. Service is exceptionally quick, and the food consistently good. Completely different from any other Abu Dhabi restaurant, this is a place where you feel briefly to have been transported back to Europe. Recommended for a boys' night out. LB

Food ●●●● Service ●●●○ Venue ●●●○ Value ●●●○

Indian

Other options → **Pakistani [p.266]**

Bukharah

Location → Al Diar Regency · Al Salam St | **676 5000**
Hours → 12:00 - 15:00 19:00 - 24:00
Web/email → na Map Ref → 8-A2

Relocated upstairs to the room once occupied by the now defunct Bellevue, Bukhara is scheduled for a major makeover. At present it feels sterile

Going Out · Restaurants

and antiseptic with nothing suggesting the upscale Indian cuisine they offer. The few patrons are overly attended by the staff, but some of the fare was quite good – if familiar. While in this limbo, the restaurant is probably not worth a visit, but when they renovate to take advantage of the stunning views, perhaps Bukhara will return to the fine, licensed Indian restaurant it once was. **CB**

Food ●●●○ Service ●●○○ Venue ●●○○ Value ●●○○

Caravan

Location → Hamed Centre · Shk Hamdan St **639 3370**
Hours → 11:30 - 16:00 18:30 - 23:00
Web/email → caravan@emirates.net.ae   Map Ref → 8-D1

An amazing place, Caravan begs the question "how do they do it?". The combination of the quality and range of dishes at such a low price – Dhs.35 for the dinner and Dhs.25 for the lunch buffet – is excellent value. This is a quiet, pleasant place to enjoy a good selection of Indian, Chinese and Thai dishes during the week, but remember it gets busy at the weekend; book in advance. Caravan offers excellent value for money, where the level of service isn't compromised by the low cost. **JVL**

Food ●●○○ Service ●●●○ Venue ●●●○ Value ●●●●

Casa Goa

Location → Zakher Hotel · Umm Al Nar St **627 5300**
Hours → 12:00 - 01:00
Web/email → zakhotel@emirates.net.ae   Map Ref → 8-B2

This funky, authentic, small but licensed eatery wins points for being delightfully rustic. Goan (Indian) cuisine is served in a no nonsense, friendly – if predominantly male – venue that feels more like a beachfront dive. Fiery vindaloo curries, fruity snacks, plus a few 'western' dishes make for a quirky menu. Service is friendly and the fare is good value for money, right down to the cheap drinks. For third world atmosphere in the Capital, this is the place. **CB**

Food ●●○○ Service ●●○○ Venue ●●○○ Value ●●●○

Foodlands

Location → Opp Etisalat · Shk Zayed 2nd St **633 0099**
Hours → 12:00 - 15:30 18:30 - 24:30
Web/email → na   Map Ref → 8-E1

Foodlands offers excellent value cuisine to suit all tastes, and has an established reputation and dedicated clientele. The restaurant is spacious and tasteful, with dining on two levels and areas defined for privacy without detachment. All are welcome, and the service is particularly attentive and helpful; Mr. Diwakar will explain the menu in detail and help you select dishes. Servings are generous and well presented (with a slant towards spicy), and there's an excellent daily lunch buffet. Unique to Abu Dhabi, Foodlands offers authentic Mogul dishes. **AF**

Food ●●●○ Service ●●●● Venue ●●●○ Value ●●●●

India Palace

Location → Opp ADNOC FOD HQ · Al Salam St **644 8777**
Hours → 12:00 - 16:00 19:00 - 24:15
Web/email → na   Map Ref → 4-C4

The unassuming exterior may border on tacky but, once inside, a burst of tasteful Rajasthani décor welcomes you. Set amidst carved teakwood doors, brocade and tapestry furnishings, an open tandoori kitchen allows you to see the chefs at work. Copper plates and cups promise the feast of kings. Vegetarians have ample choice; the rice with fruit and nuts is a must try. Cottage cheese is surprisingly the dominant ingredient, served on fritters and naan bread too! The ambience is pleasant and the staff is polite, efficient and friendly. Despite that, should you require more privacy, a secluded dining area and carved screens ensure that. **LR**

Food ●●●● Service ●●●○ Venue ●●●○ Value ●●●○

Kwality

Location → Opp Blue Marine · Al Salam St **672 7337**
Hours → 12:00 - 15:00 19:00 - 24:00
Web/email → na   Map Ref → 8-A2

The imaginative décor, friendly staff and fabulous aromas are enough to convince you that this is more than your average Indian restaurant. An impressive menu offers both typical and unusual dishes that are delicious, generous and very good value for money – and you can watch them being prepared! Cubed hammour makes a delicious starter and the palak paneer with pilau rice rounds off a fabulous main course. The service is excellent and after a visit, the restaurant's popularity among all nationalities and ages is not such a wonder. A quick call to reserve your table would therefore be wise. **EG**

Food ●○○○ Service ●●●○ Venue ●●●○ Value ●●●●

Maharaja

Location → Le Meridien · Tourist Club Area |644 6666
Hours → 12:30 - 15:30   19:00 - 24:00   Closed Sat
Web/email → www.forte.com   Map Ref → 7-D1

From start to finish, a dining experience at Maharaja is a delight. With attentive, knowledgeable service and dishes cooked and spiced according to your taste and to perfection, diners ranging from the novice to the expert Indian food lover will find palatable pleasure here. Nibble on complimentary popadums and chutney while you decide. The tandoori chicken is highly recommended and will not disappoint. Seating options range from the tastefully decorated main dining area with views of the chef's tandoori oven, to opulent private rooms, or weather permitting, the ever popular outdoor patio. **PG**

Food ●●●● Service ●●●● Venue ●●●○ Value ●●●○

Maharaja Terrace

Nihal Restaurant

Location → Nr Sands Htl · Shk Zayed 2nd St |631 8088
Hours → 12:00 - 15:00   18:30 - 24:00
Web/email → na   Map Ref → 8-C1

Nihal Restaurant is almost an institution in Abu Dhabi – it's been here for years and for good reason. The emphasis is on serving authentic Indian food at reasonable prices. The menu has a good variety of chicken, tandoor, lamb and seafood as well as breads, rice and a few Chinese dishes. Try the sweet lassi drink – it's the perfect accompaniment to a meal. A buffet is served Thursday evening and Friday lunch and is usually popular. The surroundings are clean and simple with a family area at the back. **AML**

Food ●●●○ Service ●●●○ Venue ●●●○ Value ●●●○

Royal Arab Udupi

Location → Opp Thomas Cook · Shk Hamdan St |674 3485
Hours → 12:00 - 15:00   18:30 - 24:00
Web/email → na   Map Ref → 8-B1

Outlets spread all over the city offer Indian and Chinese food at very reasonable prices. Fine cuisine is served in clean and simple settings and the service is excellent. The fact that most of its patrons are Indian lends credence to the quality and authenticity of the food, which is extensive, offering both vegetarian and non vegetarian dishes. Pretty much whichever dish emerges from the kitchen, looks good. Choosing what to eat will be about as much trouble as polishing it off, for portions are very generous! Whatever you do, save room for dessert; the 'gulab jamuns' are worth the calorie kick! **KU**

Food ●●●● Service ●●●● Venue ●●○○ Value ●●●○

Tanjore

Location → Htl Inter-Continental · Al Khubeirah |03 768 6686
Hours → 12:30 - 15:00   19:00 - 23:00   Closed Mon
Web/email → na   Map Ref → 15-E4

Al Ain's decidedly most popular restaurant for north Indian cuisine offers an extensive selection of richly flavoured traditional and less traditional dishes, keeping customers loyal for ten years and counting. A relatively small space

Restaurants · **Going Out**

houses a central court and the rough stone and wood décor is dotted with displays of spices and brass utensils, exuding an ethnic and intimate atmosphere. Ten different draft beers include the Indian 'Kingfisher' for homesick patrons. Promotions include Curry & Pint (Dhs.58+) on Thursdays.

Food ●●●● Service ●●●○ Venue ●●●○ Value ●●●●

International

Other options → Fusion [p.249]

Airport Golf Club Restaurant

Location → Airport Golf Club · Abu Dhabi | **575 8040**
Hours → 08:00 - 20:00
Web/email → golfclub@emirates.net.ae | Map Ref → na

The Al Ghazal Airport Golf Club Restaurant has the feel of an old boys' club: cool and dark, and the perfect spot to take a break before, during or after your game. The menu is however anything but old, offering a variety of traditional and non traditional clubhouse food at reasonable prices. Soups, salads and sandwiches are made fresh, and there are a number of hot entrees for the hungrier patron. The food is acceptable and the service pleasant and polite. Alcohol is served. KU

Food ●●○○ Service ●●○○ Venue ●●●○ Value ●●○○

Dining on the Breakwater

Al Fanar

Location → Le Royal Meridien · Al Khalifa St | **674 2020**
Hours → 06:00 - 11:00 12:30 - 15:30 19:30 - 23:00
Web/email → www.rotana.com | Map Ref → 8-B2

A restaurant that revolves 360 degrees (and at two speeds!) unveiling beautiful views of the city is a dining experience not to be missed. The décor is classically elegant without being too stiff and the presentation and service is precise. The menu is interestingly full of choices and even though the snapper may be a bit 'fishy', the steaks are positively delectable. A meal for two will cost about Dhs.150 - 300 plus, exclusive of alcohol – expensive, but a worthy option on special occasions. Keep your valuables well away from the windowsill; they've been known to revolve well away from your table! JG

Food ●●●○ Service ●●●● Venue ●●●○ Value ●●●○

Al Hosn

Location → Sheraton Residence · Shk Zayed 1st St | **666 6220**
Hours → 06:00 - 09:30 12:30 - 15:30 19:00 - 22:30
Web/email → www.sheraton.com | Map Ref → 9-B1

Residents and guests of the hotel comprise the majority of diners at this pleasant, buffet style restaurant. Located on the seventh floor with a good view of the Corniche, lovely wrought iron and marble tables enhance the bright atmosphere and continental decor. Standard cuisine served at reasonable prices makes for a convenient meal at good value. A basic menu offers a variety of Arabic and Asian salads, soup and a selection of cheese, with a main course of curries, chicken, beef and fish with rice. Round off your meal with pickings from the small but assorted desserts table. JG

Food ●●○○ Service ●●○○ Venue ●●○○ Value ●●●○

Beach Club Brasserie

Location → Beach Rotana · Tourist Club Area | **644 3000**
Hours → 11:00 - 22:00
Web/email → beach.hotel@rotana.com | Map Ref → 4-B3

Scheduled to open in July 2003, this beachy restaurant promotes a casual atmosphere and enjoyment for both children and adults. The menu comprises of light bites and

Restaurants

Going Out

refreshments; a special kids menu for the tots and drinks for adults as you dine on the beach amidst relaxed surroundings.

Food – na Service – na Venue – na Value – na

Club Restaurant, The

Location → Club, The · Al Meena
Hours → 12:00 - 15:30 19:00 - 24:30
Web/email → www.the-club.com

| 673 1111

Map Ref → 7-A2

The Club Restaurant is a refined venue with a comfortable, intimate atmosphere. Together with friendly yet discreet staff, good food and very reasonable prices, it offers a great all round experience. The marvellous selection of well priced theme nights could tempt you to eat there every night: Arabic, Asian, fusion & seafood to name but a few. Weekday lunches and Saturday evenings have an à la carte menu; there's a brunch on Friday. Only open to members of The Club and their guests, perhaps the above will persuade you to join! EG

Food ●●●○ Service ●●●○ Venue ●●●● Value ●●●●

Falcon Restaurant

Location → Shk Khalifa St · Al Ain
Hours → 11:00 - 16:00 18:30 - 24:00 Fri 13:00 - 16:00
Web/email → na

| 03 764 5414

Map Ref → 15-C3

This small, very basic restaurant offers Indian, Chinese and continental dishes, and is a popular place with locals and expats alike. In the low-ceilinged dining room, seven tables seat groups of four. The chefs are from India and the menu lists Mughlai cuisine, along with tikkas, tandooris, kormas, biriyanis and vegetarian specialities, as well as delicious breads. Sandwiches, steaks, chicken and salads are also available. Servings are generous and appetites can be pleasantly appeased for Dhs.30. The waiters are friendly and the service speedy and courteous. HK

Food ●●●○ Service ●●●○ Venue ●●○○ Value ●●●○

Flavours

Location → Hilton Al Ain · Al Ain
Hours → 06:30 - 10:30 12:00 - 15:00 19:00 - 23:00 Closed Fri pm
Web/email → www.hilton.com

| 03 768 6666

Map Ref → 15-D4

The new name reflects the spirit of the restaurant, which now caters to the widest possible audience, offering an alternative world taste daily. A Mediterranean décor with Arabic undercurrents allows privacy for families; this appeases the National clientele. A different theme night shapes the menu; Saturdays and Sundays feature extensive salad buffets and hors d'oeuvres, steaks on Monday, seafood on Tuesdays, a Mongolian barbecue on Wednesdays and Oriental night on Thursdays. A fixed charge per head includes food and entertainment that can range from bellydancing, oriental music, or live cooking shows. RP

Food – na Service – na Venue – na Value – na

Garden, The

Location → Crowne Plaza · Shk Hamdan St
Hours → 12:00 - 16:00 19:00 - 23:00
Web/email → www.crowneplaza.com

| 621 0000

Map Ref → 8-C1

Staying true to its name, diners are surrounded by plants and flowers with a fountain in the centre, thus creating a fresh, garden atmosphere. Seafood lovers can indulge in the various stations attractively set up in the middle of the restaurant. Large bowls of mussels and beautifully presented sushi is a diner's delight, while tasty dipping sauces accompany the grilled lobster and shrimps. Salads are fresh and colourful and a vast choice is available. Theme nights every week make for an affordable meal and most include house beverages. KW

Food ●●●● Service ●●●○ Venue ●●●○ Value ●●●○

Sundowners

Captain's Arms	Vasco's
El Torito	Waka Taua

The Garden

surrounding countryside. Don't be put off by the drive; the view, the improbable location and the restaurant itself make the trip well worth it.

A lengthy wine list complements the mainly French and Mediterranean buffet and à la carte menu. The look is contemporary and both food and service are appealing. The Friday lunch buffet is particularly popular with families.

Bookings are recommended at weekends, and why not make full use of the hotel facilities (including two tennis courts) by staying the night?

Food ●●●○ Service ●●●○ Venue ●●●○ Value ●●○○

Le Jardin

Location ➜ Al Diar Dana Hotel · Tourist Club Area | **645 8000**
Hours ➜ 06:30 - 23:30
Web/email ➜ www.aldiarhotels.com   Map Ref ➜ 4-B4

🍷 100

A variety of Arabic and international cuisine and light meals are served in a garden style cafe. The service is friendly and eager and the clientele consists mostly of businessmen staying at the hotel and walk in bachelors. Women may not feel comfortable dining here for sheer lack of female presence. Choose from a small buffet meal (Dhs.25 - 45) or go à la carte (average cost Dhs.60 exclusive of alcohol). The Pizzeria Italiana is the recommended deal for two, covering a large pizza, soup, salad and soft drinks, all for Dhs.27.

Food ●●○○ Service ●●○○ Venue ●●○○ Value ●●○○

Le Jardin

Location ➜ Khalidia Palace Htl · Khalidiyah | **666 2470**
Hours ➜ 07:00 - 10:30 13:00 - 16:00 19:00 - 23:00
Web/email ➜ kphauh@emirates.net.ae   Map Ref ➜ 10-E2

🍴 100

A French style outdoor café looks over the hotel's green lawns, pool deck and animal enclosures; the Friday buffet shifts to an outdoor air conditioned tent. A simple buffet meal is the attraction for regulars. Food is standard fare: international cuisine with Arabic salads and appetisers, Asian salads, veggies and dip. The bright atmosphere is popular with many for the cheap beach and child friendly atmosphere and makes for a relatively inexpensive day out.

Food ●●●○ Service ●●○○ Venue ●●●○ Value ●●○○

Hamptons

Location ➜ Hilton Residence · Corniche | **627 6000**
Hours ➜ 06:00 - 10:30 12:30 - 15:30 19:00 - 23:00
Web/email ➜ corexflr@emirates.net.ae   Map Ref ➜ 8-D3

📞 100

This restaurant is located on the first floor of the Corniche Residence Apartments & Hotel. The décor is modern and plain, with seating for about 100 and plenty of space between tables. The dining choice is always buffet style with a change of theme each night. The food is plentiful and the choice reasonable, if unimaginative, but the service is slow. There is a live-cooking pizza station with mix-your-own ingredients. The fresh squeezed fruit juices are truly delicious and help relieve the plain eating choice.

Food ●●○○ Service ●●○○ Venue ●●●○ Value ●●○○

Le Belvedere

Location ➜ Mercure Grand Htl · Al Ain | **03 783 8888**
Hours ➜ 12:00 - 15:00 19:00 - 22:30
Web/email ➜ www.mercure.com   Map Ref ➜ 17-B4

  🍷 150

Le Belvedere is a relatively new arrival on Al Ain's restaurant scene. Located in the Grand Hotel Jebel Hafeet, it commands a spectacular view of the

Restaurants

Going Out

It's Theme Night every night at the Crowne Plaza

Surf 'n' Turf* = Dhs. 149 net

Arabian Nights* = Dhs. 99 net

Ribs, Bibs & Pitchers* = Dhs. 99 net

Seafood Night = Dhs. 149 net

Curry Garden* = Dhs. 99 net

Taste of Italy* = Dhs. 99 net

Emirates Buffet = Dhs. 80 net

* Unlimited
House Beverages Included

CROWNE PLAZA
ABU DHABI

Crowne Plaza Abu Dhabi
PO Box 3541, Sheikh Hamdan St.,
Abu Dhabi, UAE.
Tel: 02-6210000 Fax: 02-6217444
Email: cpauh@emirates.net.ae
Web: www.crowneplaza.com

Level 2

Location ➔ Baynunah Tower · Corniche Rd West | **632 7777**
Hours ➔ 06:30 - 22:30
Web/email ➔ baynunah@emirates.net.ae   **Map Ref ➔** 9-A2

Located on level 2 of the Hilton Baynunah
Residence, Level 2 overlooks the greenery of the
British Embassy and the Corniche. It's a quiet and
unassuming restaurant that has an extensive à la
carte menu of Arabic, Italian, Tex-Mex and
continental cuisine, plus a selection for kids. The
staff is cheerful, prices moderate and the quality of
the food is good. A stylish round area is available
for private dining. Ideal for a pleasant meal and a
quiet chat. **AML**

Food ●●○○ Service ●●○○ Venue ●●○○ Value ●●●○

NRG Sports Cafe

NRG Sports Café

Location ➔ Le Meridien · Tourist Club Area | **644 6666**
Hours ➔ 16:00 - 01:30
Web/email ➔ www.forte.com   **Map Ref ➔** 7-D1

With a fresh innovative design, this double storey
café/bar subtly evokes a stadium theme in its
décor and seating structures. The interior is
bright and the food prepared in the show kitchen
is innovative and complements the surroundings.
The mezzanine floor with its own bar overlooks
the dance floor, band (Wednesdays and
Thursdays), ground floor bar and gardens; an
ideal spot to people watch. There's a flip a coin
happy hour and plenty of strategically positioned
screens showing sport. **AF**

Food ●●●○ Service ●●○○ Venue ●●●○ Value ●●○○

Palm, The

Location ➔ Al Diar Capitol Hotel · Mina Road | **678 7700**
Hours ➔ 06:30 - 10:30 12:30 - 15:30 19:00 - 23:00
Web/email ➔ adcaphtl@emirates.net.ae   **Map Ref ➔** 7-E2

This low stress, buffet dining option is now serving
up theme nights as an affordable meal for the
whole family. Feast on European a' la carte cuisine
on Sunday, try the shellfish sizzlers on Tuesday, or
treat your brood to the Thursday brunch. The
starters and salads are standard fare, but the
Peking duck carved by a smiling chef is indeed
impressive. Wait staff is friendly and the
atmosphere is clean, plain and functional with
large windows providing a view of the street.
Expect to pay around Dhs.50 - 55 per head, not
including alcoholic beverages. **JG**

Food ●●○○ Service ●●○○ Venue ●●●○ Value ●●○○

Park Residence

Location ➔ Opp Hamdam Post Office · Al Khalifa St | **674 2000**
Hours ➔ 06:00 - 24:00
Web/email ➔ na   **Map Ref ➔** 8-B2

Located on the ground floor of a tower block, this
coffee shop is handy for tenants and guests alike.
The furniture is basic and the surroundings simple,
airy and with lots of light, but not much
atmosphere. Prices are reasonable, however, the
food is uninspiring, although this could be an ideal
stopping off point for a quick, cheerful snack and a

Restaurants

Going Out

cuppa if you want a quiet and discreet place. A breakfast buffet operates between 06:00 - 10:30 for only Dhs.20.

Food ●●○○ Service ●●○○ Venue ●●○○ Value ●●○○

Rosebuds

Location → Beach Rotana · Tourist Club Area | **644 3000**
Hours → 11:30 - 03:30
Web/email → na | **Map Ref** → 4-B3

 150

Ignore the rather soppy name and enjoy one of the best truly international buffets in town! Choose from a vast selection of attractively arranged food from all around the world. There really is something for everyone here; from Thai, Indian, Italian, sushi and Mexican to Arabic, seafood, a carvery, salads, pastries and delectable delicacies for pudding! Theme nights run through the week with unlimited wine for Dhs.97 net, plus there's an excellent Friday brunch complete with kids sized portions and entertainment, allowing you to relax and enjoy your meal.

Food ●●●● Service ●●●● Venue ●●●○ Value ●●●●

Italian

Other options → **Pizzerias [p.266]**
Mediterranean [p.262]

Amalfi

Location → Le Royal Meridien · Shk Khalifa St | **674 2020**
Hours → 12:30 - 15:00 19:30 - 23:30
Web/email → www.rotana.com | **Map Ref** → 8-B2

 150

Amalfi offers the highest quality of food and service to rival anywhere in the city. One really feels like they have been treated to a high class dining experience, a million miles away from the busy streets below. The ambience is both relaxed and refined. If you are willing to spoil yourself somewhat, then this is the perfect dining experience, attaining the highest standards in all areas of service, and especially choice and quality of the menu. This is a real treat for the food connoisseur.

Food ●●●● Service ●●●○ Venue ●●●○ Value ●●●○

Casa Romana

Location → Hilton Al Ain · Al Ain | **03 768 6666**
Hours → 12:00 - 15:00 19:00 - 23:00
Web/email → www.hilton.com | **Map Ref** → 15-D4

 100

Casa Romana offers an extensive range of Italian favourites and introduces a few new flavours. Overlooking the hotel foyer, the initial feeling is of being in a goldfish bowl, but after a while the passing traffic is neither distracting nor intrusive. Overall, the atmosphere works, helped by low lighting and plush decoration, and the service is efficient and attentive. The fare is simple, generous and authentic, particularly the vegetable dishes. Desserts feature a few old favourites and offer a delicate end to a meal.

Food ●●●○ Service ●●●○ Venue ●●○○ Value ●●●○

Ciro's Pomodoro

Location → Al Diar Capitol Hotel · Mina Road | **672 7357**
Hours → 12:00 - 15:30 19:00 - 03:00
Web/email → adcaphtl@emirates.net.ae | **Map Ref** → 7-E2

 100

An interesting range of Italian food served in a lively atmosphere. Pizzas, pastas, grills and a number of salads are coupled with options such as sushi! Do not be swayed by the corny names – they make a pretty mean pizza. Don't spend too much time on the starters – just sink your teeth into a main course. Funky décor, a dance floor, stage and live acts, provide all the ingredients for a convivial night out.

Food ●●●○ Service ●●●○ Venue ●●●○ Value ●●●○

European

In Abu Dhabi, the most dominant of European cuisine is Italian; there are numerous restaurants around offering the 'best' tiramisu in town, plus the usual selection of pasta and pizzas. The atmosphere of many of these outlets aims for an 'authentic' Italian feel with whitewashed walls, jars of pasta, wood fired pizza ovens, checked tablecloths and even singing staff (in Italian of course!).

Within this style of cuisine, there are a growing number of independent restaurants springing up around the city, offering good value for money but no chance to indulge in a glass of Chianti with your cannelloni. Check out the following varieties in cuisine:

Fish & Chips, French, German, Italian, Mediterranean, Pizzerias, Portuguese and Spanish.

Restaurants

Going Out

Il Palazzo

Location → Al Ain Palace Hotel · Corniche Rd East | **679 4777**
Hours → 12:00 - 15:00 19:00 - 24:00
Web/email → www.alainpalacehotel.com   Map Ref → 8-B3

Brick walls and ceiling, and windows overlooking the Corniche enhance an already rustic Italian ambience. The menu is regular Italian (no surprises) and offers a range of antipasti, soups, salads, pastas, pizzas etc, and a variety of main dishes cater to different clients, not overlooking children's needs. The 'Pranzo Veloce' for Dhs.38+ offers a set lunch menu daily.

Food – na Service – na Venue – na Value – na

La Mamma

Location → Sheraton Abu Dhabi · Corniche Rd East | **677 3333**
Hours → 12:00 - 16:00 19:00 - 24:00
Web/email → Sheraton@emirates.net.ae   Map Ref → 8-A3

To the delight of its regulars, La Mamma is open once again after a major revamp. The focal point is the marble circular display, which houses the spectacular antipasti buffet for which this restaurant has always been known.

A tempting array of fresh salads and vegetable dishes nestle alongside platters of cold cuts, fish, seafood and cheese. The courteous staff will guide you through the menu, which includes popular pasta and pizza choices, as well as some more unusual and enticing meat dishes.

Food ●●●● Service ●●●● Venue ●●●○ Value ●●●○

La Mamma

La Piazza

Location → Sands Hotel · Shk Zayed 2nd St | **633 5335**
Hours → 12:00 - 15:30 19:00 - 23:30
Web/email → www.sands-hotel.com   Map Ref → 8-C1

Away from the hustle and bustle of the streets below, La Piazza presents a quiet and friendly atmosphere in cool yet traditional Italian surroundings. The good range of Italian food, from generous salads to pizzas and pastas is complemented by efficient service from the staff. This is an ideal restaurant for families, couples or hotel guests, providing a reasonably priced menu without compromising on quality or style of presentation. An evening at La Piazza will leave you feeling both satisfied and relaxed.

Food ●●○○ Service ●●○○ Venue ●●○○ Value ●●●○

La Piazza

Luce Ristorante Italiano & Club

Location → Htl Inter-Continental · Al Khubeirah | **03 768 6686**
Hours → 12:30 - 15:30 19:30 - 01:00
Web/email → www.interconti.com   Map Ref → 15-E4

A really big entrance door opens into Al Ain's hippest eatery. Carefully arranged modern industrial furnishings, an open kitchen and splashes of orange are soothed by music from an unobtrusive live band. An inspired menu comprises aesthetically enticing (but not so savoury) fare, including updated classic Italian dishes, pizzas and pastas. Attentive service and attractive ambience, with a little improvement in cuisine, could easily class this dining experience amongst the most magnificent. The bar area doubles as a nightclub, undoubtedly for Al Ain's cooler set.

Food ●●●○ Service ●●●○ Venue ●●●○ Value ●●●○

Luce

Pappagallo

Location → Le Meridien · Tourist Club Area | **644 6666**
Hours → 12:30 - 15:30 19:00 - 24:00
Web/email → www.forte.com   Map Ref → 7-D1

With a visit to Pappagallo you could be forgiven for thinking you were in the heart of Tuscany! Situated in Le Meridien's culinary village, the diner has the freedom of the livelier outdoor terrace or the intimacy of the piazza style area inside. The reasonably priced menu ranges from a variety of antipasti, 'make your own pizzas' and traditional desserts, all of good quality. If you're looking for a fun family night out or a more intimate dining experience, then both may be found here. AMK

Food ●●○○ Service ●●●● Venue ●●●○ Value ●●●○

Peppino

Location → Grand Continental Htl · Shk Zayed 1st St | **626 2200**
Hours → 12:00 - 15:00 19:00 - 23:30
Web/email → grand-continental-flamingo.com   Map Ref → 8-B2

An intense search is required before you finally stumble upon this place – but it's worth the effort.

For the dinner span, you will be seemingly transported to Italy (provided you stay away from the window). An endless assortment of pastas and pizzas are on offer – the problem lies in narrowing down your choice – but whatever, your order, it's bound to be a home run. Authentic (and delicious) southern Italian flavours and a pleasant low key atmosphere ensure an unforgettable dining experience. EF

Food ●●●● Service ●●●○ Venue ●●●○ Value ●●●●

Pizzeria Italiana

Location → Al Diar Gulf Htl · Al Maqtaa | **441 4777**
Hours → 12:00 - 24:00
Web/email → adglfhtl@emirates.net.ae   Map Ref → 1-D3

This welcoming, cosy establishment specialises in simple pizza and pasta dishes. The food is tasty, and includes an Italian salad buffet and fruit salad or ice cream as dessert. The place is small and cheerful, and its location close to the hotel swimming pool makes it a very casual affair. It is also possible to order from the poolside menu, which includes kiddie meals. Food portions are good and the service friendly and efficient – ideal for a quiet and inexpensive meal. AMK

Food ●●○○ Service ●●●○ Venue ●●○○ Value ●●●○

Portofino

Location → Marina & Yacht Club · Tourist Club Area | **644 0300**
Hours → 12:00 - 15:00 19:00 - 23:30
Web/email → www.abudhabimarina.com   Map Ref → 4-B4

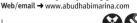

Portofino's overlooks the pool and beach at the marina. It's partially open air and has a better atmosphere in the late evening when it's busy and once the in house band (Fridays only) starts to play.

The restaurant is a basic pizzeria that offers a good mix of Italian favourites (some are heavy on the grease). The portions of food and drink are generous and most dishes are good value for money. Shisha is available and it's a pleasant place to chill out of an evening and people watch. AML

Food ●●○○ Service ●●●○ Venue ●●○○ Value ●●●○

Restaurants

Going Out

Prego's

Location → Beach Rotana · Tourist Club Area | **644 3000**
Hours → 12:00 - 15:00 19:00 - 23:00
Web/email → na   **Map Ref →** 4-B3

  150

Make reservations. This hot and trendy, contemporary new place fills up early and the customers keep coming – and with good reason. It has a menu to satisfy all tastes with an emphasis on a large variety of pizzas and pastas that can be customised to your taste. The open kitchen area allows you to watch your food being prepared. Outdoor seating overlooks the beach and water while the bright and busy indoors is never overly noisy, thanks to the high ceilings. The combination of atmosphere, food and service slot this under 'must visit'. **EF**

Food ●●●● Service ●●●● Venue ●●●○ Value ●●●●

Prego's

Sevilo's

Location → Millennium Hotel · Khalifa Bin Zyd St | **626 2700**
Hours → 12:00 - 15:00 19:00 - 24:00
Web/email → www.millenniumhotels.com   **Map Ref →** 8-B2

   150

Located beside an elegant poolside terrace with a splendid view of the city and gardens, Sevilo's is one of the newest Italian restaurants in town. The décor is 'traditionally' Italian with a conservatory style, iron gates and an open kitchen.

The varied menu offers very good choices of antipasti, pasta, seafood and meat, and portion sizes are spot on. Complimentary appetisers are served and the wine list boasts good quality wines at reasonable prices. On Wednesday evenings, there's an excellent value and very impressive seafood buffet. **AML**

Food ●●●○ Service ●●●○ Venue ●●●○ Value ●●●○

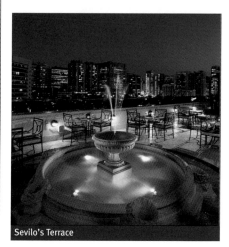
Sevilo's Terrace

Japanese

Benihana

Location → Beach Rotana · Tourist Club Area | **644 3000**
Hours → 12:00 - 15:00 19:00 - 23:00
Web/email → beach.hotel@rotana.com   **Map Ref →** 4-B3

Benihana is known to be among Dubai's liveliest Japanese eateries, and the Abu Dhabi branch, soon to open in the summer, will quite likely follow suit. Also judging from its sister outlets, the standard menu generally caters to those not particularly familiar with Japanese cuisine. Novice eaters will appreciate elastic bands tied around the ends of chopsticks and the 'Americanised' Japanese menu, whereas fans of hardcore Japanese cuisine may be disappointed. **RP**

Food – na Service – na Venue – na Value – na

Restaurants

Going Out

Just a taste of Abu Dhabi's seven wonders!

Brauhaus, Rosebuds, Rodeo Grill, Trader Vic's, Prego's, Café Columbia and The L.A.B. - seven ways to experience the best of dining and entertainment in Abu Dhabi. Little wonder our guests are often spoilt for choice!

BEACH ROTANA
HOTEL & TOWERS
ABU DHABI

THERE'S ONE FOR YOU

reservations and more information please call 02-6443000   www.rotana.com

Bonsai

Location → Health & Fitness Club · Al Mushrif
Hours → 12:00 - 23:00 Fri 13:00 - 22:00
Web/email → www.adhfc.com   **Map Ref** → 3-D2

Bonsai is a calm, relaxing venue for a traditional Japanese meal – a perfect location for a quiet meal with friends in a private cubicle.   Service is impeccable, and the wait staff friendly and helpful. The food is reasonable, fresh and healthy, and the ideal cuisine to be served in the Abu Dhabi Health and Fitness Club!   The portions are ideal for sharing and the choice of a sushi and sashimi is vast.   Round off the meal with Japanese green tea ice cream for the ultimate in good health! **KW**

Food ●●●● Service ●●●● Venue ●●●○ Value ●●●○

Zen

Location → Al Ain Palace Hotel · Corniche Rd East   **679 4777**
Hours → 12:00 - 15:00 19:00 - 24:00
Web/email → www.alainpalacehotel.com   **Map Ref** → 8-B3

This upscale, somewhat pricey restaurant is quite popular among Japanese expats, which is a good sign.   You can choose to sit at a table or on cushions placed on the floor, as a true traditionalist.   Alternatively, the teppanyaki bar offers communal dining and the opportunity to watch your food being prepared – the chef entertains with flamboyant knife tricks and suave organising of the food on the hotplate.   Choices start with a bowl of savoury soup with tofu, which should be sipped from the dish without a spoon.

Sushi

To really participate in the atmosphere, use chopsticks and drink sake. **EF**

Food ●●●○ Service ●●●○ Venue ●●●○ Value ●●○○

Korean

Arirang

Location → Khalidia Palace Htl · Khalidiyah   **665 0563**
Hours → 12:00 - 15:00 19:00 - 23:00
Web/email → khalidiapalacehotel.co.ae   **Map Ref** → 10-E2

100

Arirang's warm welcome and reputation for serving excellent Japanese and Korean food at reasonable prices keep its clientele coming back.   The teppanyaki table is highly recommended; reserve at weekends.   The dextrous chefs keeps you entertained, as they chop and prepare the food with dazzling speed and expertise.   The menu price is inclusive of soup, starters and dessert.   The Korean food focuses on barbecues.   There's a separate dining room for karaoke. Although the hotel doesn't serve alcohol, you can order wine or beer here. **KW**

Food ●●●○ Service ●●●○ Venue ●●○○ Value ●●●○

Mediterranean

Other options → **Italian [p.257]**
Pizzerias [p.266]

Casa Verde

Location → Golf Club by Sheraton · Umm Al Nar St   **558 8990**
Hours → 12:00 - 15:00 18:00 - 23:00
Web/email → www.adgolfsheraton.com   **Map Ref** → 1-A1

This is an upscale, pricey restaurant that delivers very good food and service in a spacious, pleasant atmosphere.   Everything is à la carte, but beware the nightly specials, which are priced well above anything else on the very extensive menu. Offerings range from continental to Mediterranean. Sadly, the restaurant is located above a very noisy lounge at the golf club, and the club itself is way out of town – almost at the airport... and it's not easy to find! **EF**

Food ●●●○ Service ●●●○ Venue ●●●○ Value ●●●○

Restaurants

Going Out

Chequers

Location → Sands Hotel · Shk Zayed 2nd St
Hours → 19:00 - 24:00
Web/email → www.sands-hotel.com

633 5335

Map Ref → 8-C1

  150

This is a cosy restaurant with nice atmosphere (trendy and modern), nice menu, nice wine list and nice live music, but the food doesn't quite meet the promise of the menu. Each dish looks wonderful when presented, but sadly not everything stands the taste test. The kitchen tries hard, but needs more work and fine tuning. The service is better – charming, but maybe this is a venue to which you're better off coming for the music, the cocktails and snacks. **EF**

Food ●●● ○ Service ●●●○ Venue ●●●○ Value ●●●○

Chequers

IL Paradiso

Location → Sheraton Abu Dhabi · Corniche Rd East
Hours → 12:00 - 15:30 19:00 - 23:30 Fri 12:00 - 16:00
Web/email → www.sheraton.com

677 3333

Map Ref → 8-A3

 150

If you want Mediterranean cuisine and delicious seafood, then trek through the Sheraton's gardens to find this popular restaurant. The inspired menu has several novel but rather delicious sounding offerings, including local fish. The lobster bisque, the smoked hammour and the prawns in garlic sauce all come well recommended. Although it has a good wine list, the house wine sold by the carafe is perfectly acceptable. Seafood night on Wednesdays. On completion of the remodelling of the Corniche in 2004, it should be a lovely location. **MM**

Food ●●●● Service ●●●○ Venue ●●○○ Value ●●●○

Il Paradiso

La Terrazza

Location → Hilton Abu Dhabi · Corniche Rd West
Hours → 12:00 - 15:00 19:00 - 23:00
Web/email → www.hilton.com

681 1900

Map Ref → 10-C2

 150

With a Mediterranean theme and décor that's not too dominant (plenty of stone and wood, and strategically placed urns and bottles of olives), La Terrazza offers an extensive à la carte menu as well as a buffet. The theme nights, which are inclusive of all house beverages, are great value for money. It has a welcoming atmosphere and a pleasant ambience. It generally gets very busy as the evening progresses, so reservations are recommended. Good value for money.

Theme nights: Tuesdays, Seafood Night (Dhs.135+15%); Wednesdays, Bacchanalia Night (Dhs.85+15%); Thursdays, Curry Night (Dhs.60+15%). **AML**

Food ●●○○ Service ●●●● Venue ●●○○ Value ●●○○

Restaurants

Going Out

Mexican

Other options → **Tex-Mex [p.271]**

Chi Chi's

Location → Le Meridien · Tourist Club Area | **644 3717**
Hours → 12:00 - 24:00
Web/email → www.forte.com   **Map Ref** → 7-D1

   100

Chi Chi's has some good points. Five dirham margaritas on Tuesdays are a plus. And so is the 'Best of the West' appetiser platter. Service is some of the friendliest in the region. And the taco from the Tres Amigos combo is delicious. The rest of the food, however, is not fantastic. Most of the entrees taste similar, except the (bad) seafood enchiladas. There are several specials throughout the week, but we recommend you go for a drink and snack before dinner elsewhere. **FVB**

Food ●●○○ Service ●●●● Venue ●●●○ Value ●●○○

Chi Chi's

El Sombrero

Location → Sheraton Abu Dhabi · Corniche Rd East | **677 3333**
Hours → 12:00 - 16:00 19:00 - 01:00 Closed Fri am
Web/email → www.sheraton.com   **Map Ref** → 8-A3

     150

For quality Mexican food in an authentic setting, the revamped El Sombrero is the choice. Kick off with a great Margarita and further indulge in hot tamales and salsa dancing surrounded by colourful sombreros. An extensive food menu includes all the popular favourites plus mouthwatering specials. The restaurant layout promotes a comfortable sense of space and corner tables offer intimacy in the busiest of hours. Live music entertains without drowning out speech, and the service is faultless. Although not cheap, this night out option is a sure shot winner. **MFW**

Food ●●●● Service ●●●● Venue ●●●● Value ●●●○

El Sombrero

El Torito

Location → Htl Inter-Continental · Bainuna St | **666 6888**
Hours → 12:30 - 24:30
Web/email → www.intercontinental.com   **Map Ref** → 10-C1

     150

Torito Mexican restaurant is the ideal venue for a large party enjoying the live music, or a quiet romantic meal overlooking the marina. The interior has a Mexican feel and has been carefully thought out. Service is prompt and friendly. The menu is wide with the usual fajitas, chimichangas, tacos and burritos; ideal choices are the combination meals, offering a bit of everything. Portion sizes are extremely generous and the guacamole is highly recommended – it's prepared tableside. Wines are also very reasonably priced. **KW**

Food ●●●○ Service ●●●○ Venue ●●●● Value ●●●○

Mongolian

Coconut Bay

Location → Hiltonia Beach Club · Corniche Rd West | **681 1900**
Hours → Fri only 18:00 - 21:00
Web/email → www.hilton.com   **Map Ref** → 10-C2

 100

The Mongolian barbecue operates only on a Friday at the Hiltonia Beach Club, and is excellent value for money. The food is all stir-fried, and there's a great selection of salads to go in the wok along with a selection of seafood and meats. It's self service, so the portions are as large or small as you wish. This is the perfect way to end a busy day on the beach – very casual, in a beautiful setting, with children very welcome. **RW**

Food ●●●○ Service ●●○○ Venue ●●●○ Value ●●●●

Moroccan

Other options → **Arabic/Lebanese [p.238]**
Persian [p.266]
Turkish [p.273]

Marakesh

Location → Millennium Hotel · Khalifa Bin Zyd St | **626 2700**
Hours → 19:00 - 01:00
Web/email → www.millenniumhotels.com   **Map Ref** → 8-B2

 **150**

Situated in the heart of the city, authentic flavours, a live band and bellydancing highlight this Moroccan style restaurant. Knowledgeable and courteous staff deliver mouthwatering Moroccan food plus typical Arabic dishes. Tabouleh, couscous and the mixed grill are served in generous portions – watch out for the beverage prices though. The Moroccan Orange sealed with cinnamon and honey syrup is the perfect end to a meal. The place opens after nine in the evening, so don't plan on an early night here. **RW**

Food ●●●○ Service ●●●● Venue ●●●● Value ●●●○

Nepalese

Kathmandu

Location → Nr Janata Bank · Elektra Street | **632 8860**
Hours → 11:00 - 15:00 18:00 - 24:00
Web/email → na   **Map Ref** → 8-D1

  50

Kathmandu is an authentic 'find' offering great tasting good value food with no frills. The basic décor belies the honest quality of the cooking and the genuinely attentive service. The menu offers familiar favourites from Indian and Chinese cuisine, but you may find some pleasant surprises in the Nepalese dishes. The chicken makhani and chicken momo are recommended. All meals are cooked to order, so don't expect fast food service. Personal service and unpretentious food for exceptional value make Kathmandu the perfect antidote to ubiquitous five star theme night dining. **MFW**

Food ●●●○ Service ●●●○ Venue ●●○○ Value ●●●●

Marakesh

Restaurants

Going Out

Pakistani

Other options → Indian [p.249]

Tabaq Restaurant

Location → Nr Sun & Sand Sport · Shk Hamdan St | **678 7349**
Hours → 06:00 - 17:00 18:30 - 01:00
Web/email → na
Map Ref → 8-A2

An interesting variety in food is delivered quickly and presented well (with whatever minimum resources are at hand). Portions are large and good value for money, and if a big meal is what you seek, you've come to the right place. There is the occasional choice from the specials of the day; all meat is served on the bone. A particular nice point is that regulars are recognised and greeted with enthusiasm – very warm and welcoming. A family room upstairs can be accessed after successfully manoeuvring up the strange stairs! Nevertheless, an ideal choice for a cosy conclusion to an evening or day.

Food OOOO Service OOOO Venue OOOO Value OOOO

Persian

Other options → Arabic/Lebanese [p.238]
Moroccan [p.265]
Turkish [p.273]

Al Khayam

Location → Hilton Al Ain · Al Ain | **03 768 6666**
Hours → 12:00 - 15:00 19:00 - 23:00 Closed Sat
Web/email → www.hilton.com
Map Ref → 15-D4

This Persian restaurant serves up tasty dishes in an authentic (but cold!) atmosphere. Menu highlights include the mixed grill, and the spinach and yoghurt appetiser – great with the bread served fresh from the oven, shortly after you arrive. Kebabs are predominant on the menu, and are cooked to perfection by the Indian chef. As with most Persian restaurants, carnivores are favoured here. Select one of the cosy alcoves if you can – while you'll get all the privacy you want, you won't lose out on the attentive service. **PG**

Food ●●●O Service ●●●O Venue ●●●O Value ●●●O

Pizzerias

Other options → Italian [p.257]
Mediterranean [p.262]

Pizzeria Italiana

Location → Al Diar Mina Hotel · Al Salam St | **678 1000**
Hours → 12:00 - 24:00
Web/email → www.aldiarhotels.com
Map Ref → 8-A2

This is a pizza joint that looks like (and should be) a takeaway. Comprising a small eating area that is adjacent to the busy lobby, its main function seems to be as a room service outlet for the hotel. The extremely limited menu offers pizza or pasta as main courses, with a salad bar sitting in a dark corner of the restaurant. The dessert too, is not a delightful surprise but an average sweet fix. Not a highly recommended dining option but more of a 'food for survival' choice in dire straits. **EF**

Food ●OOO Service ●●●O Venue ●OOO Value ●●OO

Trattoria Pizzeria Del Centro

Location → Novotel Centre Hotel · Shk Hamdan St | **633 3555**
Hours → 12:00 - 15:00 19:00 - 23:00
Web/email → novoad@emirates.net.ae
Map Ref → 8-D2

In the heart of the city, this is a traditional Italian restaurant with a reputation for good food, service and value for money. The food is typically Italian and includes a range of pizzas. Alternatively, ask for your own to be tailormade. Portions are generous, if not terribly exciting, and should your choice be unavailable on the à la carte menu, there's an appetising daily buffet, plus theme nights (Saturdays, seafood; Mondays, beef). This is a good stop for a quick, inexpensive meal in an authentic Italian ambience. **AML**

Food ●●OO Service ●●●O Venue ●●●O Value ●●●O

Merry Zoos

Hemingway's	Rock Bottom Café
Luce	Trader Vic's

Restaurants

Going Out

Polynesian

Other options → **Chinese [p.242]**
Thai [p.272]

Trader Vic's

Location → Al Ain Rotana Htl · Al Ain | **03 754 5111**
Hours → 11:30 - 15:30 19:30 - 23:30 Bar 12:30 - 01:30
Web/email → www.rotana.com | Map Ref → 15-A3

 150

From the inviting Polynesian décor to the inventive cocktails and signature dishes, Trader Vic's continues to please. Sit in the lounge and enjoy the sounds of the Cuban band while snacking on an appetising array of finger foods and sipping one of their exotic (and quite potent) cocktails. If you're feeling brave, try the Tiki Puka Puka – you'll only need one! Or, for a full meal, move to the dining room; the Peach Blossom Duck and the San Francisco Steak are both delicious. This is a good venue for groups out on festive occasions. **CM**
Food ●●●● Service ●●●○ Venue ●●●○ Value ●●●○

Trader Vic's

Location → Beach Rotana · Tourist Club Area | **644 3000**
Hours → 12:30 - 15:00 19:30 - 23:30
Web/email → na | Map Ref → 4-B3

 150

Whether for business or pleasure, Trader Vic's is one of the longstanding favourite restaurants in Abu Dhabi. The consistent quality of the food, the attentive staff and the relaxed tropical ambience keep people coming back (except maybe those on a tight budget). Try one of their world famous cocktails as you peruse the exciting menu – it's always difficult making the final choice from the tantalising French-Polynesian dishes! A discreet trio provides entertainment without disrupting conversation. Enjoy their fabulous cocktails in happy hour, 17:30 - 19.30; there's 20% off. **MM**
Food ●●●● Service ●●●○ Venue ●●●○ Value ●●●○

Waka Taua Terrace

Location → Le Meridien · Tourist Club Area | **644 6666**
Hours → 17:00 - 24:00 Closed Mon
Web/email → www.forte.com | Map Ref → 7-D1

 100

Situated next to the water with a large outdoor patio, this bar is a popular spot for sundowners. Sporadic service does not deter the crowd from sampling the tasty cocktails – and there are lots to choose from! You won't actually see the sunset, but the lapping waves and the resident ducks entertain during the day and a resident band takes over later. For nibbles, the sampler snack tray is an option. Better still, have a cocktail and move on to another restaurant in the Meridien Village for dinner. All of Friday is happy hour. **PG**
Food ●●●○ Service ●●○○ Venue ●●●○ Value ●●●○

Waka Taua Terrace

Portuguese

Other options → **Spanish[p.271]**

Vasco's

Location → Hiltonia Beach Club · Corniche Rd West | **692 4328**
Hours → 12:00 - 15:00 19:00 - 23:00
Web/email → www.hilton.com | Map Ref → 10-C2

 200

An extensive menu blends international/fusion and Pacific Rim dishes with European styles and Asian herbs and spices served in generous portions. The salad bar is a delight, service is

Restaurants

Going Out

efficient, friendly and unobtrusive, and the staff knows their 'stuff'. During the winter months, the patio is an ideal place to sit and take in the view. The whole place has a relaxed atmosphere with a hive of activity near the open kitchen. This is one of the busiest restaurants in town; booking is essential for both lunch and dinner. **RW**

Food ●●●● Service ●●●○ Venue ●●●● Value ●●●○

Vasco's Terrace

Seafood

Other options → **Fish & Chips[p.247]**
International [p.252]

Al Sofon Dhow Restaurant

Location → Breakwater · Al Ras Al Akhdar | **681 6134**
Hours → 13:00 - 15:30 20:00 - 23:00 Closed Sat
Web/email → na   Map Ref → 9-E4

 **100**

It's worth a visit here, just for the spectacular panoramic view from the deck of this two storey dhow floating off the Breakwater. Tables are set in booths in the form of a fishing boat. Although there is an à la carte menu, starters are chosen from the usual Arabic salads and meze. The artistically arranged display of seafood on offer will help you decide what you'd like to eat, and the food served up is delicious. The number of Emiratis dining here proves the quality of service and food. **MM**

Food ●●○○ Service ●●●○ Venue ●●●○ Value ●●●●

Al Sofon

Fishmarket, The

Location → Htl Inter-Continental · Bainuna St | **693 5233**
Hours → 12:30 - 15:00 19:30 - 23:00
Web/email → abudhabi@interconti.com   Map Ref → 10-C1

 200

The Fishmarket is the most highly recommended and costly seafood restaurant in town, well established in the art of 'choose your own ingredients' dining. You'll find a tempting array of fish and vegetables laid out market-style, priced by the kilo. The friendly wait staff advise on selection, cooking options and sauces

The Fishmarket

_Le_ MERIDIEN
ABU DHABI

the way hotels should be

THE LUXURY OF CHOICE.

NOT ONLY DO WE HAVE OVER 200 LUXURIOUS ROOMS AND SUITES - AND STATE-OF-THE-ART CONFERENCE FACILITIES - WE ALSO OFFER YOU FIFTEEN DIFFERENT RESTAURANTS AND BARS SET AMID OUR AL FRESCO MERIDIEN VILLAGE. ADD TO THAT AN ARRAY OF EXTRAORDINARY FACILITIES INCLUDING THE EDEN SPA. AT LE MERIDIEN ABU DHABI YOU'LL BE QUITE LITERALLY SPOILT FOR CHOICE

- POOLS AND BEACH
- HEALTH SPA, GYM, AND TURKISH HAMMAM
- MASSAGE AND TREATMENTS
- TENNIS AND SQUASH
- FISHING AND DIVING

_Le_ MERIDIEN
ABU DHABI

Tel: +971 2 644 6666
Fax: +971 2 6440348
e-mail: meridien@emirates.net.ae
www.lemeridien-abudhabi.com
www.lemeridien.com
IN PARTNERSHIP WITH NIKKO HOTELS

available, before taking your food to be cooked. Be warned, the price mounts quickly; don't let your eyes rule your stomach! This place is excellent for special occasions or business meals where you won't be picking up the bill.

Food ●●●○ Service ●●●● Venue ●●●○ Value ●●○○

Golden Fork

Location ➜ Opp Al Noor Hospital · Khalifa Bin Zyd St | **627 4308**
Hours ➜ 09:00 - 01:00
Web/email ➜ na   Map Ref ➜ 8-B2

Cheap seafood rather than the décor, is the draw of the Golden Fork chain of restaurants dotted around the UAE. Far from the sophisticated Fishmarket in style, quality and price, Golden Fork is great if you're in the mood for an inexpensive, simple, yet fresh seafood meal. Filipino, Indian, Chinese and continental dishes are on offer and fresh fish dishes come with complimentary soup (the fish is recommended, the soup is not). It's not gourmet food and you won't find spectacular service, but for the price, it's a bargain.

Food ●●●○ Service ●●●○ Venue ●○○○ Value ●●●●

Golden Fork

Location ➜ Opp Union Bank · Shk Khalifa St | **03 766 9033**
Hours ➜ 09:00 - 01:00 Fri 13:30 - 01:00
Web/email ➜ na   Map Ref ➜ 15-A3

For restaurant information, see review above.

Palm Beach Restaurant & Oyster Bar

Location ➜ Al Diar Gulf Htl · Al Maqtaa | **441 4777**
Hours ➜ 12:00 - 23:00
Web/email ➜ adglfhtl@emirates.net.ae   Map Ref ➜ 1-D3

Overlooking the calm Gulf waters on the outskirts of Abu Dhabi, this comfortable and relaxed venue appeals to many. An impressive menu boasts oysters, octopus, shrimps and lobster, cooked in a variety of styles, but unfortunately lacking in quality and flavour. The wine list is non descriptive and we do not recommend asking the somewhat ignorant staff. Delicious seafood you will not find. But it does work as a quick fix after lounging at the pool or beach, or for enjoying delicious cocktails and a sunset.

Food ●●○○ Service ●●○○ Venue ●●●○ Value ●●●○

Palm Beach Restaurant

Pearl, The

Location ➜ Hilton Abu Dhabi · Corniche Rd West | **681 1900**
Hours ➜ 12:00 - 15:00 19:00 - 23:00
Web/email ➜ www.hilton.com   Map Ref ➜ 10-C2

Overlooking the Abu Dhabi Breakwater and Corniche, the Pearl is renowned for it's fabulous food, service and charm. An international menu with French inclination boasts specialities such as Fois Gras, smoked quail, venison and monkfish, all wonderfully prepared and presented. Seafood night every Tuesday may not be quite so luxurious but decidedly delicious, with a fair selection of sushi and fish dishes and interesting salads – quite a hit. A good selection of wines, impeccable service and a live (and pleasing) band elevate this restaurant on the premier dining venue list.

Food ●●●○ Service ●●●● Venue ●●●○ Value ●●●○

Spanish

Other options → **Tapas Bars [p.290]**

Teplancha

Location → Htl Inter-Continental · Bainuna St | **666 6888**
Hours → 18:00 - 24:00
Web/email → www.intercontinental.com   Map Ref → 10-C1

 100

Terraced and overlooking the marina, this hit restaurant is a simple, unique concept – unfussy and unpretentious and the food can only be described as very very tasty. Spanish tapas with an Asian touch and various other creations tantalise with sizzling sounds, smell and smoke, creating an atmosphere of true Mediterranean magic. Chat away with close friends while 'picking' on an array of fine foods and sampling an extensive (and very reasonable) wine list – ideal for a lazy and pleasurable evening. SBV
Food ●●●○ Service ●●●○ Venue ●●●○ Value ●●●○

Steakhouses

Other options → **American [p.237]**

Ponderosa

Location → Hamed Centre · Elektra Street | **639 3375**
Hours → 12:00 - 24:00 Fri 13:00 - 24:00
Web/email → na   Map Ref → 8-D1

V 50

Try and control the urge to 'hee haw!' as you enter this restaurant. Open daily from noon to midnight, fast food served in a cowboy style environment is convenient for a quick meal, especially if you enjoy grilled steak. The menu is based around a Dhs.29 buffet, which includes starters and dessert. For a more substantial meal, try the individually prepared steak, lamb, chicken or fish dishes accompanied by fries or a scrumptious baked potato. Keep the kids in check around the self service whipped ice cream machine – it's bound to become very popular with them. JVL
Food ●●○○ Service ●●●○ Venue ●●●○ Value ●●○○

Rainbow Steak House

Location → Nr BHS Bld · Shk Hamdan St | **633 3434**
Hours → 12:00 - 15:30 18:30 - 24:00
Web/email → na   Map Ref → 8-C1

100

This functional dining experience offers friendly and polite service and a good selection of reasonably priced steak. Alternatives include some variations on Indian and Chinese cuisine, but the lobster is undoubtedly the best! Lunch and dinner buffet meals are great value and offer the traditional selection of salad starters ie, a variety of hot meat and fish dishes and a good choice of desserts. Close to Hamdan Street, this is a good stop for quick, no nonsense food at a reasonable price. MFW
Food ●●○○ Service ●●●○ Venue ●●○○ Value ●●●○

Rodeo Grill

Location → Beach Rotana · Tourist Club Area | **644 3000**
Hours → 12:30 - 15:30 19:00 - 24:00
Web/email → beach.hotel@rotana.com   Map Ref → 4-B3

 150

Spilling out into the new wing of the Beach Hotel, Rodeo is poised to become one of the top restaurants in town – if you like steak. Simple but sophisticated, the menu offers various cuts of beef cooked to your preferred temperature and accompanied by a choice of side dishes. This winning formula is executed to perfection and administered by a well trained and genial staff. Cosy and confident, this is an adult restaurant that focuses on fine food, proper service, and leisurely indulgence. CB
Food ●●●● Service ●●●● Venue ●●○○ Value ●●●○

Tex-Mex

Other options → **Mexican [p.264]**

Alamo, The

Location → Marina & Yacht Club · Tourist Club Area | **644 0300**
Hours → 12:00 - 15:00 19:00 - 24:00 Fri 11:00 - 15:00
Web/email → www.abudhabimarina.com   Map Ref → 4-B4

 100

Decorated with Alamo memorabilia, this place is renowned for its great succulent ribs and fajitas.

On Wednesday and Thursday nights, the Alamo really comes alive with a vibrant Latino atmosphere. Arrive early if you want conversation or take beginners salsa lessons (Dhs.35) and work up an appetite to do justice to the belly-busting portions. At 21:00 the Cuban band belts out lively music so join in or sit back and enjoy the sizzling gyrations of the dancers over a jug of margaritas. **MM**

Food ●●●○ Service ●●●○ Venue ●●●○ Value ●●●●

Rodeo Grill

Chili's

Location → Grand Al Mariah Cineplex · Umm Al Nar St | **671 6300**
Hours → 11:00 - 24:00 Fri 13:30 - 24:00
Web/email → www.chilis.com   Map Ref → 8-B2

Chilis attracts a clientele of a wide variety of nationalities who know they will be attended to by enthusiastic and efficient wait staff. The atmosphere is open and friendly, and the time of day and week will dictate how busy you'll find it. Their extensive Tex-Mex menu is bursting with dishes to tantalise the taste buds, and the dessert menu is not to be missed! Although the prices may seem a little on the more expensive side, satisfaction is almost guaranteed. **MSG**

Food ●●●○ Service ●●●○ Venue ●●●○ Value ●●○○

Ranch, The

Location → Al Diar Gulf Htl · Al Maqtaa | **441 4777**
Hours → 12:00 - 01:00
Web/email → adglfhtl@emirates.net.ae   Map Ref → 1-D3

Lots of wood and saddles adorn the walls of this western bar and restaurant and the atmosphere is pleasant (most days of the week have live music). The menu is good and varied, offering mainly Tex-Mex dishes such as fajitas as well as steak or salmon, and desserts are classics such as meringue or bread and butter pudding. Generous portions, friendly and polite service (with preferably lesser gap between courses) and moderate prices make this a popular out of the city venue and quite busy on the weekends. When the band isn't playing, television screens entertain the sports fanatics. **AML**

Happy hour: *12:00 - 19:00 & 19:00 - 22:00.*

Food ●●●○ Service ●●○○ Venue ●●●○ Value ●●●○

Thai

Other options → **Chinese [p.242]**

Royal Orchid, The

Location → Al Salam St | **644 4400**
Hours → 12:00 - 15:30 19:00 - 24:00 Fri 12:00 - 16:00
Web/email → na   Map Ref → 8-A1

The spectacular entrance over a glass covered fishpond containing huge Koi carp, attention to detail, and calming atmosphere keep this popular restaurant busy (if it sold alcohol, it would be full every night!). While the prawn dishes are recommended in particular, the polite and efficient staff serve delicious, beautifully prepared Chinese, Thai and Mongolian food at very competitive prices. The takeaway and home delivery option (the food arrives in microwave containers) is worth remembering, as is the Friday brunch (12:00 - 15:30). This restaurant is a must for visitors and residents alike and one of Abu Dhabi's best kept secrets. **MM**

Food ●●●● Service ●●●● Venue ●●●○ Value ●●●●

Restaurants

Going Out

Talay

Location ➜ Le Meridien · Tourist Club Area | 644 6666
Hours ➜ 12:30 - 15:30 19:00 - 24:00
Web/email ➜ www.forte.com Map Ref ➜ 7-D1

Dine on the terrace overlooking a quiet beach, and embark on a delightful adventure of sampling beautifully prepared food and exotic tastes. Fresh seafood is displayed market style and a personal server advises each diner about selection and cooking style – steamed, grilled or deep-fried. Fresh vegetables can be picked from baskets. Once you've done your groceries, delicious authentic Thai dishes are served. The menu, however, is limited to chicken and fish, with some beef dishes. Watch out for the chillies (hot!) – be smart and use the code on the menu.

Food ●●○○ Service ●●●○ Venue ●●●○ Value ●●●○

Taste of Thailand

Location ➜ Al Ain Palace Hotel · Corniche Rd East | 679 4777
Hours ➜ 12:00 - 15:00 19:00 - 24:00
Web/email ➜ www.alainpalacehotel.com Map Ref ➜ 8-B3

Offering you just as the name suggests, staff donning traditional Thai silk garb welcome you into a dimly lit space with a smile. The décor is charming and the quality and presentation of the food, mouthwatering. Traditional favourites include 'satay' with a delicious peanut sauce while the 'drunken noodles' is a meal in itself. Thai food is definitely for spice lovers – less palate burning dishes can be whipped up on request. Nothing is too much to ask – not even a third refill of the complimentary prawn cracker snacks and spicy sweet dip! Reservations are only necessary at weekends or if you desire window seating.

Food – na Service – na Venue – na Value – na

Business Dinners	
Amalfi	Le Rabelais
Chequers	Rodeo Grill
Fishmarket	Zen

Turkish

Other options ➜ **Arabic/Lebanese [p.238]**
Persian [p.266]
Moroccon [p.265]

Istanbul

Location ➜ Le Meridien · Tourist Club Area | 644 6666
Hours ➜ 19:00 - 24:00 Closed Fri
Web/email ➜ www.forte.com Map Ref ➜ 7-D1

If you've been to Turkey and loved the food, rely on your memory to save the day. The venue however, both indoors and terrace seating, is superior. Well meaning servers seem harried and

Far Eastern

For lovers of light, generally healthy food with an emphasis on steamed or stir-fried cooking methods, Far Eastern cuisine is an excellent option either for dining out or takeaway. Seafood and vegetables dominate the menu, but the staples are rice and noodles with dishes enhanced by the use of delicate and fragrant herbs and spices like ginger, lemon grass, and coconut milk. Dishes can be spicy, but generally less so than a fiery, denture melting Vindaloo curry.

The décor of Thai and Polynesian restaurants often reflects a stereotypically exotic view of the Far East, with bamboo beach huts and 'demure' oriental waitresses. Sometimes this combines to create a tasteful, relaxing and classy ambience and sometimes it doesn't quite make it. With the exception of Chinese outlets, Far Eastern restaurants are generally located in hotels in more upmarket surroundings, with prices that match.

Japanese restaurants generally offer a choice of seating options, from teppanyaki tables where the entertainment is provided by the chefs as they juggle, dice and slice, to private tatami rooms or the sushi option, where dishes pass before your eyes on a conveyor belt. Any way you like it, the standard of Japanese food is high, with prices to match.

Abu Dhabi has a great number of Chinese restaurants and standards vary greatly from monosodium glutamate-laden, taste killing dishes to light, nourishing and delicious cuisine. Many of the independents (ie, those not linked to a hotel or club) offer good value for money with large portions and quality food. As with Indian outlets, many Chinese restaurants offer tasty takeaway and home delivery, giving residents even less incentive to learn how to use their wok. Check out the following variety in cuisine:

Chinese, Japanese, Korean, Polynesian and Thai.

Restaurants

Going Out

confused, and the menu itself is a bit tricky. The meze sampler is an amusing assortment of micro appetisers, and the pide (Turkish pizza) makes a great snack. Main courses vary in quality; the chef's special our night was a spectacular lamb shank in aubergine strips. The venue and a change of pace should be your prime purpose for dining here, and not the fare. CB

Food ●●●○ Service ●●○○ Venue ●●●● Value ●●○○

Manhattan skyline from the water! The themed hot and cold buffet changes each evening, but offers excellent Italian, Arabic, seafood and Mediterranean dishes, plus delicious desserts – dinner more than compensates for the dubious pre dinner cocktails. The yacht is available for private functions, so call ahead to check that it's sailing. AML

Sunset cruise 17:30 18:30, Dhs.45 net (welcome drink only); dinner cruise 20:30 - 23:00, Dhs.130 +17% (seafood buffet); Friday lunch cruise, 13:30 - 15:30 (excluding summer).

Food ●●●● Service ●●●● Venue ●●●● Value ●●●○

DINNER CRUISES

Other options → **Boat, Dhow & Yacht Charters [p.119]**

Al Falah

Location → Al Dhafra · Al Meena | **673 2266**
Hours → 20:30 - 22:30
Web/email → www.aldhafra.net   **Map Ref** → 7-C4

Try this unique way to enjoy spectacular views of the Corniche. A traditional Arabic dhow cruises every evening along the calm waters while the guests enjoy a leisurely meal in relaxed surroundings. The dhow is double decked and air conditioned, has a music system, and takes a maximum of 70 people on its lower deck and 20 people on the upper one. A variety of dishes are on offer, including a lavish, freshly cooked barbecue of assorted seafood and meats, plus salads and a dessert buffet. Only soft drinks are served, and the net cost comes to Dhs.100 per person for a two hour trip.

Food ●●●○ Service ●●●○ Venue ●●●● Value ●●●○

Shuja Yacht

CAFÉS & COFFEE SHOPS

Abu Dhabi is a great city for those who love café culture – take a break from work or shopping, relax with a cup of tea, a cake and the newspaper, or simply enjoy the chance to catch up on gossip with friends.

There's a wide range of cafés around the city. Some border on being a restaurant serving excellent cuisine from cake to a full blown, three course meal. Others have more of a coffee shop approach with cake and coffee and a few sandwiches. Because of the limitations on opening a restaurant outside of a hotel or club that serves alcohol, coupled with the high number of non alcohol

Shuja Yacht

Location → Al Meena Zayed Port | **695 0539**
Hours → 17:30 - 23:00 20:30 - 23:00 Closed Sat
Web/email → restaurants@leroyalmeridien-abudhabi.com **Map Ref** → 7-D4

An evening cruise on the luxurious yacht *Shuja* is high on the list of must dos when visiting the capital – what appears to be a concrete jungle at street level is transformed into a magnificent

drinkers, cafés here enjoy a popularity otherwise missing in other parts of the world.

The following section encompasses cafés, coffee shops, ice cream parlours, Internet and shisha cafés.

Al Finjan

Location ➔ Le Meridien · Tourist Club Area | **697 4204**
Hours ➔ 08:00 22:00
Web/email ➔ www.forte.com | Map Ref ➔ 7-D1

Translated as 'the cup', this bright and airy venue offers a relaxing atmosphere in which to enjoy a large selection of fine teas (the Belgravia tea is a real treat), coffees, fresh pastries and tempting cakes. The menu also includes sandwiches, omelettes, burgers and salads, if you're after something more substantial. In fact, this is an ideal location for a business meeting, or just to watch the world go by, as it looks out over the lush gardens and ponds in the hotel grounds. **SBV**
Food ●●●○ Service ●●●○ Venue ●●●○ Value ●●●○

Al Hawwara Restaurant & Café

Location ➔ Opp Al Noor Hospital · Khalifa Street | **626 1112**
Hours ➔ 07:00 - 23:30
Web/email ➔ na | Map Ref ➔ 8-D2

This previously French café underwent a drastic makeover (and management change). Now a typical Arabic restaurant, the menu may offer classic Arabic tastes but the ambience does not. In fact, the newness of the place appears almost clinical. The upper level seats families while the lower level has a shawarma stand that caters to passers by, dropping in for a quick snack. The staff is pleasant and helpful and the prices moderate. Home delivery options are available and the takeaway menu is very popular. **AML**
Food ●●○○ Service ●●○○ Venue ●●○○ Value ●●●○

Al Maha Suite City Café

Location ➔ Al Maha Rotana | **610 6666**
Hours ➔ 24 hours
Web/email ➔ na | Map Ref ➔ 8-B1

Nestled in the heart of the city centre this café serves the local business people, and the

sophisticated ambience makes it a popular meeting spot for lunch. The attractively laid out buffet is good value for money, however, for a lighter lunch, there's a variety of great combo deals of soup with sandwich, salads or wraps. Comfortable armchairs set around low tables provide alternative seating for those just wanting tea or coffee with, perhaps, one of the delicious looking cakes. **MM**
Food ●●●○ Service ●●●○ Venue ●●○○ Value ●●●○

Arlequin

Location ➔ Nr 3 Sails Tower · Corniche Rd West | **666 6856**
Hours ➔ 09:00 01:00
Web/email ➔ na | Map Ref ➔ 9-D2

The venue (in the penthouse of a tower) is not ideal for those suffering from vertigo. Amazing views of the Corniche, Breakwater and Marina Mall area lure you initially, but it is the quality and choice of food that will have you back for more! For the faithful lunchtime crowd, the buffet (Dhs.45) always has a rotating variation of chicken, beef and fish dishes. They can even text you on the days when they serve your favourite dish. Friday brunches offer a great meze and the evenings have a good European à la carte menu. **MM**
Food ●●●● Service ●●●○ Venue ●●●○ Value ●●●○

Art Cauldron

Location ➔ Opp Navy Gates · Al Falah St | **644 4309**
Hours ➔ 12:00 - 16:00 18:30 - 23:30
Web/email ➔ na | Map Ref ➔ 4-C3

Trying to locate this café is quite akin to embarking on a 'voyage of discovery'. However, once you do find it, you will return time and again. The menu is quite extensive and deliciously unpretentious, albeit steep. Mouth watering food (the 'Bruschetta' certainly is different) and exceptional presentation and service coupled with a charming venue, make this an experience not to be missed. The ambience (novel, arty and laid back) is ideal for a quiet chat or a romantic rendezvous. Parking can be a problem. **AML**
Food ●●●● Service ●●●● Venue ●●●○ Value ●●●○

Café & Coffee Shops

Going Out

Bistro Med

Location ➜ Grand Continental Htl · Shk Zayed 1st St | **626 2200**
Hours ➜ 06:45 - 10:30 12:30 - 15:30 19:00 - 24:00
Web/email ➜ rand-continental-flamingo.com   Map Ref ➜ 8-B2

   100

This small, very unassuming restaurant is a passable lunch option but good value for money. While the food is classified as 'Mediterranean', it's really more of an international mix with Chinese noodles (somewhat tasteless) and spring rolls listed alongside sandwiches and fish dishes. The food is average and the buffet may be more suited for the carnivore preferring quantity rather than quality. More of a convenient venue for hotel guests rather than a destination to seek out. PG

Food ●○○○ Service ●●○○ Venue ●●○○ Value ●○○○

Café Cappuccino

Location ➜ Hilton Residence · Corniche | **627 6000**
Hours ➜ 10:00 - 17:00
Web/email ➜ corexflr@emirates.net.ae   Map Ref ➜ 8-D3

 100

Well secluded from the main reception of the Corniche Residence Apartments and Hotel, this clean and airy café can seat a maximum of about 60. Chintz curtains and matching cushions make for a homey and comfortable setting. The dining choice is essentially coffee, pastries and snacks, however, a daily lunchtime salad buffet from 12:30 – 15:00 offers a fairly limited choice that is fresh and nicely presented. The fruit juices are all freshly squeezed and make a pleasant alternative to the routine coffee. GK

Food ●●●○ Service ●●○○ Venue ●●●○ Value ●●○○

Cafe Ceramique Abu Dhabi

Location ➜ Nr Choithrams, 26th Street · Khalidiyah | **666 4412**
Hours ➜ 08:00 - 24:00
Web/email ➜ www.café-ceramique.com   Map Ref ➜ 9-C1

  50

Indulge your flair for art as you select your bisque, brushes, and non toxic ceramic paint and embark upon your next masterpiece at this trendy studio. Order a designer bagel, salad, sandwich and a cup of tea, coffee or fresh juice as you dabble about with paint. The food is good and the portions

generous. They even do a Friday breakfast and the venue is available for birthday parties. The ambience is pleasant and membership to the studio is available with an enrolment fee. AML

Food ●●●○ Service ●○○○ Venue ●●●○ Value ●●●○

Cafe Columbia

Location ➜ Beach Rotana · Tourist Club Area | **644 3000**
Hours ➜ 08:00 - 24:00
Web/email ➜ na   Map Ref ➜ 4-B3

 50

Tucked away next to the foyer, this café is ideal for a classic English afternoon tea. A choice of seating ranges from sofas and armchairs to tables with comfy chairs. Smartly dressed servers offer a range of flavoured teas or coffee, kept on a warming device and constantly replenished. Smoked salmon and cucumber sandwiches served on traditional tiered silverware complement a wide selection of cakes, pastries, scones, cookies and chocolates. Priced at Dhs.50 per person, an afternoon spent in this spacious and relaxing atmosphere is pure indulgence. KW

Food ●●●● Service ●●●● Venue ●●●○ Value ●●●●

Café de Foyer

Location ➜ Sheraton Abu Dhabi · Corniche Rd East | **677 3333**
Hours ➜ 07:00 - 24:00
Web/email ➜ www.sheraton.com   Map Ref ➜ 8-A3

 50

Set amidst opulent surroundings, white cane chairs, although comfortable, still seem rather incongruous when paired with marbled floors and tables. The menu has a fascinating range of special coffees and flavoured herbal infusions such as 'Queen of Cherry' or 'Jasmine Tea with Petals'. Light snacks include sandwiches and scones, and are a tad pricey, but the delicious looking cakes on promotion will surely weaken your resolve. The venue is great for watching people and the general hustle and bustle of the hotel. VM

Food ●●●○ Service ●●●○ Venue ●●●● Value ●●○○

Café de la Paix

Location ➔ Fotouh Al Khair Centre · Abu Dhabi | **621 3900**
Hours ➔ 08:30 - 22:00
Web/email ➔ na | **Map Ref** ➔ 8-E1

 50

After indulging in a bit of retail therapy at the Marks and Spencer, hop over to this café for a light bite to eat or a reviving cuppa. The ambience is pleasant and very French (as is the menu) with an outer area overlooking the shopping centre – great for a spot of people watching. On offer is a choice of salads and light meals, and the daily set menu provides good value for money. **MM**
Food ●●●○ Service ●●○○ Venue ●●●○ Value ●●●○

Cafe du Roi

Location ➔ Al Hana Centre · Corniche Rd West | **681 5096**
Hours ➔ 07:00 - 23:00
Web/email ➔ na | **Map Ref** ➔ 9-E2

 50

Now relocated to its new position at the front of the building, the Café Du Roi aims to continue providing quality food and good service in a congenial atmosphere. The large terrace at the front of the café overlooking the Corniche will undoubtedly be very popular during the cooler months. The cakes and patisserie that this café was known for still feature on the menu alongside toasted sandwiches, omelettes and freshly baked pizzas. A busy breakfast venue with a popular takeaway trade. **MM**
Food ●●●○ Service ●●●○ Venue ●●○○ Value ●●●○

Cafe Firenze

Location ➔ Nr British Council · Al Nasr St | **666 0955**
Hours ➔ 07:00 - 24:00
Web/email ➔ na | **Map Ref** ➔ 9-B2

 50

Although Café Firenze serves the usual range of patisserie, sandwiches, salads and meals, it is the ambience created by the Italian décor that makes this busy café more upmarket than its competitors. Of great value are the Thursday and Friday brunches that have attracted a regular cosmopolitan clientele. Especially popular is the spacious terrace during cooler months, for a coffee and a croissant or a quick snack. Nearby home deliveries, takeaway and catering services are available. **MM**
Food ●●●○ Service ●●●○ Venue ●●●● Value ●●●○

Cafe Mozaic

Location ➔ Nr Corniche Tower Residence · Khalidiyah | **681 7377**
Hours ➔ 09:00 - 23:00
Web/email ➔ na | **Map Ref** ➔ 9-D2

100

Interesting furnishings and bright terracotta walls invite you to chill over a relaxed breakfast or lunch. Tiled mosaic tables line a wall offering partial sea view, and raised areas provide space for groups to eat, drink and chat. A separate room with comfy seating lets you rest with a magazine or while watching the telly. The menu consists of salads, burgers, rolls and wraps, breakfast choices and hot meals. Food portions are generous and good value for money. A sushi bar and a gallery (in the offing) definitely seem worth a visit. **KW**
Food ●●●○ Service ●●●○ Venue ●●●● Value ●●●●

Cappuccino's Lobby

Location ➔ Crowne Plaza · Shk Hamdan St | **621 0000**
Hours ➔ 13:00 - 02:00
Web/email ➔ www.crowneplaza.com | **Map Ref** ➔ 8-C1

 50

Situated on the first floor by the hotel lobby, Cappuccino's Lobby is probably the place for coffee, cake and a chat, rather than lunch. The tasteful modern décor lends itself to relaxation with a variety of seating arrangements; from comfortable sofas to more formal coffee tables. On offer are a range of snacks, sandwiches and cakes, and the food is reasonable, although perhaps a little pricey. The staff is friendly enough, but it's not the place to go if you're in a hurry. **AF**
Food ●●○○ Service ●●○○ Venue ●●○○ Value ●●○○

Citrus

Location ➔ Millennium Hotel · Khalifa Bin Zyd St | **626 2700**
Hours ➔ 12:00 - 15:30 19:00 - 23:00
Web/email ➔ www.millenniumhotels.com | **Map Ref** ➔ 8-B2

100

The lobby of the Millennium hotel houses this well laid out, comfortable and spacious restaurant that ranks high with the business lunchers. The buffet is simple, attractive and very tasty, and oozes class. Hence, the need for a fat corporate wallet! The à la carte menu boasts the common favourites, including Caesar salads, seafood soups and sumptuous burgers. Service is attentive and friendly without being overtly

Café & Coffee Shops

Going Out

obtrusive. A perfect spot for a one on one or a reflective mood.

Food ●●●○ Service ●●●○ Venue ●●●○ Value ●●○○

Gerard Patisserie

Location → Marina Mall · Breakwater | **681 4642**
Hours → 08:00 - 02:00
Web/email → marinamall@emirates.net.ae   **Map Ref →** 10-B4

 50

Following in the footsteps of sister outlets scattered around Dubai and Sharjah, the patisserie in Abu Dhabi too serves some of the best coffees and pastries in town. A longstanding favourite in the other cities with locals and European residents, the branches here seem no different and will no doubt remain popular. Both outlets have a pleasant atmosphere, so far as mall cafés go, and they're great for people watching while you sip your coffee (or delicious hot chocolate) and nibble on the various freshly made cakes and sandwiches.

Food ●●●● Service ●●●○ Venue ●●●○ Value ●●●○

Havana Cafe

Location → Breakwater · Abu Dhabi | **681 0044**
Hours → 08:00 - 23:00
Web/email → www.havanacafe.co.ae   **Map Ref →** 10-B4

100

Located above the noisy Sheikh Hamdan Street, Havana Cafe provides a haven where light music and a trickling fountain provide the only distractions. The days are ideal for a quiet coffee, as the evenings are vibrant and busy. Part of the café has a number of computers allowing you to browse the Internet and a small in house library satisfies the bookworms. The speciality of the kitchen is Italian with a good choice of more traditional pasta dishes, and an early breakfast (continental included) has tasty omelettes. An added attraction is the 'Shisha man' in traditional costume selling smoking pipes.

Food ●●●○ Service ●●●○ Venue ●●●○ Value ●●●●

Hut, The

Location → Nr Pizza Hut · Shk Khalifa St | **03 751 6526**
Hours → 08:00 - 01:00
Web/email → na   **Map Ref →** 14-D3

 50

Situated in the heart of Al Ain, this cosy café will make you feel right at home with its French provincial styled interiors and comfortable couch alcoves. Browse through a diverse selection of reading material, watch football or just indulge in the all time favourite pastime of people watching. The menu offers a simple selection of continental European and American café styled bites. Always welcoming, this café is popular with the expats and the locals, and is a relaxing place to unwind after a long workday or to grab a quiet cuppa.

Food ●●●○ Service ●●●○ Venue ●●●● Value ●●●○

L'Opera

Location → Novotel Centre Hotel · Shk Hamdan St | **633 3555**
Hours → 12:02 - 24:00
Web/email → novoad@emirates.net.ae   **Map Ref →** 8-D2

This compact, European style patisserie offers great cakes, ice creams and pastries for those not worried about their waistline! Popular for quick business lunches, the menu is somewhat limited, but the meals on offer are positively delicious. However, if you're a non smoker, you might want to avoid the 12:00 - 13:00 lunch rush. Despite high calorific content, the desserts are not to be missed and the croissants are highly recommended. Cakes are available for takeaway – order ahead to avoid disappointment.

Food ●●●○ Service ●●○○ Venue ●●○○ Value ●●●○

La Brioche

Location → Marina Mall · Breakwater | **681 5531**
Hours → 09:00 - 23:00
Web/email → marinamall@emirates.net.ae   **Map Ref →** 10-B4

 100

With a great location in the Marina Mall, La Brioche is a bistro type restaurant, serving Mediterranean delicacies. An extensive, reasonably priced à la carte menu is available, together with buffet

Café & Coffee Shops

Going Out

By all means, explore the deserts, the souks and the beaches.
But, be sure to return to civilization.

With breathtaking views of the Arabian Gulf, 325 luxurious guestrooms, stylish dining options, extensive business facilities, a health and fitness club and much more, the Millennium Hotel Abu Dhabi is about as civilized as it gets.

MILLENNIUM HOTEL
ABU DHABI

TEL +971 2 626 2700. FAX +971 2 626 0333. PO BOX 44486, ABU DHABI.
www.millenniumhotels.com   sales.abudhabi@mill-cop.com

lunches and dinners on Thursdays and Fridays. The food is good (mouth watering desserts!), portions are generous and the service is cheerful and pleasant. An ideal place for a break while shopping or simply to meet friends.

A sister shop has opened in the same building as the Al Noor Hospital on Khalifa Street, 626 9300.
Food ●●●○ Service ●●●○ Venue ●●●○ Value ●●●○

Le Boulanger

Location ➜ BHS Bld · Shk Hamdan St | 631 8115
Hours ➜ 08:00 24:00
Web/email ➜ tenchi@emirates.net.ae | Map Ref ➜ 8-C2

Enjoy the newspapers or a chat with a friend over a tea or coffee at this busy little café, which specialises in good quality European food. French cuisine dominates, but Arabic and international dishes are also available.

There's a fine soup, salad and sandwich bar for the health conscious or an extensive à la carte; excellent value for money, especially the daily specials. A mouth watering selection of fresh bread, cakes and pastries are available at the bakery. Very busy at peak hours.

Friday brunch, 10:00 - 15:00, costs Dhs.40 net per person, half rate for kids aged 4 - 8 years and free for the under threes.
Food ●●○○ Service ●●●○ Venue ●●●○ Value ●●●○

Le Boulanger

Olive Tree, The

Location ➜ Howard Johnson · Khalifa Bin Zyd St | 671 0000
Hours ➜ 24 hours
Web/email ➜ www.ebmanage.com/howards | Map Ref ➜ 8-B2

With a pleasant ambience and bright furnishings, this outlet is a basic hotel coffee shop. While the portions are generous, the quality of food from the reasonably priced buffet and à la carte menu is uninspiring. The staff is friendly and cheerful.
Food ●●○○ Service ●●○○ Venue ●○○○ Value ●●○○

Pool Café

Location ➜ Htl Inter-Continental · Bainuna St | 693 5214
Hours ➜ 06:30 - 10:30 12:00 - 15:30 19:00 - 23:00
Web/email ➜ abudhabi@interconti.com | Map Ref ➜ 10-C1

Treating its customers to a uniquely relaxing setting, large windows on three sides give panoramic views of the swimming pool and the sea. The layout and furnishings are pleasant and functional, and the reasonably priced dinner buffet is plentiful, although the atmosphere at dinner would undoubtedly have improved, had there been more patrons. The wine list, although limited, is acceptable. The efficient service came with some helpful comments from the maitre d' and on request, a tasty, individual cheese platter was provided as an alternative to dessert – quite a culinary treat.
Food ●●●○ Service ●●●○ Venue ●●●○ Value ●●○○

Sheherazade

Location ➜ Al Diar Gulf Htl · Al Maqtaa | 441 4777
Hours ➜ 06:00 - 23:00
Web/email ➜ adglfhtl@emirates.net.ae | Map Ref ➜ 1-D3

Located at the ground floor of Al Diar Gulf Hotel, this bright restaurant has an extensive selection of hot and cold items on the buffet, catering for breakfast, lunch and dinner. So as a guest of the hotel, you could dine for a several days and not tire of the choices. The buffet is fresh serving quality cuisine and the presentation entices you to try everything. The attempt at creating international themes is a token and often inaccurate. However, seafood lovers must try the Thursday evening buffet by the beach (Dhs.95). Alcohol is available.
Food ●●●○ Service ●●●○ Venue ●●●○ Value ●●●○

Café & Coffee Shops

Going Out

Starbucks

Location → Opp BHS Bldg · Shk Hamdan St | **626 1001**
Hours → 07:30 - 24:00
Web/email → na | Map Ref → 8-C3

 50

This internationally recognised chain of caffeine brews is not alien to many. In classic American coffee shop style, the layout is self service, and its location on Hamdan Street attracts a lively student clientele from the nearby University. If you need respite from the young friendly and bustling atmosphere, look for a private booth with comfortable armchairs, or request the assistance of helpful wait staff to find one. This place is ideal for your regular coffee 'fix' and the lattes are plenty and delicious; don't mistake it for anything else and avoid the food. **LR**

Food ●●●○ Service ●●●○ Venue ●●●○ Value ●●●○

Tea Lounge

Location → Le Meridien · Tourist Club Area | **644 6666**
Hours → 09:00 - 21:00
Web/email → www.forte.com | Map Ref → 7-D1

50

Located in a quiet corner of the lobby with an enormous painted glass ceiling and a view of the lush garden, the Tea Lounge provides a relaxed setting for a serene cup of tea. The menu focuses on snacks and traditional afternoon teas, but sadly, the food can be indistinguishable and at times, inauthentic (eg, fake whipped cream instead of clotted cream). Service is friendly but sporadic, however, if you're looking for a spot of quiet time and refreshment, the Tea Lounge will satisfy. **PG**

Food ●●○○ Service ●●○○ Venue ●●●○ Value ●●●○

THE One

Location → Nr BMW Garage · Shk Zayed 1st St | **681 6500**
Hours → 08:00 - 21:00 Fri 14:00 - 21:00
Web/email → abudhabi@theone.com | Map Ref → 1-C3

 100

Surround yourself with the store's designer furnishings and achingly hip, low lit décor, as you mull over the delights of the 'fusion' menu. Consider the daily specialities; an all day breakfast and a mouthwatering selection of exotic sounding dishes are hard to choose from. With the weekend crowd, expect to wait around

20 minutes for your order – dive into a selection of reading material and daily newspapers available to bide time. Traditional English cream teas are served in afternoon and a kids' menu has interesting choices that go beyond the expected fast food. **GK**

Food ●●●○ Service ●●○○ Venue ●●●○ Value ●●●○

Vienna Plaza

Location → Hilton Abu Dhabi · Corniche Rd West | **692 4171**
Hours → 08:00 - 23:00
Web/email → www.hilton.com | Map Ref → 10-C2

 50

Situated at the far end of the lobby, this light and airy café overlooks the Corniche and is a popular informal meeting place. Enchanting notes from a resident harpist accompany morning coffees. A standard coffee shop style menu ranges from pasta to salads and the range of ice creams is impressive. Their speciality, without a doubt, is cakes and pastries – delicious and very very rich! **RW**

Food ●●●○ Service ●●●○ Venue ●●●● Value ●●○○

Windows Coffee Shop

Location → Int Rotana Inn · Shk Hamdan St | **677 9900**
Hours → 05:30 - 24:00
Web/email → www.rotana.com | Map Ref → 8-A1

 50

This is a typical small hotel coffee shop, but in a very convenient location as the hotel is in the heart of the city. It's on the second floor and caters mainly to hotel guests. Choose from a standard à la carte or the breakfast, lunch and dinner buffet, which incorporates a range of local and international dishes, including healthy salads and tempting desserts. The décor is chic, service is good and the staff is very pleasant; overall, cheap and cheerful. **AML**

Food ●●○○ Service ●●●○ Venue ●●●○ Value ●●○○

Zyara Café

Location → Nr Hilton Residence · Corniche Rd West | **627 5006**
Hours → 08:00 - 24:00
Web/email → na | Map Ref → 10-C2

 50

This trendy Lebanese cafe recently opened its doors and the relaxed atmosphere, eclectic

Going Out — Café & Coffee Shops

décor and laissez-faire service are all conducive to taking your time over a drink or light meal. 'Zyara' is Arabic for visit, and a wide variety of magazines, books and games help you pass the time while you wait for your order. The mainly Arabic buffet contrasts nicely with the predominantly sandwich and salad menu. The café will soon become a popular lunch spot, as have its sister branches in Dubai. **MM**

Food ●●○○ Service ●●●○ Venue ●●●○ Value ●●○○

Internet Cafés

If you want to surf the Web, visit a chat room, email friends, or play the latest game but want to be a little bit sociable about it, or when you do not have your own facilities for being online, Internet cafés are a perfect location to visit. Over the last few years, this type of café has become a more common feature throughout Abu Dhabi. The mix of coffee, cake and technology has proved an irresistible draw, and this particular niche will doubtless continue to expand.

As always, facilities, ambience, prices and clientele vary considerably, so poke your head in the door and then make your decision. Prices are typically around Dhs.15 per hour. Happy surfing!

Shisha Cafés

Other options → **Arabic/Lebanese [p.238]**
Persian [p.266]
Moroccon [p.265]
Turkish [p.273]

Shisha cafés are common throughout the Middle East, offering relaxing surroundings and the chance to smoke a shisha pipe (aka Hubble Bubble or Narghile) with a variety of aromatic flavours. They are traditionally the retreat of local men who meet to play backgammon and gossip with friends, but over the years have gained popularity with locals and visitors alike, especially in the cooler winter evenings. Most outlets offer a basic menu; generally Arabic cuisine and a few international options, plus coffees, teas and fruit juices.

Just choose your flavour of shisha and sit back – this is what life is all about! Prices are typically around Dhs.15 - 25, and flavours range from strawberry to mint, cappuccino to rose and apple to mixed fruit.

There are numerous places around Abu Dhabi where you can indulge. Your best plan of action for finding a place is to first decide if you'd like to go a bit more upscale, or if you'd prefer a more authentic experience. For the upscale option, go to the Marina Club or head to the Breakwater and you'll find the Havana Café as well as a row of Arabic restaurants serving shisha. Take in the view of the sparking city lights as you relax with friends, shisha pipe in hand. For something a little more downscale, but with character nevertheless, wander along any of the interior blocks between the main thoroughfares in town and you'll come across numerous local, back alley shisha spots. Sit yourself down with the locals and observe the action on the streets.

During Ramadan, most five star hotels have a shisha tent set up. This experience is one not to be missed as these tents become cultural melting pots with a great mix of nationalities enjoying the fragrant aromas of shisha tobacco as they nibble on tasty Arabic meze.

In Al Ain, the Heritage Village is recommended for an 'authentic' local shisha experience while the Hiltonia Club at the Hilton Al Ain and Al Naswer at the Hotel Inter-Continental are relatively good options. For an added treat, head to Min Zaman at the Al Ain Rotana Hotel and appreciate some bellydancing as you puff away. Other spots worth checking out are Al Dihleese (Al Ain Public Gardens), Dot com (Khalifa St), La Marquise (Al Ain Mall), Al Nakheel (Al Ain Oasis) and Ya Leil Ya (Ain Al Jimi Mall).

If you get 'hooked' (pun intended), and would like to purchase one, try the Carrefour Hypermarket and plenty of smaller places around the city. They offer a variety of pipes and some basic tobacco flavours. Puffing on a pipe around a campfire in the desert while watching the stars can be a very satisfying experience indeed.

FOOD ON THE GO

Bakeries

Other options → **Arabic/Lebanese [p.238]**

In addition to bread, bakeries here offer a wonderful range of pastries, biscuits and Lebanese sweets. Arabic eatables include 'borek' (flat pastries, baked or fried with spinach or cheese)

Going Out · Food on the Go

and 'manoushi' (hot bread, doubled over and served plain or filled with meat, cheese or thyme seeds). Biscuits are often filled with ground dates.

Bakery Items

Foodcourts

Most shopping malls have a foodcourt as part of their facilities. These are a particular favourite among tired shoppers looking to rest their aching feet after an intense shopping spree. Reasonably priced meals or snacks are promptly served from numerous outlets and you will find that many of the fast food hamburger chains have outlets here. The

Abu Dhabi Mall Foodcourt

range of cuisine otherwise, is quite multicultural and diverse.

Popular with all ages and nationalities, the variety of food provides something for every palate; even the fussiest of eaters should find their nibble of choice! The casual and relaxed environment is ideal for families, for most food courts house a play area that keeps the children more than occupied and very happy!

Fruit Juices Etc.

Fresh juices are widely available, either from the shawarma stands or juice shops. They are delicious, healthy and cheap, and made on the spot from fresh fruits such as mango, banana, kiwi, strawberry and pineapple (have the mixed fruit cocktail if you can't decide).

Yoghurt is also a popular drink, often served with nuts, and the local milk is called 'laban' (a heavy, salty buttermilk that doesn't go well in tea or coffee). Arabic mint tea is available but probably not drunk as widely as in other parts of the Arab world. However, Arabic coffee (thick, heavy and strong) is extremely popular and will have you buzzing on a caffeine high for days!

Shawarma

Other options → Arabic/Lebanese [p.238]

Throughout the city, sidewalk stands sell 'shawarma', which is made from rolled pita bread filled with lamb or chicken carved from a rotating spit, and salad. Costing about Dhs.3 each, these are inexpensive and well worth trying, and an excellent alternative fast food to the usual hamburger. The stands usually sell other dishes, such as 'foul' (a paste made from fava beans) and 'falafel' (or ta'amiya), which are a small savoury balls of deep-fried beans.

While most shawarma stands offer virtually the same thing, slight differences make some stand out from the rest. People are often adamant that their particular favourite serves, for example, the best falafel in town. These stands are often the first place you eat when you come to the UAE. However, look around – every restaurant has its own way of doing things and you might find that the best is, surprisingly, the smallest, most low key restaurant you happen upon by chance.

Food on the Go

Going Out

FRIDAY BRUNCH

An integral part of life in the capital, Friday brunch is a perfect event for a lazy start or end to the weekend, especially once the hot weather arrives. Popular with all sections of the community, it provides Thursday night's revellers with a gentle awakening and some much needed nourishment. For families, brunch is a pleasant way to spend the day, especially since many venues organise a variety of fun activities for kids, allowing parents to fill themselves with fine food and drink and to simply relax.

Different brunches appeal to different crowds; some have fantastic buffets, others are in spectacular surroundings, while still others offer amazing prices for all you can eat.

CATERERS

A popular and easy way to have a party, business lunch or celebrate a special occasion is to have it catered in house. This lets you concentrate on everything but the cooking and allows you to relax and enjoy yourself. Numerous outlets offer catering services, so decide on the type of food you want – Indian, Chinese, Italian, Lebanese, finger food etc, and check with your favourite local restaurant or café to see if they do outside catering.

Alternatively, most of the larger hotels have an outside catering department, usually capable of extravagant five star functions. There are also specialist companies providing a range of services at very reasonable prices. You don't even have to stay at home to get in-house catering – how about a catered party in the desert?

Depending on what you require, caterers can provide just the food or everything from food, crockery, napkins, tables, chairs and even waiters, doormen and a clearing up service afterwards. Costs vary according to the number of people, dishes and level of service etc, required.

| Friday Brunch | | | | | | | | | | | Cost | | |
Restaurant	Location	Phone	Buffet	À la carte	Breakfast	Lunch	Kid Friendly	Alcohol	Outside Terrace		Adult	Child	Timings
Al Fanar	Abu Dhabi Grand Marina	674 2020	Y	N	Y	Y	Y	Y	N		85*	43*	12:30 - 16:00
Café Firenze	Al Nasr St	666 0955	Y	Y	Y	N	Y	N	Y		35	20	08:00 - 12:00
Chi Chi's	Le Meridien Hotel	644 3717	Y	Y	Y	Y	Y	Y	N		45	45	12:00 - 16:00
Flavours	Sheraton Abu Dhabi	677 3333	Y	Y	na	na	na	na	na				
La Brasserie	Le Meridien Hotel	644 6666	Y	Y	Y	Y	Y	Y	Y		79	40	12:30 - 16:30
La Mamma	Sheraton Abu Dhabi	677 3333	Y	Y	Y	Y	Y	Y	N		85	42	12:00 - 16:00
La Piazza	Sands Hotel	633 5335	Y	Y	Y	Y	Y	Y	N		65*	32*	12:00 - 15:30
Level 9	Crowne Plaza Hotel	621 0000	Y	N	Y	Y	Y	Y	N		85	42	12:00 - 16:00
Restaurant, The	The Club	673 1111	Y	N	Y	Y	Y	Y	N		40	20	11:00 - 15:30
Rosebuds	Beach Rotana Hotel	644 3000	Y	Y	Y	Y	Y	Y	N		90*	45*	11:30 - 15:30
Sherlocks	Grand Continental Hotel	626 2200	Y	Y	Y	Y	Y	Y	N		60	30	12:00 - 16:00
Gardinia	Al Ain Rotana Hotel	751 5111	Y	Y	Y	Y	Y	Y	Y		75	35	12:00 - 16:00
Hiltonia Clubhouse	Hilton Al Ain	768 6666	Y	Y	Y	Y	Y	Y	Y		40	20	12:00 - 16:00
Luce Ristorante	Hotel Intercontinental Al Ain	768 6686	Y	Y	Y	Y	Y	Y	N		65	33	12:30 - 16:00

*plus 16% tax

For a list of hotel numbers, check out the hotel table in General Information [p.28]. For restaurant and café names browse the Going Out section of the book. You can also refer to the catering section in the telephone books, especially the Hawk A - Z Business Pages, or www.yellowpages.co.ae.

In-House Catering	
Abu Dhabi Catering & Services Est.	575 7321
Four Catering & Services Co. Ltd.	677 7307
Happy Home Catering	552 9035
Ramla Catering & Foodstuff Est.	552 1262

ON THE TOWN

Other options → Leisure [p.212]

You will soon discover that Abu Dhabi has a surprising variety entertainment options. The city may not have the quantity of outlets of a big city like New York, but there's plenty to keep visitors and residents merrily occupied! The following section includes the cultural entertainment on offer, such as theatre and comedy clubs, cinemas, bars, pubs and nightclubs.

To complement the bars and nightclubs, refer also to the information on Eating Out [p.234]. Many restaurants have a very good bar as well as a dance floor, which kicks in towards midnight. However, since they are usually reviewed only once, they will be listed in the restaurant section.

In Abu Dhabi, people tend to go out late, usually not before about 21:00. Even on weeknights, kick off is surprisingly late and people seem to forget, after about the tenth drink, that they really ought to be at work the next day. If you're venturing out to Arabic nightclubs or restaurants before 23:00, you're likely to find them almost deserted.

Wednesday and Thursday, being the start of most peoples' weekend, are obviously busy, but you will also find that during the week many bars and restaurants offer promotions and special nights to attract customers, hence creating a lively atmosphere. Particularly popular is Ladies' Night, which is traditionally on a Tuesday (and the busiest night of the week for some places). Women are given tokens at the door offering them free drinks – the number varies from one to an endless supply, and it may be limited to certain types of drink. This ploy certainly seems to attract male customers too. With men outnumbering women in Abu Dhabi (by two to one), women, for once, can take full advantage in this unbalanced world.

In this section you will find the main places that have a Ladies' Night/s at some point during the week.

Generally cafés and restaurants close between 23:00 and 01:00, with most bars and nightclubs split between those who close 'early' at 01:00 and those who stay open 'late' until 02:00 or 03:00. Few are open all night.

Refer to the *Eating Out* section for further information on, for instance, the alcohol laws.

BARS

Other options → Pubs [p.290]
Nightclubs [p.292]

Abu Dhabi has a decent number of bars of various different styles. Most are located in hotels and while many bars come and go, the more popular ones are always busy.

The city's more upmarket locations range from terminally hip cocktail lounges to decadent wine bars, from jazz bars to cigar bars – all providing salubrious surroundings for those opulent and self indulgent moments.

For more details on when and where to go for a drink in Abu Dhabi, refer to the start of the section 'On the Town'. For information on the individual bars read on...

Ladies Night	
49er's The Gold Rush	Sat/Tue/Wed
Gauloises Club	Sun
Harvester's Pub	Tue
Hemingways	Tue/Wed/Sun
Heroes Diner	Tue
Tavern	Wed/Tue
Mood Indigo	Sun
Paco's	Sun/Wed
NRG Sports Café	Wed

On the Town / Bars

Going Out

Door Policy

Abu Dhabi is a relaxed place when going out, and the easygoing atmosphere means there are few restrictions or problems getting into places. Understandably, anyone who is drunk or rowdy may find their entry refused.

Dress Code

Most bars sport a reasonably relaxed attitude towards their customers' dress sense. Some places, however, will insist on no shorts, jeans or sandals, while others require at least a shirt with a collar. Most nightspots do not permit the national dress and nightclubs generally have a dressier approach – dress to impress.

Specials

Many places have occasional promotions with different themes and offers. These run alongside special nights, such as Ladies' Night, and are usually held on a weekly basis. You can find out which promotions are coming up from the weekly and monthly entertainment publications, as well as directly from the venues concerned. Special nights such as the popular quiz nights are mainly promoted in a bar or pub, and many attract quite a following. Delightfully, the prizes are often fab.

American Bars

Hemingway's

Location → Hilton Abu Dhabi · Corniche Rd West | 692 4567
Hours → 12:00 - 01:00
Web/email → www.hilton.com   Map Ref → 10-C2

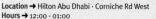

Named after the famous author, who is infamous for his love of a beverage or two, Hemingway's is celebrating over 14 years of business and is one of the capital's premier venues for all ages – it has a reputation for hosting excellent colourful bands from all parts of the globe. The interior, a blend of Mexican and American décor, is well laid out with the bar and band podium in view of everyone. The menu offers a varied Mexican cuisine, but desserts are of the warm apple crumble variety and do not disappoint. An event not to be missed is the Friday brunch (Dhs.48).

Food ●●●○ Service ●●●○ Venue ●●●○ Value ●●●○

Beach/Waterfront Bars

Beachcombers

Location → Marina & Yacht Club · Tourist Club Area | 644 0300
Hours → 21:00 - 02:30 Thu 21:00 - 02:30 Closed Mon
Web/email → www.abudhabimarina.com   Map Ref → 4-B4

A popular weekend spot to dine and dance under the stars with an interesting mix of people. Set on the beach, you can shake rattle and roll, eventually settling down on tables and chairs. Mouthwatering aromas of the Mongolian stir-fry (Dhs.35) and the shawarma stand (Dhs.10) tantalise your taste buds while a DJ plays a classic mix of music that appeals to all generations. Don't miss the biker boys as they make an impressive entrance parking their Harley Davidsons around the poolside!

Food ●●●○ Service ●●○○ Venue ●●○○ Value ●●○○

L.A.B. – Lounge at the Beach Bar

Location → Beach Rotana · Tourist Club Area | 644 3000
Hours → 17:00 - 15:00 17:00 - 03:00
Web/email → na   Map Ref → 4-B3

Before ten, this is a sophisticated meeting place for those who want to chat. Arrive later if you'd rather party in a cross between a futuristic, all flashing nightspot and an Ibiza rave. In contrast to the loud but attractively lit bar area, the spacious terrace

L.A.B.

overlooking the beach is relaxed and welcoming. Not the cheapest drinking hole in town but certainly a stylish venue with potential for a good time. Don't be deceived by the refreshing taste of the cocktails (from Dhs.20 - 25), they're strong!

Food ●●●○ Service ●●●○ Venue ●●●● Value ●●●○

Cigar Bars

Cloud Nine – Cigar & Bottle Club

Location → Sheraton Abu Dhabi · Corniche Rd East | **677 3333**
Hours → 15:00 - 02:00
Web/email → www.sheraton.com　　　Map Ref → 8-A3

    150

This posh bar is the venue for enjoying a sleepless night in sophisticated intimacy. Seek out one of the cosy little rooms for privacy; alternatively, leather armchairs in public rooms are great to just relax. Ideal for pre dinner drinks or a post dinner cognac and cigar (the choice is impressive) as the pianist plays unobtrusively. Nibble away on caviar and oysters to complement the champagne cocktails (also very tasty). Guests can buy their own bottle, which is kept until the next visit. Polite, friendly and attentive staff spoils you thoroughly, making the entire experience a luxurious treat. MFW

Food ●●●● Service ●●●○ Venue ●●●● Value ●●●●

Cristal Cigar & Champagne Bar

Location → Millennium Hotel · Khalifa Bin Zyd St | **626 2700**
Hours → 15:00 - 01:00
Web/email → www.millenniumhotels.com　　Map Ref → 8-B2

This slick, upmarket, international champagne and cigar bar has an ambience reminiscent of the colonial gentlemen's club. With a top quality package of venue, service and food, this is the perfect place to begin or end an evening. Sip a happy hour glass of Moet or Mumm's between 17:00 to 19:00, or sink into a leather sofa for a post prandial cigar and cognac; the selection of canapés, mainly eastern in style, only enhance the appetite. Far from disappointing, a visit to Cristal punctuates the evening with unashamed luxury and style. MFW

Food ●●●○ Service ●●●○ Venue ●●●● Value ●●●○

Cocktail Lounges

Other options → **Nightclubs [p.292]**

Balcony Bar, The

Location → Hilton Abu Dhabi · Corniche Rd West | **681 1900**
Hours → 12:00 - 15:00　18:00 - 24:00　Closed Fri
Web/email → www.hilton.com　　　Map Ref → 10-C2

 50

Do champagne, canapés and sophisticated music from a harp sound inviting? Combine this with comfortable seating arrangements and you have an ideal venue for pre dinner cocktails or a relaxing nightcap. Catch happy hour from 18:00 - 21:00 and try out the champagne cocktails for only Dhs.15 with complimentary munchies. A popular starting point for hen nights etc, or a warm up before you head off to paint the town red. RW

Food ●●●○ Service ●●●○ Venue ●●○○ Value ●●●○

General Bars

a.m.p.m.

Location → Htl Inter Continental · Bainuna St | **666 6888**
Hours → 18:00 - 03:30　Wed 21:00 - 03:30
Web/email → abudhabi@interconti.com　　Map Ref → 10-C1

 100

An ideal hangout for those craving a Euro flavoured chill out session. A chrome bar, leather cream sofas, easy jazz and a candlelit terracotta ambience settles you into a 'round the evening off' mood. As the night wears on, you can hit the dance floor to the beat of guest DJs. Food is Euro fusion with finger food complemented with some energising pasta dishes. Standards of presentation, flavour and service are Intercontinental hallmarked. Enjoy contemporary cocktails as you groove into the late night hours. Happy hour from 18:00 - 21:00. MFW

Food ●●●○ Service ●●●○ Venue ●●●○ Value ●●●○

Top Posh

Chequers	Le Rabelais
Jazz Bar & Dining	Rodeo Grill

Bars

Going Out

a.m.p.m.

Cheers

Location → Al Ain Palace Hotel · Corniche Rd East | 679 4777
Hours → 18:00 - 02:30 Thu 18:00 - 03:30
Web/email → aphsales@emirates.net.ae
Map Ref → 8-B3

Living large, the bar tries to keep up with its name by making theme nights a daily occurrence. Rock away on Sundays and Name That Tune on Thursday. For that matter, exercise the lungs with daily karaoke sessions or listen to a live band as you down your pint. Happy hour everyday from 19:00 - 20:00. **RP**

Food – na Service – na Venue – na Value – na

Club Bar, The

Location → Club, The · Al Meena | 673 1111
Hours → 12:00 - 24:30
Web/email → www.the-club.com
Map Ref → 7-A2

One of seven venues in the club complex, this bar tends to be a hub for people meeting before a function or enroute one of the various restaurants. Basic pub style menu offers excellent value for money, as do the beverages and the daily specials. The overall atmosphere is welcoming and homely, the staff courteous and friendly, and the clientele an international mix. The club is members only so guests pay a minimum fee (which can be deducted from the food bill). The ideal choice for a cosy yet classy atmosphere without digging a hole in your pocket – the prices for beverages, some say, are 'the best in town'. **RW**

Food ●●●● Service ●●●○ Venue ●●●● Value ●●●●

Hiltonia Clubhouse

Location → Hilton Al Ain · Al Ain | 03 768 6666
Hours → 10:30 - 23:00
Web/email → alhilton@emirates.net.ae
Map Ref → 15-D4

Overlooking the gardens, the poolside location makes an attractive venue for a casual drink or lunch. An ultra modern decor complements the attractive bar. The raised outdoor terrace is busy during the day with the odd monthly poolside party. The menu is not extensive, but includes imaginative and well presented snacks. Salads are the strong point; generous portions of fresh, colourful and crunchy ingredients are served with hot salmon, tenderloin beef medallions, beef burgers or spicy Cajun chicken. Alternatively, try the jacket potatoes, huge toasted sandwiches or the chef's weekly specials.

Food ●●●○ Service ●●●○ Venue ●●●○ Value ●●●○

Opus Bar

Location → Le Meridien · Tourist Club Area | 644 6666
Hours → 12:30 - 15:00 19:00 - 23:30
Web/email → www.forte.com
Map Ref → 7-D1

This rather elegant hotel bar is located just off the main reception area and is mainly frequented by hotel guests. It's an ideal venue for a quiet chat or as a rendezvous prior to sampling the variety of entertainment available at Le Meridien's 'culinary village'. Enjoy a snack from the bar menu or sit back and people watch. **AF**

Food ●●○○ Service ●●●○ Venue ●●●○ Value ●●○○

Paco's

Location → Hilton Al Ain · Al Ain | 03 768 6666
Hours → 12:00 - 15:00 20:00 - 24:00 Wed 19:00 - 03:00
Web/email → www.hilton.com
Map Ref → 15-D4

Paco's is an institution in Al Ain. The décor may be aging but the bar is a cosy squeeze and features a dance floor surrounded by a sprinkling of tables, ideal for a noisy but engaging evening. The

Bars

Going Out

emphasis is on music, food and conversation. Food wise expect generous portions of pub grub with a Tex-Mex twist and relaxed but efficient service. Live music five nights a week (regular band changes, expect a noisy evening if the band is in), plus the Saturday quiz and Sunday televised football ensure a lively pub atmosphere.

Food ●●●○ Service ●●●○ Venue ●●●○ Value ●●●○

Rockwell Café

Location ➜ Zakher Hotel · Umm Al Nar St |627 2266
Hours ➜ 12:00 - 02:30
Web/email ➜ zakhotel@emirates.net.ae   Map Ref ➜ 8-B2

🎸 🍸 50

Newly opened, Rockwell may also serve to try and improve the image of the hotel. Refreshingly tacky, this is a simple pub/club that threatens to succeed. Basic bachelor nosh, sports TV and a mostly unadorned room define a place for serious drinking. Strict door policy lets the lads be lads, although the promised Latino salsa band may shift the mood slightly. A place to note, particularly for a cheap night out without the frills of the larger, five star venues. CB

Food ●●○○ Service ●●○○ Venue ●●○○ Value ●●●○

Jazz Bars

Other options ➜ **Pubs [p.290]**

Jazz Bar & Dining

| Location ➜ Hilton Abu Dhabi · Corniche Rd West | 681 1900 |
Hours ➜ 19:00 - 02:00   Closed Fri
Web/email ➜ www.hilton.com   Map Ref ➜ 10-C2

     100

You may be tempted to stop awhile at Hemingway's, but the Jazz Bar will entice you to stay the rest of the evening. A sophisticated venue with classy décor, excellent food, great music and service, cultivates a truly inviting atmosphere. The menu offers many choices and the delicious main courses come in two sizes (and two prices!). But if you're there for just a drink, choose from an extensive wine list or better still, experiment with the various delicious and tempting cocktails. Seating cannot be reserved so get there early. With all the ingredients for a perfect night out, this hugely popular haunt fills up very quickly! EG

Food ●●●○ Service ●●●○ Venue ●●●○ Value ●●●○

Jazz Bar

Sports Bars

Other options → **Activities [p.166]**
Television/Satellite TV [p.40]

La Pergola

Location → Novotel Centre Hotel · Shk Hamdan St | **633 3555**
Hours → 12:00 - 02:00
Web/email → novoad@emirates.net ae   **Map Ref →** 8-D2

After a hard workout in the gym, it's refreshing on a cool evening to sit under the stars in the heart of the city and indulge in shisha and snacks. Alternatively, take a dip in the temperature controlled pool or simply lounge in the Arabic tent on the low seating. During the day, the fifth floor sundeck offers privacy for sun lovers. Both food and beverages are good value for money and service is attentive. A large television screen is available for sports addicts. **AML**

Food ●●○○ Service ●●●○ Venue ●●●○ Value ●○○○

Sports Bars

Top Trendy Venues

90 Degrees	**L.A.B.**
Al Fanar	**Luce**
a.m.p.m.	

Tapas Bars

Other options → **Spanish [p.271]**

Bravo Tapas Bar

Location → Sheraton Abu Dhabi · Corniche Rd East | **677 3333**
Hours → 12:00 - 01:00
Web/email → www.sheraton.com   **Map Ref →** 8-A3

A brand new addition to the Abu Dhabi dining scene, this bar offers a classic Spanish ambience, hot and spicy snacks, a selection of wines and Sangria and, of course, Latino hits played live. Dinner is the only meal served and under the stars, the rooftop venue assures a breathtaking view of the Gulf. **RP**

Food – na   Service – na   Venue – na   Value – na

PUBS

Other options → **Bars [p.285]**

Pubs in the UAE generally look quite close to the real thing. Close enough to transport you from the brown desert to the green, green grass of home – a thought very unlike most preconceived notions of the Middle East! Popular with all nationalities, a good number of pubs manage very successfully to recreate the warm, fuzzy atmosphere of a typical hostelry. Thousands of miles from their proper location, these places have become genuine locales for many people, offering just what they've always done – good beer, tasty food and a chilled hangout.

Ally Pally Corner

Location → Al Ain Palace Hotel · Corniche Rd East | **679 4777**
Hours → 12:00 - 01:00   Thu 12:00 - 01:30
Web/email → www.alainpalacehotel.com   **Map Ref →** 8-B3

Affectionately known as the Ally Pally, this old establishment boasts one of the original watering holes of Abu Dhabi, refusing to succumb to the 'plastic veneer' refurbishment that seems to be the modern trend. Hence,

Going Out   Pubs

the place remains a popular haunt with 'old timers' enjoying the calm atmosphere and a drink and a chat without being bombarded by multiphonic vibrations at mega decibels! The pub grub is not gourmet, but offers a good variety at reasonable prices. Special nights include Wine & Spirits and Quiz Nights, but the Corner is, in essence, a haven to escape the discos and live music of similar outlets. Happy Hour daily between 15:00 - 18:00.
Food ●●●○ Service ●●●○ Venue ●●●● Value ●●●○

Captain's Arms

Location → Le Meridien · Tourist Club Area | **644 6666**
Hours → 12:00 - 24:30
Web/email → www.forte.com   Map Ref → 7-D1

A perennial favourite with pub lovers, this venue pulls large crowds nightly. With its lively terrace and cosy interior, it's one of the default options for a casual sundowner. The food however, does not offer any surprises or excitement. Just good, old fashioned pub grub that aims to satisfy the appetite. As a busy tavern, service can be difficult, but in the end proves to be friendly. Rotating drinks specials take an already strong value for money and make it better.
Food ●●○○ Service ●●○○ Venue ●●●○ Value ●●●○

Cellar

Location → Howard Johnson · Khalifa Bin Zyd St | **671 0000**
Hours → 12:00 - 15:30 19:00 - 24:00 Thu 19:00 - 02:30
Web/email → www.ebmanage.com/howards   Map Ref → 8-B2

The ersatz pub may be a familiar concept, but it still draws a decent crowd. The Cellar is another example of a passable rendition that offers acceptable food, good drinks specials, a loud band and a cosy atmosphere. Special events occur at random, but the convenient location seems to draw a cast of regulars that swear by the place. Worth a look if on a pub crawl or as an alternative to the usual suspects.
Food ●●○○ Service ●●●○ Venue ●●○○ Value ●●●○

Harvesters Pub

Location → Sands Hotel · Shk Zayed 2nd St | **633 5335**
Hours → 12:00 - 01:30
Web/email → www.sands-hotel.com   Map Ref → 8-C1

As close to a 'local' as one can find in Abu Dhabi, this unassuming pub attracts a mostly male clientele with its reasonable food and drink. The bar menu strangely includes dubious German dishes (pork neck anyone?) meshed with English favourites like pies, bangers & mash, or fish & chips. The fried snacks are not extraordinarily delicious, but adequately serve their function. The band is decent but loud; quiz night however, would not merit a thumbs up. Service is pub standard – just flap your arms in the air and shout.
Food ●●●○ Service ●○○○ Venue ●●●○ Value ●●●○

Horse & Jockey Pub

Location → Htl Inter-Continental · Al Khubeirah | **03 768 6686**
Hours → 12:00 - 00:30
Web/email → www.interconti.com   Map Ref → 15-E4

As is quite obvious with that name, this is a typical English pub popular with expats dropping in for a drink and a bite to eat. Choose from a menu of classic pub grub like bangers and mash or fish 'n chips. Entertainment is varied, including bingo, ladies' night, karaoke, sports and quiz nights. Whatever the mood, a fun evening is ensured. On pleasant evenings, you can also choose to sit on the terrace outside, kick back and savour the good food, service and unpretentious atmosphere.
Food ●●○○ Service ●●●● Venue ●●●○ Value ●●●○

Mood Indigo

Location → Novotel Centre Hotel · Shk Hamdan St | **633 3555**
Hours → 12:00 - 02:00
Web/email → novoad@emirates.net.ae   Map Ref → 8-D2

Despite its name, Mood Indigo isn't a sultry cocktail lover's den, but rather a drinker's pub. The standard happy hour (Dhs.10 pints) runs from

Pubs

Going Out

noon till 22:00, while on Friday it's all day! Bar snacks are the typical choices, such as chicken wings or battered calamari, and the surroundings are dark and a little dingy. For three nights a week, a band drowns out idle conversation, but the Saturday quiz can be quite engrossing. Not a venue for the faint hearted. **AF**

Plans are afoot to change the name and remodel this outlet in the near future.

Food ●○○○ Service ●●○○ Venue ●○○○ Value ●●●○

P.J. O'Reillys

Location → Le Royal Meridien · Al Khalifa St | **695 0515**
Hours → 12:00 - 15:30 18:00 - 22:30 Fri 11:00 - 01:30
Web/email → www.rotana.com   **Map Ref →** 8-B2

Known around town as P.J.'s, this traditional Irish pub probably serves the best pint of Guinness in Abu Dhabi. It has an attractive menu with a distinctive Irish bias, which is echoed by the mock Irish surroundings.

The menu is good quality and good value for money, but the service is not as attentive as it could be. Happy hour runs 12:00 - 20:00; Friday afternoon is particularly popular, with happy hour extending all day and entertainment provided by a live duo. **MM**

Food ●●●○ Service ●●○○ Venue ●●○○ Value ●●●○

Red Lion

Location → Int Rotana Inn · Shk Hamdan St | **677 9900**
Hours → 12:00 - 01:30
Web/email → www.rotana.com   **Map Ref →** 8-A1

Amongst the oldest watering holes of Abu Dhabi, an interior laden with wood and leather announces a typical, traditional pub offering an adequate selection of lagers and other drinks, but only boxed wine. It gets busier by the evening and is a popular spot with offshore workers and divers, looking to fill up on some reasonably priced pub grub and enjoy the live music. A usual range of theme nights also includes the darts fraternity. **RW**

Food ●●●○ Service ●●●○ Venue ●●○○ Value ●●●○

Sherlock's

Location → Grand Continental Htl · Shk Zayed 1st St | **626 2200**
Hours → 12:00 - 02:00
Web/email → grand-continental-flamingo.com   **Map Ref →** 8-B2

Although a relative newcomer, Sherlock's is established as one of the default venues for an evening out. A hybrid British pub/American bar, the large room feels lively and offers an array of seating options. Drinks specials, promotions, quizzes, and other antics keep the feel of the venue changing daily. The kitchen is actually part of the appeal as their 'bar food' is surprisingly good, from burgers to fish & chips to a few Tex-Mex options. Good value for money and well worth the praise. **CB**

Food ●●●○ Service ●●○○ Venue ●●●○ Value ●●●○

Tavern

Location → Sheraton Abu Dhabi · Corniche Rd East | **677 3333**
Hours → 12:00 - 01:00 Thu 12:00 - 02:00
Web/email → www.sheraton.com   **Map Ref →** 8-A3

Opened at the end of March after refurbishment, the Tavern has a 'typical' woody pub atmosphere and décor. Smaller and cosier than previously, it offers a pleasant mixture of seating and is great for a drink or a meal – the Shepherd's pie is well recommended. Ladies are offered two free drinks on Wednesdays, and there's a daily happy hour, 16:00 - 20:00. Service is good, but the live band may be a bit loud for some. **AML**

Food ●●●○ Service ●●●○ Venue ●●●○ Value ●●○○

NIGHTCLUBS

Packed with all nationalities, the UAE's nightclubs are very popular from about 23:00 till the wee hours. Abu Dhabi has a reasonable number of dedicated nightclubs, as well as numerous other venues with schizophrenic personalities that are bars or restaurants earlier in the evening, then later

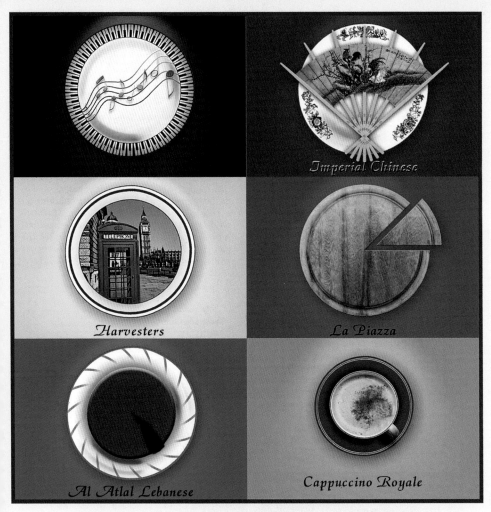

Imperial Chinese

Harvesters

La Piazza

Al Atlal Lebanese

Cappuccino Royale

Because Variety is the Spice of Life!

Sands Hotel Abu Dhabi offers you Six Varieties of the Finest Cuisine from around the world. Try the famous Italian and international line-up at La Piazza. Modern European Cuisine with live music at Chequers Restaurant. Authentic Chinese dishes at the Imperial Chinese. An assortment of delicious Lebanese dishes at Al Atlal. Authentic English delicacies at the Harvesters. Furthermore, you can relax with a cup of tea or coffee with a great selection of bakery & cakes at Cappuccino Royale.

SANDS
HOTEL
Abu-Dhabi

فندق
ساندز
ابوظبي

The best value ★★★★★ hotel in Abu Dhabi

Al Diar Hotels & Resorts ◆ فنادق ومنتجعات الديار

P.O.Box 32430, Abu Dhabi, U.A.E. / Tel: 02 6335335 / Fax: 02 6335766
E-mail: sandshot@emirates.net.ae / www.sands-hotel.com

turn into the perfect place to cut loose and shake your thang! For some authentic clubbing, look out for the increasingly common visits by international DJs and the special nights by various event organisers.

Additionally, since you're in the Middle East, do not overlook the option of Arabic nightclubs. This is your chance to sample diverse Arabic cuisine and enjoy a night of traditional Arabic entertainment, usually with a bellydancer, a live band and a singer. These venues start buzzing very late in the evening, so they may still be empty during normal packed hours at other nightspots – a classic reflection on the Arabic way of starting late and finishing, well... later.

For information on door policy and dress code, refer to Bars [p.286].

Cave De Rois

Location → Al Ain Rotana Hotel
Hours → 21:00 - 03:00
Web/email → www.rotana.com | 03 754 5111
Map Ref → 15-A3

A lively nightclub that attracts a young, predominantly male, Arabic crowd. Outfitted with a stage, the Filipino band is highly entertaining but the show really starts when the popular DJ takes over and the floor is crawling with aspiring street dancers. Serving light snacks and a standard range of alcoholic beverages, the Cave provides all the typical trappings of a late night joint. CM
Food – na Service – na Venue – na Value – na

Cave De Rois

Colosseum

Location → Marina & Yacht Club · Tourist Club Area | 644 0300
Hours → 21:00 - 02:30 Thu 21:00 - 03:30 Closed Mon
Web/email → www.abudhabimarina.com | Map Ref → 4-B4

Still one of the only late night, upscale dance clubs in town, this longstanding favourite continues to draw the young, beautiful and on-the-prowl clubbers of Abu Dhabi. With its faux stone walls, candlelit interior and hip DJs, this haunt has a rare energy level which kicks in well in the night. So don't go early unless you're desperate to avoid the cover charge or itching for a sofa overlooking the dance floor. Even on weekdays, a slightly smaller coterie of 'socialites' turn up to dance into the wee hours of the morning. Entrance is free for females; males pay a Dhs.50 cover inclusive of one free drink. CB
Food – na Service – na Venue – na Value – na

Gauloises Club

Location → Le Meridien · Tourist Club Area | 644 6666
Hours → 21:00 - 01:00 Thu 21:00 - 02:30
Web/email → www.forte.com | Map Ref → 7-D1

A fading star of the nightclub scene, Gauloises seems to have lost its identity. As an erstwhile favourite, the club generates ample traffic, but most stay for one drink and then leave. Innovative theme nights (eg, salsa dancing, live bands and themes) still attempt to occasionally spice things up. To its credit, the bar attracts a diverse assortment of ethnic patrons. However, the location is great, hence the place has potential. CB
Food – na Service – na Venue ●○○○ Value ●●○○

Peach Garden Filipino Club

Location → Hilton Al Ain · Al Ain | 03 768 6666
Hours → 21:00 - 03:00 Closed Sun
Web/email → www.hilton.com | Map Ref → 15-D4

Packed to overflowing some nights of the week, this tiny Filipino nightclub attracts a wide variety of patrons (though locals, Filipinos and Eastern Europeans are predominant). Most people seem to share a couple of things in common, such as enjoying the band's (rather good) renditions of everything from Tom Jones to Abba, and even more so, the scantily clad girls gyrating on the dance floor! A door policy in effect on Wednesday, Thursday and Friday nights requires men to pay a Dhs.20 cover charge. PG

Food – na Service – na Venue ●●○○ Value ●●●○

Tequilana Discotheque

Location → Hilton Abu Dhabi · Corniche Rd West | **681 1900**
Hours → 22:00 - 02:30 Thu 22:30 - 03:30 Closed Sat
Web/email → www.hilton.com   Map Ref → 10-C2

 50

Designed to resemble a beach hut and tropical coast environment, this curious club opens into Hemingway's and the Jazz Bar, and seems to be a place to escape the crowds at its sister venues. Lacking in distinction or particular charm, Tequilana benefits from the late night spill over when sophistication gives way to an urge to dance or sing karaoke in one of the semi private dedicated rooms. Dark and sultry, the club has potential and offers a slight variation to the usual Hemingway's routine. CB

Food – na Service – na Venue ●●○○ Value ●●○○

Tequilana

Zenith

Location → Sheraton Abu Dhabi · Corniche Rd East | **677 3333**
Hours → 20:00 - 03:00 Closed Sat
Web/email → www.sheraton.com   Map Ref → 8-A3

This newbie to the Abu Dhabi clubbing scene is all set to target the multicultural 'in crowd'. Classic

cocktails will satisfy your thirst as you nibble away on bar snacks. Crank the style up a notch with a cigar (choose from a quality range) and settle back to decent chillout music – does Buddha Bar appeal to you? RP

Food – na Service – na Venue – na Value – na

ENTERTAINMENT

Cinemas

Other options → **Theatre [p.298]**

A trip to the cinema is one of the most popular forms of entertainment in the Emirates and movie buffs here are relatively well catered for, although showings are generally limited to the latest Arabic, Asian or Hollywood films. At present there are 4 cinemas in Abu Dhabi and 2 in Al Ain showing English language films, with another few showing Indian and Arabic films.

Most of the newer cinemas are multi-screen mega sites, while the older cinemas tend to be larger, with fewer screens and a traditional, crowded cinema atmosphere.

Cinema timings can be found in the daily newspapers, as well as the Entertainment special of Gulf News every Wednesday.

Al Mariah Cinemas

Entertainment

Going Out

Release dates vary considerably, with new Western films reaching the UAE from anywhere between four weeks to a year after release in the USA. New movies are released every Wednesday. Films often don't hang around for too long, so if there's something you really want to see, don't delay too much or it will be gone!

The air conditioners inside are on super high and the cinema hall tends to become very cold, so make sure you take a sweater. During the weekends, there are extra shows at midnight or 01:00 – check the press for details. Tickets can be reserved, but usually have to be collected an hour before the show, and sales are cash only. However, with so many screens around now, you will often find cinemas half empty, except for the first couple of days after the release of an eagerly awaited blockbuster.

Comedy

Other options → **Theatre [p.298]**

The regular comedy scene in Abu Dhabi is unfortunately quite limited. However, there are regular visits from the Laughter Factory, as well as the occasional comical theatre production or one off event. Comedy shows tend to be aimed at the British population; hence, other nationalities may not find the sense of humour as funny as the Brits in the audience do.

Events are often promoted only a short time before they actually take place, so keep your ears to the ground for what's coming up.

Laughter Factory, The

Location → Crowne Plaza · Shk Hamdan St | **621 0000**
Hours → Timings on request
Web/email → www.crowneplaza.com   Map Ref → 8-C1

Based on a concept that has been tremendously successful in the UK, America and Hong Kong, this comedy club provides established as well as upcoming comedians as acts. The artists are imports from the UK comedy scene, carefully selected to entertain the Middle East expats. However, three different styles offered in one show manage to cover a broad spectrum of humour, appealing to a wider audience. Shows are usually held bimonthly, except in the summer months. Call for information.

Concerts

There's not really a regular calendar of events for music lovers in Abu Dhabi. However, at different times of the year (mainly in winter) at festivals or international sporting events, concerts and festivals are held with visits from international artists, bands and classical musicians. Ticket prices are around the same, or a bit higher than you would expect to pay elsewhere.

Visits by international bands are not very common, but they do happen, so stay tuned. In the past, club events such as Ministry of Sound nights have visited Abu Dhabi.

Cinemas

Name	Tel No.	Map	Location	No. of Languages	Prices	
					Normal	Special
Al Jazira Cinema	443 1116		Al Jazirah Sports Club	H, M, T	15	20
Al Massa Cineplex	633 3000	8 - C2	Hamdan Centre	A, E	25	30
Century Cinemas	645 8988		Abu Dhabi Mall	A, E	30	45
CineStar	681 8484		Marina Mall	A, E	30	30
Cultural Foundation	621 5300		Shk Zayed Rd 1st St	E	5	
Eldorado	676 3555	8 - B1	Electra Street	M	15	20
Grand Al Mariah	678 5000	8 - B2	Opp Zakher Hotel	E	25	30
National Cinema	671 1700	8 - B1	Umm al Nar St	H	20	15
Al Massa	03 764 4447		Nr Rotana Hotel	A,E	25	30
Club Cinema	03 722 2255	17 - A4	Nr Oasis Hospital	H, M	15	20
Grand Cineplex	03 751 1228		Al Ain Mall	E	20	25

Key: A = Arabic; E = English; H = Hindi; M = Malayalam; T= Tamil

Entertainment

Going Out

Promoters usually have no long term programmes, and details are only available about a month in advance. So for details of events, check the daily press or monthly magazines, and listen out for announcements and advertisements on Emirates 1 and 2 FM, and the northern radio stations, Channel 4 FM and Dubai FM. Tickets go on sale at the venues and through other outlets, such as Virgin Megastore. Tickets for some concerts can also be purchased online at www.ibuytickets.com or www.itptickets.com.

Concert Venues	
Club, The	673 1111
Colosseum	644 0300
Cultural foundation	621 5300
Hotel Inter-Continental Abu Dhabi	666 6888

If you suffer from severe withdrawal symptoms from live music, Dubai does sometimes have a little more going on. Again, check the press.

Theatre

Other options → Cinemas [p.295]

The theatre scene in Abu Dhabi is rather limited, with fans relying chiefly on touring companies and the occasional amateur dramatics performance. One regular highlight is the British Airways Playhouse, which tours the world.

The amateur theatre scene always welcomes new members, either on stage or behind the scenes. There is also the occasional murder mystery dinner where you are encouraged to display your thespian skills by being part of the performance.

British Airways Playhouse

Location → Htl Inter-Continental · Bainuna St **666 6888**
Hours → na
Web/email → www.intercontinental.com   Map Ref → 10-C1

Renowned for providing regular theatre and comedy evenings for nearly two decades, the British Airways Playhouse is a favourite among theatregoers and was the first dinner theatre to be staged in the Emirates. The Playhouse stages four seasons every year. Shows are rehearsed, produced and cast in London and in the past have starred such names as Leslie Phillips, Patrick McNee, Alfred Marks, Dora Bryan and John Inman. Events are not regular; call for details on upcoming ones.

British Airways Playhouse (Al Ain)

Location → Htl Inter-Continental · Al Khubeirah **03 768 6686**
Hours → na
Web/email → www.interconti.com   Map Ref → 15-E4

For information, refer to British Airways Playhouse in Abu Dhabi (see above). Events are not regular; call for details on upcoming ones.

Cinema

Entertainment

Going Out

www.factoryproduct.com

00% entertainment

Factory Productions
04 355 1862
Music
Comedy
Parties
Djs

Maps

EXPLORER

Maps

Map Legend

Corniche Hospital	Embassies / Hospitals
Al Meena	Areas / Roundabouts
Crowne Plaza	Hotels
Bowling City	Activities
City Centre	Shopping/Souks
National Cinema	Cafés/Cinemas
Clock Tower	Important Landmarks
Etisalat	Business
Wadi Tawia	Exploring

Map pages 1-3 are at a scale of 1:25,000 (1cm = 250m)
Map pages 4-10 are at a scale of 1:10,000 (1cm = 100m)
Map pages 12-15 are at a scale of 1:25,000 (1cm = 250m)
Map pages 11,16-17 are at a scale of 1:50,000 (1cm = 500m)

Techie Info

The maps in this section are based on rectified QuickBird satellite imagery taken in 2002.

The QuickBird satellite was launched in October 2001 and is operated by DigitalGlobe™, a private company based in Colorado (USA). Today, DigitalGlobe's QuickBird satellite provides the highest resolution (61cm), largest swath width and largest on-board storage of any currently available or planned commercial satellite.

MAPS geosystems are the Digital Globe Master resellers for the Middle East, West, Central and East Africa. They also provide a wide range of mapping services and systems. For more information, visit www.digitalglobe.com (QuickBird) and www.maps-geosystems.com (mapping services) or contact MAPS geosystems (06 572 5411).

User's Guide

To also help you locate your destination etc, we have superimposed additional information such as main roads, roundabouts, and landmarks on the maps. Many places listed throughout the guidebook also have a map reference alongside, so you can know precisely where you need to go (or what you need to tell the taxi driver).

To make it easy to find places and give better visualization on the Abu Dhabi maps, they have all been orientated parallel to the coastline of the Corniche which runs along the northwest side of the island (not north orientated). While the overview map on this page is at a scale of approximately 1:130,000 (1cm = 1.3km), all other maps range from 1:10,000 (1cm = 100m) to 1:48,000 (1cm = 480m).

Abu Dhabi Zones, Sectors & Streets

Abu Dhabi island is split into two zones, using New Airport Road (Sheikh Rashid Bin Saeed Al Maktoum Street) as the dividing line. The area to the east is zone 1 (east) and to the west is zone 2 (west). The zones are further divided into numbered square sectors, which are bordered by the main streets (creating a road network that is based on a grid system).

All streets (main and secondary) that are parallel to the New Airport Road are given even numbers, with the numbers increasing as they move away from New Airport Road to either coast. Those streets that are parallel to the Corniche (ie, at right angles to New Airport Road) are given odd numbers, which increase as you move away from the Corniche. At the main street intersections, blue road signs show the zone and sector names, while at secondary streets, green road signs are used. To confuse matters, many roads have different names. Listed in the index are the main roads with their official or map name, their common name, their street number and their position in relation to New Airport Road or the Corniche.

Intro

Maps

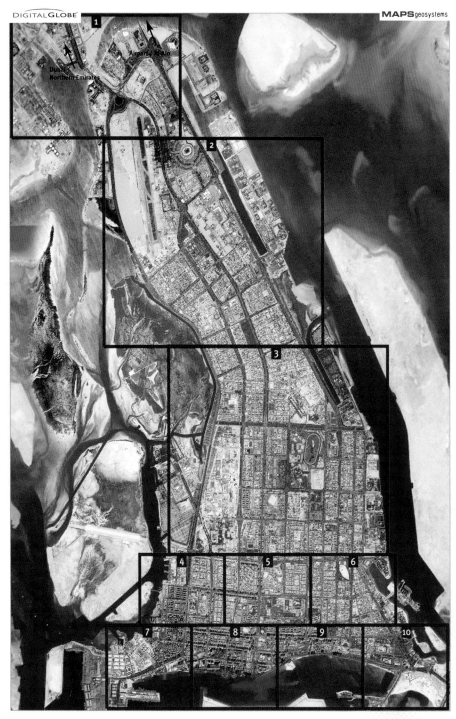

DIGITALGLOBE

MAPSgeosystems

1

Airport / Abalo

Dubai /
Northern Emirates

2

3

4

5

6

7

8

9

10

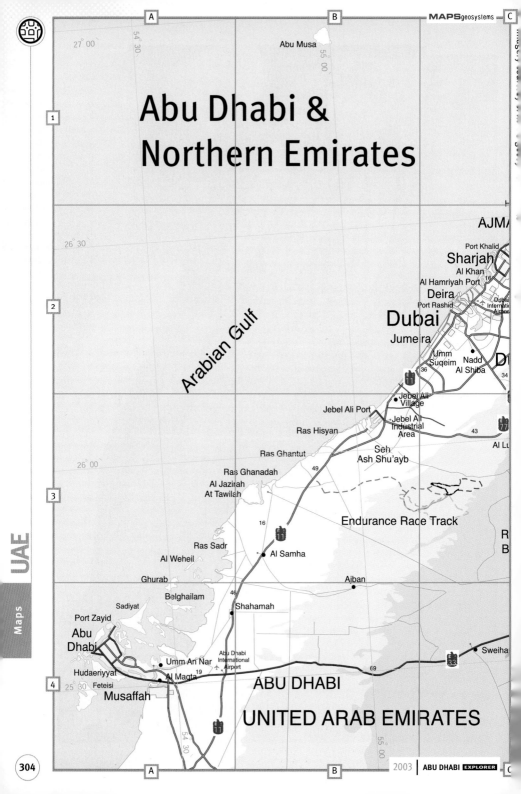

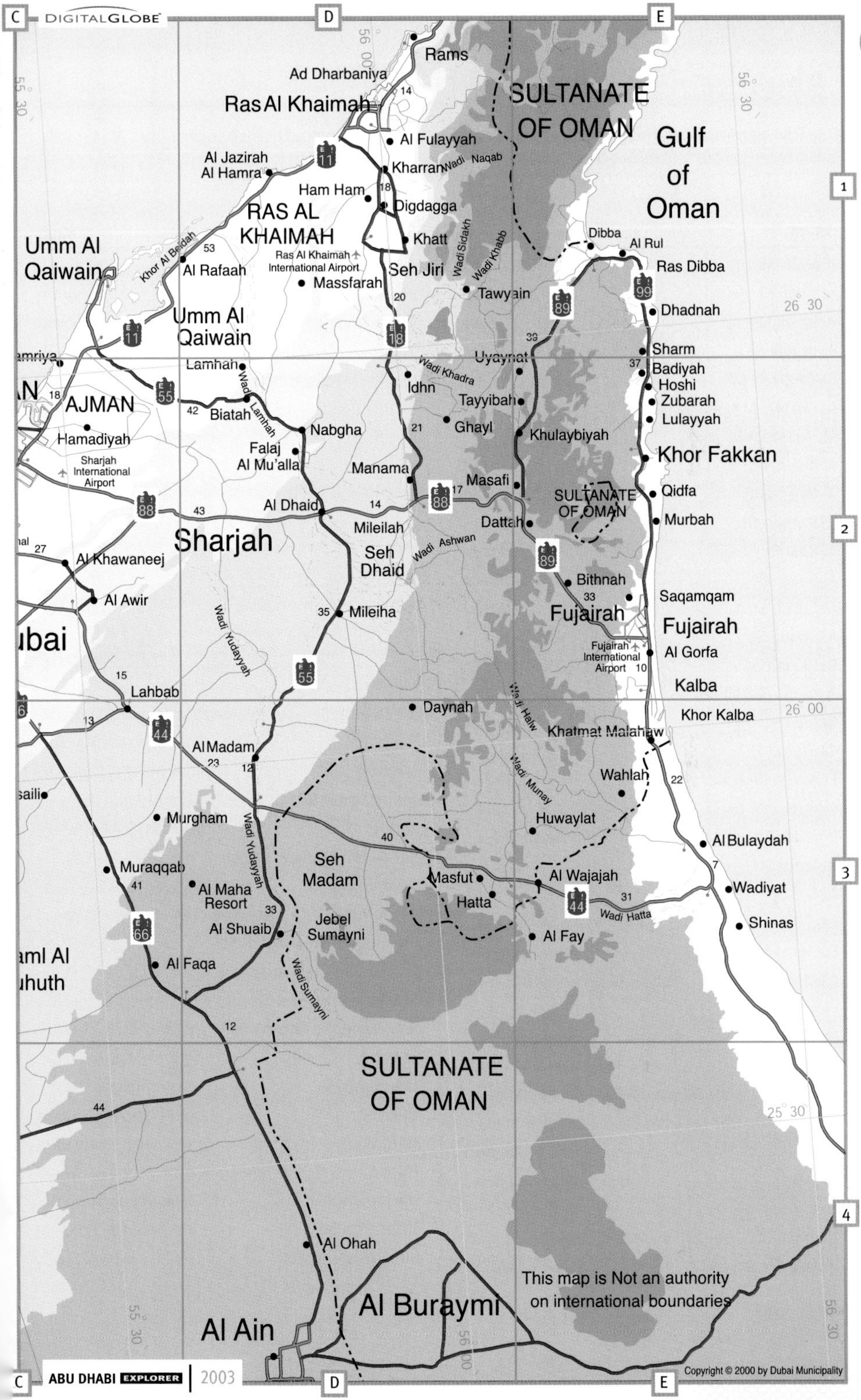

Rams
Ad Dharbaniya
Ras Al Khaimah
SULTANATE
OF OMAN
Gulf
of
Oman
Al Fulayyah
Al Jazirah
Al Hamra
Kharran Wadi Naqab
RAS AL
KHAIMAH
Ham Ham
Digdagga
Umm Al
Qaiwain
Khatt
Al Rafaah
Ras Al Khaimah ✈
International Airport
Massfarah
Seh Jiri
Dibba
Al Rul
Ras Dibba
89
99
Umm Al
Qaiwain
Tawyain
Dhadnah
amriya
Lamhah
Uyaynat
Sharm
Badiyah
Hoshi
Zubarah
Lulayyah
N
18
AJMAN
55
Biatah
Idhn
Tayyibah
Khulaybiyah
Falaj
Al Mu'alla
Nabgha
Ghayl
Khor Fakkan
Hamadiyah
Manama
Sharjah
International Airport
88
Al Dhaid
Mileilah
Masafi
SULTANATE
OF OMAN
Qidfa
Murbah
43
Seh
Dhaid
Dattah
89
ubai
Al Khawaneej
Mileiha
Bithnah
Saqamqam
35
Al Awir
Fujairah
Fujairah
55
Lahbab
Daynah
Fujairah ✈
International Airport
Al Gorfa
Kalba
44
Al Madam
Khatmat Malahah
Khor Kalba
sailie
Murgham
Wahlan
Seh
Madam
Huwaylat
Al Bulaydah
Muraqqab
Al Maha
Resort
Al Shuaib
Masfut
Hatta
Al Wajajah
Wadiyat
44 Wadi Hatta
aml Al
uhuth
Jebel
Sumayni
Al Fay
Shinas
66
Al Faqa
SULTANATE
OF OMAN
UAE
Maps
Al Ohah
This map is Not an authority
on international boundaries
Al Ain
Al Buraymi

The following is a list of the main streets in Abu Dhabi, which are referenced on map pages 1 - 10. Many roads are longer than one grid reference, in which case the main grid references have been given.

Street	Map	Street	Map
Airport Rd	1-D4; 2-C2; 3-C1	Juwazat St	see Al Manhal St (West)
Al Falah St	4-D3; 5-A3	Khalid Bin Waleed St	9-A2
Al Istiqlal St	8-E2	Khalidiyah St	9-E1/E2
Al Ittihad St	8-E1/E2/E3	Khalidyah St	see Shk Zayed First St (West)
Al Karamah St	3-C3; 5-D2	Khalifa Bin Shakhbout St	3-D3; 6-A2/A3
Al Khaleej Al Arabi St	3-D4; 6-B3; 9-D1	Khalifa Bin Zayed St	8-A1; 8-B2/B3
Al Maktoum St	5-B3/B4; 8-E1	Khalifa St	see Al Istiklal St (East)
Al Manhal St	5-C3/D3/6-A3/B3	Khubeirah St	10-B2/C2
Al Meena Rd	7-B3/C3/D3/E2	King Khalid Bin Abdel Aziz St	3-D3; 5-E3/E4; 9-C1/C2
Al Nahyan St	3-D4; 5-E1		
Al Nasr St	8-E2; 9-A2/B2	Liwa St	8-D2/D3
Al Saada St	3-B2/C2	Lulu St	8-C2/C3
Al Salam St	3-A4; 4-C3/C4; 8-A1/A2	Mohammed Bin Khalifa St	3-C3/C3/D3
Al Sharqi St	8-C1	New Airport Rd (Muroor Rd)	2-B3/C3; 3-B1/B2/B3/B4
Bainunah St	6-C2/D3/D4; 10-C1/C2		
Bani Yas (Najda) St	4-E1/E2/E3/E4; 8-B1	Nineteenth St	see Al Saada St (East)
Bateen St	5-D1; 6-B1	Nineteenth St	see Saeed Bin Tahnoun St (West)
Coast Rd	1-E3; 2-D2; 3-D1	Ninth St	see Al Falah St (East)
Corniche Rd (East)	8-B3/D3	Ninth St	see Al Manhal St (West)
Corniche Rd (West)	9-a2/C2/E2; 10-A2/B2	Old Passport Rd	see Al Falah St (East)
Defence Rd	see Haza'a Bin Zayed St (East)	Port Rd	7-B3/C3/D3/E2; 8-A2
Defence St	3-B4/C4	Saeed Bin Tahnoon Street	3-C2/D2/E2
Delma St	3-D4	Seventh St	see Shk Zayed First St (West)
East Rd	3-B3/5-A1/A2/A3/A4/8-C1	Seventh St	see Shk Zayed Second St (East)
Eastern Ring Rd	1-D3; 2-A3; 3-A1	Shk Hamdan Bin Mohd. St	7-E1; 8-B1/B2
Electra St/Rd	see Shk Zayed Second St (East)	Shk Rashid Bin Saeed	3-C2/C3/C4;
Eleventh St	see Bateen St (West)	Shk Zayed the First St	8-E1; 9-C1; 10-A1
Eleventh St	see Haza'a Bin Zayed St (East)	Shk Zayed the Second St	7-E1; 8-A1/B1/C1/D1
Eleventh St	see Sudan St (Middle – West)	Sultan Bin Zayed St	3-E3; 6-C2; 9-E1/E2
Fifteenth St	see Mohammed Bin Khalifa St (West)	The Corniche	see Corniche Rd (East)
Fifth St	see Shk Hamdan Bin Mohammed St (East)	Third St	see Al Istiklal St (East)
First St	see Corniche Rd (East)	Third St	see… Khalifa St
First St	see Corniche Rd (West)	Third St	see Khalifa Bin Zayed St (West)
First St	see The Corniche	Thirteenth St	see Delma St (West)
Hamdan St	see Shk Hamdan Bin Mohd. St (East)	Thirteenth St	see Defence St (East)
Haza'a Bin Zayed St	4-D1/E1; 5-A1/B1	Umm Al Nar Street	8-B1/B2/B3

DIGITALGLOBE™

C L E A R L Y   T H E   B E S T

61 cm QuickBird Imagery is the highest resolution satellite imagery available. We offer products and resorces to both existing GIS users and the entire next generation of mapping and multimedia applications.

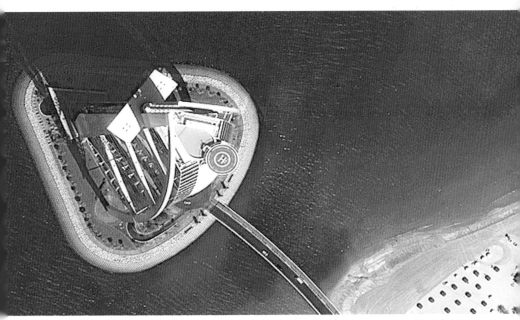

Burj Al Arab, Scale 1:2500, dated October 2002 © DigitalGlobe

MAPSgeosystems

DigitalGlobe's Master Reseller serving the Middle East and East, Central and West Africa

MAPS (UAE), Corniche Plaza 1, P.O. Box 5232, Sharjah, UAE.
Tel : +971 6 5725411, Fax : +971 6 5724057
www.maps-geosystems.com

For further details, please contact quickbird@maps-geosystems.com

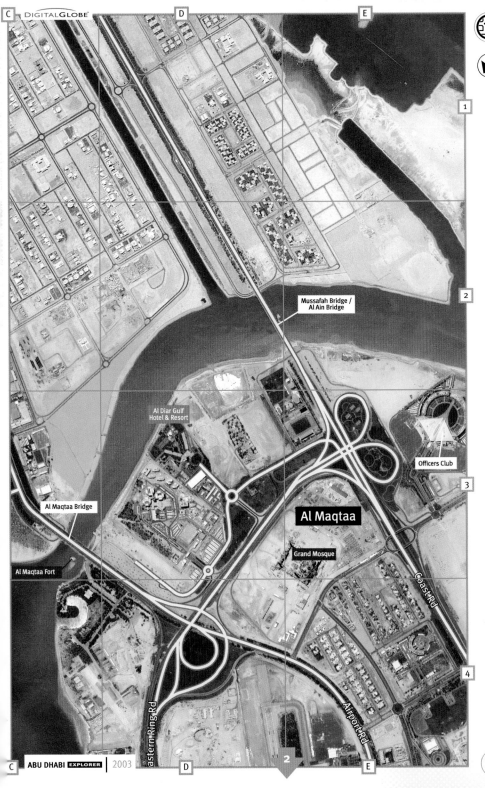

Mussafah Bridge /
Al Ain Bridge

Al Diar Gulf
Hotel & Resort

Officers Club

Al Maqtaa Bridge

Al Maqtaa

3

Al Maqtaa Fort

Grand Mosque

Coast Rd

1

Maps

4

Eastern Ring Rd

Airport Rd

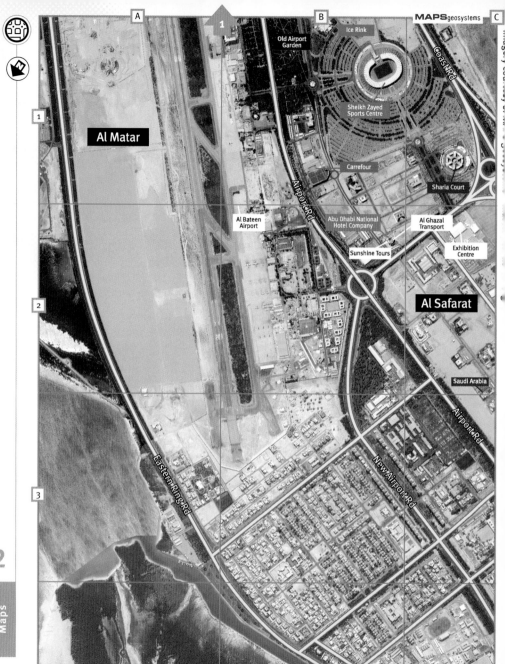

Al Matar

Old Airport Garden

Ice Rink

Sheikh Zayed Sports Centre

Coast Rd

Carrefour

Sharia Court

Al Bateen Airport

Abu Dhabi National Hotel Company

Al Ghazal Transport

Sunshine Tours

Exhibition Centre

Airport Rd

Al Safarat

Saudi Arabia

Airport Rd

Eastern Ring Rd

New Airport Rd

Mangroves

DIGITALGLOBE

Grand Stand

Heritage / Bedouin
Vilage

Qasr El
Shatie

Coast Rd

Yemen

Qatar

Coast Rd

Airport Rd

New Airport Rd

2

Maps

1

2

3

4

Mangroves

Al Saadas

New Corniche

Qasr El Bahr

Eastern Ring Rd

New Airport Rd

Airport Rd

Hadbat Al Zaafran

Traffic Police

Al Saada St

Immigration Department

Churches Area

Al Khubairat School

Shk Mohd Bin Zayed Mosque

National Theatre

Chouiefat School

Shk Rashid Bin Saeed Al Maktoum St

Ministry of Information & Culture

New Airport Rd

Eid Prayer Yard

Defence St

Al Wahdah

Al Karamah

3

Maps

Qasr El Shatie

Al Mushrif

Coast Rd

Saeed Bin Tahnoon St

Oman

Abu Dhabi Health &
Fitness Club

Race Track

Abu Dhabi Golf &
Equestrian Club

Al-Karamah St

Khalifa Bin Shakhbout St

Sultan Bin Zayed St

Al Mushrif
Childrens
Garden

Mohammed Bin Khalifa St

Al Bateen

Al Nahyan St

Gulf Diagnostic
Centre

Ministry of
State

Delma St

Al Rowdah

3

Maps

Qasr El Bahr

Al Falah St

Ministry of Labour

Al Meena

City Terminal
Abu Dhabi Airport

Beach Rotana
Hotel & Towers

Abu Dhabi Mall

Century Cinema

AUH Co-operative
Society

Bam Bu!

Ninth St

Old AUH Co-operative
Society Bld.

Al Diar Dana
Hotel

Abu Dhabi Marina
& Yacht Club

4

Maps

Haza'a Bin Zayed St

Al Dhafrah

School Area

Water & Electricity HQ

Emirates Computers

Al Falah St

Bani Yas St

Finland

Municipality &
Town Planning
Department

Ministry of Finance
& Industry

Madinat Zayed

Al Futtaim
Motors

Abu Dhabi
New Primary School

Al Salam St

Bani Yas St

Etisalat

Ninth St

Bahrain

A & E

ADNOC-FOD

Maps

4

3

Main Bus Terminal

Al Wahdah

Taxi Stand

1

Haza'a Bin Zayed St

4

Al Dhafrah

2

Al Diar Palm Hotel

Al Falah Plaza

Al Falah St

3

Al Manhal St

5

Maps

4

Central Post Office

Madinat Zayed

Gold Souk

Shk Rashid Bin Saeed Al Maktoum St

East Rd

4

Madinat Zayed Shopping Centre

Homes R Us

DIGITALGLOBE

Al Karamah

China
Jordan
Greece

Al Rowdah

Al-Karamah St

Al-Nahyan St

Kuwait Korea

Dar Al Shifa
Hospital

USA

Bateen St

AUH Co-operative
Society

Al Jazeira
Hospital

Sheikh Khalifa
Medical Centre

Central Hospital

Al Manhal

King Khalid Bin Abdel Aziz Saeed St

Al Manhal St

Al Manhal

Maps

5

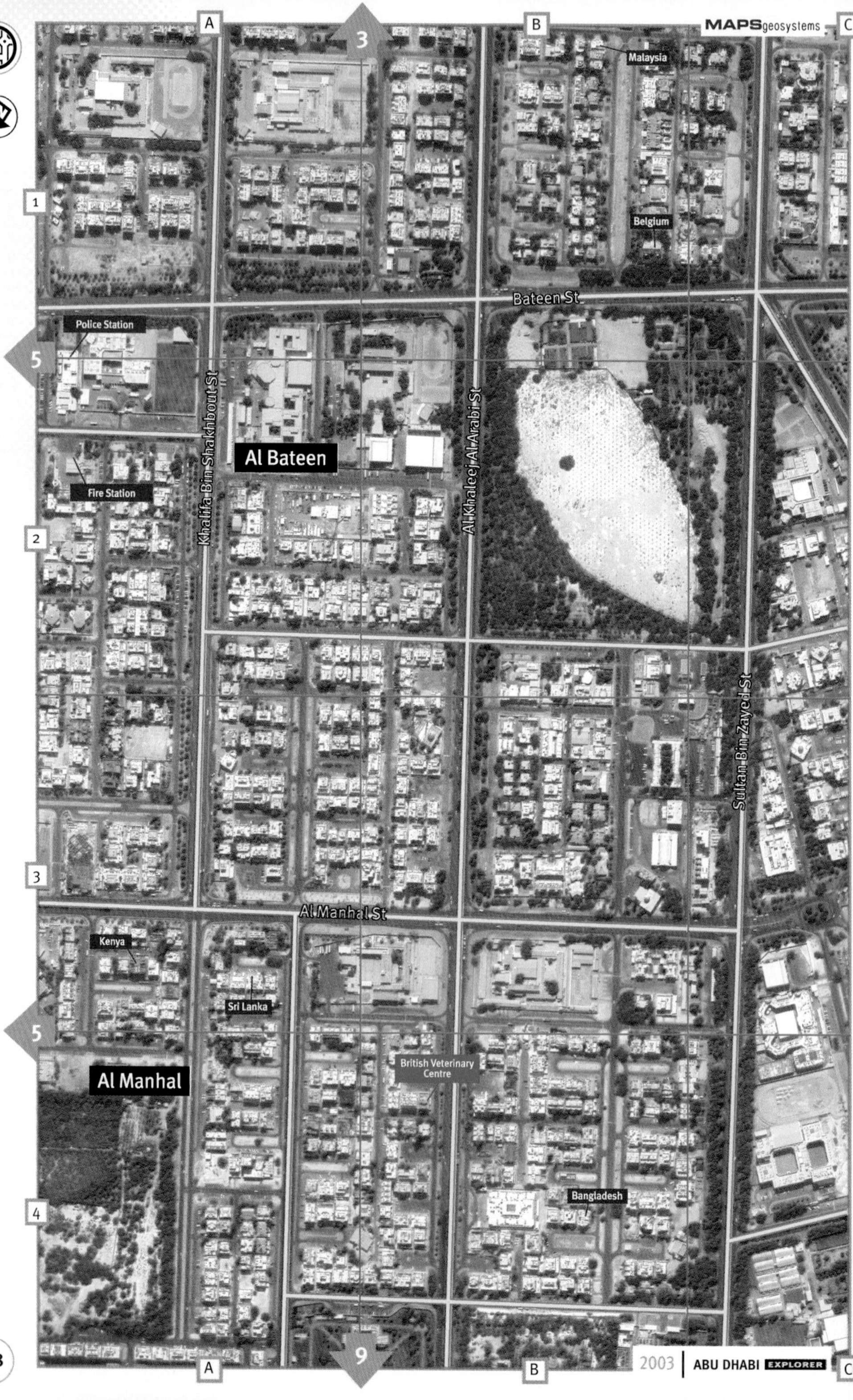
A
B
C
3
Malaysia
Belgium
1
Bateen St
Police Station
5
Khalifa Bin Shakhbout St
Al Khaleej Al Arabi St
Al Bateen
Fire Station
2
Sultan Bin Zayed St
3
Al Manhal St
Kenya
Sri Lanka
5
British Veterinary Centre
Al Manhal
Bangladesh
4
9
A
B
C

DIGITALGLOBE

Bainunah St.

Bateen Dhow
Shipyard

Abu Dhabi Woman's
Association

Al Bateen

Ministry of Planning

Ministry of
Public Works

Ministry of Agriculture
& Fisheries

6

Maps

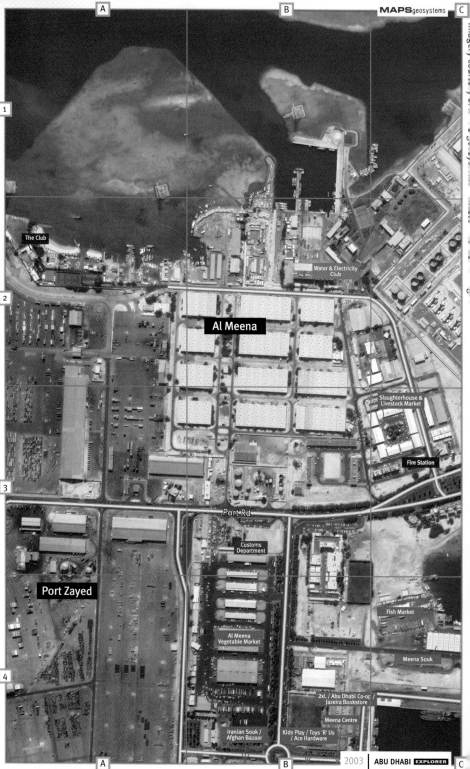

The Club

Water & Electricity Club

Al Meena

Slaughterhouse & Livestock Market

Fire Station

Port Rd

Customs Department

Port Zayed

Fish Market

Al Meena Vegetable Market

Meena Souk

2xL / Abu Dhabi Co-op / Jazeira Bookstore

Meena Centre

Iranian Souk / Afghan Bazaar

Kids Play / Toys 'R' Us / Ace Hardware

7

Maps

C · D · E

Le Meridien Hotel

Beyond the Beach

Post Office

Shk Zayed the 2nd St

Mosque Gardens

1

Abu Dhabi Tourist Club

Shk Hamdan Bin Mohd St

Al Salam Hospital

8

Power & Desalination Plant

Al Meena

Emirates Plaza Hotel

2

Al Diar Capitol Hotel

Corniche Hospital

Meena St

American Veterinary Clinic

3

7

8

Dhow Harbour

Al Dhafra

Maps

4

C · D · E

4

Al Hamra Plaza
Residence

Sands Hotel

Shk Zayed the Second St

1

Eldorado Cinema

Sahara
Residence

Al Markaziyah

Dr McCulloch's
Clinic

National Cinema

Al Maha
Rotana Suites

Crowne Plaza
Hotel

International
Rotana Inn

7

Shk Hamdan Bin Mohammed St

Sun & Sand Sports

Havana Café

British Dental
Clinic

Swiss

Al Mariah
Cinema

City Centre

Lulu Centre

Grand
Continental

Bowling City

2

Russia

Zakher Hotel

Capital Gardens

Al Diar Mina
Hotel

Howard Johnson
Diplomatic Hotel

Millennium Hotel

Khalifa Bin Zayed St

Post Office

Al Diar
Regency Hotel

Khalifa Bin Zayed St

Le Royal
Meridian Hotel

ADMA-OPCO
ADGAS

Austria

Sheraton Abu Dhabi
Resort & Towers

ZADCO

Al Ain Palace
Hotel

Corniche Rd (East)

3

7

8

Maps

4

Lulu Island

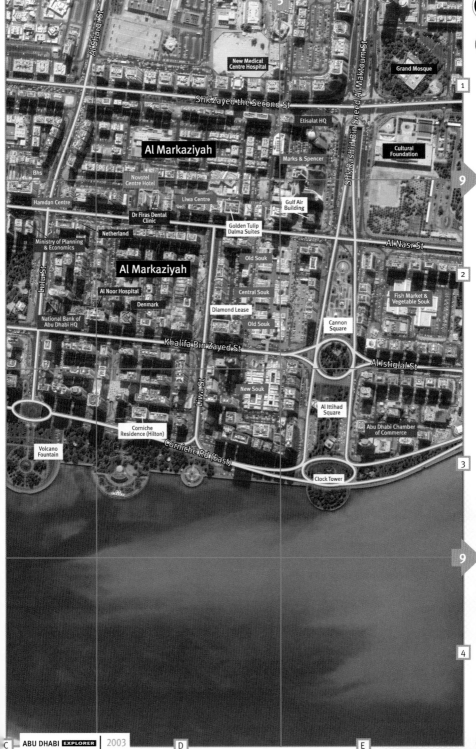

DIGITALGLOBE

Al Sharqi St

New Medical Centre Hospital

Shk Zayed the Second St

Etisalat HQ

Al Markaziyah

Marks & Spencer

Bhs

Novotel Centre Hotel

Hamdan Centre

Liwa Centre

Gulf Air Building

Dr Firas Dental Clinic

Golden Tulip Dalma Suites

Netherland

Ministry of Planning & Economics

Al Markaziyah

Lulu St

Old Souk

Al Noor Hospital

Central Souk

Denmark

Diamond Lease

National Bank of Abu Dhabi HQ

Old Souk

Khalifa Bin Zayed St

Liwa St

Cannon Square

Al Istiqlal St

New Souk

Al Ittihad Square

Corniche Residence (Hilton)

Abu Dhabi Chamber of Commerce

Corniche Rd (East)

Volcano Fountain

Clock Tower

Shk Rashid Bin Saeed Al Maktoum St

Grand Mosque

Cultural Foundation

Al Nasr St

Fish Market & Vegetable Souk

1

9

2

3

9

8

Maps

4

Al Manhal

Al Muhairy Centre

1

Grand Stores

Sheraton Residence Abu Dhabi

Shk Zayed the First St

Platinum Residence

Al Hosn Plaza

Khalidiyah Centre

Old Fort & Qasr Al Husn Palace

Al Hosn

British Council

India

Abela Superstore

Al Nasr St

Al Markaziyah West

Al Hosn

Al Ghazal Rent A Car

2

Britain

Bainunah Hilton Tower

Corniche Rd (West)

Khalid Bin Al Waleed St

Tariq Bin Zayed St

King Khalid Bin Abdel Aziz Saeed St

3

9

4

Lulu Island

Al Bateen

Khalidiya Garden

Sultan Bin Zayed St

The One

Shk Zayed the First St

Dana Plaza

Lamcy Department Store

Al Khalidiyah

Khalidiya Childrens Garden

Corniche Towers Residence

Eldiar Furniture & Interior Design

ADCO

Al Hana Shopping Centre

Khalidiyah St

Ali & Sons Car Showroom

Corniche Rd (West)

Al Khaleej Al Arabi St

Breakwater

Al Sofon

Al Ras Al Akhdar

Abu Dhabi Womans Association Centre

6

E

1

10

2

3

10

9

Maps

4

A B C

6

Bainunah St

Ministry of
Communications

Ministry of Labour &
Social Affairs

Al Bateen

1

Shk Zayed the First St

9

Police Station

Council of
Ministries

Etisalat

Spinneys

Ministry of
Cabinet Affairs

Federal Supreme
Court

Ministry of
Islamic Affairs &
Justice

Federal National
Council

Al Khubeirah St

2

Al Khubeirah

Corniche Rd (West)

Hilton
Abu Dhabi

Hiltonia Club

3

10

Maps

9

Breakwater

4

Al Safina

Local Cafe &
Restaurant

Havana Café

Heritage Village

Carrefour / IKEA / Sun &
Sands Sports / CineStar

Abu Dhabi International
Marine Sports Club

Marina Mall

A B C

DIGITALGLOBE

Ministry of Petroleum
& Mineral Resources

Hotel Inter-Continental
Abu Dhabi

Bainunah St.

ADNOC

Khalidia Palace
Hotel

Al Ras Al Akhdar

Conference Palace
Hotel (u/c)

Abu Dhabi
Ladies Club

Cleopatra's
Spa

Ladies Beach

1

2

3

4

10

Maps

Al Ain – Street Index

The following is a list of the main streets and hotel buildings in Al Ain, which are referenced on map pages 1 - 10. Many roads are longer than one grid reference, in which case the main grid references have been given.

Street	Map	Street	Map
Abu Bakr Al Siddiq St	15-B3	Hazzaa R/A	17-A1
Abu Obaida Bin Al Jarrah St	13-A3/B3	Hilton R/A	15-C4
Al Ain R/A	14-E4; 17-C1	Hospital R/A	14-E2
Al Ain St	15-A2/A4; 17-C1	Khalid Bin Al Waleed St	12-E4
Al Asar St	see Al Athar St	Khalid Bin Sultan St	14-D4; 15-B4
Al Athar St	13-B1/C1	Khalid St	see Sultan Bin Zayed Al Awwal St
Al Baladiyya St	12-E4; 14-E1/D3	Khalifa Bin Zayed Al Awwal St	14-E3/E4
Al Basra R/A	14-C2	Khalifa Bin Zayed St	16-D1
Al Bourj R/A	14-E3	Khalifa Bin Zayed St	14-B3; 16-B1/E1
Al Buraimi R/A	15-B2	Khata Al Shikle St	15-D4/E4
Al Falah St	13-B3	Lotus R/A	13-B1
Al Falaheya St	see Othman Bin Affan St	Lulu St (North)	see East Rd (New Airport Rd)
Al Forousiya St	see Khalifa Bin Zayed St	Mohammed Bin Khalifa St	13-A4/B1; 15-A1
Al Gaba St	see Abu Bakr Al Siddiq St	Mubarak St	see Hamdan Bin Zayed Al Awwal St
Al Ghozlan Garden R/A	11-E4	Municipality R/A	14-E1
Al Ghozlan R/A	16-D2	Municipality St	see Al Baladiyya St
Al Hili R/A	13-A2	Nahyan Al Awwal St	17-B2
Al Hili St	see Mohammed Bin Khalifa St	Najda St	see Bani Yas Rd (Najda Rd) (East)
Al Istraha R/A	15-C3	Old Airport Rd	see Maidan Al Ittihad St (North)
Al Ja'amah R/A	15-A2	Omar Bin Al Khattab St	15-C3
Al Jamia St	see Tawam St	Othman Bin Affan St	15-C3
Al Jamia St	14-C4/D3; 16-E1	Oudh Alttoba St	see Ali Bin Abi Taleb St
Al Jimi R/A	14-E1	Saeed Bin Tahnoon Al Awwal St	14-D3/D4
Al Khabisi R/A	12-C4; 14-C1	Salahuddeen Al Ayyubi St	15-B3
Al Khaleej Al Arabi St	11-B2/E2	Salana St	see Salahuddeen Al Ayyubi St
Al Kharis R/A	15-A1	Second St	see Airport Rd (South)
Al Khatem R/A	15-D4	Second St	see Maidan Al Ittihad St (North)
Al Khatem St	see Khata Al Shinkle St	Selmi St	see Hamdan Bin Mohammed St
Al Mahad R/A	14-D3/E3	Shakboot Bin Sultan St	11-D4; 14-A3/E3; 15-A2/C2; 16-B1
Al Markahniya St	see Shakhboot Bin Sultan St		
Al Mashatel R/A	15-C2	Shk Zayed Bin Khalifa St	see Shakhboot Bin Sultan St
Al Masoudi R/A	12-E3	Silmi R/A	15-A1
Al Mira St	see Al Salam St	Sixth St	see Bani Yas Rd (Najda Rd) (East)
Al Muraba R/A	15-B3	Sultan Bin Zayed Al Awwal St	15-A4
Al Muttarath R/A	14-D4	Tahnoon Bin Zayed Al Alawal St	14-A1/B2
Al Nadi R/A	15-A4	Tahnoon St	see Nahyan Al Awwal St
Al Nakheel St	12-E3; 13-A4	Tawam R/A	16-D1
Al Salam St	15-C4/D4	Tawam St	see Khalifa Bin Zayed St
Al Salama R/A	15-B3	Tawam St	16-E2
Al Thakteet St	see Al Ain St	Thirtieth St	see Al Khaleej Al Arabi St (West)
Al Thakteet St	17-C1	Thirty Fourth St	see Bainona St (West)
Ali Bin Abi Taleb St	15-A2/B2	Tourist Club Area	see Al Salam St (Corniche Rd)
Arah Al Jaw St	13-C1/C2	Twenty Eighth St	seeKhalifa Bin Shakbout St (West)
Bani Yas St	12-E3; 13-B2	Twenty Fourth St	see Al Karamah St (West)
Clock Tower R/A	15-A3	Twenty Second St	see Khalid Bin Al Waleed St (West)
Eighth St	see Al Salam St (Eastern Corniche Rd)	Zakher R/A	17-A2
Fourth St	see East Rd (New Airport Rd)	Zayed Al Awwal St	12-B2; 14-C3; 17-B1
Hamdan Bin Mohammed St	14-B1/D1	Zayed Bin Sultan St	14-D3/E3; 15-B3; 17-E2
Hamdan Bin Zayed Al Awwal St	14-C1	Zoo R/A	17-B1
Hazah St	see Khalid Bin Sultan St		
Hazzaa Bin Sultan St	11-E3; 17-A3		

Maps

Al Ain Overview Map

1

2

3

11

Maps

4

Salamat

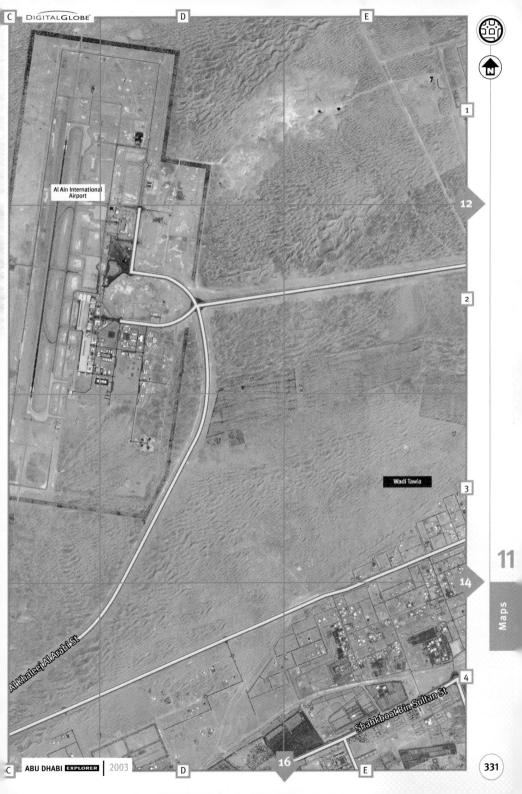

DIGITALGLOBE

Al Ain International Airport

Wadi Tawia

Al Khaleej Al Arabi St

Shahkboot Bin Sultan St

1

12

2

3

14

4

16

11

Maps

Zayed Al Awal St

1

11

2

3

12

Maps

11

Al Tawia

4

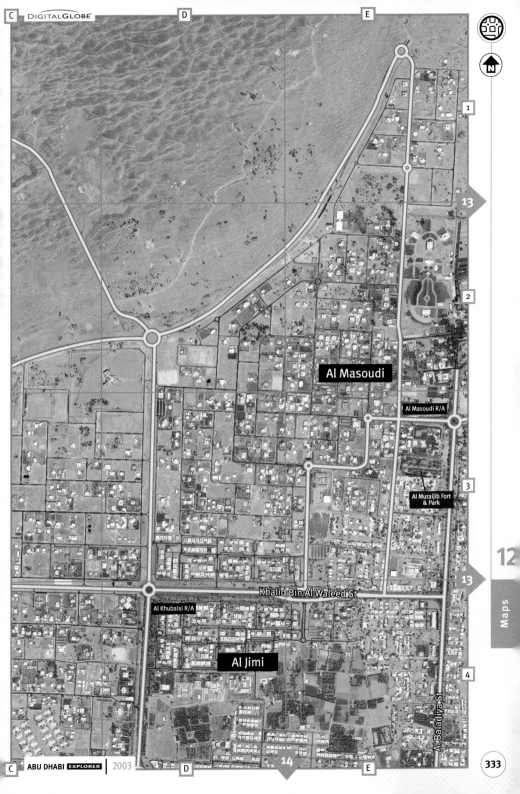

C   D   E

1

13

2

Al Masoudi

Al Masoudi R/A

Al Muraijib Fort
& Park

3

12

13

Maps

Khalid Bin Al Waleed St

Al Khubaisi R/A

Al Jimi

4

Al Baladiya St

14

C   D   E

Al Masoudi

Al Athar St

Lotus RA

Al Qattara

Mohammed Bin Khalifa St

Al Hili RA

Bani Yas St

Qattara Sports Club

Al Falah St

Al Qattara

Abu Obaida Bin Al Jarrah St

Al Nakheel St

Mohammed Bin Khalifa St

Hill Fun City & Ice Rink

Maps

3

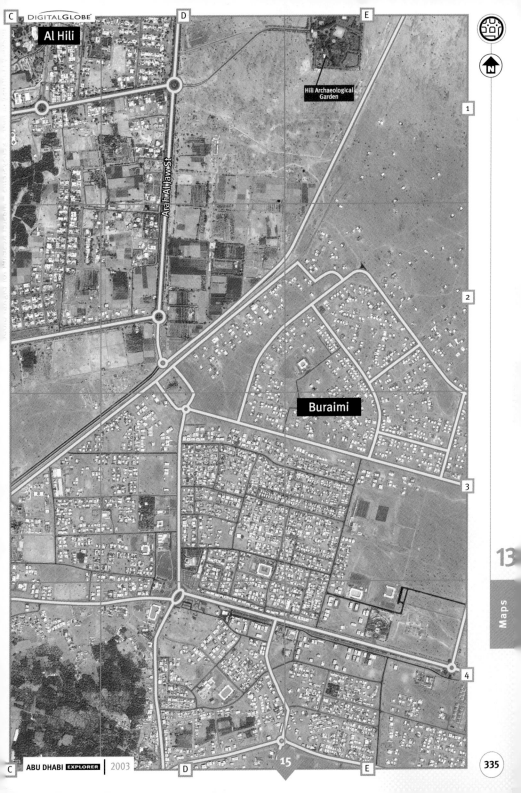

Al Hili

Arch Al Jaw St

Hili Archaeological Garden

Buraimi

Hamdan Bin Mohammed St

Tahnoon Bin Zayed Alawal St

Al Khabisi

Shakhboot Bin Sultan St

Wadi Al Jimi

Muwaiji Fort

Khalifa Bin Zayed St

Deer Park

14

Maps

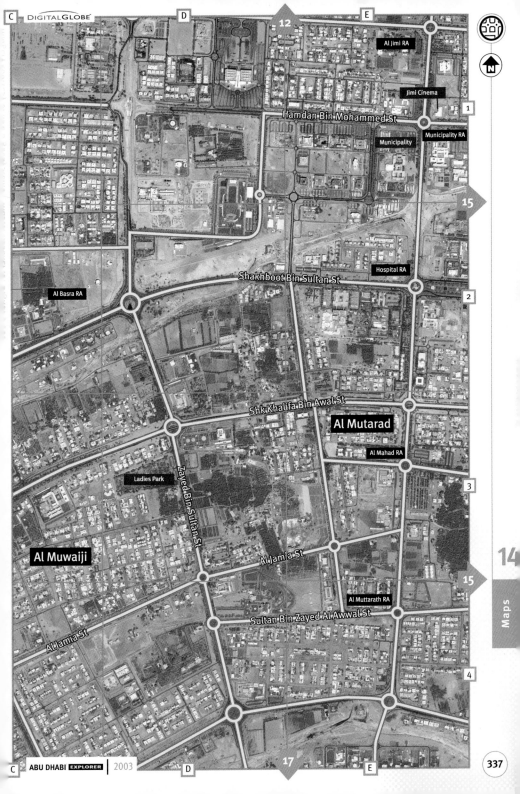

DIGITALGLOBE

Al Jimi RA

Jimi Cinema

12

1

Hamdan Bin Mohammed St

Municipality RA

Municipality

15

Al Basra RA

Shakhboot Bin Sultan St

Hospital RA

2

Shk Khalifa Bin Awal St

Al Mutarad

Al Mahad RA

3

Ladies Park

Zayed Bin Sultan St

Al Muwaiji

Al Jamia St

15

Al Muttarath RA

Sultan Bin Zayed Al Awwal St

14

Maps

Al Jamia St

4

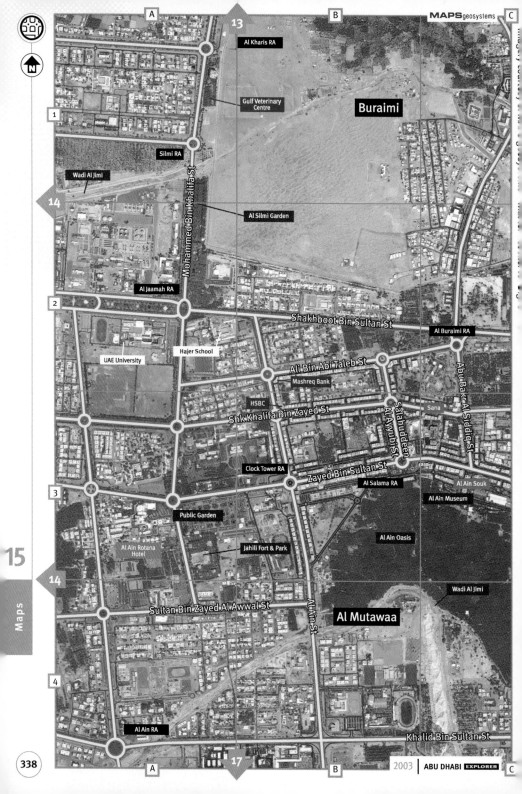

Al Kharis RA

Gulf Veterinary Centre

Buraimi

Silmi RA

Wadi Al Jimi

Mohammed Bin Khalifa St

Al Silmi Garden

Al Jaamah RA

Shakhboot Bin Sultan St

Al Buraimi RA

Hajer School

UAE University

Ali Bin Abi Taleb St

Mashreq Bank

Abu Bakr Al Siddiq St

HSBC

Shk Khalifa Bin Zayed St

Salahuddeen Al Ayyubi St

Sana

Clock Tower RA

Zayed Bin Sultan St

Al Salama RA

Al Ain Souk

Al Ain Museum

Public Garden

Al Ain Rotana Hotel

Jahili Fort & Park

Al Ain Oasis

Wadi Al Jimi

Sultan Bin Zayed Al Awwal St

Al Ain St

Al Mutawaa

Al Ain RA

Khalid Bin Sultan St

15

Maps

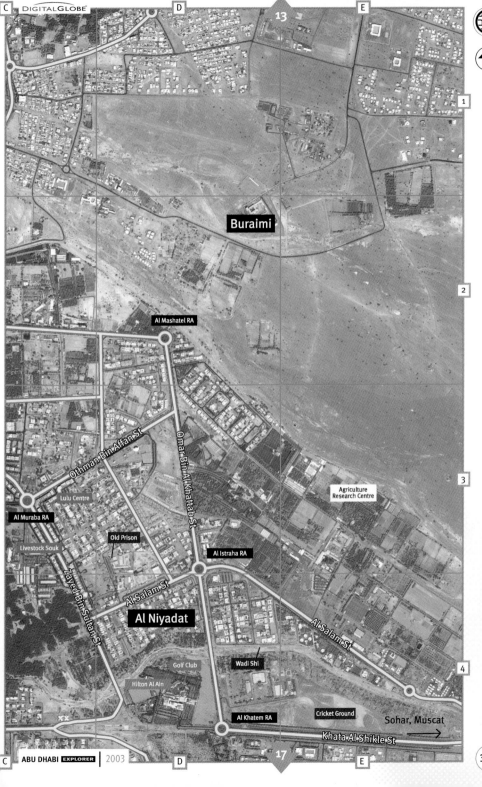

13

1

Buraimi

2

Al Mashatel RA

Othman Bin Affan St

Omar Bin Al Khattab St

Lulu Centre

Al Muraba RA

Old Prison

Livestock Souk

Agriculture Research Centre

3

Al Istraha RA

15

Maps

Zayed Bin Sultan St

Al Salam St

Al Niyadat

Al Salam St

Golf Club

Wadi Shi

Hilton Al Ain

4

Cricket Ground

Al Khatem RA

Sohar, Muscat →

Khata Al Shikle St

11

Abu Dhabi

Al Bateen

Shakhboot Bin Sultan St

Ghrebah

Abu Dhabi

Maps

Tawan RA

Khalid Bin Zayed St

Maqam

Khalid Bin Zayed St

Wadi Al Ain

Tawan St

Al Agabiyya

16

Maps

17

3

4

Hazzaa St

Al Ghozlan RA

Hazzaa RA

Falaj Hazzaa

Zoo RA

Nahyan Al Awwal St

Zayed Al Awwal St

Zakher RA

Zoo District

Nahyan Al Awwal St

Hazzaa Bin Sultan St

Al Ain Fayda

Jebel Hafeet

2003 | **ABU DHABI** EXPLORER

17

Maps

DIGITALGLOBE

15

Al Ain St.

Zayed Bin Sultan St.

Industrial Area

Al Ain Zoo & Aquarium

1

2

3

4

17

Maps

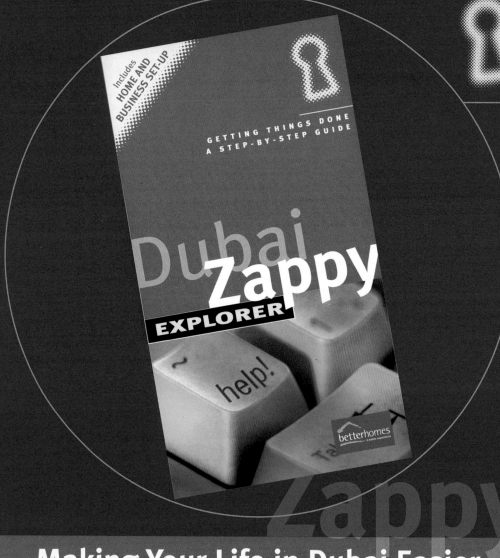

Making Your Life in Dubai Easier

A complete step-by-step guide for getting things done, the **Zappy Explorer** leads you through procedures on all aspects of life, whether business or personal – in a zap! This authoritative guide contains over 100 well thought out, clear and easy to follow procedures, and tips and advice for everything from obtaining visas and permits to telecommunications, housing, transportation, licences, banking, education and health, making it your best chance for navigating through Dubai's administrative mysteries.

- Immigration
- Residence
- Communications
- Transportation
- Personal Affairs
- Business
- Maps

Available from leading bookstores, hotels, supermarkets or directly from Explorer Publishing

Index

EXPLORER

INDEX

Index

Index

Insiders' City Guides

EXPLORER

These are no ordinary guidebooks. They are your lifestyle support system, medicine for the bored, ointment for the aimless, available over the counter and prescribed by those in the know. An essential resource for residents, tourists and business people, they cover everything worth knowing about the city and where to do it.

Abu Dhabi Explorer

The third edition continues to be the authoritative leading lifestyle guidebook to Abu Dhabi and the Oasis town of Al Ain. In keeping with the style of the **Explorer** series, this comprehensive, fun and easy book provides exhaustive information on anything worth knowing about Abu Dhabi and where to do it. Providing in depth, practical and accurate coverage on the emirate of Abu Dhabi, there really is no alternative to satisfy your entertainment and leisure needs.

ISBN 976-8182-38-5 **Retail Price** Dhs.55, €18

Dubai Explorer

Now in its seventh edition, the **Dubai Explorer** is firmly established as the leading annual lifestyle guidebook to Dubai. Comprehensive, fun and easy to use, the meticulously updated content covers general information & orientation to specifics on home, work and leisure, leaving no questions unanswered. This is the insiders' guide to what's hot and what's not in Dubai and the Emirates, perfectly suited to residents, short term visitors, business people and tourists – an essential resource for anyone exploring this vibrant and surprising city.

ISBN 976-8182-33-4 **Retail Price** Dhs.65 €18

Geneva Explorer

Following the hugely popular style of **Explorer** guidebooks, a resident team of writers, photographers and lovers of life have sold their soul to exhaustive research. The result is a comprehensive insiders' guide with practical and accurate coverage and recommendations. This lifestyle guidebook is ideal for residents, short term visitors, business people and tourists, and an essential resource for anyone exploring this beautiful, historical and multicultural city. **(Due out 4th quarter 2003)**

ISBN 976-8182-44-x **Retail Price** Dhs.65 €18

Hand-held Explorer (Dubai)

This downloadable and ultra-comprehensive version of the **Dubai Explorer** transfers the world of happening Dubai straight to your Palm Pilot with just a click of a button. Interactive, informative and innovative, the **Hand-Held Explorer** is easy to install, a breeze to use and packed with useful information.

ISBN 976-8182-40-7 **Retail Price** Dhs.65 €18

Kicking boredom's butt since 1785!

EXPLORER

Insiders' City Guides • Photography Books • Activity Guidebooks • Commissioned Publications • Distribution

Insiders' City Guides

Oman Explorer

Formerly known as the **Muscat Explorer**, the scope of this comprehensive leisure and entertainment guidebook has been broadened to cover the rest of this beautiful and largely unspoiled country. Including a new business section, the latest, up to date restaurant reviews, heritage, culture and much more, this is the only definitive and essential guidebook to Oman. **(Due out 4th quarter 2003)**

ISBN 976-8182-07-5 **Retail Price** Dhs.55 €18

Street Map Explorer (Dubai)

Find your way effortlessly through the streets of Dubai with this first ever detailed and indexed street guide. An absolute essential for every home and car, this street atlas holds map pages of concise street names and numbers, a quick reference section of popular locations and public facilities, and an extensive index that allows easy access to locations through the most convenient routes. Now, you'll never be lost again! What's more, the handy and compact size is a snug fit for your glove box.

ISBN 976-8182-10-5 **Retail Price** Dhs.45 €18

Weekly Explorer (Dubai)

This free concise weekly guide is the most up to date, central source of information on life in Dubai. One A4 page gives the low down on special events, such as sports, restaurant and bar promotions, exhibitions, what's on at the movies, home, outdoors, business tips and more.

ISBN – **Retail Price** Free

Zappy Explorer (Dubai)

A complete step-by-step guide for getting things done, the **Zappy Explorer** leads you through all the procedures involved in settling into life, home or business in Dubai – in a zap! This authoritative guide contains over 100 well thought out, clear and easy to follow procedures, tips and advice for everything – from obtaining visas and permits to telecommunications, housing, transportation, licences, banking, education and health. This is your best chance for success while navigating through Dubai's administrative mysteries.

ISBN 976-8182-25-3 **Retail Price** Dhs.65 €18

Kicking boredom's butt since 1785!

Photography Books

Where words fail, a picture speaks volumes. Look at the world though new eyes as the lens captures places you never knew existed. These award winning books are valuable additions to bookshelves everywhere.

Dubai: Tomorrow's City Today

Stunning photographs shed light on the beauty and functionality of contemporary Dubai, a city that is a model of diversity, development and progress. Explore its historical highlights, municipal successes, innovative plans and civic triumphs, as you wonder at the grandeur in store for the future. **(Due out 4th quarter 2003)**

ISBN 976-8182-35-0 **Retail Price** Dhs.165 €45

Images of Abu Dhabi & the UAE

This visual showcase shares the aesthetic and lush wonders of the emirate of Abu Dhabi as spectacular images disclose the marvels of the capital and the diversity of astounding locations throughout the seven emirates. **(Due out 4th quarter 2003)**

ISBN 976-8182-28-8 **Retail Price** Dhs.165 €45

Images of Dubai & the UAE

Images of Dubai is a visual showcase, sharing the secrets of this remarkable land and introducing newcomers to the wonders of Dubai and the United Arab Emirates. Journey along golden beaches under a pastel sunset, or deep into the mesmerising sands of the desert. View the architectural details of one of the most visually thrilling urban environments in the world, and dive undersea to encounter the reef creatures that live there. This book is for all those who love this country as well as those who think they might like to.

ISBN 976-8182-22-9 **Retail Price** Dhs.165 €45

Sharjah's Architectural Splendour

Take a guided tour of some of the highlights of Sharjah's architecture. Through the lens, this book captures small, aesthetic details and grand public compounds, the mosques and souks of this remarkable city. Striking photographs are linked together with text that is both analytical and informative. Whether you are a long term resident or a brief visitor, this volume of images will undoubtedly surprise and delight.

ISBN 976-8182-29-6 **Retail Price** Dhs.165 €45

Kicking boredom's butt since 1785!

Activity Guidebooks

EXPLORER

Why not visit stunning marine life and mysterious wrecks, or stand poised on the edge of a natural wadi or pool in the mountains? Get a tan and a life with our activity guidebooks.

Family Explorer

This is the ONLY family handbook to Dubai and Abu Dhabi. Catering specifically to families with children between the ages of 0 - 14 years, the easy to use **Explorer** format details the practicalities of family life in the northern emirates, including information on medical care, education, residence visas and numerous tips on indoor and outdoor activities for families and kids. **(Due out 4th quarter 2003)**

ISBN 976-8182-34-2 **Retail Price** Dhs.55 €18

Off-Road Explorer (UAE)

Containing 20 adventurous off-road routes with clear and easy to follow instructions, this is an invaluable tool for exploring the UAE's 'outback'. Satellite imagery of every stage of the route is superimposed with the correct track to follow. For each route, points of interest are highlighted, along with distances and advice on driving the more difficult parts. Outstanding photography peppers this guide and additional information on topics such as wildlife and archaeology complement the off-road routes.

ISBN 976-8182-37-7 **Retail Price** Dhs.95 €29

Underwater Explorer (UAE)

Packed with top 58 dive sites covering both coastlines and the Musandam, this dedicated guidebook is ideal for divers for all abilities. It includes all the crucial information you need to know about diving in the UAE – from suggested dive plans and informative illustrations to marine life photographs and more.

ISBN 976-8182-36-9 **Retail Price** Dhs.65 €18

Kicking boredom's butt since 1785!

Abu Dhabi Explorer – Quick Reference

Emergencies

General

Police	999
Ambulance	998 / 999
Fire	997
ADEWA	991
Abu Dhabi Police HQ	446 1461
Municipality 24 Hour Hotline	677 7929
Operator	100

Pharmacies/Chemists – 24 hours

Each emirate has at least one pharmacy open 24 hours. The location and telephone numbers are in the daily newspapers. The Municipality has an emergency number (677 7929) which gives the name and location of open chemists.

Hospitals

Al Noor Hospital Emergency	626 5265
The Corniche Hospital Emergency	672 4900
Golden Sands Medical Hospital	642 7171
Mafraq Hospital Emergency	582 3100
National Hospital Emergency	671 1000
New Medical Centre Hospital	633 2255
Shk Khalifa Medical Centre Emergency	633 1000

Al Ain Hospital (Al Jimi) Emergency	03 763 5888
Emirates International Hospital	03 763 7777
Oasis Hospital Emergency	03 722 1251
Tawam Hospital Emergency	03 767 7444

Dentists/Orthodontists

American Dental Clinic	677 1310
Austrian Dental Clinic	621 1489
British Dental Clinic	677 3308
Dr Firas Dental Clinic	633 5988
Gulf Diagnostic Centre	665 8090
International Dental Clinic	633 3444

Canadian Dental Clinic	03 766 6696
New Al Ain Dental Clinic	03 766 2059
Thabit Medical Centre	03 765 4454

Medical Centres/Clinics

Centre Medical Franco Emergency	626 5722
Gulf Diagnostic Centre	665 8090

Emirates Medical Clinic Centre	03 764 4744
Family Medical Clinic	03 766 9902
New Al Ain Medical Clinic	03 764 1448

Emergency Denotes 24 Hour Emergency

Hotels

Abu Dhabi Airport Hotel	575 7377
Al Ain Palace Hotel	679 4777
Al Diar Capital Hotel	678 7700
Al Diar Dana Hotel	645 6000
Al Diar Gulf Hotel & Resort	441 4777
Al Diar Mina Hotel	678 1000
Al Diar Palm Hotel	642 0900
Al Diar Regency Hotel	676 5000
Beach Rotana Hotel & Towers	644 3000
Crowne Plaza	621 0000
Emirates Plaza Hotel	672 2000
Grand Continental Flamingo Htl	626 2200
Hilton Baynunah Tower	632 7777
Hilton International Abu Dhabi	681 1900
Hotel Inter-Continental	666 6888
Howard Johnson Diplomat Htl	671 0000
International Rotana Inn	677 9900
Khalidia Palace Hotel	666 2470
Le Meridien Abu Dhabi	644 6666
Le Royal Meridien Hotel	674 2020
Mafraq Hotel	582 2666
Millennium Hotel	626 2700
Novotel Centre Hotel	633 3555
Sands Hotel	633 5335
Sheraton Abu Dhabi	677 3333
Zakher Hotel	627 5300

Ain Al Fayda	03 783 8333
Al Ain Rotana Hotel	03 754 5111
Al Diar Jazira Beach Resort	03 562 9100
Dhafra Beach Hotel	03 877 1600
Hilton Al Ain	03 768 6666
Hotel Inter-Continental Al Ain	03 768 6686
Mercure Grand Jebel Hafeet	03 783 8888

Cinemas

Al Jazira Cinema	443 1116	H, M, T
Al Massa	633 3000	A, E
Century Cinemas	645 8988	A, E
CineStar	681 8484	A, E
Cultural Foundation	621 5300	E
Eldorado	676 3555	M
Grand Al Mariah	678 5000	E
National Cinema	671 1700	H

Al Massa	03 764 4447	A, E
Club Cinema	03 722 2255	H, M
Grand Cineplex	03 751 1228	E

Lang: A=Arabic, E=English, H=Hindi, M=Malayalam, T=Tamil

Airlines

Air France	621 5815
Air India	632 2300
Air Malta	621 2100
Alitalia	622 6957
American Airlines	627 1111
Biman Airlines	634 2597
British Airways	622 4540
Cathay Pacific	800 4343
China Airlines	621 5500
Cyprus Airways	626 7055
Egypt Air	634 2333
Emirates Airline	691 1600
Gulf Air	633 1700
KLM	632 3280
Kuwait Airways	631 3200
Lufthansa Airlines	627 4640
Malaysia Airlines	645 4050
Oman Air	626 6800
Pakistan Intl Airlines	635 2600
Qatar Airways	632 5777
Singapore Airlines	622 1110
Swiss Air	622 6640
Thai Airways	621 2900
United Airlines	622 6162
Yemen	632 3675

Telephone Codes

Directory Enquiries	180
Operator	100
Etisalat	633 311
Etisalat Information	144
Fault Reports	170
Billing Information	142
Internet Service	222 81
Mobile Customer Care	101
Speaking Clock	140

Taxis

Al Ghazal Taxis	444 7787

Al Ghazal Taxis	03 751 656

Flight Enquiries

Flight Enquiry	575 7500
Abu Dhabi Airport	575 7500

Al Ain Airport	03 785 55